Car Crazy

By

Scott Faragher

Porsche 928, Mercedes 450 SL, Jaguar XJ-S

5

Car Crazy!
ISBN: 978-1-7344528-0-8
Copyright 2021 Scott Faragher
Published by Deathcat Media
Website: deathcatmedia.com

1976 Cadillac Fleetwood Brougham, last of the real Cadillacs

DEDICATION

This book is gratefully dedicated to Tom Strickland, my automotive mentor and friend, who in my early 20s, was kind enough to help me learn basic mechanics which have served me well. He was never too busy to provide help with any problem either over the phone or in person. Through him I met Craig Harper, and Glenn Hall, the latter who allowed me to enjoy some really great cars before I could actually afford to keep them.

My sincere thanks also to my lifelong friends, Bruce Shelton, Clark Conn, Steve Vassallo, Tom Crockett, Randy Smith, Jay Page, Bard Selden, Chad Selden, Tait Selden, Mike Cofer, Albert Marlowe, Walter Wilson, Charlie Kimball, Clay Yager, Richard Jett, Mike Wade, Kingsley Hooker, Jeff Nunnally, all of whom have accompanied me or inspired me in my automotive journey, and new friends Fred Harvey, John Ferguson, and those friends I've yet to meet.

Thanks also to my Nashville mechanics past and present, Dainey Canfield, Joe Robinson; Alex Davidoff and Mark Bowden at Euro Auto Body; David Blanks at TGC; Erol at Erol's Autobahn; and Mike Wurster and the crew at Wurster's in Franklin, Tennessee.

If there are some typos or anything wrong editorially, or with formatting, I beg your indulgence. Thanks for your purchase.

Contents

I. Bikes

II. Family Cars

III. Oldsmobile 1967-1970 442s &W-30

IV. Lincoln 1960 & 1959 & a Chevy Nova

V. Jaguar MK VIII, MK IX, & X Sedans

VI. Jaguar E-Types 1961-1968
1968 Jaguar XK-E Roadster
1961 Jaguar XK-E Roadster
1964 Jaguar XK-E Coupe
1967 Jaguar XK-E Roadster
1967 Jaguar XK-E Roadster
1964 Jaguar XK-E Roadster
1967 Jaguar XK-E Coupe
1965 Jaguar XK-E Roadster

VII. Jaguar XK 140s, etc.
XK-140 Roadster
XK-140 Roadster (2)
Jaguar 3.8 S
Jaguar XK-150 Drophead
Jaguar XK-120
1998 Jaguar XJ-S

VIII. JAGUAR XJ-S
1988 XJ-S V-12

IX. 1962-1965 Lincolns & Convertibles
1964 Lincoln Sedan
1965 Lincoln Convertible
1964 Lincoln (2)
1964 Lincoln Sedan (3)
1964 Lincoln Sedan (4)
1963 Lincoln Sedan
1964 Lincoln Convertible
Next! 1964 Lincoln Convertible (2)
1962 Lincoln Convertible
1962 Lincoln Convertible (2)

X. The Big Lincolns 1977-1979
1979 Town Car
1977 Town Car
1979 Collectors Series
1978 Town Car
1977 Continental

XVII. Fomoco or Mofoco?
1984 Jeep

NOTE: The cars presented here are not all of the cars I've ever owned, or even all of those that have passed through my hands at one time or another, but they are the ones which I've selected to include for one reason or another.

Inspired by country singer Marty Robbins' album cover `Gunfighter Ballads,' and 1960s T.V. western `Have Gun Will Travel,' I `Have Keyboard, Will Write.'

There was an old abandoned fairgrounds racing car very similar to the one shown here (which belonged to singer Marty Robbins) parked behind a small house down the street from my grandparent's house formerly on Nashville's Castleman Drive. It was gold and had `44 Jr.' painted in big letters on each side. I'd climb through the window and sit in it for hours, back when I was eight or nine years old. I'd shift the gears, imagine the sound of that flat head V-8 and dream of the day when I'd have my own hot rod. I never did get a hot rod (though I still want one), but, in time, I made up for it.

INTRODUCTION

My love affair with cars began when I got my first toy car at age three. I could get on my hands and knees roll it across the floor. And I still remember my first plastic model car, a 1959 Buick convertible made by a company called AMT. The 1/24th scale cars were called `3 in 1' meaning that there were extra parts included in the box so that the car could be put together as stock, custom, or competition. There were other plastic model car makers then including Ideal, Revel, Monogram, Lindberg, and Pyro, that I remember off the top of my head. From assembling them I learned the names and placement of their different components, and their functions. There were several `hobby shops' in Nashville back then, including Austin's Electric, located where 440 crosses West End Avenue, near what used to be a railroad trestle. There were also Miller's on Church Street, and Martin's, on 8th Ave. N. which sold model cars, electric trains, and other things like raw balsa wood, Thimble Drome gas-powered airplanes and cars, fuel, and engines, propellers, balsa airplane models, and even balsa wood model cars. There were also two Phillips Toy Marts, with the first originally on 8th Ave. S. with a later store in Belle Meade, which is still in operation.

Later, when I was around twelve years old, I was given a real Ford Model A touring car by two older friends who lived on Sneed Ave., one street behind mine. It was complete, and as I recollect even ran, but my father wouldn't let me have `a junk car.' It could have been a great father and son project, but my father had no use for cars over and above their mere function.

We'd drive to Daytona Beach, Florida every summer for a two week vacation in the days before the interstate. We'd pass through small towns and I'd see cars at gas stations, and hot rods parked around them. I still remember a `32 Ford coupe at one with a for sale sign for $150. Each town had its own famous restaurant or hotel then, none of which were chain restaurants, and each city and town were unique. In Florida, I was aware of cars which, while occasionally seen in Nashville, were common there. 1955-1959 Eldorados, Coupe DeVilles, and convertibles, and King Midgets, were plentiful. I wanted one. I wanted many. The same for Jaguars, Rolls-Royces, Bentleys, Lincolns, and convertibles of all types. And back then, in the days before portable crushers, there were real junkyards, with cars from the 1920s to the present, rusting in peace, like Packards, Cadillacs, and some cars I'd heard of but never seen before. And every gas station had mechanics on duty, many of whom had worked on tanks, airplanes and other machines during World War II. Any fairly competent mechanic could pretty much fix anything that was likely to go wrong with any American car, and sixty years ago, most cars in the U.S. were American made.

Much has changed in the past fifty years, and no doubt, I've changed too, hopefully for the better. Ultimately, I'm just an average guy who's always loved cars, and if you're reading this, chances are you're as fascinated with cars as I am. Though our choices in cars may be or may have been different, it's likely that many of our experiences have been similar. I hope this book finds you well, and that you enjoy taking a spin with me at the wheel.

NOTE: My opinions and conclusions with regards to the merits or lack of, as well as to the desirability of one car, or one model of a particular marque as opposed to another of the same brand, or a different one, are strictly my own. Some cars I used to consider ugly, like the AMC Pacer, the VW Bug, or the Porsche 911, for example, appear interesting to me now with the passage of time. The fact is, I like all cars. Each is a unique expression of its time, place and purpose, and every car has its admirers as well as its detractors. All interest me now. Again, my observations and conclusions are my own, and not necessarily true or accurate.

1976 Cadillac Eldorado Convertible, top down on an open road: 500 cubic inches of fuel-injected power! Economy? Not really, but then, so what?

There is one other thing. Since my automotive experiences involve parallels with many of my friends who had often similar cars before and concurrent with mine, I will introduce some of them now as their names and pictures will pop up from time to time.

Bruce Shelton: I met him on the steps of Julia Green Elementary School when I was in the 2nd grade and he was in the 1st. He wore a canvas knap sack on his back with his name `Bruce' written with a magic marker. He looked just like Dennis the Menace, a popular comic book figure at the time. I addressed him and said `Bruce the Goose' to which he replied "Go to Hell!" As it turned out, his father and my grandfather knew each other well since my grandfather supplied Esso gas to his father's `Automatic Car Wash' at the corner of 15th & Hayes, in the heart of the car dealerships which were for the most part located on Nashville's upper Broadway in the 1950s and 1960s.

Bruce was exiled to Castle Heights Military School at age 10. I'd later be sent to Columbia Military Academy and we'd frequently come home on weekends with my godfather providing us written medical excuses, basically weekend passes. Later, in 1983, as president if In Concert, I'd hired him as an agent even though he had no experience whatsoever. He turned out to be one of the best agents I've ever known and basically became the company's main agent for Jerry Lee Lewis.

Bruce was the first person my age who had his own Cadillac, a 1969 Coupe DeVille which he'd driven up from Florida in the early 1970s where he'd moved with his parents after he'd left military school. People thought we were both in the music business, but neither of us had any idea then, that we ever would be. For me it was just around the corner, for Bruce, ten years later.

The Three Stooges: Tom Crockett, Bruce Shelton, and the author 1977 at former Nashville International. I always hired my friends.

Tom Crockett: I remember the first time I saw him. I was sitting in the Hillsboro High School lunch room with my pal Alan Williamson. Crockett had this incredibly sarcastic smirk on his face as he walked, surveying his new surroundings. I was a freshman too, but I remember saying to Alan, "There's something about that guy that just makes you want to kick his ass." We became best friends and he really was the wildest person I ever have known. There was nothing he wouldn't do, automotively or otherwise. He also, like Bruce and I, attended Columbia Military Academy at one time or another.

Steve Vassallo: "They probably have wine for breakfast," Bruce's mother once observed in regards to Steve. I don't know when or where I met him, but I've known him since I was around twelve. Another true wildman.

Randy Smith: I met Randy at Hillsboro High School my senior year. He was ex-MBA and Brandon Hall. I was ex-BGA, Baylor, and Columbia Military Academy. We hit it off immediately and have been friends ever since. By way of Randy, I became familiar with mid-1960s Mercedes SLs, since his father had three of them at the same time.

Bard Selden: I'd just stepped off the bus in Oxford, Mississippi coming to visit my pals Randy Smith and Steve Vassallo for the first time at Ole' Miss, preparing to ride with Steve to Mardi Gras. I was wearing a Confederate officer's uniform as I walked toward the campus. Suddenly, a Rambler pulled up beside me and someone I'd never met reached across the seat, opened the door, and said "You must be Scott Faragher, hop in," he said. Truly astounded, I asked "How could you possibly know that?"

"I recognize you by your sword," he answered. That was more than fifty-three years ago, and we're still friends.

Me, Bard Selden, and Randy Smith, 1968. We shot up some abandoned cement block building with this .45 that Bard had brought from Mississippi, in what used to be called the country, outside of Nashville. Nothing says fun for teenagers like cold beer and the smell of gunpowder!

At Oxford, Mississippi a couple of years ago. The author, Steve Vassallo, Randy Smith, Bard Selden. It was the first time we'd all been together in Oxford in fifty years.

Steve Vassallo today. He still lives in Oxford.

OK, technically this is a book about cars, so feel free to skip this part if you like, but since I still ride bikes, and they were my first set of wheels, I include it anyway.

I.

Bikes

1. Western Flyer For most of us, bicycles were our first set of wheels. They belonged to us and nobody else, and gave us our first true taste of independence. On my bicycle, I could go to school, the shopping center, the baseball field, friend's houses, or just ride around aimlessly. I got my first bicycle for Christmas the same year that my best friend and his older brother got their bikes. We were both ten years old and my friend's brother was twelve. My bike was a fat-tire Western Auto Western Flyer, red with white stripes, chrome wire wheels, white wall tires, Bendix rear brakes, and allegedly some sort of nebulous automatic transmission in the rear hub. Despite the high sounding talk in that regard, I always had to dismount the bike and walk it to the top of any hill at some point because it became impossible to go any further in the ascent. There were no front brakes and the rear brake was contained within the hub of the rear wheel. To slow or stop the bike it was necessary to put backward pressure on the pedals. It was consequently possible to slam on the brake and slide in gravel or even on the road. Even at ten years old I remember remarking to a friend that bicycles should have front and rear springs and knobby tires like motorcycles.

My friend and his brother both received what were known as `English Bikes' which were either made or sold by J.C. Higgins. They were different and cooler than mine, in the same sense that a Jaguar XK-E was cooler than a Corvette. Their English bikes were black with skinny black wall tires and chrome wire wheels. They looked neater in a way than American bikes because they had separate hand brakes front and rear, and separate gears settings (high, low, & neutral) which could be shifted by a lever. The shift lever, as I recollect, when moved, lengthened or shortened a small chain extending horizontally from the starboard side of the rear wheel hub. These alleged gears didn't really do anything either, at least nothing we could notice, but for us, mobility was now a daily option, and we could literally ride anywhere we wanted to go around the neighborhood. I would subsequently have many bicycles but my first bike hooked me on fat-tire bikes, a passion I still enjoy.

2. Puch

By the time I was 26, I'd been running three miles a day for about five years, and decided I wanted to do some roadwork with a bicycle to augment that. To that end I bought several different bikes at the monthly Nashville flea market over a several year period. Most people who remember bikes like the popular Schwinn Varsity and the Continental will, remember them as durable and above all `heavy,' I mean really heavy. There was no such thing around Nashville in 1977 as a mountain bike. One day, tired of the primitive and really heavy bikes I'd been experimenting with, I stopped in at Cumberland Transit, a Nashville bike and camping store owned by a childhood friend of mine, Allen Doty. I saw one I liked which was called a Puch. I didn't especially care for the name, but it was a visual work of art, a deep high gloss royal blue with gold pin striping. It was also state of the art at the time, which meant that it was a ten-speed and while heavy, didn't weigh as much as an old Schwinn. The salesman asked me if I wanted to take it for a test ride. I didn't know that was even possible. I showed him my driver's license which he copied, and was on my way. I felt like the wind, everything worked like it was supposed to, and the gears shifted perfectly. The frame was actually too tall, though I didn't know it at the time, and the handlebars were those type that curl down in such a way that you end up looking and feeling like Quasimodo after a long ride, and can't stand upright for a couple of hours afterwards. I bought it and wrote a check for $379, the most money I'd ever spent on a bicycle at the time. I'd literally bought running cars for less. Still, it was new, beautiful, and everything worked.

I rode it around the neighborhood and would frequently ride to Franklin from Belle Meade Blvd. down Chickering to Old Hickory, and to Old Natchez Trace to Franklin and back, around thirty miles each way. Once while riding with a friend way, way out in Williamson County one Sunday afternoon, a large dog came running after me and tried to bite my right leg. I should have sped up and just outrun him. Instead, being combative as I was, I reached out to kick him in the chops. It would have been no problem except that my bike frame was too tall, and I'd slowed down to be sure that I got the bastard. I lost my balance and hit the road, breaking my collarbone and getting a concussion. This, of course, because I had no helmet. I'd never worn a helmet, considering it too restrictive. I was semi-conscious as the ambulance driver asked me to which hospital I wanted to be delivered. The words of my late godfather Dr. S.W. Ballard, a surgeon and longtime Williamson County resident came to mind. "Never go to the Williamson County Hospital." I asked them to take me to St. Thomas Hospital, in Nashville, to which the ambulance driver said, "We don't go that far." I ended up at the old Williamson County Hospital anyway, where I was given a sling for my broken collarbone and taken home by my friend. I should have been given x-rays or brain scans, but nothing. I wasn't home long before I was sick at my stomach. I had my ex-wife drive me to St. Thomas where I ended up staying for three days of tests and monitoring. I never ride anywhere for any reason without a helmet now, and anybody who does is crazy. I'd been lucky and knew it. In a misguided attempt at Charity I photographed this beautiful bike then gave it to Goodwill in 2007, along with a nice, heavy Raleigh road bike. It was the second new bike I'd ever had in my life and I'd had it since 1977. It was in perfect condition, having always been stored indoors. I'm sorry now that I didn't keep it. It wasn't worth anything and probably was scrapped, as so many bikes are.

3. Specialized Stumpjumper

I first became aware of mountain bikes in the late 1980s. There was a place which rented them for $50 a day somewhere in the Green Hills Village part of Nashville, fairly near my office on Music Row. I'd already bought one bike from Nashville's Cumberland Transit and thought I'd look and see what they had in the way of mountain bikes. They always had a bulletin board as soon as you walked in the door where people could post pictures and information about used bikes private individuals had for sale. I thought this was a very generous service for a retail bike shop to offer. Anyway, there was a red Specialized Stumpjumper for sale for $125. It didn't have any sort of suspension, front or rear. It was just a rigid frame bike with fat, knobby tires and 18 or 21 speeds. I'm six feet tall, but even so the Stumpjumper's frame was also too tall, but I loved the bike and rode as long as weather permitted at Nashville's Percy Warner Park on the horse trails were where I'd ride. I'd take the road from the Belle Meade entrance and head up the hill on the pavement, find a horse trail and take off. It was illegal to ride on the horse trail as they were for horses only. But the stables which had been located down from the entrance from Cheekwood Botanical Gardens were long gone, and there were seldom any equestrians on the trails, especially during really hot summer afternoons. I'd been raised around horses so if I encountered someone, I'd dismount, stand still until after he or she passed. The way I saw it was that anyone riding a horse up and down what was in some cases, rather rough terrain in 100 + degree heat was a sadist anyway.

4. Specialized Hard Rock
One day in 1993 I stopped in at Cumberland Transit and found a new Specialized Hard Rock with a shiny black frame and orange lettering, like Halloween colors. It had a front suspension fork and was priced at $500, a price I was willing to pay. Of course,

I wanted a full suspension bike because I've always been fascinated by suspensions of all types, especially automotive rear suspensions, but the prices were artificially inflated on bikes with a rear suspension then. What was interesting about rear suspension bikes of the late 1980s and most of the 1990s was that they were constantly being refined and changed, with different manufacturers trying different designs. I bought the bike, and had a great time with it riding by myself up in the woods. It was my third new bike, and the first one I'd bought as an adult that had a frame of the right size. The bike professed to be made from `chromoly' whatever the hell that is. When late autumn came, I hung it on a hook from the garage ceiling. The following year, when I got it down for spring, the front suspension no longer worked. It was bottomed out, apparently from hanging there all winter. It was my fault. I should have left it sitting upright on the garage floor, but I hadn't known any better. Again, I gave away another bike I should have kept, but didn't, this time to the veterinarian down the street.

5. Trek 9000
I soon saw an ad for a full suspension Trek 9000 in a local paper. It was nearly new, and I think had cost around $1,500. I traded a 1976 Cadillac Fleetwood for it and was on my way. It took a little getting used to but I loved it. It wasn't so good ascending steep hills however, due to the rear suspension's high pivot point. So when I had to stand on it to climb a hill, there was a pronounced pogo effect as the tightening chain pulled the rear wheel forward, raising the rear frame and seat post a couple of inches up with each cycle, a constant up and down, a lot like `posting' on a horse. In addition to the pogo effect, there was the loss of energy wasted on the up and down movement, which should have

been applied to the rear wheel, and moving the bike forward. Be that as it may, I loved that bike and had more fun with it up in the woods than I'd ever had with any bike. In reality, it's just worn out. The rear suspension bushings are degraded to the extent that if you lift the bike by the top rail, the rear suspension drops an inch or so, and it also wobbles from side to side. Ideally, I'd just replace the rear bushings, but alas, none were available. Trek should have these parts on hand forever, but their intention, understandably, is to sell new bikes, not to repair old ones. Also, rear suspension technology (with some manufacturers) has advanced to the extent that my Trek 9000 was now obsolete, even if I could get new rear suspension parts.

I think *Mountain Bike Action* rated the Trek 9000 as one of the worst mountain bikes available, but you had to know how to ride it and what to expect, sort of like with an old Porsche. I still have it nearly thirty years later. Despite its faults, it was revolutionary for its day especially during a transitional period of bike suspension design. And I must say, there was nothing like being up in the woods by oneself on what is referred to as a `technical trail' on a hot summer day.

6. Trek 9200 Despite its inherent faults, I really liked my 9000, and sought to find another one on ebay. They'd show up occasionally but most of them were as beat up as mine. After a casual and sporadic search on ebay and

elsewhere, I eventually found a Trek 9200, which was the same bike as the 9000 but with negligible improvements. The one I found was like a mid-1990s time capsule. It was as new, having been used slightly, if at all, and was literally in perfect condition. In my zeal, I bought it and was thrilled when it arrived. It was everything I'd hoped it would be. In reality, the frame was taller than my 9000, and a shorter frame is more desirable for serious riding. Its rear suspension bushings were perfect, so I transferred them to my 9000 in less than fifteen minutes. This colorful 9200 has now moved into the realm of an art object given its perfect, unused condition. I ride it briefly, upon occasion, but that's it. I enjoy looking at it and like its bright colors.

7. Trek Fuel One April morning in 2007 on the way into Nashville, I stopped at Trace Cycles, a bike shop which was then located in part of the

famous Loveless Motel's surrounding shops. My intention was to look specifically for a new road bike. I was planning to do some serious roadwork  riding on the nearby Natchez Trace during the upcoming summer months. I'd recently sold my house in Nashville and would no longer have instant access to Percy Warner Park's horse trails since I'd moved to my girlfriend's house in the country, forty miles away. To my surprise, there was a new Trek Fuel mountain bike which caught my eye. It was flat black, with flat black wheels, neither of which I found visually appealing, as I like bright colors, but it sat up high in the front with its Rock Shox front suspension and looked like it could probably handle anything I might give it. The rear suspension was of the rocker type and didn't appear to have as much travel as I would have liked, and instead of a simple spring, it had some sort of air shock which made a hissing sound when compressed (so much for sneaking up on rattlesnakes in the woods). So, even though I'd stopped by to merely look at some potential road bikes, I left with this brand new Trek Fuel. It cost $928 and change, more than I'd paid for several really wonderful cars in my twenties. I figured that this bike was 'state of the art' at the time, a logical evolutionary step up from my beloved Trek 9000.

It had been spontaneous purchase, but after I bought it, I realized that I was not going to be able to ride it as intended, without transporting it to Nashville to Percy Warner Park. By the third time I'd done this, I was finishing up my ride in the woods and just happened to notice that one of the rear suspension screws had fallen out. On the way home I stopped at Trace Bikes and ordered another screw for twenty something dollars in advance. It arrived a week or so later, and after I picked it up and got back home it didn't fit. I subsequently removed another screw of the same size, from the other side of the suspension and took it to the local hardware store and bought several identical screws for $1.50 each. Honestly, this bike was a piece of junk. Screws routinely fell out of the rear suspension, which had to be tightened constantly at every place a screw existed. Each screw had to be torqued down before, during, and after each ride, which reduced the intended function, and thus the purpose of having a rear suspension to begin with. It reminded me of several really nice looking women in my past, who despite being attractive, quickly proved to be more trouble than they were worth.

One day on impulse, I took it for a loop I'd carved out of the heavy brush in the back field bordering the woods. I hadn't gone more than a hundred feet when I decided enough is enough. The thing was wobbling so much that I considered it dangerous to ride at all, anywhere. I dismounted and walked it back to the garage. A few days later, I happened to notice that the port side chain stay had literally crystalized and broken in half. What would have happened if I'd been descending a steep hill fast when it snapped in half without notice? Perhaps I should have it repaired? Replace the rear suspension

triangle with a new one? The thought never entered my mind. It was a piece of junk from beginning to end. Not only that, it got flat tires regularly, unlike my Trek 9000 which still has the same tires it had in the early 1990s. I removed what parts were salvageable such as the wheels, brakes, front suspension fork, seat, etc. and applied them to one of my subsequent Walmart mountain bikes.

Genesis V-2100

I don't like snobs of any sort, especially snobs without portfolio, and bike snobs are some of the worst. They have to have the newest and what they've been told by advertising, to be the absolute `best' of every possible thing, even down to irrelevant minutiae such as the bicycle seat post, crank, wheels, tires, and pedals. Consequently, the idea of a Walmart bicycle would be inconceivable to the bike snob. I'll admit that some equipment is superior to other equipment, but newer is not always better. Carbon fiber is certainly lighter than steel or aluminum in terms of bike frames, but it is not as durable and does not hold up over time under hard use. Everybody had to have an aluminum frame, then chromoly (whatever that was), then a carbon fiber frame, and now, in some cases back to steel. Next it was 29" wheels, or 27.5". Pushed by heavy advertising from the companies who'd already sold all of the 26" bikes they could, the suckers bought 29" bikes. There's nothing wrong with them, they just don't handle as well as bikes with 26" wheels. Hell, I knew that to begin with. "Well, it's been discovered that 27.5" wheels bridge the gap between the better handling characteristics of the 26" while maintaining the blah blah blah offered by the 29" wheels," a bike shop owner told me yesterday. In another eight months or so, it will be again `discovered' that the 26" really is more `user friendly,' or some other such term, after all.

Anyway, in Holly Springs, Mississippi, where I spend as much of my summer as time permits, the Walmart or 'Walmark' as it's sometimes known, is the go to place for necessities. I'd been looking at bicycles every time circumstances required me to be there. I'd been noticing a particular dual suspension mountain bike called a Genesis V 2100. It looked cool, had a rocker type rear suspension, and was priced at approximately $150. I already had several bikes so I really didn't need another one, but all of my bikes were in Tennessee and I used all of them up there. At length I decided to buy one and was literally on the way to get it but decided to stop at the post office first. There was some guy sitting on the steps who was an off duty fireman and one of these bikes was parked next to him. I asked him if it was his bike and we began talking about it. He said that he really liked it and that it was fine for his purposes, but added that he had several other bikes. I told him that I was literally on the way to buy an identical bike right then, and he offered to sell me his for $75. I took it for a spin and told him I'd take it and to wait there while I drove down the street to the bank to get some money. I returned, paid him, and loaded the bike into my car. I got it home and stripped the garish identifying stickers off of the body, then looked at the bike in detail. It had a simple rocker type rear suspension which was similar to that of my Trek Fuel, the only difference being that this was more simply executed, and in that sense superior. Additionally the rear fork had an extra, pivot point as opposed to the Trek's rigid rear triangle, and was thus superior. Most importantly, none of the screws in the rear suspension bolts by design, ever came loose, ever. They never needed tightening.

In actual use over rough but moderate terrain this bike is superior to either of my three Trek full suspension bikes, proving again that the simpler anything is the better it is likely to be. The only complaint I have, if any, is that the front fork's suspension is 'spongy' for lack of a better word, and cannot be adjusted. If I intended to engage in any seriously rough terrain or downhill riding, I'd replace the front suspension with something from Rock Shox. The rear suspension spring is adjustable, however, and should be tightened to reduce bounciness. The tires are tougher than those of my Trek Fuel and infinitely less subject to puncture. I liked this bike so much that I bought three new identical bikes for Tennessee. Simple is usually better.

9. Kestrel Road Bike

This was the first carbon fiber bike I'd ever had, and likely my last, not that there is anything wrong with carbon fiber. This bike really was that lightweight, but by the time I ended up with it, I was living in the country and not about to ride on Hwy 100, a curvy two-lane road with no shoulder. The Natchez Trace Parkway was close enough, that is, within fifteen miles, but I really didn't want to fool with it. I did ride it on the road in Nashville's Percy Warner Park a couple of times, and after riding heavy mountain bikes on the road as well as in the woods for years, hills were a breeze. I rode for about an hour and a half around Belle Meade and in the park once or twice with my friend Jeff Nunnally who I used to ride with on weekends from Nashville to Franklin and back in the '80s. Now, the population of Nashville has exploded over the last thirty years to the extent that riding a road bike anywhere within twenty miles of Nashville is more dangerous than it's worth. A cyclist was even mowed down and killed near Nashville on the Natchez Trace fairly recently, a place generally considered to be safe for cyclists. I kept this bike as a work of art for several years without riding it, but decided at length to sell it since I had no intention of ever riding it again. Besides, it seemed to flex a bit at speed which was a bit disconcerting. That, along with those really minimal high pressure tires made even a small piece of gravel potentially treacherous. I sold it to a physician from Vanderbilt who was glad to have it. It really was the most beautiful bike I've ever seen, and if I'd had a place to display it, I probably would have kept it for the thing of beauty which it is.

As an afterthought, my friend the veterinarian, to whom I'd given my Specialized Hard Rock used to road bike 5000 miles a year, often on dangerous roads, and frequently in the dark. He'd taken his carbon fiber bike in for service and was told that it had stress cracks throughout the frame and was unsafe to ride at all. His technician refused outright to even minimally service the bike. My point here, as relates to cars, is that I don't think carbon fiber as a structural component of automobiles is desirable for any number of reasons, and I doubt that it will stand the test of time. Again, this is merely my opinion and, I could be wrong.

I still ride daily weather permitting, but I'm no longer actively seeking new and better mountain bikes. The latest Genesis V 2100 is the same dual suspension frame as my earlier ones with bright red and black colors which I really like. It has 27.5 inch wheels which I kept on one of them although I replaced the larger wheels with 26 inch wheels from something else on another. I'm not saying I'll never buy another high end mountain bike, but it will have to be superior to the cheap Walmart bikes, which except for the front suspension is unlikely.

Throughout this book, I'll be inserting some pictures where space permits, some of which may have nothing to do with the subject under consideration at the time, as is the case here in which we're talking about bikes. One day while driving down Charlotte in Nashville, I saw a very rare (no doubt the only one in existence) three-finned 1959 Cadillac Fleetwood. Since I knew I'd never see another one I stopped and had my picture taken. In honor of the occasion, I'm holding my red Hoo Doo bag, which contains a lodestone, High John the Conqueror, and some other powerful items I'm not at liberty to mention due to considerations pertaining to national security. That's my faded blue 1969 to the right of the image, my first Cadillac convertible.

Who wouldn't want one of these?

At my first Fan Fair at Roger Miller's King of the Road Hotel, across the river from downtown Nashville. At this time, it was called the `Dee Jay' Convention, then Fan Fair, and now I think it's Country Music Week or something like that. Cadillacs were definitely in my future!

Conrad Belisle (center) owned the Cadillac and Oldsmobile dealership in Ottawa, Ontario. That's me on the left as a young whipper snapper at Le Dome in Ft. Lauderdale in 1973. I told him that foreign cars were getting ready to invade the US in mass, especially from Japan and Germany, England (not so much). He angrily told me "I've forgotten more about cars than you'll ever know." I said, "You're probably right, at least about the first part of your observation." The truth is, nobody then had any idea what was on the horizon. The Datsun 240Z had already made a strong showing in the US, and the so-called muscle car era was on the way out, though unknown to the average consumer. The early `70`gas crisis' was real enough with cars lined up by the dozens to get gas anywhere they could. Whether the gas crisis was manufactured or actual, the consequences for the average American motorist were significant. By the mid-1980s American cars sucked, and that bumbling Jimmy Carter hadn't helped matters with his desire to bring America down a few notches. By 1973 my mom had bought a couple of Subarus, another friend had a small Datsun pickup, and a girl I knew also had a Suburu coupe. Mercedes SLs and sedans were beginning to show up around Nashville's Music Row for the first time, interspersed among the Lincoln MK IVs, MK Vs and large Cadillacs. They were more of a curiosity at first, but by 1977, who wanted a new Cadillac?

My grandfather Arthur McCalmont at the wheel of something.

II

Family Cars

The '51 Ford is built to stay in style,
to stay young in performance, to stay thrifty . . . for the years ahead!

No seatbelts or headrests. Steel dashboard, long rigid steel steering column aimed at your chest. No problem!

1951 Ford Sedan

This was the first car I remember, as I was born in 1949. I remember it for two reasons. First of all, it had a metal dashboard. One afternoon I was riding with my mother in front of Vanderbilt Hospital in Nashville, heading toward what is now known as Hillsboro Village. I was sitting in the front passenger seat next to her when she had to make a sudden stop. Back then, there was no concern whatsoever for passenger safety, let alone that of children, who were routinely permitted to ride standing up, lying down, or even lying on the area behind the back seat under the rear window, formerly known as the package shelf. When she hit the brakes, my forehead hit the heavy steel dash, causing me to acquire a subarachnoid brain cyst which would only be discovered thirty years later after a biking accident.

The second reason I remember that car is because it was where I had my first lesson in what would become a fairly wonderful lifelong relationship with women. I was three or four years old, and she was six, and my first girlfriend. She didn't know it, but I did. One warm summer evening we were sitting in the car, just the two of us, just like grownups while my mother was in the house visiting my grandparents. I was sitting in the driver's seat and she, Brent, in the passenger seat. We were talking, that is, she was doing most of the talking and I was just looking at her, entranced by her incredible beauty. I never wanted this night to end, but knew that would, and probably sooner than later. I wanted to memorize every moment.

Suddenly, she pushed the cigarette lighter into its receptacle, and when it popped out she grabbed the knob and withdrew it. "Isn't it pretty?" she asked. And indeed it was, glowing bright red in the semidarkness. "Touch it," she said. I knew that it was red and beautiful, but not that it was hot. I was reluctant, but her voice was soft and sweet and she was so beautiful, and I trusted her. So, I touched the end of my finger to the hot surface. Totally surprised, I Immediately began howling. She quickly replaced the lighter and left the car. My finger was hurt, but my feelings much more so than my finger. I couldn't believe that she'd intentionally done that to me. In tears, I returned to the house, told my grandfather what had happened, and asked `why'? "That's just the way girls are," he told me.

After this, my grandfather bought a new 1957 Ford coupe. It had mild fins, a V-8 engine and he drove it fast. It was white with some sort of gold metallic stripe down the side. His wife, my grandmother, had died in 1955 or 1956, and by 1959 he'd retired and remarried and moved to South Peninsula Drive in Daytona Beach. By this time he had a white 1959 Plymouth sedan, the most basic model available and drove it at a creeping intolerably slow pace. The Plymouth sedan had big, bulbous, but not what I'd call `precise' fins as with the Cadillacs of the era.

1961 Plymouth By the time I returned to spend a month or so with my grandfather in the summer of 1961, he had a new Plymouth sedan, a 1961. This was one of the strangest looking cars I'd ever seen. Visually, it resembled a fiddler crab from the front. My grandfather who'd once hauled ass around Nashville for decades, now crept at a snail's pace around Daytona Beach in this absurd four-door conveyance. But that was then. Now the car looks very desirable, mainly because automobile designers are really limited by so many arbitrary governmentally imposed restrictions that no designer is truly free to just create anything he wants. What I especially like about this car now is that no auto manufacturer will ever conceive of, let alone put into production anything as visually extravagant as this ever again, and as a society, we are doubtless

poorer for it. I do suspect, however, that the face of the current Lexus lineup will seem every bit as strange fifty years hence as this `61 Plymouth does today. That said, I cannot but detect a strong resemblance in any modern Toyota Lexus to this 1961 Plymouth, which is perhaps the Lexus design team's greatest stylistic influence, at least from the front. But judge for yourself!

1958 Chevrolet Biscayne

My parents bought this car when I was eight years old. It was the first new car I remember us having. The 1951 Ford which it replaced had probably been bought new, but I don't remember. The `58 was a white four-door sedan with a straight six-cylinder engine. When I was eight years old I didn't know anything about cars at all. By age ten, I knew that it was next to the least expensive Chevrolet one could buy, only slightly less desirable than the even lesser `Delray.' I was somewhat embarrassed by this time. My best friend's parents, who lived two doors down had a really cool 1960 Pontiac station wagon and a black 1957 Chevrolet convertible. Dr. Martin who lived down the street, had a 1959 Ford convertible. Elm Hill had a strange looking Volvo which he considered a sports car. The Fesseys, one street over, on Esteswood, had a 1960 Thunderbird convertible, and one of my best friend's parents had two chauffeur-driven Cadillac Fleetwoods.

The '58 sat low and didn't look too bad, if you like white cars, which I don't, except in a dry climate. I used to have to wash this car and it always streaked, with grey patches even when new. And a white car in any climate, especially a humid southern climate, will eventually mildew just sitting still. The Biscayne's interior was light green cloth with vinyl bolsters. The car had no air conditioning, power brakes, radio, or power steering. Back then, those features, now standard on most cars, were all optional at extra cost. It also had roll-up windows, something 'younger people' (I can't believe I'm actually in a position to use that term), are unfamiliar with. Since the car didn't have power steering, the steering wheel was nearly as big as that of an ocean liner. Back then, on most cars other than Cadillacs, Lincolns, and Imperials, power steering was optional, so the same steering wheel was generally used for each model whether or not it had power steering. This meant that if a car didn't have that option, the large steering wheel was necessary in order to manhandle the wheel.

I didn't know back then that Chevrolet, Cadillac, Buick, etc. were all made by the same company, though I couldn't help but notice that the front end of the Chevy looked a lot like the front end of the 1958 Cadillac. This was the car I learned to drive with, and it really was a wonderful car, in retrospect. It took us literally all over the country. We traveled in this car with an Apache camper in tow, and vacationed in different parts of the country. We went to the Alamo in San Antonio, swimming at Barton Springs in Austin, to Jamestown, Yorktown, and Williamsburg, Albuquerque, Carlsbad Caverns, and Santa Fe in New Mexico, Washington, DC to the Smithsonian, crab fishing on the Delaware River, Mt. Vernon, Monticello, etc. Additionally, we went to Daytona Beach, Florida for two weeks every summer to visit my grandfather.

The Biscayne never conked out on us, or left us stranded, although once, somewhere, it did require a new generator. At some point, it had its aging six-cylinder engine replaced with a rebuilt one, as was the custom at the time when few American cars ever exceeded 100,000 miles. I remember that car fondly now, and it's worth mentioning, that as a child, I travelled to more places by far than any of my friends whose families had more expensive cars. This was our only car until we got a 1964 Olds F-85 Cutlass.

1964 Oldsmobile F-85 Cutlass

This was the second new car we ever had as a family, and it became my mother's while the 1958 Chevy, as a second car, enabled my father to drive to work for the first time, rather than having to take the bus, or have my mom pick him up downtown. It was a metallic green four door sedan with a matching fabric interior, and a small V-8 with plenty of power. Unlike the '58 Chevy, it had air conditioning, power steering, power brakes, and above all, a radio. It was a pretty car with clean, crisp lines and I never felt ashamed to be seen in it. Later, I would enjoy driving it.

By this time, I was fourteen, and fully aware of cars and music, two of my early passions which would remain lifelong. There were great cars all around me. My next door neighbor had a perfect black 1952 Buick and a mid-1950s Packard Clipper. Nashville's Green Hills Market was next door to the Green Hills Theatre building, which also contained a hobby shop, where we bought model cars. It was a prosperous area then, as now, and anything could be seen there anytime. I remember regularly seeing Cadillacs, Lincolns, Packards, and everything else. One day there were two identical black 1948 Lincoln Continental V-12 convertibles parked side by side at Green Hills Market.

All of us hitch-hiked around the neighborhood back then or rode our bikes. If there were any maniacs out and about, we didn't see them. I often got a ride in an older boy's XK 120, or in one of the McClure's two 1962 Lincoln convertibles. The McClellans, who lived on Lynwood, one street over, had two faded 1949 Lincoln Cosmopolitans which resembled large cockroaches. An old man who also lived on Lynwood, had a 1936 Lincoln Coupe which he drove regularly. A friend's mother had a 1959 Mercedes 190 sedan which she drove with her nose in the air, as if she were the Queen of England. We mockingly referred to her as 'The Goddess of Green Hills Pharmacy.' A family up the street from me had a French Citroen and would pick me up from time to time. It was a four-door sedan, long and low with a very strange appearance, a cross between a space ship and some peculiar member of the insect world. Its steering wheel had one spoke, and was very unique. As I said, there were many great cars around my part of town in the 1950s and 1960s. I even remember looking up one day and seeing a D-Type Jaguar with a fin headrest flying down the street in front of my house.

I got sent to Battleground Academy for the seventh and eighth grades, starting in 1960. I generally rode the thirty or so miles to Franklin on this horrible stinking bus with Lori Ghertner and his older brother Gary, who lived on nearby Esteswood. The bus bounced up and down, swung wildly around corners, was filled with exhaust fumes to the extent that I felt sick everyday by the time I reached school. Eventually, Gary got a driver's license and a brand new 1961 Pontiac Le Mans coupe. It was white with red bucket seats, the immediate predecessor of what would soon become the Pontiac GTO. It was an interesting car technically, though I didn't know it then. It had a torque tube rather than a driveshaft, its transmission at the rear of the car, just ahead of the differential, and an independent rear suspension, although of the primitive and dangerous swing-axle type used by Mercedes and Porsche at the time. Their parents already had a 1960 Thunderbird coupe, white with tan bucket seats, power windows, and air conditioning, which we often took. It was so far above and beyond our 1958 Chevy that it seemed to be from another dimension. When Lori's parents bought a new silver Buick Riviera in 1963, they offered the Thunderbird to Gary, who elected to keep his Pontiac, so the Thunderbird was traded in. The Riviera was solid, exotic, and elegant, silver with black bucket seats and a futuristic console. What a car!

BGA had students from the seventh grade through high school, mostly from fairly well to do families. One of the boys had a new metallic blue 1962 Chevy 409. When I first saw it, I expected something exotic since I'd heard so much about the 409. It was anything but, with bench seats, no air conditioning, and small hubcaps that looked like cake pans that barely covered the lug nuts. About the only thing that could be said about the car was that it was a 409 with a manual 4-speed floor mounted shifter. I didn't see what the big deal was.

There was one student with a new 1962 Corvette, and several more with sports cars. One boy who lived behind me on Sneed Road had a Triumph TR-3 in which I often received a ride home. Another kid who lived one street behind me drove a strange French Renault Dauphine with a rear mounted air-cooled engine. It was small, underpowered, and scary to ride in due to its size. Another BGA student, who lived one street over on Esteswood subsequently got a mid-1960s 421 Pontiac 2+2 coupe.

At about this time, when I was ten years old, I joined the Boy Scouts, Troop 31, at St. George's Episcopal Church in Belle Meade. My scoutmaster lived up the street from me on Estes Road in a big two story brick house. His son Ross was my age, a friend of mine, and also in my scout troop. We'd ride to the scout meeting every Monday night with his father, either in an MG TD, with the top down, or in a 1961 Rambler convertible, with the top down. I usually got stuck in the back seat, which was no problem in the summer, but the scoutmaster always had the top down, regardless of the temperature, unless it was raining. He must have been almost as cold as I was in that MG, given the uselessness of heaters in British sports cars of the era.

One afternoon after school, I was visiting his son Ross, and we were in the yard. We were both around eleven years old. Ross was suddenly struck in the ass without notice by a BB fired from John Drury's yard. Ross jumped, and I laughed, but he was pissed. We took cover upstairs over the garage, raised the window and started shooting back. From our high vantage point we got the best of the three boys and their guns, and made them jump, but they managed to shoot out some of the garage windows. When the battle was over I walked home, thrilled by the exchange, but thankful that nobody had been blinded. When old man Perry had returned from home that night, he ran over some of the glass and got a flat tire, as if it were my fault.

At the end of the eighth grade, which I flunked, I returned to Julia Green School, near my house. When I started to school at Hillsboro High School, the following year, it was a different world, and there were students my age and older, with some great cars. A girl I'd gone to grammar school with, had a fairly new Rolls-Royce Silver Cloud as a daily driver. Her father had a 1956 Lincoln MK II, and several early Rolls-Royce Silver Ghosts. At Hillsboro there was also an XK 120 roadster, an XK 140 roadster, a black 1958 Fleetwood, new Pontiac GTOs, multiple Grand Prix, Oldsmobile 442s, and one kid my age alternated between an XK-E roadster and a Jaguar 3.8 S sedan. Several kids had new 427 Corvette coupes and roadsters. There were also some really nice 1955, 56, and 57 Chevy Bel Aires, and by the time I was a senior, one student had a metallic blue 1967 Impala SS 427 convertible.

My grades weren't very good so I got sent to Baylor one summer in Chattanooga, where I made great grades, but was not allowed to return as a student in the fall because I'd sold beer signs to some of the students and made some money. Back then, at Baylor, if you got caught smoking, even once, you were expelled. No questions, no second chances. I would have thought that the school would have applauded and encouraged my success in free enterprise, in selling beer signs, but no.

After Baylor, I spent my junior year at Columbia Military Academy in

Columbia, Tennessee (1966-1967) as a boarding student. There I saw my first 1967 Cadillac Eldorado Coupe in person. It was grey with red leather, and unlike anything I'd seen before. It had received the prestigious `Car of the Year' award from one of the motoring magazines for 1967, and had been presented by General Motors as a `personal luxury car,' which it was. It was big, with a really long front end, and a shorter, but perfectly proportioned and sculptured stern. The disappearing headlights only added to its allure.

One of my new friends at CMA was from Leland, Mississippi, and his grandmother lived 40 miles away from school in Nashville at Windsor Towers apartments. She had a 1963 Cadillac Sedan DeVille which she would let us drive when we came to town on weekends. My friend Elliot always wanted me to drive, which I enjoyed, but he was nuts. One time we went to Burger King on West End in the Vanderbilt area and got a couple of burgers to go. When we returned to his grandparents' apartment, he closed the door to one of the bedrooms, and removed the ketchup and mustard-soaked lettuce and tomato from his sandwich, opened a chest drawer, and placed the whole mess on top of some clean and nicely folded clothes. I just knew that his grandmother would think that I did it, and said so, but that didn't stop him. He did this on more than one occasion but it was never mentioned. Of course, I was appalled by his actions, but couldn't help laughing because it was such a crazy thing to do. And of course, the more I laughed, the more it looked like I was the guilty party. Elliot died a year later on the way home from summer school at Chamberlain-Hunt school in Port Gibson, Mississippi, when his 1966 GTO ran off the road. It was subsequently determined that carbon monoxide from the air conditioner had caused him to pass out at the wheel.

There wasn't much to do at CMA, but I did read car magazines, some of which had cars for sale, listed and pictured at the end of the magazines. In 1966 one could buy a Mercedes 300 SL for around $1,500, or an aluminum bodied 1930s Rolls Royce, for about the same amount that my mother was paying for walking horses back then. I remember saying that cars would be a much better investment, in that horses invariably died. I was right, of course, but the fact of the matter was that Mom liked horses, not cars.

Another friend of mine, Alex Steel, and I, had stopped by his grandmother's apartment building on Belle Meade Blvd. in Nashville one afternoon, to see if he could put the touch on her and get some money. When we entered the lobby, he walked over to the large radiator in the hall and pissed right on it. I was horrified, but laughed, as usual. He died in a new Aston Martin fifty years later. That's part of the problem with the newer cars, they're so fast and so silent, with almost no true sense of actual speed, that it's easy to lose control of one of them. By the time you realize how fast you are really going, it's too late to make any correction, and that's that. All of the computerized traction management, antilock brakes, and other features, as good as they are, can't override the laws of physics. With the older cars, especially with the top down, there was a more accurate sense of speed, and the driver was more attuned to the sound of the engine and the feel of the road through the steering wheel. Cars are `better' and safer now than they've ever been, but in a sense, easier to get killed in if you don't know what you're doing. Most drivers aren't experienced enough, myself included, to be playing around with 500 horsepower in residential areas.

I'd actually studied hard for the first time in my life at CMA, made the highest grades I'd ever earned, before or since, and was allowed to return to Hillsboro High School in Nashville my senior year. But for graduation at CMA, several seniors received new cars, whatever they wanted. One student received a brand new red 1967 XK-E roadster, and another, a new 1967 Shelby GT 500.

My pal Clay Yager of Memphis. I met him at CMA 54 years ago and we still like cars, music, and beer signs. Here he stands with one of his Chrysler Crossfires. He also has a convertible.

1966 Plymouth Satellite Convertible

While I'd been stuck at Columbia Military Academy, my mother bought a 1966 Plymouth Satellite convertible from some guy my younger sister had been dating. It was white with a black convertible top, bucket seats, and an automatic transmission with a console-mounted floor shifter. I really liked the car but didn't get to drive it much as I was away at school most of the time that my parents owned it. I thought it was an attractive car with sleek lines and like most convertibles of its era looked good with the top up or down.

The interior was some vague sort of burgundy with a vinyl, western-themed design, which I liked, but the car lacked AC and power steering, both of which were extra cost options for most cars in the 1960s. I drove it back to CMA one bright Saturday afternoon to visit  some of my former classmates, and had a pleasant drive down and back with the top down. There was some mechanical problem on the way home, which I don't specifically recollect. I'd made it home as far as Franklin, stopped somewhere and it wouldn't start. I think it had something to do with the distributor. After it had been towed to wherever, and I'd flagged a ride home, my father grabbed his head in both hands (as usual), and stomped around the house, again telling me that I was going to bankrupt him and force all of us to move to the dreaded 'east Nashville.' I wasn't too worried about that, because I'd heard it said many times, and all of us were all still on Estes Road. I imagined that if he elected to move to east Nashville, for whatever reasons he might decide to do so, it wouldn't affect me, as I had friends in Belle Meade whose parents liked me, where I could stay until the end of my senior year. No big deal! I don't remember the exact circumstances under which the Plymouth departed, but it was gone by the end of my senior year of high school. The Olds F-85 stayed with us until Mom bought a new 1970 Olds cutlass sedan. By this time nearly every middle class family had two cars and getting a new car was not the big deal it had been in the 1950s, when almost everyone in the neighborhood would come look at and admire whatever new car anyone bought.

1969 Volkswagen

There weren't that many VWs around Nashville in the late 1960s, and most of them, I assumed were owned by beatniks, although that wasn't always the case. I sometimes rode back from BGA in Franklin with an acquaintance who lived two streets over when I was ten or eleven. We were driven on these rare occasions by his absolutely beautiful older sister in her VW bug convertible, always with the top down. It was love at first sight. Not the car, but my friend's sister. The VWs looked like bugs, and the acceleration? Not really. Even the convertible with its top lowered looked strange, specifically the top frame, which in my estimation even then, should have had another hinge at each side so that when down it wouldn't extend so far behind the rear seats. One of my good friends, Winky Pilcher lived across the street from the girl with the VW convertible, and eventually got a new VW coupe. He was older than me by two years and I'd occasionally ride around with him and friends through Percy and Edwin Warner Parks in our neighborhood. I'd always be in the back seat, and he'd drive fast along the curvy roads which wound around, up and down and through the parks. It seemed to me that the car was top heavy with more than one person inside and likely to flip over at any moment without notice, which it did one day, although I wasn't on board at the time.

Anyway, my mother frequently got on various tangents concerning one thing or another, often involving cars. Both of them were 1969 Volkswagen Automatics, cars with stick shifts, but without manual clutches, an unnecessarily complex and pointless exercise in futility, which also extended to some Porsche 911 models of the era, including the 912. It debuted in 1968 as the 905 Sportmatic, consisting of a fully synchronized four-speed gearbox developed from the original 901. A hydraulic torque converter and single disc clutch operated through an electrically activated vacuum control unit set in motion by the floor-mounted shift lever. Every time the shift lever was moved, the clutch released. There was a 'D' mode for shiftless driving but I recollect that it was confusing to operate. Instead of having a linear from front to rear PRND1234, from front to rear, you had to move the shift lever around with no idea where it was really supposed to be positioned.

Mom bought two of these VW bugs, though nobody knew why. They just showed up one day at her house, both brand new. One was brown, and the other was British racing green. I remember being stopped beside the road with both hands on the shifter cursing it and attempting to choke it. They could have just given it an automatic transmission to start with. At that time I hated Volkswagens, mainly because they were always holding up traffic, especially those obnoxious VW vans that looked like an oversized loaf of bread, with a top speed of fifty off the side of a mountain with a strong tailwind. The brakes always sounded like a bunch of spiders rolling around inside a tin can, and beginning with 1968 models, God help you if you were the least bit claustrophobic. The front seats had built in headrests giving the seat backs the appearance of a tombstone from an old cowboy movie, and completely obscured the forward vision of whoever had the misfortune to be stuck behind them. That in addition to the fact that the rear windows did not lower, at all, made the situation even worse. And they all sounded like lawn mowers. The Karmann Ghia, on the other hand, was really beautiful by anyone's standards with its Ghia designed body, and low profile. There was even a convertible available. Now that I'm not regularly being held up by them in traffic, I look upon all air-cooled VW Bugs as interesting, curious, and actually somewhat desirable, especially the pre-1968 models. This may also be a good time to mention the lasting power of advertising. "Just drop in to Jenkins & Wynne-they're the folks with the Volks-wagens." I still remember the words to that tune and its melody as played on the radio sixty years ago. As far as our two VWs were concerned, I came home one day and they were gone, and even though I hadn't especially liked them, I was mildly disappointed.

1969 AMC Javelin

Another of my mother's purchases was a 1969 American Motors Javelin. Other than the 1966 Plymouth Satellite convertible, it was the only car she ever bought that I really liked. The Javelin debuted as a 1968 model, supposedly to cater to the Camaro and Mustang buyer, which I guess it did. Ours was a Javelin SST, sort of copper/bronze color with a black vinyl top and black vinyl bucket seats, and a V-8 with a floor-mounted automatic, and some sort of rally wheels as opposed to plain hubcaps. When I returned home from the navy, there it was. I liked it immediately. In the first place, it was a very attractive design, a good looking two-door coupe. It also had really cold air conditioning, a V-8, and perhaps even a stereo radio. It also had what sounded like a `cricket' in permanent residence somewhere within the dashboard.

When fall 1970 arrived I went to the University of Tennessee in Chattanooga. I had just squandered all of my school book money for the semester, having purchased a flintlock pistol at a place downtown called the Antique Armory. As fate would have it, I was walking down McCallie Avenue on my way back to campus when to my surprise, who pulls up alongside me totally unannounced, but my Mom in her Javelin. To say she wasn't pleased to see me walking down the street with a pistol in my hand, would be a great understatement. She couldn't have cared less about the pistol, but knew on some level that I'd bought it with money intended for legitimate purposes. And even though Chattanooga wasn't Manhattan, how is it that she happened to drive the 120 miles or so from Leiper's Fork, Tennessee on a whim, and just happen to drive right up to me? I could've been in class, or anywhere else in the city, for that matter, but here she was. How do they know? It must be some sort of Zen thing.

And while I'm thinking about McCallie Avenue, I remember cutting through the parking lot of the girls' dorm one afternoon. I couldn't help but notice a good looking girl walking in the other direction. `Poetry in Motion.' As I stepped out of the parking lot a campus police car entered the small lot. In a matter of seconds there was a loud crash as its driver rammed a parking light post head on, in broad daylight, his attention obviously focused on something other than his driving. As Muddy Waters observed, `the whole world's thinking about the same old thing.'

III.

1967-1970 Oldsmobile 442s, Coupes & Convertibles

1967 Olds 442

By the beginning of my senior year in high school, several of my friends and acquaintances had died in car accidents, some as a result of speed, others, alcohol, or a combination of the two. My friend Jay had a new yellow 1968 Camaro SS with a black vinyl top and I rode around with him for most of my senior year. When his parents moved to Ft. Lauderdale for the winter, it was party time. Jay let me drive his father's 1961 Sedan DeVille daily, which I enjoyed, as I'd always loved Cadillacs. The crisp lines of the 1961s always appealed to me. During spring break, we took his Camaro to their place in Ft. Lauderdale.

I'd also reconnected with my friend Steve Vassallo, who was in school at Ole Miss. He'd wound up with his grandmother's white 1955 Chevy four-door sedan. It was in good shape, but not much fun. One weekend, Vassallo came home from Ole Miss with one of his student friends, Steve Bowman, a Sikeston, Missouri native. Bowman was driving a 1967 Oldsmobile 442. It was red, with red bucket seats, a white vinyl top, and a four speed floor shifter. They wanted me to skip school and ride back to Ole Miss with them, which I did. The car was extremely fast, and Bowman drove like a bat out of hell. I liked Oxford and spent much of my senior year of high school there, drinking beer, occasionally smoking weed, (when we could get it), listening to the ever changing music, going out with college girls, and understandably, as a result of these and other indiscretions, not graduating from high school. But that car was a rush. Bowman often let me drive, giving me drunken instructions from the back seat while trying to make time with some girl. I don't approve of drunk driving, but in high school or college in the late 1960s, it wasn't uncommon. Back then, you couldn't buy beer in Oxford, although whiskey was sold at liquor stores. I thought this was a strange law, even then, since whiskey and other alcoholic beverages sold at liquor stores were of a much higher alcohol content than beer. The liquor stores in Oxford at the time didn't have windows, so people passing by wouldn't be tempted by actually seeing whiskey bottles displayed on shelves. All this stupid law did was to encourage under age liquor sales since police driving by couldn't see kids inside the liquor stores. It was also easier to buy liquor locally than to drive the winding two-lane road thirty-something miles to Holly Springs to get beer.

There was a joint in Holly Springs then called the Hitching Post, where students from Ole Miss would drive to eat, drink beer, listen to the jukebox, and hang out. It was a fun, jumping place, and of course there were plenty of places to buy beer to go in Holly Springs. Many Ole Miss students were needlessly injured or killed in motoring accidents back then as a result of having to drive to Holly Springs to buy beer, solely as the result of moronic laws. Fortunately, this is no longer the case, but I do remember the Oxford police stopping us, with me at the wheel of that 442, drunk as hell, on the way back to the dorm. We were stopped by a black officer, unusual in Oxford at the time. He wanted to see my license, shined his flashlight around the inside of the car, looking for beer, empty bottles, or other signs of alcoholic consumption. Finding nothing, but clearly noticing that the three of us were really drunk, he asked where we were going. We told him that we were heading back to the dorm. Bowman, who was even more inebriated than I was, offered to drive, but the cop, noting his condition, returned my billfold, told me to be careful, and to drive straight to the dorm.

In the mid- and late 1960s, it wasn't an especially big deal for teenagers to drive drunk as long as it wasn't recklessly, and generally confined to their own neighborhood, at least as far as the Belle Meade, Green Hills, and Hillwood areas of Nashville were concerned. It was never advisable, and some kids were taken to `juvenile,' meaning juvenile court. Basically their parents were called down there in the middle of the night, admonished, and told they were responsible for their minor children, and then the children briefly lost some privileges. Generally, if you were stopped by the Belle Meade police, they'd dump your beer onto the street and send you on your way with a warning. If you were well-mannered this is usually what happened. If you were a smart ass, however, they'd call `Metro,' meaning the Metro Nashville police, who weren't especially favorably inclined toward intoxicated `rich kids' on general principles.

You didn't want to be detained by a Metro policeman, and when a Belle Meade policeman had to call one or more of them to take a drunk and belligerent teenager `downtown,' it was best to sober up quickly and be on especially good behavior. While Belle Meade wasn't generally Metro's beat, they would drive down Harding Road from time to time, especially by Nick Varallo's, a popular teenage hangout where you parked in the gravel parking lot and black waiters in white cotton coats took your food and drink orders. The place also sold bottled beer, and most of us had credible IDs.

One of my best friends, Tom Crockett, who I've already introduced, was drunk and disorderly one night and had been either detained by two Metro Policemen, or transferred to them by the Belle Meade Police. In any case, my friend was underage, and a smart ass with a big mouth. He was placed in the backseat of the patrol car and immediately lit a cigarette. The cop told him to put it out, and he loudly mumbled something like, "Fuck you. I don't have to do shit. My father…." Smack! He was taken behind the restaurant and physically admonished, so to speak, and then taken to night court, and his parents called. He was sore all over from `resisting arrest' and missed school for several days as a result of his big mouth and bad attitude.

On weekends, most teenagers reluctantly threw whatever beer they had left in their cars out of the window before they headed home for the night. It was always 'a gift from above' when on a Saturday or Sunday morning a couple of us would be walking down a neighborhood street an find some full beer bottles or cans by the side of the road.

As my senior year in high school wound down, I was understandably depressed as all my friends were accepted at various colleges and universities. The reality of the poor decisions I'd made began to become obvious. My friend Jay didn't graduate from Hillsboro that year, and neither did I. He ended up at Riverside Military Academy in Georgia, and I ended up joining the navy to keep from being drafted. I had no interest in being killed in Viet Nam, or killing anyone else, for that matter. I wasn't a peacenik, I just felt that our national interests weren't being threatened, and didn't wish to be cannon fodder for some large corporations profiting off the war effort at the expense of kids who weren't rich enough, lucky enough, or smart enough to avoid it. Interestingly though, my father who'd been a tank commander, and wounded on two separate occasions in WW II, ended up teaching at Riverside briefly during the waning days of WW II.

By the end of the summer of 1968, I returned to Ole Miss for a last hurrah, but I knew the clock was winding down and soon I'd have to be off to the navy. The sick feeling I'd experienced at having to return to Columbia Military on a Sunday afternoon after having been given a medical excuse from a relative so I could spend the weekend in Nashville, was nothing compared to the increasing dread of knowing that soon I would lose my freedom altogether, and that by the time I got out, most of my friends would have already graduated from college and either have good jobs or be in law or medical school.

The 'last hurrah' consisted of Steve Vassallo, myself, and Steve Bowman hauling ass to Clarksdale in Bowman's 442, which he called the 'Red Whore' to a party where Bowman had a good looking hot date. We were all going to party at some trailer owned by a friend of his. Vassallo and I both had dates with girls we'd never met. The drive down from Oxford was fun and as soon as we arrived, we stopped at some joint for beer. The cold beer and the air conditioning were in stark but pleasant contrast to the summer heat of Mississippi. We had some time to kill before we picked up our dates so we went to the local Budweiser distributor where my friends waited in the 442 while I went inside and talked somebody into giving me a nice lighted Budweiser beer sign with a Clydesdale encased in a plastic bubble.

To make a long story short, the party was a bust, neither my, or Vassallo's dates liked us and we didn't like them. The trailer, however, was not what I'd expected. In the first place, it was larger, but more significantly, it resembled the inside of a 1930s yacht. Be that as it may, Vassallo decided to split and return to Oxford, notwithstanding the late hour, or that we didn't have a ride back since we'd arrived in Bowman's car, and he wasn't about to leave. This girl was really good looking and ready, so I didn't blame him. I suggested that we just wait it out and go back to Oxford with Bowman tomorrow. Vassallo insisted that we return right then, so we got a taxi. Needless to say, we didn't get far, basically just outside Clarksdale and on the two-lane highway north, before we both ran out of money. I traded the cab driver my recently acquired beer sign to take us a bit further, but we didn't get far.

Hitching a ride was a good idea in theory but at nearly midnight, there wasn't any traffic, and absolutely no lights anywhere. After walking God knows how many miles in nearly total darkness along a two-lane road, we hailed a ride with someone who was on his way to work the night shift at some gas plant a couple of miles up the road. "This is as far as I'm going," he said as he dropped us off and turned into the loose gravel parking lot of the gas plant. We stood there in the darkness and realized that we were going to walk to Oxford since we weren't going to get a ride until daybreak. Neither of us had any idea what time it was, exactly where we were, just that it was after midnight, and we were both very tired. Vassallo suggested that we find a couple of unlocked cars and sleep until morning and then start over. I located an unlocked pickup truck and climbed in. Vassallo hopped in the metal bed and we both dropped off to sleep quickly. I was in the middle of a good sleep when I was awakened by the truck's owner at around 5 am. He told us to beat it and that he was heading home, back toward Clarksdale.

It wasn't long until we got a ride all the way back to Ole Miss and decided to have some fun at Bowman's expense. I boosted Vassallo through the back window of Bowman's rented trailer. Then we opened several cans of chili, then summoned the trailer park's dog, `the whore dog' as we'd dubbed her. We fed her all she could eat, and then locked her in the trailer on our way out the front door. When Bowman got back to his trailer, the front door was wide open. Apparently the whore dog had begun howling and was extracted by its owner. We'd expected it to have excreted through every orifice inside the trailer, but alas, this had not happened. Bowman was pissed but soon got over it. After all, he'd had a great time in Clarksdale.

In the navy, I got sent to Great Lakes, Illinois for basic training, where I met a guy who was a Christian Scientist. He suggested that I go to church with him. There were many advantages as he pointed out. In the first place, since there was no Christian Science church on the base, we got to actually leave base twice or more a week, which otherwise was not yet permitted to new recruits. Secondly, there were girls at the church, and thirdly, good food. My friend, Dana, explained the basic tenets of the religion, all of which sounded as logical to me as anything else I'd been exposed to so far, so hell yes!

One night a week, Canon Ballard came to pick us up in his 1963 Lincoln Continental sedan. It was silver with black leather, and the church was located in nearby Lake Forest, a well-to-do suburb of Chicago. I enjoyed riding in that fabulous car, as well as getting off the base. All of the people I met were incredibly nice. They opened their homes to the two of us and treated us like kings. Lake Forest had large, older expensive houses like many in Nashville's Belle Meade, or parts of Memphis, but on smaller parcels of land. I remember seeing a light blue `59 Aston-Martin drophead on a used car lot in Lake Forest as we drove by. How I wanted it, but it didn't matter what it cost, I couldn't afford it, and wouldn't have been allowed to keep it on base if I could have bought it.

I came home for the Christmas Holidays, went to Ft. Lauderdale with Jay Page for the holidays and went to the Orange bowl, then back to Great Lakes, for electronics school. By this time I frequently went to Chicago and stayed at the Sheraton Blackstone, which had a discount for servicemen. One day I rode with a friend to the Ford dealer at Des Plaines, Illinois, and put a down payment on a two year old 1967 Shelby GT 500. It was white with blue stripes, a 428 with two four-barrel carbs. It hauled ass. I knew that I wouldn't be able to afford it, but at least I got to take it for a nice spin around the area, and I had the warm feeling, a glow actually, which lasted for several weeks. Someday, I knew I would have a really cool car, but it seemed so far away, and I didn't know when that would be or how it might come about.

After several months I left Chicago and went to Key West, Florida for Advanced Undersea Weapons School in February. Key West was heavily populated with old Jaguars in 1969. There was an XK 120 drophead, which ran, was in good shape, and for sale for $250. I was making around $40 a month then, so, as cheap as it was, it was still well beyond my reach. The guy that owned the Pier Hotel at the time, had a 1928 Rolls-Royce drophead with a Pontiac Tempest engine. There were other old Jaguars all over town, XK 120s and 140s, all roadsters or dropheads. When I returned ten years later on business, I was told by a native who remembered them, that they'd mostly been thrown into the sea to be used for fishing reefs. What a waste.

After weapons school, I was sent to Newport, Rhode Island, where the navy war college was. It was an area which had been populated by the very rich since the era before an income tax, and there were wonderful cars everywhere. I remember walking down the street one day as a wrecker was removing a dirt covered 1953 Cadillac Eldorado convertible from a garage where it had been parked for no telling how long. A couple of its tires were flat, but those chrome wire wheels still glistened. There was a desert rose colored 1958 Lincoln MK III convertible for sale at a local dealership for $300, an XK 140 roadster for $500, both beyond my reach. Although I didn't have any money, I was certain that, as desperate as things appeared then, that one day I would be on my own, and I'd have whatever cars I wanted, but I knew I had a while to wait.

I was out of the navy for good in January, 1970, much better for the experience. I'd been to Chicago, Key West, Newport, Guantanamo Bay, Cuba, France, England, Holland, Germany, and Denmark. I'd increased my knowledge of things mechanical and electrical, and I'd crossed the North Atlantic in winter, and enjoyed floating blissfully in the Caribbean. Like my father had told me, it was over before I knew it. I was discharged from Newport, Rhode Island, and flew to Memphis where my friends picked me up at the airport and took me back to Oxford and Ole Miss. By this time, Bowman was no longer living in the trailer park and had gotten a different `67 442. This one was metallic blue, with air conditioning, bucket seats, and an automatic. Apparently, Bowman had traded cars with his sister for some reason. This car was better, if not as much fun, and Bowman's driving had toned down also. He didn't keep this one long and soon had a 1968 MG B roadster, which as usual, he preferred for me to drive so he didn't have to fool with it. As winter headed into spring, I realized that I wasn't going to be able to start to school at Ole Miss without a job, even though I did have the G.I. Bill which would defray costs. Oxford wasn't like it is now, and the square was about as exciting as a graveyard. I couldn't find a job of any kind anywhere in Oxford.

I returned home, which was now in Leiper's Fork outside of Franklin, TN. and enrolled at Belmont College in Nashville for the spring semester. I'd ride to school with my father every weekday on his way to work. My parents soon bought a new 1970 Oldsmobile Cutlass four door sedan, keeping the 1964 Oldsmobile Cutlass as a second car, and finally getting rid of the long serving and faithful 1958 Chevy Biscayne. By 1970, the Cutlass had become a much larger car and had switched its rear suspension from leaf springs to coil springs. The `F-85' designation had been largely dropped, as the F-86 Sabre Jet, which had likely inspired its name, was now obsolete. The car was new, and nice, but somewhat bulbous, for lack of a better word. Its handling was, I thought, less precise than the 1964, but the ride was softer.

I drove my friend Jay's mother to Jay's high school graduation at Riverside Military Academy in Georgia, in her 1969 Cadillac Sedan DeVille, and then the three of us returned to Nashville for the summer of 1970. Within a week or so, his new car, a graduation present, was ready. We drove to someplace in Georgia to pick it up in one of Fleet Transport's company cars, some sort of new Mercedes diesel sedan. That thing barely made it to the top of Monteagle Mountain, literally. Anyway, Jay's car was a brand new, custom ordered 1970 Oldsmobile 442 W-30 coupe. It was gold with a 455 engine, Ram Air, a fiberglass lock down hood with two large air intakes, red plastic inner fender wells in front, and some sort of finned aluminum cover for the differential. The interior featured a gold console and bucket seats, and what was then referred to as a `his n' her' automatic transmission with a floor shifter. It was quite an iron with blinding acceleration and a top speed in excess of 150 mph.

1970 Olds 442 W-30

Jay would soon be heading to Miami, Florida for college. I, on the other hand would soon be attending U.T. Chattanooga. We'd taken my sister back to the University of Southern Mississippi at Hattiesburg, in his mother's 1969

Cadillac Sedan DeVille, a car which I really liked. We then returned to Nashville, picked up his 442, and then off to Daytona Beach for a few days and then to Ft. Lauderdale for an end of summer trip. It had been the best summer of my life to date.

This picture shows me standing in front of the pier on North Atlantic on Daytona Beach in the late summer of 1970.

When we reached Daytona, we stopped in to visit my grandfather and his wife at their house on South Peninsula Dr. where we'd be staying, and then off to the beach. We were both underage but had acceptable fake IDs. When night fell, we hit the bar at the shore end of the pier on North Atlantic. Jay made some comment to one of the waitresses. It was nothing rude or suggestive, but she ignored him. Another waitress stopped by our table and, addressing me, said something to the effect that the other girl wasn't very nice, and that I might do better with her. She introduced herself as Vicky, and told me she lived at one of the apartments there, on the shore side of the pier. She gave me its number, and told me when she got off. I said I'd see her then. It was strange to me to have been sought out and solicited by an attractive girl for the sole purpose of an anonymous sexual encounter, which it turned out to be. I was 20 years old at the time and pleasantly surprised. She was 26, and from New Jersey. This had never happened to me before, and was the perfect end of a perfect summer.

As this relates to this Olds 442, by 1974, Jay no longer wanted it and so I borrowed the $1,600 I needed from Tom McNiel at what was then known as Commerce Union Bank in Nashville. This was the first business dealing I'd ever had with him, but over the next decade he'd finance much of my hobby. By this time, I'd determined that I probably needed a dependable car. I'd gone with Jay to pick this one up new from the dealer in Georgia, knew its history, and was glad to have it. Additionally, I had a long personal history with this car and liked it.

My favorite 442 of all time was the 1967, but as much as I liked it, this 1970 W-30 was much more formidable in many ways. It was more substantial physically, that is, bigger. It was without doubt the fastest car I'd ever owned up to that point, although I never personally tested its limits. Once on the interstate somewhere in Florida Jay had buried the speedometer needle. I'd guessed we were approaching 150 mph.

I guess the 455 engine wasn't that good to begin with, as it had been completely replaced while it was still under warranty a couple of years earlier. I kept the car for a couple of years and it was enjoyable and fun to drive. Back then, in Nashville, there was only one real Mexican restaurant in town, so people from Belle Meade and Green Hills would drive out to Rivergate to eat at some chain joint at the mall. Anyway, once I got rammed in traffic out there. It dented the rear bumper and one of my flared trumpet exhaust pipes. The accident was clearly the other driver's fault, and his insurance company sent me a check. I would have preferred to have had the car fixed but was inexperienced since I'd at this point never been rammed before, an event that would be repeated often in the future. I was making around $200 a week by this time which was twice what I'd been making a year or so earlier, but it was fall, and rainy, and since the damage was minor, and I needed the money, I'd get it fixed in the spring.

Before that happened, the engine `died a death' as they say in New York. I had it towed somewhere, and sold the car for $500. I had no idea what it would cost to fix, and although I knew the owner of Hippodrome Oldsmobile on Broadway, I was certain that I couldn't afford to get it fixed, whatever it cost.

In the meantime, I still had a beautiful 1967 E-Type roadster.

Several years went by, and I saw the 442 one more time. It was parked on Broadway next door to the Great Escape, a Nashville used record store. When I exited the store, there it was, with its current owner standing next to it. I spoke with him and saw that it had been repaired and still had the original paint. The only problem, he said, was that somebody had placed some hay in the trunk at some point and that it had fallen down in the lower rear fenders, and had caused some rust behind the rear wheels at each side. I remembered that the trunk floor did not run all the way from left to right as it should have. There was about an inch and a half, or thereabouts space between the sides of the floor, and the insides of the rear fenders, leaving space on each side for anything to slip down inside the lower fender edges, settle there and collect water. Apparently, this is what had happened with the hay. Water had collected there somehow, and it had rusted both lower rear fender edges. I told him it was no doubt my fault, remembering that I'd brought hay back from my parents' farm to the place I was living at the time.

I still remember the car fondly and my association with my friend Jay Page. We'd been inseparable from ages 17-22 and then life sort of took us in different directions even though we both continued living in Nashville. He worked for Fleet Transport, then at Jim Reed Chevrolet, and then became the head of Mercedes Benz of Nashville, for several years before voluntarily relinquishing that position to be head of their used car department. He always liked cars of all types but I don't know if he ever really had another one that he actually loved, or if he just grew up. Most of his adult life was spent in the car business. I'd see him from time to time around town and we'd always speak, but sadly, he'd gone his way, and I'd gone mine. He died several years ago from the delayed effects of a ruptured aneurysm, but I miss him still. I miss us being teenagers, having fun and not worrying about anything at all, just having fun.

Bruce Shelton, Jay Page, and me, 1968

1970 Olds 442 Convertible

I had no intention of ever getting another 442, although I still loved them. It's just that I was more interested in Cadillacs, Lincolns, and Jaguars, and hadn't satisfactorily explored them, but then all of a sudden, I bought another one from a co-worker, a 1970 convertible, sight unseen, in another state. It was an action I'd repeat often in the future, usually with satisfactory results. In this case, it was in Waco, Texas, and I didn't want my wife to know about it, because I just didn't want to have to explain myself and I could afford it.

I called my pal Albert Marlowe. He didn't have to be anywhere at any particular time and had been brave enough to drive his 1958 Eldorado convertible all the way around and across the country many times. Anything that could have gone wrong with his car had done so on many occasions, and usually under the worst imaginable circumstances. He could handle whatever might come up. I don't remember what I paid him to fly down to Waco, Texas and pick up the Olds. I suggested that he use a pseudonym if he happened to call me anywhere other than my office. He selected the name 'Jack Stowage,' which I thought was rather inventive. Hopefully there wouldn't be any problems. Well, of course there were. I should have had the car hauled up here by a proper transporter but I didn't know any better at the time. It certainly would have been less expensive.

As I remember, the car actually caught on fire, and also had to have a complete transmission rebuild en route. I think when it was all told, I'd paid him $1,800 or thereabouts to bring the car to Nashville. He provided me with receipts for his hotel rooms, fuel, food, airline ticket down, and for repairs.

By the time it was delivered, it ran great and had a new transmission. The interior was nice with a floor mounted in console automatic shifter. I was disappointed that it didn't have the sport steering wheel that my W-30 had. I had other cars at the time and this one didn't get that much use. The top was fine and the paint was worn, but original. I made the mistake of letting some dumb ass English friend of mine use it for a few weeks. He was really a moron. If this wasn't a car book, I would literally astound you with tales of his incompetence. Anyway, when he brought it back, I could hear him coming down the street long before he reached my house. He'd been too cheap or stupid to put any steering fluid in the power steering pump and it sounded like an airplane engine. I was lucky it hadn't locked up and caught on fire. What a dumb ass!

I think I kept it about a year before I decided to sell it. My wife and I were going on a sea cruise in the Caribbean and I could use the money for that. I placed an ad in some local paper and sold it immediately. The buyer arranged to come pick it up and pay me cash. He was to meet me at my office on Music Row one Friday afternoon. On that day I drove it to work, but went to Williams Aviation way out I-65 North for something, in the late afternoon. Our company had two Beechcraft Barons out there. Anyway, on that afternoon a large storm was imminent. The sky was angry, dark, and churning, with lightning flashing as I hauled ass out the interstate with the top down and the wind blowing through my hair. I wound the car out to somewhere between 85 and 90 mph. I'd never driven it anywhere but around town or back and forth to work a few times. On this occasion I was amazed by its performance. It was as fast as I had the courage to drive it. I hoped that the buyer didn't show up, because now, I was actually in love with the car. If he didn't, I wouldn't sell it to him at all. What an amazing afternoon drive in a fabulous car.

The lesson I learned from buying this car is that it's best to have any car bought in another city to be delivered by a professional transport service. And don't loan any car to anybody for any reason, as the potential legal ramifications for misuse can be significant for the car's real owner. I had given the buyer my word, and unfortunately, he was at my office when I arrived. I wanted to tell him that I'd changed my mind, but I wouldn't want anyone to disappoint me in a similar way, so I accepted payment, gave him the title, and watched him drive away, but I missed it immediately.

A couple of years later I received a call from my Mom saying that the transmission had gone out on her 1970 Oldsmobile Cutlass sedan. She asked if I wanted it. I didn't especially, but it was in good shape so I had the transmission fixed and then sold it. They didn't want it anymore and while it was still a good car, it just wasn't my type of car.

After that wonderful summer of 1970, I went away to the University of Tennessee at Chattanooga, during its second year as part of the UT system. I preferred Chattanooga to Knoxville as it was closer to home, and I was already familiar with Chattanooga, and loved the place. I'd gone away to school my freshman year without a car, and completed the year without one still, but my girlfriend's parents let her use their metallic green 1969 Ford sedan, and. friends at Sigma Chi also had cars, so I was seldom without a ride.

Charlie Kimball with his 1991 Cadillac Allante.

I met Charlie at UT Chattanooga my first year, at which time he had a 1971 Plymouth Barracuda convertible, and his grandmother's 1963 Lincoln which by the time he ended up with it, several years later, he said, had a dent somewhere on almost every surface. He's had a number of interesting cars in his time including a 1963 Oldsmobile 98, a 1967 Plymouth Fury convertible (which he says we double-dated in), a 1969 Triumph Spitfire, a 1967 MGB, among others. His favorite car? A 1974 Oldsmobile Toronado. Today in addition to `normal' transportation, he has this Allante and a Morris Minor.

As regards his Allante, he says that despite the visual overall similarity, there were numerous changes to the cars from year to year, including horsepower, engines, seat controls, and modifications to the top release mechanism. He recommends a parts car.

Native Nashvillian Fred Harvey with his Willis. I met Fred at a mutual friend's wedding a couple of years ago. He's an interesting guy and has a great shop at his home in Fairview. He's into hot rods and performance cars and also has a beautiful 1957 Ford coupe, and an open wheel Ford hot rod. Like many of us, he grew up making model cars. He is an accomplished mechanic and is capable of fabricating suspensions and working with engines, especially American V-8s.

54

IV.

Lincoln, 1960 & 1959

1960 Lincoln Continental MK V

I returned to Chattanooga for the 1971/1972 school year without a car, again, but would soon, unexpectedly have one, which would be my first car. I'd been in love with the MK V from the first time my godfather drove up in his new baby blue 1960 Lincoln Continental Mk V sedan, sometime in late 1959. He was a surgeon, and this was the second car of his I remember. The first was his 1957 Lincoln Premier, a pale yellow boat that featured factory air conditioning. Like the early similarly equipped Cadillacs, it had large clear plastic tubes emanating from the trunk-mounted air conditioning unit just behind the top of the rear seat back. His new 1960 Lincoln was the most magnificent thing I'd ever seen. It made our 1958 Chevrolet Biscayne four-door, of which I was already ashamed, even more of an embarrassment. This Lincoln had several long, narrow tear-shaped `ridges' on the hood, for lack of a better description, similar to those found on the wing surfaces of a Russian Mig 17 jet. The Lincoln star hood ornament placed at the far end of what seemed like the length of a football field was truly impressive. There was a space of nearly a foot between an adult's shoulder and the outside door skin. The door itself was more than six inches thick. The instrument panel consisted of four chrome rimmed metal dials, each mounted within descending concentric circles above a flat, machine-turned metal surface, as with a 1930s Cord, or a 1970s Pontiac Trans-Am. The steering wheel itself was massive. I mean massive, and the steering column appeared to be nearly eight inches in diameter. Furthermore, the car had power windows, and vents, power steering, and air conditioning which was channeled through the arm rests of the front doors to the rear passengers. And the rear window, that is, the rear windshield, had a center panel which slid down behind the back seat. Everything about the car exuded wealth, prestige, and power. There was even an engraved heavy brushed metal plate on the dashboard, positioned above the glove box door which had a small Lincoln star and the letters MK V followed by my godfather's name, `S.W. Ballard, M.D.' If that wasn't enough, the gear shift selector had an indicator which displayed the selected gears in different colors. This was a heavy, heavy car, and it did not budge, rattle, or bounce when it hit bumps or crossed railroad tracks.

 I should perhaps mention the late Dr. Ballard at this point, since he was such a great influence in my life. He was a self-made man in the truest sense of the word, had come from nowhere, Montana, put himself through Northwestern, and become a surgeon. He didn't take any crap from anybody, and did whatever he wanted. He felt that he deserved the best, and he went out and got it. If he didn't know something, he found out about it. He accepted no excuses from anyone, especially himself. He was an inspiration to me, and one of the great influences on me personally. I loved to ride in that Lincoln of his, but riding with him in any car he drove was absolutely terrifying. When he'd made the decision to pass somebody, anybody, that's what he did, and he would accelerate as fast as the car would go, until he achieved his objective. He'd pass entire lines of cars, pass on hills and around blind curves, at full speed, and seemingly without any concern for what or who might be on the other side of the hill or around the bend. Old Hillsboro Road around Leiper's Fork, is curvy two-lane road, with plenty of Hills, and back then, one was likely to suddenly come upon a tractor with a trailer load of hay or tobacco, without notice. These possibilities were of no concern to him at all. Ultimately my godfather gave his car to one of the nurses at his office and bought a new 1964 Lincoln sedan. Before that, however, l was taken in his 1960 on my first date. One of my first model cars was also a 1960 Lincoln Mk V, so I felt that I had a history with that particular make and model to start with. By the time I got back from the navy, nearly all of my friends had new cars even though they were still in college, and I envied them. I didn't want theirs, I just wanted my

own.

"An incomparable sense of security and command" Indeed!

Anyway, one day, my godfather and my mother showed up unexpectedly at my apartment in Chattanooga, where I was in college, on their way to Clement's Antiques in Hixon, just out of town. I joined them and was glad to get a free meal and the opportunity to go someplace cool. We stopped to get some gas at a Gulf station, and parked to one side of it was a black 1960 Lincoln MK V coupe with a `for sale' sign and a phone number. It also had a posted price of $250. This was really disheartening to me, because they'd made a special trip from Nashville for the sole purpose of looking at a piece of furniture, an English Chinese Chippendale secretary, which was priced at $10,000 in 1971 money. And I couldn't even afford $250 for an eleven year old car. I was really depressed. Two of my friends had new Oldsmobile 442s, another friend's father had given him a new Mercedes 250 SL, at a time when such a car was extremely rare. I determined that I could and would get that car if it was possible, by any means necessary. After they dropped me off I called the gas station, got the phone number of the owner, called, and asked him about it. He said that he'd be willing to hold the title and take payments if I could come up with a hundred dollars down payment. I literally sold everything I had of any value and came up with ninety-five dollars, which he accepted along with my agreement to pay him five dollars a week. It was the happiest day of my life when I got that car. I didn't just have a car, I'd never merely wanted a car, ever. I now had an incredible car, something unique, something which had slanted headlights and big chrome bullets mounted on the front bumper. What an iron! But, even though I had the car in my possession, I still had to pay for it. To that end I got a job as a tour guide at Ruby Falls where I was paid $5.00 for each tour I conducted. I also worked briefly at some lab where one of my Sigma Chi fraternity pledges had married the owner's daughter and had a new Porsche 911. The job at Ruby Falls was interesting and helped develop my people skills. It consisted of taking s dozen or so people in an elevator down to the cave where the waterfall was located. The guy who ran the place pronounced `tour' as `ture.' He'd announce that a new ture would be commencing in fifteen minutes or so.

The job at the laboratory wasn't so much fun, but it was strange, because I'd never been in a place where women performed jobs like driving fork lifts, and other functions traditionally considered `men's work.' I thought this is what it must be like in Russia.

The 1960 Lincoln MK V was the first car I really fell in love with.

The headlight arrangement wasn't considered strange at the time, although it seems so now. In fact, both Rolls-Royce and Bentley subsequently adopted a similar headlight arrangements for some of their later convertibles and coupes, which are generally still referred to privately as `Chinese Eye' cars. And furthermore and on top of that, other American cars had similar headlight arrangements, The 1962 Chrysler 300 H, for example.

Not every original feature worked, as I'd hoped, like the air-conditioning. It didn't work at all, and the heater and defroster didn't work either, well, that's not exactly true, the heater worked once and actually put out hot air for about fifteen minutes on that singular occasion. The hood, like that of a Jaguar XJ-S, opened from the windshield forward. It had two massive L-shaped steel pegs which were supposed to lock into place into two receptacles on the firewall when the hood was closed, but didn't. What happened, was that as I drove and picked up speed, air would pass over the front of the hood causing it to pivot downward at the front and lift near the windshield, somewhat like the air intake grill of a Porsche Carrera, opening above 40 mph. The constant airflow and the overall weight of the hood kept it from ever opening fully when the car was in motion, no matter how fast the car might be going, but it was an interesting visual quirk. And of course, any window was likely to defy the laws of gravity in reverse. That which went down, might not necessarily go up. The paint was a beautiful high gloss black and was in very good condition. The body was rust free, and the chrome, of which there was plenty, was bright and shiny, and the interior was as new. And most importantly, it ran like a bat out of hell.

But barring its eccentric quirks, it was an amazing machine. I felt secure in that car at any speed due to its sheer weight and bulk. People in newer, smaller cars, especially older women, would literally change lanes if they saw me approaching from the rear, most likely fearing that anyone who would drive `something like that' could be capable of anything, and had nothing to lose. Cars changed noticeably from decade to decade back then. A car from the 1940s generally looked like one from that period, same for the 1950s and 1960s. By 1971, this car no longer resembled anything else on the road in current production. It was my pride and joy and I was every bit as thrilled with this car as if I'd had a new Lincoln Mk III. I'd step out of a building and see my car parked there and was amazed by its beauty, especially from a side view. From the front, the car wasn't so attractive, with its slanted headlights, and Pepsi crate grill, but I liked it anyway, and often thought how the front might have been better designed while still maintaining the same side profile but determined that it wouldn't have been possible, and ultimately, that it really didn't matter anyway. My first car, as all cars have always been to me, was a visual and engineering work of art, elegance in steel. Everything about it was designed to be the best that the engineers of Detroit could come up with at the time. I'd have been thrilled to have one of these cars literally in the den of my house one day, just so I could look up and see it anytime I wanted to.

Driving it was an amazing experience. The view down the hood was incomparable, certainly one of the best on any passenger car. That Continental star affixed to the front of the hood looked like a gun sight. Despite the car's immense weight and size, it was extremely agile with plenty of power. Gas mileage? I didn't know and didn't care. It wasn't that I was rich like my friends. I literally had to gather pennies and dimes to buy gas at times, living as I was on $25.00 a week, but there was a place in Chattanooga where I could buy self-service horse piss gas for 26.9 cents a gallon. I knew nothing at all about cars, and even less about gasoline. I bought the cheapest fuel I could find and figured that it was all of more or less the same quality. It was worth whatever gas cost to be able to drive a car like that.

The engine was a 430 cubic inch displacement V-8 with a two-barrel carburetor, and a 10 to 1 compression ratio, which produced a whopping 315 horsepower at 4100 rpm, and 465 foot pounds of torque at 2200 rpm, not that I had a tachometer, or would have cared. It ran well, and that was enough for me. It also had a three-speed automatic transmission.

It's strange now to think how many different models of the same car were produced by Detroit's `Big Three' in that era. In the case of the 1960 Lincoln, they were listed in the showroom catalog as follows: Lincoln Coupe, Four-Door Sedan, Landau-Lincoln Premier Coupe, Four-Door Sedan, Landau-Lincoln Continental Coupe, Four-Door Sedan, Landau, Convertible, Town Car, and Limousine. Despite the number of various models, they all used the same engine and all had essentially the same dimensions of a 131" wheelbase, a width of 80.3" and an overall length of 227.2"

The 1960 Lincoln was the last of the series which had started with the 1958 model year. They all had the signature slanted headlights, and the Continentals all had the `breezeway' rear windshield, but they were in truth different cars despite their visual similarities at first glance. They evolved each year, but the 1958 and 1959 were more similar to each other than to the 1960, but all of them are wonderful cars, if you like their looks.

"Superb performance from the finest engines in our history"

By this time, I was renting a downstairs apartment in an old house on the edge of campus. My first roommate, had had a new blue 1970 Pontiac Trans Am which I really liked. He moved somewhere else mid-semester and I got a new roommate. Mike Cofer, a Chattanooga native, had a 1955 De Soto Firedome coupe. It was two-tone, white over dark blue. It had an angry looking front grill which made it look like a large prehistoric fish with a mouth full of gleaming chrome teeth. It had some sort of Hemi engine, not that I knew what that meant at the time. The engine looked bigger than my 430, and it probably was. What I did know was that it was incredibly fast. It was also lighter in weight than my Lincoln, and more aerodynamic. Both of our cars were pillarless two-door coupes, lacking posts behind the front doors. His car rattled every time it hit any sort of uneven road surface. The windows rattled within the door whether they were raised or lowered. It didn't have the build quality that the Lincoln had. I didn't know why it rattled and my car didn't, but in retrospect, I think it was because my car had a unibody as opposed to body on frame construction, that and a much greater curb weight.

Much was made of the `unibody' structure in Lincoln's advertising of the day (1958-1960), and with good reason. As opposed to the traditional body bolted to a frame, the body and chassis were integrated into one `immensely strong unit' with more than 5,000 welds. What this meant in practical terms was a more spacious interior, a lower center of gravity, a smoother, more stable ride, and increased safety because the body panels are a part of the entire unibody unit. It's worth mentioning that the unibody concept wasn't adopted by Rolls-Royce and Bentley until 1966 with the introduction of the Silver Shadow and Bentley T Series. It is now nearly universal in its application.

"Unibody-Key to a stronger, safer, quieter, motorcar"

In addition, Lincoln was one of the first automotive brands to take rust prevention seriously, by submerging the body of every Lincoln and Continental into a rust inhibiting bath allowing it to penetrate areas which would have been impossible to reach with traditional spraying methods (when used at all). For this reason, Lincolns from this period forward seldom, if ever, have rust problems.

In any event, my roommate Mike already knew a hell of a lot about cars, electrical systems, and other things. One day he fixed the electric rear window of my car to the degree that it would raise and lower half way. We had a lot of fun fooling with our cars.

One of the most interesting, actually terrifying experiences I ever had with my first car had to do with the brakes. Of course, I knew nothing at all about how brakes actually worked, but I began to suspect that perhaps the brakes were not fully disengaging when I took my foot off the pedal. To remedy this, I would sometimes pull the brake pedal away from the floor after an application with the top of my right foot. Well, one day I was flying through an intersection, slowed, and then pulled the brake pedal upward with my foot. When I needed to slow the car again, I applied the brake pedal, and to my absolute terror, it instantly went all the way to the floor without the car slowing at all. By the grace of God I somehow managed to dodge the other cars around me and coasted to a stop further down the road, with the car in neutral. I placed it in park, applied the emergency brake, opened the door, and then got down on the floor to examine the brake pedal. To my surprise, I realized that there was a two inch long metal pin about the diameter of a pencil, which was hinged at the underside of the brake pedal. The other end of this pin was normally situated in a corresponding receptacle on the surface of the floor. When I'd retracted the brake pedal with the top of my shoe, it dislodged this crucial pin from its housing, leaving it dangling from the bottom of the brake pedal, and me without brakes at all. Surely, Ralph Nader should have known about this and mentioned it in `Unsafe at Any Speed.' I'd been lucky and never repeated the mistake. It was an unpardonable design flaw which shouldn't have even been possible.

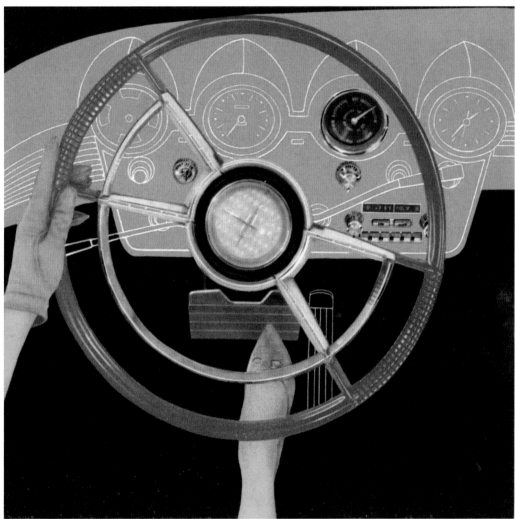

Look at that dainty wee toe!

That Lincoln got me through both semesters and back and forth between Chattanooga and home many times. In any case, I left U.T. Chattanooga at the end of the spring semester in 1972 with my tail between my legs after having been dumped by my first real girlfriend after a year and a half. In retrospect, it was one of the best things that ever happened to me, although it sure didn't seem like it at the time, and my young heart had been broken. As I looked back, she had every right to dump me, given my extreme level of immaturity and lack of direction. I transferred to MTSU in Murfreesboro, about forty miles from my parents' house in Leiper's Fork, near Franklin, Tennessee. So I returned home for a few weeks and then packed up my Lincoln and moved to Murfreesboro to start summer school there.

Eagerly awaiting its new engine!

One day, my car no longer had reverse gear. It had just simply stopped working at all. This made parking anywhere a really serious consideration, but I soon learned to leave myself an out no matter where I parked. Eventually the car began losing power. The engine was tired, and the owner of a Gulf station where I bought gas from time to time in Murfreesboro offered to rebuild the engine for $350. I had a Gulf credit card which I'd been given solely for emergency use only by my parents, and the station owner said that would be an acceptable form of payment. He assured me that the task could be accomplished in three days. Thirty days later, the car was finally ready. You can't possibly imagine how thrilled I was to get my car at last. I had walked over to the station nearly every day, checking on its progress. On that glorious day when I walked to the Gulf station to pick up my car, I was told that it was ready, but that there was one minor problem, however, in that it had ended up costing "a little more than we anticipated." The bill was $750. Not the $350 as promised. When I went to pick up the car the owner wasn't there, so some lackey took an imprint of the credit card. And I signed it for $400. There was at that time, some rule that it was not permissible to put more than that amount on a Gulf credit card during any one day period, probably for security reasons. The attendant kept the credit card and I told him that I would be back the following day to sign the slip for the other $350.

I knew that I was going to be in big trouble when my parents got the bill. I was certainly apprehensive but I figured that I'd been intentionally lied to, as well as overcharged. My father was a Federal attorney could sue the station owner and everything would be fine. The main thing was to have physical possession of the car, for as I'd always heard, `possession is 9/10s of the law.' More than that, I'd missed my car and just wanted it back. But any fear I had of my mother's shock and my father's rage were, for the moment dwarfed by the realization that my pride and joy, the greatest personal statement of my being, my ultimate freedom of movement and expression, had `a new engine!'

It was summer, so I put down all of the windows that worked and hit the interstate, heading from Murfreesboro to Nashville. I couldn't wait to get on the road, to hear the sound of that engine and feel its power. I had, however, been cautioned not to drive it over fifty miles an hour for the first five hundred miles. The car ran smoothly with plenty of power, but then why shouldn't it? Everything within the engine had been replaced. It was an amazing experience. What speed! What power! I had no idea anything could run this well. I was about ten minutes into my magnificent drive when the red oil light suddenly began flashing. I stopped at the next exit and checked the dipstick. The oil level was a quart low. "Well," I thought, "they must have just forgotten to top it up." I added a quart and went on my way, none the worse for the experience. A few minutes later the oil light came on again, only this time it was down two quarts. To make a long story short, the car used more than a gallon of oil by the time I reached Franklin. I was sweating blood, the car was barely running by this time, I was out of money, and I still had another fifteen miles to go to make it home. I literally wanted to kill the two stooges at the gas station, the stupid station owner and his dimwitted mechanic, the moron responsible for this problem.

My father was really pissed, not at the station owner who had ruined my car, but at me for having an old car in the first place. He hated that car from the moment he saw it, especially after he backed into it one morning on the way to his office, as if he couldn't see the big son of a bitch. His crappy four-door Chevrolet Nova's rear bumper hit one of the large chrome bullets on my front bumper, somewhat denting his car, but leaving mine unscathed. As angry as he was, he had no idea how mad he was going to be in another two weeks or so, when the credit card bill came.

I kept the car in oil for another two or three days, drove back to the Gulf station in Murfreesboro and told them that they'd ruined my car, that they had misrepresented their competence and had lied to me and overcharged me. I stated furthermore that I had no intention of signing the credit card for the other $350. The station owner was there on that day and said that "...cars are like people. Sometimes they need to spend some time at the hospital," and suggested that I should let them look at it and see what the problem was. I replied that my car had already been at his hospital for more than a month and had been discharged as fully recovered. Another trip to his particular facility would, I reasoned, cause my car to end up in the morgue.

The gas station owner was indignant that I should be offended that he had ruined my car and overcharged me for doing so. I correctly determined at this point, that most, if not all service station owners and attendants of that era were indeed morons by nature. This particular stooge was named `Leolie,' as if that could be considered an acceptable name anywhere in the civilized world. Perhaps his parents had been unable to spell `tea olive,' who knows? I told him that he would never touch my car again and that the next time I saw him would be in court.

I limped into the service department at the Lincoln dealer in Nashville to find out what those idiots had actually done to my car and how much it would cost to have it properly repaired. Their diagnosis was that it needed something that was going to cost another $250. I didn't have that much money, and no way to get it. So, that in addition to the $400 I'd already spent would have come to $650. As to the other $350, the service station could eat it. There was no intention on my part that it should ever be paid.

The car made it back to my parents' house, but that was it. It was not drivable. I parked it out in front of the barn in the back yard and that was the end of the matter. In the meantime, I awaited the certain fallout from the impending arrival of the credit card bill. I didn't have long to wait. It showed up one afternoon for $750. The $400 which I'd signed, and the additional $350 which had my father's forged signature. Forged, not printed, not initialed, but forged by that stooge at the gas station. My father was a longtime federal attorney with the IRS. He could've made one phone call to Leolie and told him that unless he not only refunded the initial $400 and notified the credit card company to drop the other $350 that his life was going to become a nightmare from that moment forward. He could have sued him for forgery and fraud, and arranged for him to be audited by the IRS every year as long as he lived. That's what I would've done for my son. Instead, my father paid the entire bill, and stated unequivocally that I had gotten exactly what I deserved for fooling with an old car. Never mind that I had the forged credit card receipt as well as the written damage estimate from the authorized Lincoln dealership to correct the station's damage to my car. It was the greatest disappointment of my life, an early education in the duplicity and incompetence of auto mechanics. I also learned first-hand that some people are outright liars, and that as country singer George Jones' late agent Shorty Lavender had said, "Some people would rather climb a tree and tell you a lie than stand on the ground and tell you the truth."

Equally as disturbing as the loss of my car which I'd worked as a tour guide at Ruby Falls for nearly a year to pay for, was the fact that my own father had not defended me. He'd unfairly abandoned me during my time of need. And his disparaging remarks about old cars were equally unkind, as if I had an old car by choice. It wasn't like I could afford to buy a new Cadillac, and had purchased an old car instead, solely with the intention of enraging him.

I miss that car even now and sometimes I still think about getting another one, but I've got enough cars already, and as with most love affairs, it's never as good as the first time. They say that you always lose your first love, and I suppose that's true. I did lose my first girlfriend at about the same time as my first car, and now, many years later I still miss my first love, not the girl, but that car. It was my first taste of real freedom, the freedom to go anywhere I could afford to go. Yes, in retrospect, it probably was `a heap,' but to me it was beautiful, and I was proud of it. I was also proud of myself for having the initiative to buy it, to negotiate the deal, and to work and pay for it, especially when I didn't have any money. Its main lesson for me was that there is always a way to do what I want to do. All that's necessary is for me to figure out how to do it.

The MK V sat in the back field in front of the barn for a year or so and nearly every time I saw it, I despaired. I knew nobody wanted it but me, but that I didn't have the money to get it repaired. I have no idea whatsoever why I suddenly disposed of it the way I did, but I called the ass hole at the Gulf station and told him if he wanted my car he could come get it. Perhaps he could fix it. It would at least still be on the road. He immediately came and got it and hauled it away. I took this image with a Minox B. It was the last time I ever saw the car. The unfortunate thing is that I would have been able to afford to fix it if I'd just held onto it for another year. In fact I called the imbecile who'd destroyed it to ask him if he still had it. I could almost feel his smirk as he told me curtly, and with some relish, that it had already been sent to the scrapyard and crushed. Although I was sad about the car's fate, it wasn't the last 1960 MK V Coupe I'd own.

In fact, I should mention that my pal Tom Crockett's parents had bought him a Lincoln MK V sedan at Lancaster's Garage in Franklin on Old Hwy 96 while we were still in high school. This was after he'd already destroyed a 1967 Mustang coupe. Lancaster's was basically a large junkyard which extended across several acres and up a couple of large hills. I'd known about it since I was a 7th grade student at BGA in Franklin. One day fellow student Jimmy Ellis and I were over there walking around and Jimmy spontaneously bought an old Triumph motorcycle of some sort for $15. It was all there and in good shape, but didn't run. My godfather had bought an old farm house down the street in 1964 or thereabouts, so I was familiar with the garage owner Clyde Lancaster, since we drove by it frequently on the way to Franklin. Everything showed up there sooner or later. I remember a black Jaguar XK 140 with red leather in good running condition for $750. A red `67 XK-E roadster turned up there in 1968 for $1250. It was in good shape and had belonged to a girl I knew who'd received it new the previous year, but had moved on to something else. There were cars there of all kinds in varying states of decomposition as well as many in good shape. There was even a black and gold Hertz Shelby 350 GT in the garage covered with dust.

Anyway, there was a white 1960 Lincoln MK V sedan sort of near the garage/office, its balding tires immersed in mud up to the wheel hubs. Tom decided he must have it and persuaded his mother to buy it for him. It cost $200 as I recollect. Clyde told us dryly "It runs and drives." Like most junk yard operators of the era, everything was for sale but it didn't matter personally to the owner whether or not he ever sold anything. I'd like to have had this car myself but didn't have any money to speak of other than what I earned by selling beer signs the distributors had given me.

Anyway, this car was a lot of fun and ran fairly well. Crockett lived in a house with his parents on Nichol Lane in the Belle Meade section of Nashville. I mention this because he developed a previously unknown desire to back this giant car up against stop signs and street signs in the neighborhood. It went like this. He'd back the car's back bumper into the desired target. As he increased the engine's speed the stern of the car would begin to ascend the steel pole to which the sign was attached. The rear bumper would get higher and higher the faster he revved the engine. At the crucial point the body of the car would have climbed as far up the pole as its rear leaf springs would allow. The tires would start spinning and smoking briefly and then the sign post would collapse, having been flattened to an angle between 80 and 90 degrees, at which time, he'd again place the car in drive, and off we'd go. It was one of those stupid and potentially dangerous things teenagers with cars did back in the late 1960s.

I remember riding in the back seat of his car one summer evening, dressed in a Nazi uniform I'd gotten somewhere. Our friend Steve Vassallo was in the front seat. That black and white leather was very slick and every time we'd round a corner I'd slide across the seat. The car didn't have any seatbelts, not that we would likely have used them then, but at least they would have helped stop me from sliding constantly from one side of the seat to the other. We'd gone over to Yates Pharmacy for a visit to the `Jett set,' which consisted of Richard Jett, who worked there, and whoever of our friends happened to be there at the time. Jett had a beautiful metallic green 1959 Chevrolet Impala bubble-top coupe with a stern that resembled the face of a fiddler crab. We paid our respects, visited a bit, and then headed back to Belle Meade to drive around some, and then over to our favorite local hangout Nick Varallo's, hopefully to get some beer.

On the way over, we cut over from Belle Meade Blvd. down West Brookfield. En Route, we noticed that on the right side of the street at John J. Hooker's house there was a party going on. Without notice, Crockett turned sharply from the street into Hooker's front yard. He began driving in tight circles, that is, as tight as any circles could be in something of that size. He was spinning the wheels and sliding around, tearing up the nice lawn and slinging mud everywhere. Suddenly, the car stopped. The engine had died. He tried repeatedly to restart it, but by this time, there were people standing inside the house looking at us through various windows, drinks in their hands. We knew that it wouldn't be long before the Belle Meade police arrived. Finally, after many unsuccessful tries as the minutes ticked very slowly by, the car suddenly started, and we were again on our way. We made it back to Randy Smith's house on Jackson Blvd. at which point we considered ourselves `safe.'

Wildman Tom Crockett in his `Adam Faith' phase.

John J. Hooker was a very controversial but interesting man, every bit as eccentric and intelligent as anyone I've ever met. He was a well-known lawyer, and "the only person at Belle Meade Club who put his feet on the table" according to W.R. Smith, my friend Randy's father. Hooker had been banned from filing anymore `frivolous lawsuits' by one judge. Hooker also once summoned late Councilman Glenn Ferguson (subsequently Metro Trustee) to a meeting at his residence. When Ferguson arrived, he was escorted by the doorman to the bathroom where he found Hooker naked in a full bath, as if this weren't an unusual place for a meeting. Hooker also was frequently seen around town wearing tails and a stovepipe hat. He also ran unsuccessfully for Tennessee governor several times. Be that as it may, he was generally well-liked by most of Nashville's so-called `silk stocking gang.' His ex-wife Tish Hooker made the cover of *Town & Country* Magazine once, and President Kennedy spent a night at old man Hooker's house near Edwin Warner Park. Anyway, in his later years, Hooker used to frequently sit in front of the Belle Meade Starbucks holding court, speaking and being spoken to by friends, fans, and well-wishers. I was writing a biography of Nashville politician Glenn Ferguson several years before Hooker's death, and we were in front of Starbucks talking about that since both of them were old-school lifelong Democrats. I reminded him of the incident with Crockett's Lincoln in his front yard, thinking that after all of this time he might find it amusing, but to my genuine, surprise he didn't.

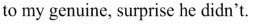

"Born to be Wild"
Jon Crockett

On another occasion, Randy's roommate, Bard Selden, was in town from Tunica and we went for a spin in Crockett's Lincoln. He was still up to the same old tricks with speed limit signs, stop signs, and mail boxes. He mowed down a couple, and we suddenly found ourselves being pursued by two guys in a Dolts-wagon (as we called them) VW bug, presumably trying to get our license number. Crockett's V-8 Lincoln had easily out run them and when they spied the car in Randy's driveway at 419 Jackson, they stopped there and got out of their car. The ever resourceful Maryanne threw a quart bottle of beer which crashed on the street, just missing one of the VW's two occupants. They got back in the car and left. We all piled back in the Lincoln and Crockett backed over a couple of more street signs and mailboxes before he damaged the transmission linkage to the extent that the car could now only move backwards. We backed the car all the way back to his parents' house and stashed it out of sight beneath the carport, hopped in Bard's 1965 Rambler sedan, and returned to Randy's house none the worse for the experience, but thankful for having evaded `the law.'

When Crockett went off to the Navy a month or so later, the car was still sitting in his driveway. When he was released from the service, it was gone. "Where's my Lincoln?" he asked his mother, who replied, "What Lincoln?" Crockett's father understandably didn't want Crockett driving his car again, not after what had happened to Crockett's father's new 1966 Oldsmobile 98, a couple of years earlier. Crockett had been driving around Belle Meade drunk late one night, his brakes already fatigued and fading due to frequent high speed stops and starts. Crockett decided he would see how long it took him to reach 70 mph. It wasn't a particularly wise thing to do in a residential neighborhood, especially while looking back and forth at his watch and the speedometer rather than at the road ahead. Crockett ran into a tree and nearly destroyed the new car, though he escaped with minor injuries. But then, his father should have known better. We were once en route to a casual rural banker's meeting at Montgomery Bell State Park outside of Nashville in an earlier Olds 98, a 1964, as I remember. I was in the back seat and Mr. Crockett, `Skull' as we called him, was letting Tom `practice' driving. Skull had a very dry sense of humor and at one point stated calmly, "Tommy, if I had my hand on my dick, you'd have jacked me off by now," meaning Crockett had been weaving all over the highway. We both laughed and laughed. It was the funniest thing we'd ever heard.

Skull gave Crockett $1,500 in 1970 when he got out of the navy, with the stipulation that he had to buy a new car. The only new car he could find at that price was a VW Beatle. This one was a British racing green with the newer one-piece bumpers and tombstone headrests on each of the front seats. Crockett immediately painted it with signs and slogans in bright dayglow colors which read LSD, SMOKE POT, and some other profanities as well as something unflattering about the police. Understandably he was stopped by the Belle Meade Police almost every time he left his driveway.

1959 Lincoln Continental MK IV Convertible

While my black 1960 Lincoln had been working, I'd noticed a white 1959 Lincoln MK IV convertible parked frequently at a gas station on the main drag in Murfreesboro. It was never parked in the same place, and it wasn't always there. This led me to believe that it was in good working condition. I'd also noticed that the top was always down, and figured that, since it was summer, this was to be expected, although the sun probably wasn't good for the leather. I also assumed that the top worked. One day, I stopped and inquired about the car. "Oh yeah, that belongs to so and so." Someone gave me his phone number. I called the owner, he said the car was for sale for $175. I went over and had a look at. It was under a tarp in the back yard with the top down. Of course, in those cars, the top, when lowered, was completely concealed beneath a steel panel with detachable fiberglass end pieces on each side. The original red leather seats looked pretty well dried out, but still useable. The car started right up. "It needs brakes," he told me, and "by the way, the top doesn't work." Well actually, it was more than that. The top not only didn't work, it was missing altogether, not just the fabric, but the entire top frame. It had stopped working, so rather than learning to operate it manually, which was a difficult, but not impossible task for several people who knew what they were doing, he'd simply removed it with a sledge hammer and other rather crude implements. It hadn't even been sawed. I told him that I'd think about it and get back to him.

This was my mistake, thinking about it. I shouldn't have thought about it at all, but with my black first car immobile behind the barn, and another similar car here, available, and affordable, I did think about it. First, of course, I had to arrange financing. I called my godfather, and, much to my surprise, he said I could have the money. I'd neglected to mention the problem with the top and the brakes. Of course I had no idea what I would do when it rained, or when the weather turned cold, but then it was summer, and I was 22 years old. I can honestly say that I never considered getting an old Plymouth, Ford, or some other lesser car, that I might actually be able to use. This Lincoln was art in motion. On the day I went to pick up the car, I paid the man, he gave me the title, and the car started right up. I imagined I could get back to my apartment using the emergency brake and driving slowly. I let the car warm up, which didn't take long, given the heat of the day. Literally, as soon as I backed out of the driveway and off of his property, the car died, blocking both lanes of the residential street. It took me a few minutes to get it started the second time. By now, I was sweating nails, hoping that I'd be able to make it back to my place. I made it, but that was all. I had to admit though, that car looked mighty fine parked on the street with its top down, right outside my front door.

Of course I had no insurance at the time, as it was not required by law in Tennessee back then, and I didn't have any money. I took the license plate off of my dead black Lincoln and put it on the back of my new car. The car, it turned out, ran pretty good for the short trips I made around town. I decided at length to drive it home to Leiper's Fork for the weekend. I knew that this would be an undertaking and that the car was prone to overheating, but it was open countryside all the way from Murfreesboro to Franklin, if I could just make it to the open road. I should interject at this point that I'd never driven it more than a few miles at one time, so I just assumed it would get me the fifty or so miles back home. On the day in question, I drove it carefully, knowing I had no brakes other than the emergency pedal. I came around the courthouse and headed down a hill toward old Hwy 96. The light changed and a car was stopped in the near distance in front of me. I had no alternative other than to hit the emergency brake pedal hard. The back wheels immediately locked up and the rear of this beast swung out sideways. A policeman had witnessed this entire event, and strangely didn't follow me in his car or give me a ticket. I actually made it back to Leiper's Fork without further incident, the reflection of my head and shoulders along with the clouds above and behind me visible in the convex center of the massive steering wheel. When my father returned home from work that day, he saw this giant car parked diagonally across the walkway in the front yard. The sight of this white elephant made him even angrier than the credit card bill. He'd grasp his head between both of his hands and go nuts on me anytime he saw that car. If it was visible in the pasture, which it frequently was, that was almost as bad.

The 1959 Lincoln looked a lot like the 1960, but they were very different cars. The instrument panel of the 1959 resembled a television screen in shape and lacked the sophistication of the 1960 Lincolns. The front end had similar slanted headlights, but the car lacked the solid feeling that the 1960 had. I was never able to afford to get the brakes fixed, and the car began to overheat, hissing steam from the cracked pipe at the top of the radiator housing. I'd just drive the car around the pasture with the top down until it heated up and shut down of its own accord. Wherever it stopped, that was it. I'd go back and start it up later, or leave it there for a couple of days. I eventually somehow got it to the house I was renting in Nashville, but was young and needed money. I sold it twice. The first buyer paid me a deposit but never returned for the car or called again. The second purchaser paid me a deposit and did come back for it. I saw it 15 years later under a tarp in someone's back yard in a less desirable part of town, looking like it hadn't moved in years.

1960 Lincoln Continental Mk V Coupe (2)

I took the money I received from the XK-E hybrid I sold (see Jaguar below) and bought this pale pink 1960 MK V coupe, the second one I ever owned. I had seen it somewhere with a `for sale' sign in the window and called its owner, Knox Baldwin, a very strange individual known in Nashville gun collecting circles. It was a pale French pink, as on a woman's Chanel ballet flats, not a bright glaring bubble gum pink, but subtle and understated. It really didn't work that well on this car, or probably anything else this big.

I had constant trouble with it after the first week or so, and it was frequently towed to Preston Lincoln Mercury, the Nashville Lincoln dealer at the time. I'd frequently call and be told that it was ready, and find that nothing whatsoever had been done to it at all. Generally speaking, it wouldn't start. A new starter and then a new a new battery were installed, and still it would be as likely not to start as to do so. My friend Kirk Preston's father owned the dealership and Kirk finally told me that his mechanics didn't want to work on it at all. I really didn't get that. They got paid for what they worked on. If it had been me, I'd have called all of them together and said "Anyone who works here in this shop is going to work on whatever Lincoln or Mercury comes through the door. If that doesn't work for you don't let the back door hit you where the good Lord split you!" He said he couldn't do that, and even though his father owned the place, he just worked there like everybody else.

Sometimes I would literally remove the heavy battery at night in cold weather and take it in the house so it wouldn't get too cold. The next morning it might or might not start. The sad truth was starting to dawn on me, that perhaps these cars really weren't very good, I mean, at all, but I still had a sentimental attachment to my first car, that black 1960 MK V. Additionally, the faded pink paint wasn't original and sometimes at the self-service car wash the high pressure wand would peel off some of the paint exposing the original faded baby blue beneath.

The supreme irony came to me in the form of a check from the Lincoln dealer personally made out to me for the amount of `one million thanks.' I was very much offended but laughed nonetheless at the blatant absurdity of the check, went to the bank, got my banker to staple a `returned for insufficient funds' notice on it and mailed it back to the dealer. I soon tired of its lack of dependability and sold it, never imagining that I would ever want or see it again. In fact, I remembered the words of Dr. Ballard, who in regard to his new 1960 Lincoln MK V sedan, "I could look at the closed door and see daylight around the cracks, from the driver's seat."

1960 Lincoln Continental MK V Coupe (3)

This was the third 1960 Mk V Coupe I had. I saw it in Hemmings or some other car magazine, called the owner in Atlanta, asked him a few questions, bought it over the phone and sent Nashville's Hillwood Wrecker Service to Atlanta to pick it up. I kept it five or six years but didn't drive it much. It ran fine, was in good shape, and there was nothing wrong with it other than that the paint was faded and the leather was dry. Leather seats were still rare on American luxury cars in the early 1960s. By the time I bought this car, I had three company cars and it just didn't get much use. One day it wouldn't start. Instead of finding out what the problem was, I kept running the starter. It overheated and actually caught on fire. I quickly extinguished it and it sat where it is shown here until I had it taken over to my mechanic around the corner several years later. My work life at that time was

very busy and I literally didn't even have time to fool with it at all. Eventually I had it scrapped. What a needless and stupid waste of a rare and wonderful car. I wish I had it now.

1973 Chevy Nova

My mother's next obsession was Chevrolet Novas, though who can say why? Not the 1967 Chevrolet Nova Super Sport, but current issue, lackluster Nova sedans. As I recollect, she bought two new 1973 four-door sedans, a yellow one for my father and a brown one for herself. They probably had six-cylinder inline engines, but I'd never been interested enough to look. I was in college at the time at MTSU in Murfreesboro, Tennessee, and had no drivable car. At this time, I still had the dead 1959 Lincoln Convertible and a deceased 1960 Lincoln Mk V coupe, both parked side by side in front of the barn in back of

my parents' house in the country, outside of Franklin, Tennessee. One day my mother called me and said that she was going to buy me a car and felt that she could afford around $4,000. You can't imagine how thrilled I was. Finally, a 1964 Lincoln convertible, a Jaguar E-Type, possibly an XK-140, or even another 1960 Lincoln MK V, perhaps even a convertible, all of which were considerably less than $4,000 at the time. My initial enthusiasm was short lived. No, she was going to buy me a new car, a real car, something I could actually use. I could get either a Chevrolet Nova or a Chevrolet Vega. She'd already spoken to Mr. Walker at Walker Chevrolet in Franklin and he was expecting us that very afternoon. Considering that I had been more or less walking since my 1960 Lincoln was murdered by an incompetent stooge, I was in no position to argue, and was grateful for the offer even though I still tried to persuade her to get me something cool.

When we got to the dealer we were greeted by salesman Flip Hood (I'm not kidding), who was only too willing to oblige. The car I ended up with was a brand new metallic blue 1974 Chevrolet Nova two-door post coupe. It did not have the optional hatchback, nor did it have carpets. Instead, it had a fully rubber covered floor. It did have power steering, a radio, and air conditioning. Most importantly, it had a 350 V-8, not suitable for racing in its factory configuration, but at least respectable conversationally. I was thankful to have this car because it provided me freedom of movement, as well as the ability to transport girls, to and from my swank bachelor pad, actually a rented porch room on the side of someone's house near campus, and I really liked the car's looks.

The Nova was not right from day one. It ran well enough, but the floor lacked any insulation at all and, with the exhaust pipe running beneath, was hot as hell, even in winter. It literally burned my feet through my shoes. To make matters worse, the car leaked water, lots of water, somewhere from the trunk lid, so that the rubber covered floor held the water. Whenever I applied the brakes the water would surge forward from rear to front, rushing beneath the front seat, hitting the floor well wall, and then cresting before covering my feet, like a breaking wave. After several unsuccessful trips to the dealer to have the matter corrected, I decided to take matters into my own hands. I called the dealership, made certain that Mr. Walker was going to be there, and then upon my arrival, invited him for a ride.

He was suspicious because I'd already brought the car in before for the same problem, but as my parents had bought several cars from him in the past, and were likely to do so in the future, he felt obligated to go for a ride with me. I asked him to join me in my car, which he did with some obvious apprehension. I took the car out on the highway in front of the dealership and hit the gas pedal. When we reached about 50 mph, I stomped the brake pedal hard, taking care to keep both of my feet above the floor. Instantly the water rushed beneath the front seat and, hit the floor well and doused his feet. "The car still leaks," I told him. "Fix it!" In it went again. It was never right the whole time I had it, but it served its intended purpose. It was indeed dependable transportation. A friend of a friend had a beautiful black 1967 Jaguar E-Type roadster with a rare detachable factory hardtop and red leather. It was one of the most beautiful cars I'd ever seen. He was driving back and forth between Nashville and UT in Knoxville and the car wasn't really suitable for that much of a drive on a regular basis. He offered to trade me even for the Nova. I can't tell you how much I wanted to make that deal but the car was in my parents' name (for good reason) and they said `absolutely not.' I lamented their decision for days. Eventually, I ended up with the `67 E-Type anyway, as I shall relate, but not before it had been sold to someone in east Tennessee.

One night I thought that I'd throw the Nova hard into a curve. I wasn't going that fast but immediately lost control nonetheless, as the rear end came around of its own accord, suddenly and with no warning, sort of like a scorpion (or an early Porsche). The car spun around in a circle two or three times before coming to a stop, leaving me both shaken and stirred. I knew at that point that the car was unsafe. But more of that later. In the meantime, I bought my first 1964 Lincoln sedan. (See `1962-1965 Lincolns & Convertibles' below).

1956 Lincoln Continental MK II

In the early 1970s there were two MK II Lincolns with which I was familiar in Nashville. One of them belonged to a man named Cheek who regularly drove a black one, on days when he wasn't driving his 1962 or 1963 Lincoln convertible. The other one, pictured below, belonged to Dr. Arnold Haber, a collector of early Rolls-Royce Silver Ghosts, of which he had several. By the mid-1970s he'd moved from Green Hills to Old Hillsboro Rd. near Leiper's Fork down the street from my parents' house. His house, at this point was newly constructed and configured in an L-shape with garage bays on the ground level for his magnificent cars, and his residence above. Anyway, he knew my parents and was known to me personally. His garage had several early Rolls radiators propped against walls. He also had a beautiful Lincoln Continental MK II. It was an expensive and limited production car when it was offered to the public in 1956.

This particular car had factory air conditioning which, as I recollect had a couple of round vents emanating from the ceiling which meant that there were two large clear plastic tubes (one at each side) extending from the flat package shelf beneath the rear windshield, just behind the back seat, to the car's ceiling. The source of these tubes was the rather large AC unit which was housed in the trunk, just behind the metal wall which separated the back seat from the trunk. Cooled air was blown from this trunk-mounted unit through these tubes and into the cars headliner, where they exited into the car's interior via several round vents. Units of this type were the norm in the early days of automotive air conditioning, an expensive option for the cars on which they were available.

I specifically remember seeing them on my godfather's 1957 Lincoln Premier, and some very early 1950s Cadillacs as I've mentioned. By 1960, and possibly earlier, the plastic tubes had been discontinued by both Lincoln and Cadillac in favor of dashboard and under dash vents.

Although I didn't have the $2,500 asking price, Dr. Haber was kind enough to let me borrow it for a few days and I enjoyed driving it around and always considered Dr. Haber to have been an inspiration. By this time I was fully in love with Lincolns of all kinds, a relationship which, for me, continues to this day, ending however, with the 2012 Town Car.

V.
Jaguar MK VIII, MK IX, & X

My mom made it clear that when I wasn't in school, I had to either be working or living somewhere else. By the fall of 1973 I'd rented a small house on Crestmoor Avenue in Nashville's Green Hills area. It was my first residence away from school. I've always liked a yard, a garage, and a driveway, and I never wanted to live in a box, no matter how nice, exclusive, or expensive. Here there would be room for more than one car. I was about to get my first Jaguar, sort of.

Jaguar Mk VIII

I'd wanted this MK VIII for years. It belonged to a friend of mine's father who'd owned it for probably 10 years. He had let it sit for several years and it hadn't moved from its spot under trees in his gravel driveway where it reposed gracefully along with a rare Alfa Romeo Coupe, which, as far as I knew, never ran under his ownership. I visited his daughter from time to time and her father and I would go outside and admire the two cars. "Look at those lines," he would say, standing there with his hands on his hips, but he never made any effort to fix either of them. He was a strange man, sort of an 'occasional aristocrat' with nice manners. As far as anyone knew didn't actually 'work' for a living like the rest of my friends' fathers did. He would take his golf bag and disappear for a couple of weeks at a time, but he was someone all of us liked.

After much persuasion over the course of several years, he finally let me have it…provisionally. I had it towed to the house I was renting on Crestmoor. It didn't run then, and hadn't. A friend of mine, Walter Wilson, who had an XK 120 and a Bentley, S-1 helped me get it running, as did my automotive mentor, Tom Strickland. The first thing I did was remove the six sparkplugs, and put some oil of some sort in the top of each cylinder, before replacing the plugs with new ones, properly gapped. As I recollect, I let it sit for awhile without doing anything else to it. Then, I got a crowbar and crawled under the car and stuck it into an open spot on the flywheel, and gently attempted to turn the flywheel with the car in neutral, as instructed. I was able to do so. Tom Strickland told me to work the flywheel a little at a time until it had made a few revolutions, which I did, although it took some time. Surprisingly, the engine wasn't seized despite the fact that the car had been sitting outside for several years in the same place without moving. Next, I got a battery and hooked it up. I'd never changed the points on any car's distributor before, which I now learned how to do. Over the phone, Tom Strickland told me to stick a screwdriver in the top of a specific cylinder and to get that piston to its highest point. I was to do this by pushing the starter button ever so slightly. The screwdriver, of course, snapped off inside the cylinder. Damn, I thought, I've ruined this car's perfectly good engine without ever driving it, or even getting it started. I freaked out. I called Tom and told him what had happened. "You may be alright," he said, "but don't do anything else until you get the piece of screwdriver out of that cylinder." I had no idea how to do that. He explained that there was a tool available at any auto parts store which would fix the problem. The tool was a long, narrow rod with a handle at one end, and a long magnet at the other. This worked, the screwdriver blade was easily extracted, and I never did that again.

I think the next thing was the fuel pump. In any case, I eventually got the engine cranked up. There was some white smoke at first, but then it actually smoothed out and ran on its own, with me controlling the throttle from under the hood. This triumph represented the zenith of my automotive experiences up to that point. I had no insurance on that car, did not have the title, and was not prepared to actually attempt to drive it since the brakes probably didn't work, might not work at all, or might partially work, and then lock up. I didn't have the money to pay to have it towed back to my place if it conked out somewhere. I proudly called the car's owner and told him of my success. As soon as I did, he wanted it back. He had it towed back to his house, where it resumed its deterioration, again sinking into the dirt completely, and was along with the Alpha, eventually hauled to the scrapyard when the house was sold, but I had actually succeeded in getting a Jaguar running on my own. Now, I really wanted one.

Jaguar MK IX

I was determined to have a MK VIII or MK IX sedan. A friend of mine, Bart Graves, had one which he used to drive around town. I called him up and he said that he still had it, but that it needed brakes. He wasn't using it anymore and it was for sale. He wanted $600 for it. "Does it run?" I asked him. "It runs good" he said. "I've got to go to work, he told me, but I'll leave the key in the ignition. Come over anytime, whether I'm here or not and you can start it up. You'll need to bring a battery though."

I was 23 at the time and still didn't know much about cars, so my friend and mentor Tom Strickland went with me to Bart's house on Battery Lane and there it was. It was black and looked good and the tan leather was in good condition. Its interior retained the exquisite fragrance of any old Jaguar. I knew immediately that I wanted it. I opened the hood and had a look. It was pretty much the same layout as the MK VIII having a dual overhead cam straight six, with twin side mounted S.U. carburetors. I put the battery in, made sure I had a good connection and it immediately started but backfired through one of the carburetors (the air cleaner had been removed) at just the moment the leaking braided metal fuel line shot a stream out its side into the carburetor. Instantly fire was everywhere as the gas continued spraying into the already burning fuel. By the grace of God there was a garden hose lying on the ground near the front door and already hooked up to a faucet. I turned off the ignition so the fuel pump shut down and immediately stopped fueling the fire, which we quickly extinguished. Lesson learned. Always have a ready hose, a fire extinguisher, or both if you're going to be fooling with fuel systems in general, and British fuel systems in particular.

The Jaguar MK IX was sportier than a Rolls-Royce Silver Cloud or Bentley S, every bit as elegant, with a better, and less complex braking system.

I was making $100 a week working as an apprentice talent agent at the Nova Agency, and paying rent, food, and expenses out of that at the time. In short, I now had a nice MK IX but I couldn't afford to get the brakes fixed. I had worked as a tour guide for Gray Line during the past summer and as part of my route in East Nashville, I'd daily passed a back yard where a white Jaguar XK 120 was in a state of permanent repose. It was devoid of a windshield, any chrome, and appeared to be just a body on a frame. It had disc wheels rather than wire. It was worth having a look at, so one Saturday I drove over there to east Nashville and knocked on the door. The owner, whose name I do not remember, was there. He showed me the 120 and it was a complete body on frame but with no seats, engine, or anything else, but…he told me, all of the parts were in one half of the garage. In the other half of the garage was another complete XK 120 roadster. The cars weren't for sale and he intended to get both of them running one day soon. I asked him if he was familiar with the MK IX, and told him about mine. The following Saturday he came to my place and looked at the MK IX. It started right up, looked and ran good. We struck a deal and I traded him my Jaguar for his two XK 120s and all of the parts he had. I ended selling the two 120s at the end of the summer for $2,400 to Glen Hall, a medical student I'd met through Tom Strickland, after I realized that I didn't have the technical skills then to get either of them running. Basically, I'd made $1,800 plus my initial $600. Not bad considering I was making $400 a month back then before taxes.

I should mention in passing that when I worked as a tour guide that previous summer, I learned a valuable lesson, as I shall relate. On the day I applied for work I was hired immediately since I was a native Nashvillian. "Here's how it works. You're going to ride on this big bus. You'll sit in one of the front seats and the tour guide will stand at the front of the bus and tell about everything the passengers will be seeing. Oh don't worry, you'll be paid for riding on this and several subsequent trips before you take over. You'll have a driver as well. Don't worry, you'll catch on quickly." So we went by the Parthenon in Centennial Park, the Upper Room Chapel, etc. No problem, but then the bus headed out the interstate toward Hendersonville, and made a loop around and through Gallatin Road, and a series of back streets, passing country crooner Hank Snow's `Rainbow Ranch' and Roy Acuff's house, before going all the way out to Johnny Cash's house, way out in the middle of nowhere. The only reason anybody from my part of town ever went to east Nashville then was to try to pick up girls or to look for old cars. Anyway, the tour took a little more than an hour and a half.

Cool. I'd know my way around after a couple of more trips over there. But…as soon as we got back to the depot which was then located at 5th and Broadway, the Gray Line manager, Terry, threw me some keys to a Dodge van and said, so and so didn't show up. "You'll have to take the tour yourself." I handled the first part of the trip with ease, and even managed to locate Johnny Cash's house way out in Hendersonville, or wherever it was. After that, people started complaining. "Where's the Rainbow Ranch? We're supposed to see the Rainbow Ranch." I explained that this was my first tour and that I would find it but I had to look for it. They could not have cared less whether this was my first tour or hundredth. They'd paid to see these things and they wanted to see them. Well, the famous Rainbow Ranch was some very small 1950s house on a side street off of Old Hickory, right off the interstate. It was anything but a `ranch' and owned by country great Hank Snow, who was himself famous, in addition for his inimitable music, for firing his violinist Chubby Wise mid-performance when Chubby's bow lifted Hank's famous `rug' from atop his head. "Chubby, you're fired!" Anyway, I couldn't find it so I picked a nearby street, selected a nondescript house of similar appearance which lacked a name on the side of the mailbox, stopped and allowed people to take pictures of some house. "This," I told them dramatically "is the famous Rainbow Ranch, home of country music legend Hank Snow."

"It isn't much of a ranch," some complained.

"It's his island in this sea of tranquility," I assured them as they took their pictures. I remembered that Roy Acuff's house was much larger. I did manage to locate the street where he lived, but I had no idea which one was his house. I picked a large, nice looking two-story house with no name on the mailbox, stopped and encouraged them to exit the van and take pictures. I have no idea whose house it was. It didn't matter, they were happy. I learned to expect no mercy in business. People don't want excuses, in fact, as Rev. Ike said, "The better the excuse, the worse it is." If you've been hired to do a job, you'd better know what you're doing. It was a lesson which has served me well.

NEW 4·2 LITRE MARK TEN SALOON

joins the famous range of Mark Ten, 'S' model, Mark 2 and 'E' Type Jaguars

Jaguar MK X

I considered the late 1960s Mk X one of the most beautiful cars of what was then the modern era. Given its sleek styling, it almost looked like it was moving even while sitting still. I think it was a unibody construction but I don't remember. The forward-slanting grill was, I think, the first for Jaguar sedans and very pronounced, at that. There weren't many MK Xs in Nashville in comparison to MK IIs, not that there were many of those either. In fact it really wasn't until the mid-1980s with the successful XJ sedans that Jaguars were seen with some frequency on Nashville streets.

The MK X had the same 4.2 liter dual overhead cam engine as the XK-E, and had the same three large S.U. carburetors as the XK-E, although the MK X had a `starting carburetor' which the E-Type lacked. I asked my friend, Walter Wilson why the E-Type had a manual choke as opposed to the starting carburetor found on the other triple-carb Jaguars of the same year models. His reply was that the MK X was a more expensive car than the E-Type and therefor was likely fitted with the `better,' more expensive starting carburetor. That sounded logical to me, but personally, I preferred to have control of the choke manually, which in the case of the XK-E was a lever fitted within a vertical chrome strip immediately to the left of the glovebox. It was easily accessed and adjustable.

The car had a fully independent suspension front and rear, much like the E-Type's in the rear, if not actually identical. The car was a technical, as well as visual work of art. It was also large and low, in keeping with Jaguar's late 60s sedan styling. The interior was an amazing sight to behold in its own right,

84

and was every bit as elegant as that of any Rolls-Royce or any of its contemporaries.

In the case of the MK X, I acquired in 1974 or thereabouts, I think I paid $500 for it and it ran fine and drove fine, but…it had been seriously hit behind the starboard rear passenger door. I'd bought it from an acquaintance who'd inherited a `36 Cord convertible, had had a 450 SL, and now a 1974 Eldorado convertible. I knew I didn't have the money to get the body fixed, but I also knew that having it for a while would allow me to gain some experience and knowledge of the car which I might not have had otherwise. I eventually sold the engine to Dr. Hall, who came over with a couple of friends and extracted the engine and transmission as a complete unit. It was interesting to watch. I've always been amazed by somebody successfully removing a heavy engine with a chain and not destroying anything, especially the three side-mounted S.U. carburetors. I sold the rest of the car to someone and pocketed three or four hundred dollars as a result. The fact of the matter was that I was making money on every Jaguar that passed through my hands, although I really wasn't buying them to sell.

The Jaguar MK X interior. Look at all of that beautiful wood and leather.

VI.

The Jaguar-E Types 1961-1968

Production plans for the Jaguar XK-E or E-Type, as it's generally referred to by purists, were officially announced in late January 1961 at the New York International Automobile Show. Rumors of the new Jaguar had been spreading for months, especially after Briggs Cunningham had entered a prototype the year before at LeMans, which was driven by Walt Hansgen and Dan Gurney, but was plagued by fuel injection problems, perhaps ultimately leading to the use of three large S.U. carburetors instead. By May, 1961, 'Car & Driver' magazine had the new car on its cover. It's visual lineage from the D-Type, and its production version the XK-SS, are unmistakable. The venerable 265 horsepower 3.8 liter engine with its three carburetors was a direct transfer from the X-150 S, and its front suspension was basically a carryover from the D-Type (I think). The car was offered in both a fastback coupe and an open roadster, the former being a complete departure from the previous production XK coupes (120, 140, 150) in that it had a fully opening rear door, a first for a Jaguar. The front was essentially built in four main sections; the center panel, lower front center, and both fenders, the intention being to minimize the cost of minor accident damage repair by removing the necessity of replacing an entire front unit. I imagine also that the production of separate panels was also less expensive than attempting to fabricate and manufacture a one-piece panel unit. As mentioned, there is a tendency by many to refer to the XKE or XK-E as the `E-Type' only, but in truth, Jaguar Cars, Ltd. referred to it as all three in advertising of the era. It was and is a remarkable car and arguably challenged the necessary acceptance of discomforts associated with most previous open British sports cars. In terms of pure engineering it was far ahead of any of its Italian or German contemporaries.

This is the new Jaguar XK-E!

This was the full back cover of the May, 1961 edition of *Car and Driver*. Even though the early cars had external hood releases (one on each side), this first ad clearly indicates that the decision had already been reached at Jaguar to have internal releases, a decided improvement.

Of course, for me none of its technical specs had any especial meaning at eleven years old, which was my age when the car debuted. I just thought it was the most beautiful car I'd ever seen. The May, 1961 *Car and Driver* concluded as follows: "The specs are sensational; that such a car could be engineered is remarkable. As usual, Jaguar adds a minor miracle by selling such a machine at an incredible price. The XKE is not expected to cost appreciably more than the XK 150S, top car of the series it completely replaces! This means we're talking about $5,500. What did the XK 120 cost when it was first introduced in the U.S. in 1948? No less than $4,900. This fantastic growth in value, at practically the same price, is dramatic tribute to the policies of Jaguar's Sir William Lyons." As a side note, it's interesting to note in looking back at this almost 60 year old issue of *Car and Driver* the large number of sports and foreign cars that fill its pages especially in light of the impending, but as yet unsuspected muscle car era. But then, what had become `*Car and Driver*' by 1961, had formerly been called `*Sports Cars Illustrated.*'

1968 Jaguar E-Type

Enzo Ferrari is reported to have said that the Jaguar E-Type was the most beautiful car he'd ever seen. Few would disagree. It debuted as a 1961 model year car and its curved lines and sensual body made it one of the most visually appealing cars anybody had ever seen, an opinion which is still prevalent today. It was every bit as exotic beneath the skin as it was on the outside, and was extremely advanced technically for its era. It had a monocoque body as opposed to a body-on-frame, as had been the case with its predecessors, the XK 120, 140, and 150. There was a rigid steel strut frame extending from the firewall forward, with hinges at the front which allowed the bonnet, or `hood' as we say, to open forward, and to be easily removed if necessary, thus providing excellent access to the engine. The new car was powered by the popular overhead cam straight six-cylinder with the same 3.8 liter displacement as the XK 150, only now equipped with three large S.U. carburetors as opposed to the dual S.U.s of the earlier XK's (three carbs were standard on the XK 150 S). The engine block was iron and the heads and carbs were polished aluminum, making the engine a visual masterpiece of modern engineering.

The rear suspension was truly independent, with two u-joints per axle, the first for a production Jaguar. By contrast Mercedes was still employing a primitive swing axle for its rear suspensions. There were also two shock absorbers for each rear axle (four in all), placed within corresponding coil springs. Maserati, in contrast, was still using a primitive live rear axle on its premier Ghibli coupes and roadsters as opposed to a fully independent rear suspension as on the XK-E. Four-wheel disc brakes were standard, and rear brakes were inboard discs, mounted on each side of the differential.

The Jaguars already had an earned reputation for speed and elegance beginning with the Jaguar SS in the 1930s. I still remember the first Jaguar XK-E I ever saw. It was in the summer of 1962 or 1963, and parked in front of Nashville's Green Hills Market, close to the street, with its top down. Of course I'd seen them in magazines, who hadn't? But this was the first one I'd seen in person. It was white and had a Colorado license plate on the back. I spoke with the owners, a young man and his pretty wife. They said they loved the car. I did too.

As memorable as seeing my first E-Type was, my first ride was even more remarkable. I was walking / hitch-hiking to my friend Tom Crockett's house on Nichol Lane. A guy picked me up in front of Belle Meade Country Club in a black Series I E-Type. He said "I'm only going to Chickering," not even a mile down the road, but it was cold and I appreciated the ride. He was dressed in tails with a high shirt collar and looked very elegant. I opened the door, and stepped down into the small leather seat. I was fascinated by the placement of the gauges and the layout of the interior. He stepped on it a bit, for my benefit, and the sound of that engine was melodic. I was awestruck and said, "I'll bet this thing corners well." "Yes it does," he replied calmly, as he sharply turned left onto Chickering. The car didn't budge and took the curve with ease. He stopped, I got out of the car, thanked him for the ride, and walked the rest of the way to my friend's house in a trance, from which I still haven't recovered. In the 1960s, as the so-called 'muscle car era' came into being, American cars became increasingly higher powered and faster. Unfortunately, their speed exceeded their handling, and many teenagers died as a result. Generally speaking, expensive sports cars handled better for the most part than did their American rivals, even if they lacked the often blinding acceleration. This did not, of course, apply to cars like the air-cooled rear engine Porsches, which were badly designed and dangerous. Three of my friends in their early 20s, died on a clear summer day in a 1959 Porsche 356, coming out of a very slight curve too fast, when the car lost control and hit a tree. Almost any other car would have handled that same curve at that speed, with ease, including any giant Cadillac, Lincoln, or Imperial of the era.

The first of many Jaguars I was to experience, was a gold 1968 roadster owned by a country music singer at the time named Anthony Armstrong Jones. It was a series 1.5 which meant that it was transitional, and had not suffered the exterior changes which were put in place for the 1969 model year, other than the removal of the distinctive glass panels over the headlights, and the replacement of the winged knock-offs with hubs which had to be removed with a wrench rather than a mallet. On the inside, the instrumental toggle switches had been replaced with the less impressive, but less intrusive rocker switches. The car also had small headrests atop of the seatbacks. The engine, still basically the same 4.2 liter used from 1965 onward, had suffered the loss of its three large S.U. carburetors in favor of two strange looking Stromberg units. As far as performance was concerned, I didn't know the difference. The car was very fast. It was for sale for $1,800 which was a lot of money at the time, considering that I was still in school. My sister worked as a receptionist at United Talent, the talent Agency which represented the car's owner, as well as other acts like country singers Conway Twitty and Loretta Lynn. The singer let her use the Jaguar indefinitely, and she let me borrow it for several weeks. I assumed at the time that all country music singers were rich and that he didn't want the car anymore. But who wouldn't want a Jaguar XK-E? The car had oxidized gold paint but was still presentable. Its top, like that of all open British sports cars, leaked when it rained, and visibility was almost zero due to the water condensation on the inside of the car. When it rained, the car would be cold and wet for days. I was fortunate enough to borrow it for those few weeks that winter, and enjoyed it immensely despite its many drawbacks.

The original leather interior seating surfaces had been either covered or replaced with some thin fabric, which appeared to have been permanently applied. Water thus leaked onto, into, and through the seats, which along with the late fall/early winter weather, were particularly uncomfortable. They were always wet, and so was the seat of my pants. But the sound of that engine was magnificent, and of course the view down the long bonnet is unequaled.

I drove the car to Chattanooga one weekend to visit my former college roommate, Mike Cofer. When we'd shared an old house, he'd had a two-tone blue and white 1955 De Soto Firedome coupe, and I'd had my black 1960 Lincoln Mk V coupe. By this time he had a Triumph Spitfire and really liked sports cars. As fate would have it, the Jaguar died in Chattanooga. Fortunately a new $2.50 alternator belt was all that was required. It was the cheapest I ever got off with any Jaguar. I stayed the weekend and had a wonderful time. On the way home it began snowing heavily and it accumulated quickly. I seriously doubted that I would make it over Monteagle Mountain, a route once as deadly to truckers as Cape Hatteras was to sailors. I felt that if I could just keep moving I could probably make it. Halfway up the mountain there stood a hitch-hiker and I gave him a ride despite the fact that I didn't want to lose my forward momentum. Back then you could give somebody a ride without being particularly worried that you might have inadvertently picked up an axe murderer. We made it all the way up the mountain and I dropped him at a truck stop and continued on my way. Surprisingly, the car never lost traction despite the heavy snow. I think now that I made it up and over the mountain because there were few other motorists on the road and the snow had not yet packed into ice, that and my incessant prayers.

My most lasting memory of that car was driving home to my parents' house in Leiper's Fork, Tennessee one night during the Christmas Holidays. It was snowing heavily by the time I left Nashville, and most anybody with any sense had already arrived home. I took the back roads, as I always do when it snows, and armed with the recent success of my Chattanooga trip and a large dose of youthful folly, I drove down Old Natchez Trace from Sneed Rd. to Old Hillsboro Rd. This was one of the most beautiful roads in the South under any conditions. In the summer, the trees on either side of the narrow stone wall-lined lane form a glorious, leafy canopy punctuated by darting rays of sunlight. On this particular night, I was the only motorist on this then lightly traveled road, and there were no sounds other than those of the engine, those three nearly useless windshield wipers, and my own breathing. The sky was absolutely dark and there were no street lights, but with the snow covering everything, it was light enough. I was cold, the seats were wet, as usual, and of course the heater didn't work at all. Visibility was minimal as well, and the windshield had more ice on the inside than on the outside, but it was one of those magical experiences which one remembers forever, the solitude, the quiet, and the thrill of driving that car through that magical snow-covered dreamscape.

One day I had to return the car to my sister, and my disappointment was great, though not unexpected. I'd finally, at least partially, experienced a Jaguar XK-E as they were generally called, back then, and I wanted more. I knew that the day would come when I would have my own Jaguar. I didn't know how or when, but of that, there could be no doubt.

I'd still never forgotten my first ride in an XK-E, and my few weeks with the 1968 had convinced me that the time for getting one was 'as soon as possible.' Fortunately I didn't have long to wait. Unbeknownst to me at the time, I'd very soon drop out of college to accept a job as a talent agent. I didn't initially know what that job entailed, but was soon working along with two experienced agents in the newly formed Nova Agency at the beginning of the so-called 'outlaw' era of country music. Our exclusive artists included Waylon Jennings, his wife Jessi Colter, David Alan Coe, Tompall Glaser, Dr. Hook, and Jerry Lee Lewis.

1961 Jaguar E-Type

If I wanted to be politically correct, I could say that I was indeed an early environmentalist in that my first Jaguar E-Type was 'a hybrid.' Specifically, it was an XK-E with a Chevrolet 350. The original engine was regrettably long gone as were its three beautiful S.U. carburetors. Of course it sometimes overheated, the brakes weren't that good, and it was often necessary to push it off to get it started at all. At that point I didn't know any of the differences between a Series 1, 2, or 3. I knew that it had a decent top, the desirable glass over the headlights, and it ran. Technically, it probably wasn't safe to drive, but I was 23 or 24 years old so, as far as I knew, was immortal. It had outside hood latches instead of the later ones, meaning it was necessary to insert a T-handle into a receptacle on each side of the hood behind the front wheel in order to close and lock, or unlock and open it. The reason this car was dangerous was that the top rail of the frame on each side of the engine compartment had been rudely cut out in order to accommodate the cylinder heads of the 350 V-8. There were actually open spaces between the cut ends of the frame on each side and the corresponding cylinder heads. I was surprised that the whole front hadn't simply collapsed.

Apart from occasionally having to push it off to get it started, it was a lot of fun. I learned to park it in such a way that I would always be able to push it off or get it rolling just in case it didn't start. I also learned the hard way to protect the nose. The front end of that car was so low that it was easy for anybody to back over it, which in fact happened in the parking lot behind my office. I came out the back door one day and noticed that someone had backed over it and dented it. Thanks Pal!

The strangest thing that happened was that someone told me the brakes needed to be bled, so I drove it to the Jaguar dealer at the time, Scott-Welch, which was located off of West End. I'd been in love with George Welch's sister Nancy, since the first time I saw her, but alas, she was 20 when I was 17. Love hurts. Anyway, I drove the car to the service department and left it off one Friday morning. I had somebody from work drive me over there at the end of the day. I paid them, got in the car, dropped the top, and headed toward my former in-laws' house, absolutely the last place I wanted to be going on a Friday summer afternoon after a full week of demanding work. Traffic on the interstate was heavy and I was a bit worried about the engine overheating as I got caught in the slowly moving, or I should say, creeping exit lane. As I was descending the hill, I noticed that when I stepped on the clutch, the car wasn't actually rolling freely like it should be. If I could just reach the Hillwood area before the brakes locked up I'd be all right, but alas, this was not to be. I was literally driving with the brakes on even though my foot wasn't on the brake pedal, intentionally revving the engine much higher than it should be under the circumstances just to keep moving. At last, a mile or so from my destination, I could see smoke, and yes, brief glimpses of flames through both the port and starboard bonnet louvers. I immediately pulled into the nearest driveway, turned off the engine, jumped out of the car and raced to the front door and began banging furiously. Some woman reluctantly answered the door only to behold me shouting and pointing at my car. Anybody could clearly see the black smoke pouring from the louvers. She calmly asked me what I expected her to do about it. A hose perhaps?! A bucket of water! Anything! By this time, her husband arrived and I had to explain all of this again. At length I was given a couple of large kitchen pans of water and was able to extinguish the fire. The brakes hissed and sizzled like an angry cobra, but after a couple of trips the fire was out, although the steam continued. I left them my in-laws' phone number, and walked over to their house, a mile or so away. Half an hour later, I received a call saying that my car had rolled nose first into a tree. Apparently, with my car on fire, and my brakes locked up, it hadn't occurred to me to engage the emergency brake. Perhaps under other circumstances…The car was picked up by Hillwood Wrecker Service, as usual, and dropped back in my front yard on Crestmoor Road, a bit worse for the wear, but believe it or not, the brakes worked fine after that.

I actually successfully drove this car without incident all the way to Sewanee, Tennessee and back for a meeting with country singer David Alan Coe at some old hotel he'd either rented or bought. The car actually made it there and back. In remembering the trip now I'm surprised the entire front end didn't just collapse at the 75 mph. interstate speed. It really was that dangerous.

As fall approached I again faced the reality that this car wasn't going to work for us during the winter months, especially with no heater or defroster. I traded it to Sam Knight, who had a fabulous junkyard on Charlotte Ave. across the street from the former Falstaff Beer distributor. The car I traded it for was a really beautiful 1960 Lincoln MK V sedan. It was a work of art, silver, slightly oxidized but presentable nonetheless. It had no rust or dents, and the interior was a blue fabric with dark blue leather bolsters and interwoven silver thread. This car was nearly perfect physically.

But first, let me tell you the story of this car. I'd seen it for the past five or six years parked at a house off of Music Row along with a 1959 Lincoln Mk IV sedan. They both belonged to a black man who lived in a nice house in the area, and I stopped one day and asked him about both of them. I told him about what had happened with my first Lincoln MK V and asked him if his was for sale. He said that neither of them were for sale. He was nice enough, but I noticed them every time I passed by. A couple of years later, I stopped by, and asked about them again, and once more, after that. Still the same response. I'd left my phone number several times and he was always cordial, but the cars weren't for sale even though they'd never moved from where I'd first seen them. Then one day, as I passed by Sam Knight's junkyard on Charlotte, there both cars were, along with the rest of Sam's stash.

Let me say a little about Sam Knight. He ran a junkyard less than three miles from the center of downtown Nashville, on the west side of town. Nearly everything showed up there sooner or later, but especially Cadillacs and Lincolns, and in time, 1967 and 1968 Cadillac Eldorados. Most of my friends didn't care one way or the other, as they all had new cars, but Sam was nice

and let us crawl around in his junkyard since he knew that those of us who visited, loved cars as much as he did. He sold parts, or entire cars, whatever anyone wanted. It was nothing short of miraculous to us that these beautiful Lincolns, Cadillacs, and sometimes even Jaguars ended up there. Most were in very good shape. We couldn't understand why everyone didn't just rush over there to buy one of these beautiful works of art. Anyway, I drove my Jaguar XK-E hybrid over to Sam's and asked about the silver MK V sedan. He told me that he had to run some errands and that if I wanted to ride with him I could. We were gone about half an hour, and during that time he was constantly looking behind houses and in back yards as he drove by, his eyes scanning, constantly looking for anything of interest. At one point, he stopped at one house where he saw some derelict car, knocked on the door, and when nobody answered, left a note with his phone number, inquiring about the car.

He said the 1960 Lincoln seemed to run fine, but that he'd recently acquired it and the 1959, and really didn't know. We agreed on an even trade. The next day I brought him my car and title, and left driving the 1960 Lincoln. I was by no means finished with XK-Es and would eagerly await the day when I could afford to buy a really nice one. I was certain that one day I'd be rich and would be able to buy anything I wanted, although my expectations greatly exceeded my prospects at the time.

A couple of days later I regretted my trade. I went back to Sam Knight and asked him if we could trade back. Sam Knight was a shrewd businessman and he made money on everything he did. But, in this instance, he said, "I'll tell you what I'll do. You give me $200 and you can keep both of them." He must have known that I didn't have any money, but I was able to come up with $200 at the end of the week and had both cars. He'd done me a big favor and I knew it. As my income suddenly began increasing I had no need to stop by Sam Knight's anymore. One day I noticed all of his cars were gone. The land was no doubt very valuable. I hope he sold it and made a lot of money. I miss him now. He was a really good guy and loved all cars as the objects of art they were at the time.

I honestly don't remember what I did with the silver Lincoln MK V. I suppose I sold it. I remember stopping by a gas station on 21st Ave S. and Blair Blvd. and having a mechanic look at it. He observed "There's some `far' (fire) somewhere deep down in the motor somewhere." I drove it home but determined that with winter approaching I needed to do something fast and I needed some money. I placed an ad in the paper in order to sell the Jaguar hybrid. At this point I had the good fortune to meet Tom Strickland, an elderly (over fifty) gentleman from Donelson who came to look at it. It was a fortuitous meeting for me because almost everything I subsequently learned about cars, I learned from him. He taught me how to install and set ignition points, among other things right off the bat. He was a very interesting man and had some unusual cars. He had a really nice 1929 Packard convertible coupe with outside door handles which resembled those of an early nineteenth century carriage. He also had some sort of large early 1920s wooden motor launch on blocks in his back yard, a couple of Jaguar XK 150 coupes, and a whole bunch of parts. He also had a Jaguar SS from the 1930s, and a giant 1911 Cadillac with wood spoke wheels. He bought the XK-E hybrid from me for $700 or $800, and eventually replaced the 350 with a correct 3.8 liter engine with the right three-carb set up. He also fixed the hole in the center of the bonnet, although he never repaired the missing upper rails which had been crudely removed from the upper struts at the front frame at each side. Tom helped me with any and every one of my questions about my subsequent Jaguars, and other cars, and when unable to adequately instruct me over the phone would come over in person. He was a good friend and mentor to several Jaguar fiends around town. He also introduced me to Glenn Hall, a medical student at the University of Tennessee in Memphis to whom I would subsequently sell several other Jaguars (see above).

1964 Jaguar E-Type Coupe

Back then in Nashville, the informal members of an unofficial Jaguar club knew each other, and if somebody heard of something for sale, word got around. A girl I had known one night during college in the biblical sense, had a brother who had a `64 Jaguar E-Type Coupe in Fairview, less than 20 miles west of Nashville. I drove out there, had a look at it and it looked good. There were a couple of problems. The bonnet, that is, the entire front section was unattached to the car, because the car had recently had engine work done. I saw my banker, Tom McNiel, got $1,200 and had it towed to the house I'd been renting in the Green Hills section of Nashville. I dropped a battery in it and it turned over, but I still didn't know enough about cars to get it started. I fooled with it as much as I knew how, but the truth was, I still wasn't making any money back then, and even if I had been, I didn't know any professional mechanic, even though Tom Strickland was as good as any of them, he was available for advice, but not for hire. One day soon, I knew that I'd be able to afford one that I could just get in and drive and not have to worry about what anything cost. Given my circumstances at the time I had no objective reason to believe this, I just knew that at some point, the right opportunities would have to present themselves, and I'd be ready when they did. In the meantime, I sold the `64 after six months to Glenn Hall, paid off my 90 day note at the bank, and made several hundred dollars.

Even though this isn't a really high definition image, just look at this engine, and the surrounding structure, as well as the beautiful chrome wire wheels and their knock-off wing nuts. The XK engine had been around since 1949 and still is both a technical and visual work of art. The XK-E was a direct descendent of the XK 120, the C Type, and D Types, all of which were proven race winners, and all of which were elegant in appearance by anyone's standards. The Series I Jaguar XK-E was understandably considered by many automotive experts of its era to have been the most beautiful car ever built. Many still consider it to be so even today. Both the coupe and the roadster were beautiful and are magnificent from any angle.

1967 Jaguar E-Type Roadster

One summer day I was detouring behind some street off of Nolensville Rd. and saw a white 1967 E-Type roadster. I went back later and looked at the car and talked to its owner. It was for sale for $2,500 and `ran good.' I called Dr. Hall in Memphis, told him about the car and received a finder's fee of two or three hundred dollars, without having to actually do anything. It was easy enough, but in the back of my mind, even then, was the knowledge that I was greatly reducing the number of Jaguars in Nashville, not that there had been that many to begin with. At some level, I sort of thought that this might work to my own detriment, which ultimately, it did. But in the meantime, it was free money.

1967 E-Type Roadster

I'd met this car in 1973 and had the opportunity to trade my new 1973 Chevrolet Nova for it as an even trade, but several years later, it showed up in the Nashville paper, only now, it was a resident of Crossville, Tennessee, former home of Renegade Resort, for which I'd worked as a phone solicitor from some building on West End, the autumn before I suddenly, and unexpectedly found myself working in the music business. My first job in the music business hadn't worked out after a couple of years, due to circumstances beyond my control, and I'd returned to Nashville's Belmont, none the worse for the experience. Now, I'd been hired as an agent again, this time at the Lavender-Blake Agency, Nashville's largest. But after my last experiences in the music business I wasn't that sure of my future, that's why I'd returned to Belmont to finish my degree and then go to law school. Shorty Lavender and Dick Blake were ok with me working in the afternoons for the remaining months of the semester, as long as I made them money, which I did.

By this time, I was making more money than most of my friends, and although I was living in the best part of town, I was still renting a WW II era clapboard house. The music business seemed to be constructed on a foundation of constantly shifting sands. However, I was good at what I did, and when the semester ended, I joined the agency fulltime. I'd unknowingly found my calling, and didn't return to school. Although I would become successful, and soon, I had no way of knowing it then. At this point I was just another agent.

I was hired, strangely enough, as the result of a casual lunch between long-time friends Louie Dunn, who was singer Marty Robbins' agent, and Shorty Lavender, agent for George Jones and Tammy Wynette, among others. I'd briefly worked with Louie Dunn at the Nova Agency before he'd resumed his representation of Robbins. While there, he'd bought the first Mercedes 450 SLC in Nashville. Somewhere I'd found a 1/16 scale plastic model of a 450 SLC and had assembled and painted it just like his. I gave it to him unannounced, and he was highly pleased to have it for his office. I'm not saying that this gift had anything to do with me being hired, but when Shorty casually asked Louie if he knew any agents who were available, he mentioned me specifically, because I was on his mind. Although I was only twenty-five, I'd already worked as an agent for Waylon Jennings, Dr. Hook, David Allan Coe, Jerry Lee Lewis, and others. My point is, that it's good to bring people gifts, something I've done all of my life, for no particular reason. If I see something I think a friend might like, I pick it up for him or her, for no reason, other than I can. Everybody likes to be thought of fondly, and everybody likes gifts. It never hurts to be remembered by people who like you.

Anyway, I bought this '67 sight unseen over the phone, without having driven it. Actually, I'd seen it two years earlier as I mentioned. I told the car's current owner that if he'd drive it to Nashville, I'd buy it. As I recollect, I sent him a $500 deposit, and on the day in question he showed up at the offices of the Lavender-Blake Agency on Music Row, which were in an old house owned at the time by Shorty Lavender, and country singer Tammy Wynette (one of the agency's clients). He'd driven the car to my office and had been followed by his wife in a new 1977 Lincoln Town Car, probably the largest production car Lincoln had ever made. I was duly impressed, even though my bosses, Shorty Lavender and Dick Blake each had new 1977 Lincoln sedans then.

As exotic and beautiful as any Ferrari

Two interesting things happened to me with this car which are worth mentioning. One cold winter day I'd gone for a spin to visit my parents at their home in Leiper's Fork, about thirty or so miles from where I lived. I was motoring along pleasantly, enjoying the heater which actually worked, and listening to the magnificent sound of that exhaust exiting those four Abarth pipes beneath the stern, when suddenly the speedometer needle began flipping around rapidly from one speed to another. I knew I was probably going somewhere around 60 mph. down this two-lane country road, not 30, or 160 mph. The needle jumped around for 30 seconds or so, and then in a final gesture, hit 160, fell to the bottom of the round gauge and died.

The other odd thing was that I locked myself out of the car one time in my driveway, with my keys to the house, my office, my other car still in the ignition. As the reality of my situation fully set in, an impending call from nature became even more urgent. Believe it or not, I managed to find a wire coat hanger in the driveway. As they say, `sometimes when God closes a door, he opens a window.' The problem was that the detachable hard top was locked in place both at the rear sides and at the top of the windshield. There was no way to angle the coat hanger between the top of either side window and the detachable top, so tight was the seal. My only possible option was to attempt to fashion a hook with one end of the coat hanger, stretch it from the center of the top at the rear, all the way across the rear of the interior, over the console and then hook the coat hanger end into the key ring, withdraw the cluster of keys from the ignition, and very carefully, without dropping them retrieve them. The only place I could pry up the edge of the removable top even slightly, was beneath the center of the rear window, and there, only minimally, less than a quarter of an inch, and then only with great difficulty. It just might work. With the tips of my fingers being mashed hard, I miraculously managed to lift the rear center of the roof beneath the rear window just enough to get the wire coat hanger inside the car. While holding the top in that position, I managed to insert the coat hanger as desired all the way across that open space, hook the keys, withdraw them from the ignition, and slowly retrieve them. I couldn't believe my luck. I'd performed this delicate operation from behind the rear window of the top. I doubted that I'd ever be that lucky again under similar circumstances and made sure that I never locked the doors from the inside before shutting them, and always locked the door with my key. Be that as it may, the fingertips of my left hand having been mashed were sore for several days. When my 90 day note became due, I sold the car to Glenn Hall, who subsequently sold it to somebody in Memphis. By this time, if I'd really thought about it, I could have converted the 90 day note to an installment loan and actually kept the car.

1964 Jaguar E-Type Roadster

I was standing next to the former Oxford Smoke Shop talking to my friend and banker Tom McNiel one bright morning when a beautiful black Series I E-Type conv. whipped around the corner and passed us. I knew its owner, Davy Jones, who worked in some executive capacity at Vanderbilt University or hospital, and lived in Hillwood. I'd spoken with him on numerous occasions and we'd passed occasionally on Belle Meade Blvd. on summer nights, him in his beautiful black E-Type, and me, in my faded XK-140, both of us enjoying the warm night air with our tops down.

"I know where I can get a Jaguar just like that for $3,200," I told Tom.

"Well, why don't you?" my banker asked, puzzled.

"I can't afford it right now," I replied.

"I think you can."

"OK."

That was that. I'd already driven the car and knew that it was excellent in every respect. It had been garaged all of its life, was rust free (a consideration on all early production Jaguars). It was a glossy black Series I roadster with red leather bucket seats. Although the term `bucket seats' was widely used in reference to any separate, that is, free-standing front passenger seats in any car at the time, the 1961-1964 E-Type seats really were buckets. They were comfortable enough, and the good thing was all that was necessary to raise the top was to reach backwards while still sitting in the driver's seat, grab it with both hands, pull the top over your head, and lock it to the top of the windshield frame. Beginning with the 4.2 Liter E-Type for 1965, the seats were higher (and better) and it was necessary to get out of the car to raise the top because the seat backs had to be folded forward a bit.

In my opinion, there really is no better view from any driver's perspective than this, and it sounds as good as it looks. This is truly as good as it gets.

As pertains to cars, I was working hard, doing a good job, and I'd never lost money on any of my Jaguar purchases, so I got a 90 day loan from Tom McNiel and bought the car. The thrill and anticipation of getting some incredible car that you really like when you're young, is hard to duplicate as you get older, if for no other reason that by a certain age, you've already had a lot of wonderful cars. I could hardly sleep the night before I went to get it.

When I picked it up it really was as nice as I'd thought when I saw it the first time. Everything worked as it should, as expected. The car ran great on dry days. Sometimes, however it wouldn't start at all. I'd let it sit for a couple of days and drive something else in the interim. As I've mentioned, one of my favorite things was to go for a drive around the neighborhood at night. One summer night I took my wife for a spin with the top down over to McDonald's in Green Hills for an icy Co-cola (as we say in Dixie). The top was down and we were caressed by the warm breezes on the way over. My mistake was parking the car and going inside. When I returned, the car wouldn't start. I don't know if the engine was flooded or wasn't getting enough fuel. I knew that any further attempts at the moment would either ruin the starter or drain the battery. I could perhaps remove the distributor cap and dry it out, not that there was necessarily any moisture inside. Maybe that would work. I got some dry paper napkins and dried everything out. I left the distributor cap off for about an hour and a half, and then it started right up.

Anyone who enjoyed the TV series `Madmen,' and has owned an XK-E, remembers when the British guy (Jarred Harris) decided to kill himself by asphyxiation. He went to elaborate preparation, hooking and taping hoses to the twin exhaust pipes, routing them precisely through the rear window and sealing it, which must have required some time to do such a thorough job. He sat down in the beautiful brand new Jaguar XK-E coupe, quietly contemplated his life and his last few remaining moments on earth, then removed his glasses, laid them carefully aside turned on the ignition and pushed the starter button. The engine turned over repeatedly but absolutely refused to start. He ended up hanging himself in frustration.

The most remarkable thing that happened with this car was that one day there developed a sound in the gearbox like someone was inside hitting it repeatedly with a hammer. The faster I went the faster the hammering. I immediately removed the console box containing the radio and speakers so I could check the oil level in the gearbox. To my displeasure, the oil was at the proper level. Of course it was. It would have been entirely too simple to have merely needed to add some oil and been quietly on my way. I reassembled everything and continued driving it for another week or so before I called a friend of mine who owned an import repair place. I explained my problem and he said to bring it in. My pal and co-worker, madman Tom Crockett, had asked me for a ride to Music Row that morning, so I swung about four miles out of my way to give him a lift. Had I not done so, I would have gone straight to the repair shop. As it was, a couple of miles before we reached Music Row, the hammering suddenly, and if I may say so, miraculously ceased of its own accord, and didn't return as long as I owned the car.

One day soon the second renewal of my 90 day note at the former Commerce Union Bank would be due, so I called Glenn Hall in Cookeville who bought the car over the phone, came down with a trailer and picked it up. I paid off my note at the bank and again made a few hundred dollars. My experience and knowledge of Jaguars had increased, and I'd had a good time, and made some money. More importantly, I was beginning to earn more money at work, which was starting to look more like a career than just a job. I knew the day would soon arrive when I would have an E-Type I could afford to keep. In the meantime, my credit was good and I could always buy another one whenever I wanted. As a result of my increasing car purchases, I'd established a personal relationship with a banker, something which proved to be a valuable asset.

1967 E-Type Coupe

A few years later, I espied a red 1967 Jaguar XK-E coupe sitting atop four jack stands minus its wheels in a Franklin, Tennessee back yard. I stopped, knocked on the door, and spoke with the owner. He said he'd sent the wheels somewhere to have them balanced and re-chromed. The car wasn't for sale per se, but might be. I handed him my business card and said that if it would be for sale, to please give me a call when it had its wheels. I heard from him a month or so later on a really cold winter day. He'd decided to sell it after all, so the forthcoming Saturday I headed to his house in Franklin. I left my coat and gloves in my car since I figured that we'd be back after a short test drive. Wrong! When any early Jaguar is involved the potential for a problem is inherently an aspect of driving it anywhere. This example was no exception. With the steering wheel in my casual but expert grip, I cut over to the next block to Hwy 96, took a left and headed toward Hwy. 100. The engine sounded great and the oil pressure gauge was ideally where it should be. I'd already made a decision to buy this car, when six or seven miles from our point of origin, the engine just stopped without notice, and wouldn't start again. Obviously it was out of gas, but no, that wasn't the case. We looked at each other in bewilderment, exited the vehicle, opened the bonnet and had a look at the engine. We closed and locked the car, and stood beside it with our thumbs extended. Franklin wasn't like it is now. When you got less than a mile out of town on Hwy. 96 toward Hwy. 100, you were in a rural area all the way. There was no sprawling Westhaven development. In other words, there wasn't any great volume of motorized traffic, and the few cars that passed us, passed us by. After ten minutes or so of freezing our asses, an old black man in a pickup truck kindly gave us a lift. He said there was no room in the cab, but that he'd give us a ride if we wanted to get in the back. The only problem was that the back was stuffed with junk, bags of leaves and garbage, and broken pieces of wood and rusted metal. It was stacked higher than the cab, and there was no place to even think about sitting down. We managed to climb atop the pile of junk, stretching across the top and lying prone, looking forward, our faces above the cab. We could have easily fallen off except that we were both holding on for dear life, and nearly freezing to death. When we reached Franklin both of my hands were nearly frozen in the shape of claws. When we got inside his house they burned as I held them under the hot water trying to thaw them. It was an interesting experience to be sure.

That was that. I told the owner to call me when and if he got it fixed. A week or so later I heard from him and he said the problem turned out to be the fuel pump, it had been fixed and was ready to go if I wanted it. Another drive and everything worked like it was supposed to. I bought the car and was glad to have it. The leather was good, it had new tires, and recently re-chromed wheels. It never overheated, despite its lawnmower-style fan blade, and the clutch was so durable it was almost necessary to raise up a bit in the seat just to push it down. Other than my first Jaguar XK 140, this car gave me the least trouble of any Jaguar I've ever owned, before or since.

There was one incident having to do with the twin exhaust pipes, as I shall relate. One afternoon I went to the gym at Green Hills, Cosmopolitan, I believe it was called. Anyway, parking was limited at times, and on this occasion I parked in a grassy median parallel to the paved parking lot. There was a cement entrance to this place, but the rest of it was grass. Anyway, when I was ready to go, I began to drive out of this space, but the bottom of the car somehow hung up on the cement. I was hot and tired and had to get back to my office. The intelligent thing to do would have been to have gotten out of the car and discovered what the problem was, then pull forward in the grass and make a different approach. But no. I didn't want to do that. I was ready to go now, not later. I backed up a couple of feet, then revved the engine, determined to just run over it, which I did. When I did so, I managed to disconnect the entire exhaust system from the bottom of the engine, and then run over both pipes as they pivoted from the central hanger on the bottom of the car, just ahead of the rear bumper. The exhaust pipes now dragged backwards behind my suddenly much louder car, throwing sparks into the air as I drove straight to Riley's Exxon, fairly close to Music Row. Riley (husband of country music singer Jeannie C. Riley of `Harper Valley PTA' fame) put my car on a rack, disconnected, and then reattached the pipes. As I watched Riley fix the problem, I recalled my father's words "If it doesn't fit, don't force it."

I'd acted impulsively and stupidly and gotten off easily and inexpensively. I had, however learned a lesson. Thirty or so years later, my Mercedes 560 SL had a flat rear tire while sitting in the garage. I'd probably run over something and it had developed a slow leak. There was a spare 450 SL wheel and tire against the wall with which I replaced the flat one, rather than unpacking the trunk and lifting the correct spare wheel from the trunk floor of the 560. I just wanted to back out of the garage, take the flat to be repaired and then put it back on the car. With the new rear wheel in place, I started the car, and was ready to back out. I put the car in reverse but it wouldn't move. I surmised that since this this new problem hadn't previously existed, it doubtlessly had something to do with the new wheel, which it did. Instead of stupidly damaging something needlessly, I removed the 14" wheel and retrieved the spare 15" wheel from the trunk, and backed out of the garage without incident. Even though these SLs looked pretty much unchanged since their introduction in 1971, by 1987 there had been many changes. Obviously the larger brakes of the 560SL would not accommodate the earlier 14" wheels.

I enjoyed this 1967 XK-E coupe. It looked, ran, and sounded great, and I kept it for more than a year before I decided to sell it. On this occasion I didn't have to sell it, but did so on impulse, a foolish one in retrospect. I had several other cars and it was a spur of the moment decision. Anyway, I placed an ad in Hemmings and received a call from someone in Virginia. After I answered some questions, he agreed to buy the car at my asking price, whatever it was. On the day in question I picked him up at the Nashville airport, and took him to my house. He got in the Jaguar and followed me to the old Howard School building downtown where I would sign the title over to him and he'd pay me. Less than a mile from our destination, I looked in my rearview mirror just as he pulled over to the side of the road and jumped out of the car, followed by a cloud of smoke. An electrical fire! In a Jaguar. What Jaguar owner could ever anticipate such a thing? Just kidding.

Understandably, he considered this to be a bad omen and changed his mind. I returned him to the airport and had the car towed to a friend's import repair facility nearby. This was before I'd become familiar with Joe Robinson and his former `Jag Cars, Ltd.' Anyway, I was called when the car was ready and went to pick it up. I was told that the fuel pump had shorted out and that it was fixed now and that I was good to go. I was pleasantly surprised until I got in the car and the clutch was as limp as a 90 year old's weiner. The clutch had been perfect, and now it wasn't, I no longer had to stomp it, but just barely touch it. Somehow this `repair' place had ruined my clutch. It must be the slave cylinder, I was told. "It was that way when we got it." I knew that was a lie, but I just wanted the car back. Now. "Fix it!"

I got it back and the clutch pedal was stiffer, but not by much, not even close to the way it had been before they `fixed it.' And the fuel pump? It was not bolted to anything anywhere, nor was it in the tank. Instead it was wrapped in electrical tape from top to bottom like a mummy, and literally rolling around on the floor beneath the spare wheel. And this place had a good reputation, if you can believe that. In the late 1970s and early 1980s in Nashville, it was difficult to locate a mechanic who actually knew anything about British cars. There are some now and they don't need to advertise. There is one even now however, that advertises regularly on so-called talk radio and professes great expertise in repairing (and then the owner basically names every brand he's ever heard of), including Rolls-Royce, Bentley and `Alfa-Romero." His inability to even pronounce the name of the latter marque would certainly cause me to doubt his proficiency in anything else. Anyway, I sold the 1967 Jaguar coupe and was almost immediately sorry that I'd done so. To this day, I still can`t say with certainty which I consider to be the most beautiful, the coupe or the roadster.

1965 E-Type Roadster

Anyway, after a couple of years my boss Dick Blake, told me that the Cadillac Fleetwood Talisman I'd gotten as a company car (see below) was costing him too much for gas and said that I should get another car. Rather than argue with him, as I usually did, I decided to hear him out, knowing full well that I had no intention of driving anything lesser or taking any sort of step backwards.

"Look" he said, "I just don't want to spend that much money on gas any more. I'll give you the son of a bitch free and clear (the Cadillac), but you'll have to pay taxes on it. Then, you can pick out another company car, one that's a bit more economical."

"I don't know," I bluffed. "I'm real attached to that car. How much money do I have to play around with?"

"How about $6,000?" he asked.

"I don't know," I told him. "Let me look around a bit."

I soon found a beautiful black 1960 Lincoln MK V convertible with original red leather seats, my favorite color combination at the time. It was located in Iowa, a consideration in that I would have to have it shipped and would be buying it sight unseen as I was too busy at work to go look at it. In the meantime, a 1965 Jaguar XK-E roadster suddenly came up for sale in the Nashville paper. It was located in Belle Meade and was familiar to me, as was its owner, John Mack, who I knew would never have sold it under any circumstances. Unbeknownst to me, however, he'd recently died in an auto accident somewhere in the Bahamas, and his widow was now selling it. I went over and had a look at it and took it for a spin. The tires were just a bit too large, but other than that it was fine. I told her I'd think about it.

There was really only one problem which really concerned me. Once in my early twenties, I'd imagined my own death in a yellow Series I E-Type roadster on the Old Natchez Trace, near Old Hillsboro Road. This was before I'd ever actually owned or even driven one. I was now married and had a two year old son. I should probably be more responsible at this point. However….maybe if I just painted it red, and stayed off of Old Natchez Trace?

I overcame my lingering psychic reluctance and decided that since I'd pretty much had to sell all of my previous XK-Es because I'd needed money, I should get the Jaguar as a company car and let Blake pay for my gas, insurance, and maintenance. Blake went along thinking that it was a good deal for him because he still had saved more than $10,000 by not having to pay for a new car to begin with. Unbeknownst to either of us, it would soon cost more in maintenance than its purchase price, an expense which would be continuous for the next several years.

1965 E-Type in its original color. My 2nd `company car.'

At this point, the relationship I'd developed over the last few years with the head of the Cadillac dealer's body shop paid off. I soon had it completely stripped to the bare metal, all chrome and trim removed, and repainted a dark bright red. He told me this would be his last job because he was going to retire as soon as it was finished. He had the car several weeks and I'd check on it periodically. He'd done an incredible job, the result of his decades of experience, and I appreciated the personal attention he'd given me.

Surprise! Surprise! That Jaguar devoured nearly as much fuel as my giant Cadillac Fleetwood with its three large S.U. carburetors, and I only fed it high octane gas. It constantly required expensive maintenance, usually costing several thousand dollars a year. But unlike with my previous E-Types, I didn't worry about whether or not it would start, or what it would cost to repair. Thanks to my mechanic, Joe Robinson at Jag Cars Ltd., it always started.

By this time, I knew that regardless of whatever I drove, it would be one of the most distinctive and exotic cars on the road in Nashville. These days there are Aston Martins, Maseratis, Bentley Continentals, and even some Lamborghinis and Ferraris regularly seen on the streets in the Music City. In fact with so many great cars on the road today, there are only a few that really make a personal style statement now. In that light, I remember seeing Father Divine's Duesenberg at the Imperial Palace Car Museum in Las Vegas. Father Divine was an extremely charismatic depression era black preacher, and one of the most interesting, successful, and significant figures in American social history. His car, the largest Model J Duesenberg ever built (178.5" wheelbase and a body 7' wide) had been ordered for him by a patron of the church and was known as the `Throne Car' and built to hold ten people. Technically Father Divine owned nothing, but possessed much. Anyway, the impression he must have made when he arrived in this chauffeur-driven masterpiece made an infinitely greater statement of wealth, power, and influence than anything anybody can do today. Yeah, you've got a Gulfstream or a Lear, so do many,

many other private individuals. Yes, you have a giant mansion. Big deal! A new Rolls Phantom? Yeah, so what? Some rock star being lowered to the stage from a helicopter? It's all been done. But in the 1930s it hadn't been done. I was never in that league, but still, my everyday cars were generally much more interesting and notable than what any of my contemporaries drove, regardless of their income, and they would become even more so as time passed.

I'd drive this car to work on nice days with the top down. Its engine sounded great with the exhaust exiting the four Ansa pipes I'd had installed when it needed a new exhaust system. When I got the car, it had been fitted with some after-market air conditioner, part of which was located behind the gear shift and in between the seats. I considered that a potential rust problem if it wasn't already, and had Joe Robinson remove it along with its associated plumbing. To my surprise the floors were solid. In fact the only rust in the entire car showed up later, in the battery compartment, always a troublesome spot for XK-Es. It was repaired with metal when I had the car completely repainted.

The car was prone to overheating in traffic in the summer, and of course it would be, given the enclosed engine, minimal airflow around it, and the thermostatically operated engine fan, which in reality was basically nothing more than a skinny, one-piece lawn mower blade. My friend Walter Wilson had solved a similar problem with his XK 120 Roadster years earlier, by placing an electric fan in front of its radiator, which I probably should have had Joe Robinson do when the car was being serviced. The fact was that it kept its cool well enough considering the summer heat, I just learned not to drive it on the interstate in rush hour traffic in the heat, not that I ever did so anyway more than once or twice. I also watched the oil pressure gauge, often in stark terror in slow traffic as the oil pressure plummeted at idle in traffic. The fact of the matter is that the XK engine was basically bulletproof, as they say, whether as a 3.4, 3.8, or 4.2 liter. Wiring and the potential for electrical

issues were greater concerns.

One fine summer afternoon as I was driving down Belle Meade Boulevard, I joyfully remarked to myself, "Damn, I love this son of a bitch!" As I stopped at the traffic light in front of Belle Meade Club, the clutch pedal went all the way to the floor, and the engine just stopped altogether. The transmission had to be removed to be repaired. $1,800 later I was again, good to go.

The gravy train kept rolling at Dick Blake International for another couple of years until Dick Blake died in October, 1983. He'd been in and out of the hospital for years, but finally died, I think from pneumonia. I really didn't believe he was going to die since he'd gone to the hospital for a week or so every five or six months for years, and would return seemingly none the worse for the experience. I'd had the 1965 Jaguar for four or five years at this point, as well as nine other E-Types during the previous decade. I was, for the moment, at least, through with Jaguars, perhaps even forever. By this time, I'd had the perfect E-Type experience, having had the car for several years at no expense to myself as a company car, and was now ready for something else. Despite having been properly repaired with metal, its sill beneath the battery, was rusting again and starting to sag. The halcyon days of Dick Blake International were behind me now. I was president of the new company, In

Concert International, and we had work to do. I would no longer have a company car, in fact, none of us would at first. My fleet at this point consisted of my 1974 Fleetwood Talisman, and a 1964 Lincoln convertible. I was now down two cars and really didn't know what I wanted to enjoy next.

Wee Scotty.

I should mention Dick Blake at this point. He was one of the most mysterious and interesting people I'd ever met. Although my association with him had begun nearly a decade earlier, I never really knew him. Nobody did, as I shall relate. He'd been a fighter pilot in the Pacific in World War II, flying P-40s and P-51 Mustangs. He'd been shot down twice, captured by the Japanese, stuck in a prison camp, and periodically buried underground with nothing but a bamboo tube to breathe through. He'd been stabbed in the chest with a bayonet, and consequently only had one lung. He'd been part of the Bataan Death March. His war record just kept going.

He'd owned a tavern in Indianapolis and become a part-time concert promoter before moving to Nashville and working as a talent agent at the Hubert Long Agency, the biggest talent agency of its era. When Hubert Long died things looked bleak, but Blake eventually started an agency with Shorty Lavender called the Lavender-Blake Agency (where I'd worked). When that company dissolved over personal differences between its owners, he started Dick Blake International, where I ended up in the late 1970s, after Barbara Mandrell's father, Irby Mandrell, had suggested he hire me.

Blake was closer to me than my own father, and even though we fought constantly over money, we respected each other. Once it cost him $200,000 to avoid giving me a raise for two weeks. I told him what I wanted and said that if he wouldn't give me what I should be making based upon what I was earning him, he should consider this my two week notice. He said, "If a man can do better somewhere else, that's what he should do. But don't think that you'll be taking Ronnie Milsap with you." I was totally loyal to Blake, but he was getting rich and we weren't. It was too late for me to stop the engine I'd put in motion for starting an agency with singer Ronnie Milsap. Blake found out from banker Clarence Reynolds that Milsap was planning to leave him, and had already funded his own agency with me at the helm.

At that point, Blake was singing a different tune and said "What will it take to make you stay?" I told him that I'd never wanted to leave in the first place, but that it was too late to stop things at this point. He said "Just give me a figure…now." I told him that it didn't matter because if I did abandon my plans with Milsap, Milsap would still leave the agency and my relationship with him would be destroyed. He replied, "I'd rather have you as an agent than Milsap as a client, if it comes to that." It was the highest compliment I'd ever received as an agent. I did get a substantial amount of money at that moment, and what I wanted to begin with. He ended up cutting Milsap's commission in half for six months to appease him. In other words, it cost Blake $200,000, plus what he had to pay me, just to tell me to kiss his ass for two weeks. What this has to do with cars, is that the main reason I didn't want to leave Dick Blake International was that I'd have had to relinquish my Jaguar. I loved that thing!

When Blake died, the company secretary secured his service records. It turned out that he'd never even left the country while in the service, and that his lung problem was the result of tuberculosis. He wasn't a war hero at all. This was the world I inhabited for twenty years in Nashville's music business.

When my colleagues and I started our own company I returned the Jaguar and the `69 Cadillac convertible (see below) to Dick Blake's wife, and never saw either of them again. I'd had the option of buying both of them from her but the truth is, it was time to move on.

Dick Blake, `Man of Mystery'

In Daytona

VII.

Jaguar XK-140s, etc. (3.8 S, XK-150 Drophead, XK-120)

1956 XK-140

I kept seeing a white XK 140 roadster parked in front of a one-story apartment building close to what was then known as Belmont College, one of my alma maters. Anyway, it was beautiful, with chrome wire wheels and a perfect burgundy interior. I noticed that it never moved and was always there. I left a note on the owner's door and received a call. He said it wasn't for sale but I kept his number. He ended up working at a gym in Green Hills, of which I was a member. Anyway somehow the car was for sale now for $600. It didn't run, and he said the engine was locked up. The car was now located in Clarksville, around sixty miles from Nashville. He offered to drive me up to see it. On the appointed day I met him at the gym and got into the smallest car I'd ever seen, some sort of first generation Honda two-door coupe. It was inconceivable that somebody would think so little of himself and his own safety, or that of his loved ones, that he would even consider having such a car. I held onto my nuts all the way up and back, but I bought the XK 140 and had it brought to the house I was renting on Crestmoor Rd. back then, in the Green Hills section of Nashville. The car wasn't in pieces, but was complete and fully assembled. And everything except the engine was in perfect condition, including the paint, the top, interior, and the side curtains.

My automotive mentor Tom Strickland came to the rescue, examined the car and loved it. The first thing was to was remove all of the spark plugs and put some sort of penetrating oil in the top of each cylinder, let that sit for awhile, and then insert a crowbar into the hole in the side of the gearbox where the flywheel was accessible and see if the flywheel could be manually turned slowly, as I'd done with the MK VIII. If so, the prognosis was good. It was a really beautiful car in truly excellent condition, and it was now in the garage and out of the elements.

To make a long story short, I kept the car for six or seven months, and realized that I didn't have the time, the money, or the ability to fool with it. Tom Strickland wanted to buy it and in the best interests of the car, I sold it to him for $800. I was still in my mid-20s and broke at the time. I was working in the music business but still wasn't making any money...yet. Tom Strickland showed up and I rode with him to the old Howard School building in downtown Nashville to transfer the title to him. When I handed it to the clerk, she went somewhere, came back a few minutes later, and returned the title to me, saying that the car had been reported as stolen. At first I really didn't understand what she meant. "No," I told her, "the car hasn't been stolen. It's at my house, in the garage. I saw it fifteen minutes ago. I'm sure it's still there."

"No, the person whose name is on the title reported the car as having been stolen."

"But that's the person who sold the car to me."

"Let's get out of here," Tom said.

I was still quite perplexed. Why would anybody report a car as stolen, keep the title and the car and then sell the car with the title as if nothing had happened?

Tom surmised that the car had probably stopped working so its owner reported it as stolen, and was paid for it by the insurance company. It was a logical supposition, but surely insurance companies do some sort of investigation, however minimal, before they pay a claim. The owner had made no attempt to hide the car at all. In fact it had been parked on a public street in plain sight in front of his apartment building. I thought that at the very least, someone in the automobile title division of the government might at least be curious that someone was attempting to register a stolen car, but apparently nobody cared one way or the other.

Since I'd determined to sell it at this point, I called a friend in Memphis, told him about the car, and the situation. I received a call from a friend of his, and sold the car no questions asked for $1,000, and he picked it up and I never saw the car again. I'd like to have it now as it was in perfect physical condition and I could afford to have it fixed.

The entire incident reminded me of a sometime friend of mine of questionable character who'd sold me some of my first weed in high school. One day during the summer, I happened to be driving to my parents' house in Leiper's Fork. As I was driving down Old Hillsboro Rd. I noticed black smoke which appeared to be coming from somewhere down a dirt road to my left. I turned down there to see what was happening, and there was Russell May, standing beside what was left of his beautiful Austin Healey 3000 roadster, which he casually admitted he'd set on fire to collect the insurance. He was subsequently paid $1,800 for having destroyed a really rare and beautiful car. Good things come to those who wait. In his case, he didn't have long to wait. He was killed in some sort of explosion while attempting to manufacture narcotics in his kitchen three or four years later.

Anyway, I'd sold the XK 140 for more than I'd paid for it, but there was still the issue of someone having knowingly sold me a stolen car, even if it had been his own. He had a new Pulsar stainless steel watch, which was one of the first digital watches ever made. It had a really dark ruby red crystal, and to see the time, you simply pushed the button located where the winding crown would be on a normal wrist watch. When you pushed that button these numbers would light up for as long as you held the button down. It had a stainless steel band, and as I recollect retailed for around $900 then, back in the early 1970s. I told him what had happened with the title and he turned white as a ghost. "Look," I told him, "I don't know what you did with the insurance company and I don't want to know, but I can't legally register the car, and there are serial numbers all over it. It's not enough to remove the information plate under the hood. Here's what I'd be willing to do. If you give me your Pulsar, I'll forget all about it and never mention it again. I don't want to be out $600, and maybe I can use some of the parts." He removed his watch from his wrist and handed it to me, glad to have done so, and that was the end of the matter. I'd sold the car to somebody, having explained the circumstances, and he sold it to somebody else. Presumably, and hopefully, it is alive and well somewhere even now. It certainly deserved to be.

XK 140 (2)

Occasionally on the way to my office on Nashville's Music Row, I'd pass or be passed by a faded red XK-140 Roadster with its canvas top up. Although my experiences with the white XK-140 had been strange, I still liked the 140s, perhaps not as well as the XK-120s, but given the extreme rarity of a flatbed wrecker in the mid-1970s in Nashville, I considered the full steel front and rear bumpers of the XK-140s to be a plus. Also the steering, if I'm not mistaken, was by then a rack and pinion as opposed to what was known as `worm gear' steering on the XK-120. One day I followed this car to a parking lot at nearby Vanderbilt University and spoke with the car's owner, a Vanderbilt professor. He told me he'd rebuilt the engine himself, but that he really didn't need it anymore, and though he hadn't thought of selling it, I could buy it if I wanted to. I think his asking price was $1400, which was the going rate at the time for one in its condition. I knew it ran fine, because I'd seen him driving it from Franklin, Tennessee (as I discovered), to Vanderbilt University in Nashville, on many occasions. I bought it from him, and had somebody drive me to Franklin to pick it up.

It ran great, although it smoked a bit, and it had the desirable `C-Type' cylinder head. This was the first Jaguar XK 120 or 140 I'd owned that I could actually drive, and I can honestly say that it was the one open Jaguar I ever owned that had the least problems. In fact, the only thing that ever happened was that once, on a summer day, it had a flat tire, which I easily replaced. Raising or lowering the convertible top was time consuming and troublesome. Rather than the top just folding back, as on the drophead version, or as on the subsequent E-Type roadster, the entire top frame had to be removed and stowed. And since the car didn't have actual windows, there were curtains with plastic (as I recollect) windows which had to be fitted to the low-cut aluminum doors. With these installed, visibility was at best minimal, and if it rained, basically nonexistent.

There was some rust in the rear fenders in front of the wheels, and the red leather was dry and worn, but otherwise the body was acceptable. Mechanically speaking, there were no problems with brakes, gearbox, steering, or engine. It really was a great car and I used to drive it on my usual loop at night with the top off, the wind blowing all around me and the cicadas and crickets raising all kinds of hell, glad to be alive on a summer night, as was I. Another wonderful feature of the early XKs were the vertical vents on each side of the car just in front of the doors. These could be opened which allowed the easy flow of outside air into the seating area. There were no motors or electric switches involved. They opened and closed manually. Of course, if it happened to be hot outside, hot air, and when cold, cold air. It was funny, because working at the Lavender-Blake Agency, as I was at the time, I frequently drove great cars to work, and Dick Blake, one of my two bosses, invariably made comments like "When are you going to come over and cut my yard with that thing?" He didn't know it then, and neither did I, for that matter, but a few years later, he'd be buying me four company cars of my choice, some of them simultaneously (see above).

I don't remember why I sold this car, but I did, probably on impulse. My usual stand-by buyer, Glenn Hall, passed on it because it needed to be stripped to the bare metal and completely repainted. I ended up selling it to Craig Harper, a Jaguar enthusiast and owner, whom I'd met through my mechanical mentor Tom Strickland, several years earlier. Craig had it completely repainted in its original red, kept it for awhile, and sold it. I've always loved the XK-140s and this one had been a wonderful experience.

At around this time, a friend of mine Glenn Proctor, who lived on nearby Warner Place, called me and said that he always saw me driving XK-Es and wondered if I knew of a good one for sale. I told him there was a nice black '64 or '65 roadster at the used lot of Scott-Welch, the Jaguar dealer at the time. It was priced at $6,000. He bought it, but didn't want his parents to know about it, so it stayed in my front yard on and off for a couple of months before he sold it, also I think, to Glenn Hall, worried that his parents might upbraid him for having done something so foolish.

Jaguar 3.8 S

At about this same time, my friend Johnny Barnett, from South Carolina, a songwriter and singer who I'd first met and represented while an agent at the Nova Agency, had bought a Jaguar 3.8 S-Type with a four-speed manual transmission and right-hand drive. We'd already had some interesting experiences. I'd booked Waylon Jennings at Nashville's Exit/In for an RCA Records party and used Johnny as the opening act. He'd basically been booed off of the stage, not that he'd done anything wrong. It was a small room and everyone was shouting "We want Waylon!" Anyway, Johnny had an early 1960s Land Rover, I believe it was a four-cylinder, and Johnny was a big talker, not a braggart, per se, but, well sort of. Anyway, "This thing can go anywhere. What it can't go around, it can go over or through." He had a big personality and a really thick Southern accent and was instantly likeable. I suggested we take it to Williamson County near Leiper's Fork, close to my parents' house for a trek through the woods where I regularly rode horses and knew we'd never see anybody else there. Anyway, off we went. We were less than half a mile off of the road, but already well into the woods when we came upon a fairly large tree branch. I suggested we either attempt to move it or try go around it. "Hell no, nothing can stop this thang!" That might've been true, but somehow as we tried to climb over it, a long, very thick tree branch managed to turn and wedge itself firmly and inextricably between the starboard side of the engine and the inside fender well. And try as he might, the highly praised, unstoppable four-wheel drive couldn't get the Land Rover off of the branch. We were stuck there. We hoofed it back to my parents' house a mile or so away and got a ride back to Nashville. I don't know how Johnny got the Land Rover out of there, but I know it took a wrecker.

On another subsequent occasion, I'd booked Johnny at a small club in Chattanooga called the Brass Register owned by Paul Boehm, who happened to have a rare a Muntz Jet coupe as a daily driver. Johnny suggested I ride the short 125 miles or so from Nashville to Chattanooga with him. "You mean in the Land Rover?" I asked. "Hell yes, that thing in the woods was just a fluke. That Land Rover will go anywhere. It's unstoppable. They use them in Africa for safaris, besides, it's on the interstate. What could possibly go wrong?"

I've always liked Chattanooga and had many friends there. My old roommate Mike Cofer, who'd had the 1955 Desoto Firedome coupe was working at the Brass Register then, and it would be fun. So, off we went on a very clear and hot summer day hauling ass as fast as a tortoise with a strong tailwind, being passed by everything else on the highway. Somehow, that underpowered thing actually made it over and down Monteagle Mountain to within forty or so miles of Chattanooga before it suddenly stopped running altogether. We hitch-hiked to the nearest interstate rest stop and gas station and I called the Sigma Chi fraternity house in Chattanooga and had somebody pick us up on the interstate about an hour later. The problem on this occasion turned out to be he fuel pump.

Johnny was quite successful in time, and had bit parts in a couple of Cheech & Chong movies. He'd also been given a solo spot in Robert Altman's controversial movie `Nashville,' and performed a song in its entirety at the Exit/In entitled `Somebody's Been Cookin' in my Baby's Pan.'

At some point, realizing the futility of attempting to use a Land Rover as a daily driver in pre-Land Rover Nashville, he'd acquired a white 3.8 S-Type

Jaguar sedan, which was a wonderful car despite its sort of rounded bug-like shape. It smelled like all old Jaguar sedans of the era, a wonderful fragrance combination of old leather and wood. The famed six-cylinder XK engine ran great. Johnny had written a song called `The Unknown Singer's Tomb' which had been recorded by Eric Burdon, former singer of the British group `The Animals,' and as a result, had been hired as Burdon's opening act for some dates in Germany in the mid-1970s. Since Johnny was going to be out of the country for a few weeks, and his wife was a stewardess and wouldn't be home, he asked if I'd mind driving his 3.8 S while he was gone, just to keep it running. Sure thing! At that point I had never driven a 3.8 Jaguar sedan and was glad to have the opportunity. It was strange enough driving a right-hand drive car for the first time because I was on the wrong side of the car, and it was necessary to shift gears with my left hand, and I'm right-handed. I got used to the shifter quickly and really enjoyed driving that car for those three weeks. I was glad that he'd had a good time in Europe but I wished he'd stayed over there a bit longer.

Dead for want of functional brakes!

As regards the Jaguar 3.8, in general, I kept seeing one behind a house on Harding Place in Nashville's Belle Meade area. It looked like it hadn't moved in years. One day I stopped by and left a note on the back door for the owner asking him about it. It was white but covered with dirt and leaves, and the starboard rear wheel was missing and the port rear axle was sitting on the ground. Shortly thereafter the owner, Foster Hume, called me. He'd bought the car new but the brakes stopped working and after several trips to the repair shop, he gave up and bought another car. Although the Jaguar was dirty, I assumed I could probably get it running. He sold it to me tor $35.00, if you can believe it. It sat in my driveway for a few months but at that time I was so busy at work that I never had time to even put a battery in it and see if the engine would turn over. I ended up selling it to Dr. Glenn Hall in Cookeville sight unseen over the phone, again.

One day, a few years or so later, I ran into a friend of mine, Steve Bennyworth, who saw me exiting my `65 E-Type roadster and said he had an incomplete MK II sedan which he'd give me if I wanted, since he realized he was never going to do anything with it. I was excited at the prospect by this time, but when I drove over to see it, the engine was missing parts, the instruments were gone, and some of the wood trim was missing. It was in pieces like a MK IX I once had, and sadly above my skill level. I thanked him, but as my yardman had once sagely observed, "That's above my knowledge box."

Jaguar XK 150 Drophead

I have no idea where I got this XK 150. I bought it from somebody because it was there, but sold it after looking at it for a few months. Like my 1959 Lincoln Convertible I sold it twice, getting a deposit both times. The second buyer ultimately came to get it. As you can see, even in this low resolution picture, it was full of rust. I never had an XK drophead, or a fixed-head coupe, although I'd like both now. In my experience there were just more roadsters around. The dropheads, unlike the roadsters, had a top which actually folded up and down, and they also had roll-up windows and much taller doors, which may have been steel rather than aluminum as on the roadsters. I think the drophead XKs had a longer wheelbase than the roadsters, though I'm not sure. And as far as XKs are concerned, all of them are beautiful, including the coupe, drophead, and roadster, and really fun.

Jaguar XK-120

One day, a member of the Nashville vocal group `The Four Guys' came by the office at Dick Blake International to visit his pal Dave Barton, a fellow agent. He noticed a photo of me sitting in an early 120 roadster (above) which had belonged to late country singer Mack Vickery, who'd written or co-written several hit songs for different artists I'd represented, including the classic and quite lewd `Meat Man' for Jerry Lee Lewis, and `I'm the only Hell My Mama Ever Raised,' which he'd co-written with Bobby Borchers and Wayne Kemp for Johnny Paycheck. My friend Walter Wilson whose knowledge of XK-120s was, and is encyclopedic, observed this car and advised me that the running lights at the top of each fender were missing, indicating that this was likely an earlier model before the lights were molded into the fender rather than attached. Anyway, this friend of Barton's said that he had one just like it.

It was sitting behind a semi-derelict building along with a 1967 or 1968

Cadillac Eldorado which had been de-crapitated as I like to say, meaning that its hardtop had been rather crudely removed, but that's as far as the conversion to a convertible had progressed before the project had been abandoned. Basically, this XK-120 was a frame and body, with no additional parts. I bought it anyway and had it towed to the small house I was renting at the time. I had no idea what to do with it, and enjoyed looking at it as a sculpture, but eventually sold it to Dr. Glenn Hall in Cookeville.

The first `Smart' car I ever saw. Not my thing, but curious nonetheless. The question still remains: Why?

My pal Glenn Ferguson with his 450 SL

VIII

Jaguar 1988 XJ-S

I never liked the Jaguar XJ-S from the moment I first saw it. It was an innate prejudice on my part based upon the assumption that it should be a sports car in the truest sense of the word, like all of the Jaguar sports cars which preceded it. The Jaguar E-Type had started its descent beginning in earnest with the 1968 (see above) and gone downhill from there. The 1969 and 1970 E-Types with their strange exhaust pipes, open headlights, and gaping mouths, were a far cry from the 1961-1967 cars. In Jaguar's defense, the company was trying to keep the car alive by complying with increasingly onerous U.S. safety regulations, but its days were numbered. The E-Type name continued, but by the time it was reintroduced with a V-12, it was a different thing altogether. The idea of a V-12 was certainly appealing, but its introduction in an E-Type seemed strange to say the least, although Ferrari had done quite well with V-12s, as had some Packards and Lincolns. Basically, the engine was too big for the car, both in terms of weight and length. To accommodate the massive engine, the E-Type was lengthened, and widened, but still nose heavy. Nobody could complain about its performance, but it did not corner nearly as well as a six-cylinder E-Type.

I remember turning on the local news one sunny, Saturday afternoon in time to hear about two teenage girls who'd been killed in a car accident when their car left the road. The feature showed a wrecker hauling a burned V-12 E-Type roadster from where it had crashed and burned when failing to make a sharp curve. It was burned to a crisp but clearly recognizable, partially due to its distinctive heater fan housing. It was a tragic situation to be sure, two young girls enjoying riding around with the top down on a summer day. The driver was probably inexperienced, and going too fast in a car which didn't really handle that well. I remember thinking at the time, this outcome would have perhaps been less likely in a six-cylinder car.

Visually, the V-12 E-Type was still attractive with its flared fenders, and louvered bonnet. The classic wooden steering wheel was gone, however, and the two round exhaust pipes had been replaced with four strange looking pressed steel pipes in an unusual cluster. Some of the E-Types also had pressed steel wheels with hubcaps instead of wire wheels, an inexcusable substitution, one which the Germans had inexplicably gotten by with for years. The car also had a grill for the first time, which suited the newer, longer body. The engine was an engineering and visual work of art, with four Carburetors as opposed to the two Strombergs used on the last of the six-cylinder models.

The V-12 E-Type had been forced to change in order to survive, and Jaguar had admirably succeeded in keeping the iconic car alive for a bit longer. More importantly, Jaguar, faced with impending and possibly unknown future regulations, had still been able to maintain a valid and clearly discernible descent from the original car. But, the handwriting was on the wall, and the E-Type was over, in all of its incarnations.

I resented the government regulations which killed the E-Type. Some of these regulations were necessary, much needed, and overdue, especially as applied to passenger vehicles, but I thought all sports cars should be exempted from any crash requirements. A sports car is not `safe' by nature, at least in the traditional sense, and a driver should be able to buy any car he wants or can afford. Period. The M.G. Midget, and MG-B had affixed huge rubber bumpers in an attempt to stay on the road, but U.S. government regulations had not only killed the E-Type, but sports cars in general. I was pissed.

The XJ-S debuted in 1976 and was definitely not a sports car, it was a closed GT coupe. I didn't find it visually attractive and never had a desire to have one. In the late 1970s and early 1980s, real E-Types were plentiful and not particularly expensive. As long as I could have a Series I E-Type, why would I (or anyone else) even consider the flat, strange looking XJ-S? And that `flying buttress' roof line had been tried by General Motors in 1966 and 1967 and done away with after a few years. No, I didn't want an XJ-S.

That all unexpectedly changed for me one day. I'd recently moved to my girlfriend's house outside of Nashville, and kept seeing a black XJ-S coupe parked under a pine tree at some repair joint in Centerville, about fifty miles from Nashville. I'd noticed it sitting there forlornly for a couple of years, and strange to say, felt sorry for it. It was the only foreign car there and was basically being allowed to rot. One day, I stopped and had a look at it. It was covered with pine needles, but the interior was in surprisingly good shape. There must be some serious mechanical issue with the V-12 engine, or it wouldn't have been sitting there for at least two years that I knew of, or possibly longer. I spoke with `Fat Boy,' the shop's owner, and he told me that the car wasn't for sale and that it was the owner's `pride and joy.' I replied that if such were the case, he should take better care of it. I persuaded Fat Boy to give me the owner's name and number. I called the owner who said he'd driven the car there several years earlier to have the idle speed adjusted down a bit and had never picked it up. "I don't know why, I just never got around to it."

Yes, the car was for sale, and it `ran fine when parked,' the last time he drove it. He said he'd take $2,000 for it. I met him over there and he'd brought a pair of jumper cables as if the car would start right up after several years with just a boost from another battery. Finally, after several more fruitless attempts, I brought a hot battery. As incredible as it seems, the car actually started up after a couple of attempts and ran fine. I thought about it for a couple of days and decided to buy it. It started, and I actually drove it the ten miles or so to the house without incident. I was sweating blood the entire way, but it did fine.

After that one trip home, it wouldn't start. I bought a new fuel pump from Auto Zone, and a filter, and strainer from Nashville's Jaguar dealer (at the time), and had a friend clean out the fuel tank, the insides of which looked like the outside of the sunken Titanic. Again, the car started up and ran wonderfully, except that it idled fast, as I'd been told. I insured it and immediately drove it to have the oil changed. The front brakes began slowly seizing on the way home from the oil change, ten miles further east, and by the time I made it home, were hotter than a two dollar pistol.

After the brake calipers and pads were replaced, the car was finally drivable. The tires that were on it when I got it had been new and were still in very good shape. Its looks slowly began to grow on me, although at times, it sometimes reminded me of a mid-1980s Camaro when viewed from the side. The view down its long hood was nothing like that of the E-Type, and was actually very disconcerting in that the front fenders seemed to converge toward the center of the car when seen from the inside of the car, making it, in my estimation the ugliest car I've ever driven, strictly from the driver's perspective. It was sort of like driving a speedboat. I was never ever really able to get used to it, but the effortless acceleration was amazing, actually breathtaking.

The XJ-S's performance was unlike anything I'd ever experienced. The original E-Types had been, in my estimation, a bit sluggish off the line, although the 3.8 seemed to me, at least, a bit faster than the 4.2. From 40 or 50 mph they got fast real quick. In terms of this car's acceleration, it seemed even faster off the line than my 1970 442 W-30 with the latter's 455 C.I. engine. One difference was that in the XJ-S, I was much closer to the ground, and the sense of motion was somehow much less pronounced, and at the same time greater than that of any other car I'd ever driven. I know this observation sounds contradictory. With large American V-8s like the Cadillac 472 and 500 cubic inch engines, both carbureted and fuel injected, the actual mass of the cars contributed to the sense of both speed and motion. Driving the XJ-S was like watching TV with the volume down, not much sense of acceleration, just scenery quietly moving very fast. On numerous occasions I'd find myself traveling at 80 mph or faster without being aware of it.

With any open Jaguar from the XK 120 through the last of the six-cylinder E-Types, there was the ever present music of the overhead cam engine always alerting the driver to its actions by the constantly changing pitch of its fabulous sounding exhaust. Despite its V-12, the XJ-S was deceptively, and annoyingly silent. I looked underneath the car and saw that there were two large mufflers and two large resonators. While living out in the country I'd become increasingly annoyed by hicks driving large, loud pickup trucks. On one hand, I certainly understood the desire to hear the sound of an engine, but on a truck? What's the point? It's a truck, not a sports car. It doesn't look that good to begin with, doesn't handle well, and is totally unsafe at its top speed. Again, what's the point? At the risk of activating my own latent but lurking rusticity, I decided to have the two large (one on each side) mufflers just ahead of the rear bumper, removed. I had a V-12, and damn, I wanted to hear something, anything. I drove my car to Nashville and an Arab on Charlotte Ave. put the car on a lift and replaced the two silencers with straight pipes. I had no idea what to expect when I cranked it up with the two back mufflers gone. Would it sound like a B-17? A truck? I didn't know what to expect. At first I was disappointed. I couldn't discern any difference. It sounded the same to me as it had when I'd brought it in.

Around town it also sounded the same. Only on the highway, at speeds between 50 and 60 mph, did it start producing any sound at all. I liked what I heard, and the faster I went the better it sounded. This was a problem for me because I wasn't happy until I could hear that engine loudly, which meant 75 mph and up. Consequently, I drove it faster than I would have if I'd been able to really hear the engine at slower speeds. I seriously thought about removing the two remaining mufflers but was certain that the car would then be really loud, so I left it the way it was.

One day, after several years, I was driving the car to Nashville, forty-five or so miles away. It was running like a rocket, and all the way into town I thought, `what a fabulous car! I love this son of a bitch!' It was the fastest car I'd ever had, and now, having owned it for several years, I clearly understood its wide acceptance and appeal. This car was wider than the V-12 E-Type and heavier, and unlike the E-Type, well-suited to a V-12. This car was meant for a V-12. Anyway, it was all I could do to restrain myself from really speeding all the way in. As I passed Edwin Warner Park the car suddenly started making a strange sound, like someone was inside the engine with a hammer. I slowed down and the sound slowed down as well, though remaining as loud. Maybe I'd done something to the engine, I didn't know. Maybe a rod was going to come flying through the side of the engine at any minute. Or it could be one of my wheels was coming loose. The starboard rear wheel of my 1974 Fleetwood Talisman had come off on the same road after sounding similarly (an unsuccessful attempt on my life by a would-be assassin). There hadn't been any vibration then, just a similar banging sound. Maybe the wheel bearings had given out. Maybe I was about to lose a wheel.

Or perhaps it was the transmission. My 1964 E-Type had sounded almost identical, like there had been someone inside the gearbox with a hammer. As with those two cars, and now this Jaguar, the volume of this banging sound remained constant, but sounded faster or slower depending on my speed. Well, there was nothing to be done about it. I was in town and had places to go, things to do, and people to see. If the engine blew, it blew, and that was that. I did immediately stop and check the oil level, which was where it should be. Given my past experiences with the Jaguar dealership, and given that Joe Robinson who'd serviced my E-Types and first Rolls and Bentley, was no longer in business, there was nowhere to take it and have it checked out. It either made it home or didn't. I went about my business, as usual and drove home at the end of the day without incident. The car hadn't overheated and the oil pressure seemed fine. I had no idea what the problem might be. I didn't drive it back to town, or anywhere else. Whenever I cranked it, it started immediately, however the banging, hammering sound remained. This is why it is so important to have a mechanic who actually knows something about one's specific car, rather than `in general.' Taking any out-of-the-ordinary car to someplace proclaiming to `service all makes and models' is just asking for trouble.

I thought about the situation for a few months, trying to decide what to do or where to take the car, and after some reflection, decided to call an acquaintance who had a Jaguar like mine. He'd also been a helicopter technician and had worked as a mechanic for several years at a shop that handled high end cars and exotics. My attempts at describing the situation to him over the phone were basically futile. He was as nice as could be but said he couldn't diagnose the problem without at least hearing the engine. I didn't want to risk driving it back to town, and given his poor health, I suggested my placing a tape recorder near the engine, recording it and then transferring it to a CD, which I did. I dropped it off in his mailbox, called him a few days later, whereupon he told me that his first impression was that the problem was most likely caused by a defective or broken spark plug. Hmmm, a spark plug? As many cars as I'd had, I'd never had anything suddenly go wrong with a spark plug. I'd had plugs fouled by oil over a period of time, but nothing else. Not certain whether or not his preliminary conclusions were right or wrong, and not inclined to go to the trouble of removing twelve hard to reach spark plugs one at a time, I decided to let the car go.

By this time, I'd bought a couple of other cars and had lost interest in the V-12. I sold it to some kid from Tullahoma, Tennessee who was in his early 20s. I'd explained the whole situation to him and he brought a trailer. The car started right up, still banging, and he drove it onto the trailer. I felt like it was going to a good home, and that I'd done my good deed in saving it from the junkyard, where it was certainly headed except for my timely intervention several years earlier.

A couple of weeks later, I called to check on the car and was told that the problem had indeed been a spark plug. It was something I'd never encountered before, and as a result, my knowledge of engines was increased. I was happy for him and glad that the problem was that minimal. Several months later I saw the car for sale on craigslist, and was tempted to go get it back, but decided against it. It was too fast and by this time I had too many cars again.

The Jaguar XJ-S was ultimately produced as a cabriolet and a convertible and approximately 125,000 were made in its twenty year production run. My mistake had been expecting the XJ-S to be a sports car, somehow a continuation of the E-Type. Only when I got beyond that unrealistic expectation, and accepted that the sports car as it had been since its inception, was dead once and for all, did I begin to really appreciate the remarkable V-12 XJ-S. The overall fit and finish of the interior were every bit as good as that of any Rolls-Royce or Bentley, and far superior to that of the Porsche 928s and Mercedes SLs of its era. There was one notable feature in common with the E-Type, perhaps a quiet nod to those who missed it, and that was its door handles. Like those of the XK-E, the most you could do was get the tips of your fingers in the space between the door skin and the handle.

I miss that car now, several years later, and may get another one, one day soon, but maybe not. The fact is, as with the E-Types, I'm thankful for the memories, but somewhat afraid of them now, not of the cars per se, but other drivers. When I was in my 20s and 30s, there weren't as many cars on the road as there are now, and there weren't large SUVs, and giant pickup trucks. More significantly, there weren't as many morons at the wheel as there are now, drivers pecking on phones, like deranged chickens.

The XJ-S interior. Leather everywhere.

Bruce Shelton, obviously at ease.

Attorney Jim Arena, the author, Bruce Shelton, In Concert ex-patriots.

IX.

The 1962-1965 Lincolns & Convertibles

1964 Lincoln Sedan

The 1964 Lincoln was an evolutionary continuation of the altogether new Lincoln Continental which debuted in 1961. Before we can talk about the `64, we must first address the 1961. Its engine, a 430 cubic inch, carried over from the 1960 Lincoln. The new four-door Lincoln completely changed the whole manufacturing game as it had previously existed for Lincoln. In 1960, for example, the Lincoln range consisted of a four-door Premier, a two-Door Premier, a two-door Lincoln Series coupe, and a four-door Lincoln Series sedan. There was also a Lincoln Series Landau, which we won't count since it had the same body as the regular Lincoln sedan. Additionally, offered were a Continental coupe, a four-door Continental sedan, and a Continental two-door convertible, and also, an extended wheelbase Lincoln Town Car, which featured a divider window. In other words, for 1960, Lincoln offered nine separate cars. For 1961, Lincoln only offered the Lincoln Continental and Lincoln Continental convertible, having dropped seven different cars in four ranges, counting the formal limousine. The automotive world was shocked. The Lincoln also abandoned the habit of changing its physical appearance completely every two years or so, a practice still maintained by Cadillac for years to come. The tail fins which had largely defined Cadillac from the 1955 Eldorado through the late 1960s (in diminishing degrees) had reached their zenith for Lincoln in 1957. Now they were gone for good, and the new Lincoln Continental sedan and convertible had the same profile and roofline in either configuration. Both were four-door cars and their appearance was identical, except one had a convertible top. Variations of this basic design would largely define Lincolns through the late 1980s.

The new car featured opposing doors, known as `suicide doors' even though I've never known of anyone who'd exited a 1961-1969 Lincoln unexpectedly as the result of an accidental rear door opening. The 1961 Lincolns exuded understated elegance both within and without. On the outside, the Continentals' lines were uncluttered with unnecessary ornamentation, but with their formal roofline, and opposing doors were visually striking. Inside, the interiors were large, yet intimate. In short, it was magnificent. In the meantime, Cadillac continued changing its overall appearance every two years or so, seemingly indefinitely.

My first exposure to the 1964 Lincoln came via my Godfather, who I've already mentioned (see 1960 Lincoln, above). He'd bought a new 1964 which was tan with tan leather. I enjoyed riding in it and hoped one day to have it, but he'd sold it while I was away at college. I liked all of the 1961-1967 Lincolns, but I wanted a 1964 specifically. It was longer than the 1961-1963 and the side windows no longer curved upward to a narrower top when they were raised, but instead went more or less straight up. The front grill on the 1961 was a bit more cluttered, for lack of a better word than those of its immediate successors, and by 1963 and 1964, somehow looked `better' to me at the time, although now, I'm not sure.

I bought my first 1964 Lincoln for $100 at some crappy car lot in east Nashville. It didn't run, but it was a nice metallic blue, with a light blue metallic leather interior. I'd long wanted a 1964 Lincoln, at that time, considering it to be the best looking of all of the so-called suicide door Lincolns. The 1961 certainly revolutionized the concept of luxury car design, and the cars steadily improved, finally shedding the 9.50 x 14 inch wheels in favor of 15 inch wheels for 1964. The Thunderbird inspired dash board had disappeared for the 1964 model, which was, as I recollect, four inches longer than its predecessors. These cars were of a unibody construction, as with its 1958-1960 predecessors. They'd been submerged in zinc and galvanized, so the rust which afflicted most other cars of the era was absent.

The car I bought was a nice example, it just didn't run. I figured it was worth a roll of the dice, so I paid for it, and had it towed to Green Hills Mobil station, where I was working that summer. For a little over $150, the mechanic got it running, and there was absolutely nothing wrong with it. Even the air conditioning worked. It wasn't perfect, but I would rather have had it than something `normal.'

I learned another valuable and early lesson as a result of having this car. There was some hick who worked as the station manager when the boss wasn't there. One Friday night, having saved what little money I had, I paid this manager a hundred dollar bill. I should have waited and paid the station owner directly since he was the one I'd made the deal with, but I was afraid I might spend the money. The manager kept the $100 and didn't tell the station

132

owner about it, and I couldn't find the receipt, which was just a credit card blank that said $100. I didn't like the bastard but figured that maybe we just had a personality clash. I'd mistakenly assumed that at least he was honest, even if he was a stupid hick. He wasn't (honest that is. He was a stupid hick). I told the station owner what happened and he said he'd never received the money, so as far as he was concerned I still owed the $150. The lessons I learned from this experience were: Always pay the person you've made a deal with, not someone underneath him. Secondly, always get a signed receipt for any money you pay anyone on any debt, ever, and keep up with the receipt.

I'd been renting the maid's room at Randy Smith's house in Belle Meade, and my friend's mother got tired of seeing both my Chevy and the Lincoln parked there, and I always needed money back then, so I eventually sold the Lincoln, and was none the worse for the experience. I still had my 1973 Nova. I would have preferred to have sold the Nova and kept the money and the Lincoln, but I knew my parents weren't going to go for that and the Nova title wasn't in my name for that very reason, as previously mentioned. I drove the car for a while without incident, and then needing money to return to school, I placed the car in the front yard of my friend's parents' fashionable Belle Meade address and wrote $300 in large numbers across the front windshield with a bar of soap. My friend's mother went nuts and couldn't believe I would do something that crass. This wasn't a used car lot. I didn't understand her outrage at the time, although I understand it now, more almost fifty years later…but still. I ended up using the car all summer and selling it for $300. I'd actually made some money and had enjoyed what I considered to be one of the most beautiful cars of all time.

The only strange thing about this car was that once I rounded a corner and ran into the back of a car owned by the State of Tennessee Insurance Commissioner. Needless to say, I didn't have any car insurance at the time. His car wasn't really damaged just sort of `scraped.' I knew his son who was about my age, and mentioned it. He again told me `not to worry about it,' but worry about it I did. I just didn't have any money to speak of even though I was working for the summer and out of college.

1965 Lincoln Convertible

As a driver and tour guide for Gray Line, one summer, I frequently passed gas stations, car lots, and junkyards in my job. One Saturday I was driving around east Nashville looking for cars, and stopped at a nondescript junkyard and discovered, much to my surprise, a 1965 Lincoln convertible reposing blissfully in the weeds way back off the street. It was metallic blue with a white top and white leather seats. It was in really good shape except for its faded, oxidized paint. I told my friend Randy Smith about it. He paid $200 for it and we agreed to split everything in excess of $200. It was towed to my office on Music Row. I cleaned it up and put a battery in it from my 1964 Lincoln but it wouldn't do anything, and wouldn't even turn over. Whatever was wrong with it would cost more money than I had so I sold it for $250. I paid Randy his $200 and we had a big lunch somewhere. I didn't know enough about cars at this time to prepare to even begin to commence to get it started, and I didn't have enough money to get it fixed, whatever it might cost. The 1965 was my least favorite of the four door Lincoln convertibles anyway. It had the same body as the 1964, but the hood was different, with the front turn signals moved from the front bumper into the leading edges of the front fenders, thus interrupting the original lines which had been in place since 1961. Worse yet, the center of the grill been bastardized to resemble that of a Mercury, a bad decision in terms of its appearance. That having been said, the 1965 was still a great looking car, and fun to drive. My best friend at Columbia Military Academy had one, that is, his parents had one, which I got to drive upon occasion so that he was free to drink beer without having to worry about driving. I knew that someday I'd have a '64 Lincoln convertible in good shape. Regrettably, it would take awhile.

1964 Lincoln Sedan (2)

As soon as I sold my first 1964 Lincoln sedan I regretted my decision, since it was at this point the nicest car I'd ever owned, and one of my favorite cars of all time, but I'd driven it all summer and actually made $50 when I sold it, and I needed the money. My kind of friend Rob Earls had a 1964 Lincoln sedan, just like my first one, a metallic blue with metallic blue leather. I don't remember where he got it, but it was nice. The metallic blue leather was a light color and sort of rolled and pleated, with buttons. It was actually quite beautiful. I'd been in love with that pattern since the first time I'd seen it, ten years earlier in my Godfather's tan 1964 Lincoln sedan. As late as the mid-1960s, leather was still a fairly rare and expensive option in American luxury cars. Most Cadillacs, Lincolns, and Chrysler Imperials, excluding convertibles, had fabric seats with leather bolsters. The fabric seating surfaces were probably less expensive to produce, and perhaps there was still some lingering memory from automotive designers of the era that in formal cars, leather was generally only used in the front seat, the chauffeur's seat, while broadcloth was used in the rear of the car for passenger seats.

The paint had not oxidized as much on his car as on that of my first 1964 Lincoln, and the car was quite presentable, and ran fine. I couldn't imagine why anyone would want to get rid of a perfectly good 1964 Lincoln sedan if he didn't have to, but Robb said he just wanted a different car, but in fact, he mistakenly thought it 'used too much gas,' unaware that during that era, anything over ten miles per gallon was a bonus. He was an amateur musician like myself, so I traded him a red Rickenbacker 360 semi-hollow body guitar for the car in an even trade. While I hated to lose my Rickenbacker, I knew there would be more to come, and I was very happy to have another Lincoln, this time, an even better one.

This 1964 Lincoln was now my primary means of transportation, while I had my first real job, in Nashville's music business. After I'd had it for a few months and was satisfied that it was dependable, and that the 1973 Nova was no longer needed, I returned the Nova to my Mom and thanked her. I'd genuinely appreciated my mother seeing that I had a reliable car, but I returned it to her as I was now old enough to be on my own. It had gotten me by and served me well in between Lincolns, and strangely enough, turned out to be the only new car I ever had. That Nova really had been unsafe, and the boy who ended up with it after, me died in it. I remember seeing the wrecked car behind the Chevrolet dealer in Franklin, where it had come from. It was absolutely destroyed. I was sorry that it ended up that way, but glad that it hadn't happened to me

My boss at the time, country singer Chuck Glaser, had a new black 1973 Lincoln MK IV, and each of his brothers, both Jim Glaser, and Tompall, had different colored Mk IVs as well. Chuck's MK IV was a large, black two-door beast with opera windows, a sunroof, and a continental kit trunk lid, an obvious carry over from the late 1960s MK IIIs and the earlier 1956 and 1957 Lincoln MK IIs. The 1973 MK IV was the second iteration of the current MK IV introduced in 1972 (the original MK IV being offered in 1959), and was generally considered to be the most exotic American luxury car of the era. A`personal luxury car' was of necessity a large powerful, expensive, low production, two-door coupe. While both Cadillac and Lincoln had produced two-door coupes since the very late 1940s, the MK II was probably the first car to which the term could legitimately specifically apply in what was then the so-called modern era. GM's Oldsmobile Toronado arrived in 1966 and Cadillac followed suit with the Eldorado in 1967. Lincoln fought back with its popular equally exotic MK III in 1969 and even more radical MK IV in 1972.

New US government safety regulations for the 1973 model year mandated a front bumper which could survive a 5 mph crash without damaging the rest of the car. This same regulation would apply as well to the rear bumpers beginning with the 1974 model year. This new regulation made sense in terms of the original function of bumpers, which had been somewhat spring loaded, and designed to protect the car's body from damage in parking incidents, etc. Over time, however, bumpers had become more or less universally integrated stylistically into the front and rear of car bodies and no longer served as originally designed or intended. The new regulations rectified that lapse, but not without visual ramifications. The new front bumpers were no longer merely front and rear styling accents, as they had been for the most part during the 1950s and `60s, and for 1973, now more or less resembled battering rams. Some manufacturers adapted to the new requirements more gracefully than others, with Lincoln being one of the worst.

On the 1972 MK IV, the front and rear bumpers blended seamlessly into the flowing lines of the body. The 1973 front bumper of the MK IV, however was nothing more than a large, cumbersome chrome plated battering ram which extended several inches from the front of the car and, beyond each fender to the sides. The rear bumper however, remained unchanged from 1972, and still blended nicely into the bodywork of the MK IV. My boss would frequently have me drive by Glaser recording studio to pick up some tapes or drop something off, and would let me drive his new MK IV. I felt like a king driving that thing. It was long and low with a hood that seemed to stretch endlessly beyond the front windshield. The famous Lincoln `star' hood ornament which had somewhat resembled a gun sight had been slenderized and placed at the top of the grill. The car was fun to drive, but when it was necessary to turn at anything less than creeping speed, the car dove like a P-47 Thunderbolt due to that weighty front bumper, long front, and short tail. It would require immediate braking, at which time, the light stern would come up like a scorpion's tail.

Anyway, his MK IV was a beautiful black with a black vinyl top and black leather seats. It had the now famous latitudinal oval opera window located in its rear roof side panels behind very minimal rear windows on each side. These opera windows were considered to be the height of 1970s automobile luxury and elegance. They were probably a styling response from Ford to the redesigned 1971 Cadillac Fleetwood Brougham's coach-like rear C-pillar running lights.

Inspired by my boss's shiny black Lincoln MK IV, I decided to have my metallic blue Lincoln painted black. The problem was that I still wasn't making any money to speak of yet, and didn't have the necessary $150 for the cheapest paint job I could find, `baked enamel.' I did however have a friend from high school who was at the time, the manager of Earl Scheib, a cheap auto painting shop located at the time on Nashville's upper Broadway. I hadn't seen or heard from him in years but called him up and made a deal with him over the phone. I knew that he was into music and I had an old but wonderful Seeburg studio monitor with a gold front steel mesh, an Altec 811 treble horn, and two 12" speakers. It had come from Mercury Recording Studio and had once been owned by legendary Nashville producer Jerry Kennedy, and had somehow ended up with country singer Bill Anderson. My sister had bought it from him, and I bought it from her. My friend accepted it in lieu of payment, and so I finally had a black 1964 Lincoln sedan.

When I got it back, it didn't look quite like I'd thought it would when I took it in. The black exterior did not compliment the metallic blue headliner and interior, and the quality of the paint job didn't meet my expectations. Still, it was a pretty cool car, although its life from that point forward, however, was unfortunately rather brief. In June, 1974, I was about to be married. I was to

be marrying a Catholic girl and, being a non-Catholic, I was `required' to visit the head priest at a Catholic church situated on a slight hill in a semi-urban part of Nashville. My future wife, myself, and this priest were in the rectory, and my Lincoln parked outside. As we chatted, we were suddenly interrupted by a loud crash which sounded like it had come from somewhere on the street below. I remember thinking, `some poor son of a bitch just got it,' and even said something to that effect. A few minutes later there was a knock on the door and someone asked if there was anyone here who happened to own a `large black car?' Of course it was mine. It had jumped out of gear and rolled backwards down the hill and been struck by a large 1970s Dodge. I had liability insurance then, but not collision, so while the other car was paid for, repairs to mine were not. The stern of my Lincoln had been pushed almost to the back seat, and probably would have been except for the spare wheel and tire resting on the floor of the cavernous trunk. That was the end of that. The car still drove fine, but looked like hell. It had been a really wonderful car and I'd confidently driven it to Chattanooga and elsewhere on multiple occasions without incident. Younger motorists with older cars have no idea of the inconvenience of a breakdown in the days before cell phones. If your car broke down, you couldn't just call a tow truck from your location or have somebody come pick you up, especially if it conked out in a rural or isolated area. For me, the joy of driving something really cool far outweighed any potential mechanical issues.

I always preferred the 1964 Lincoln sedans and convertibles, but now, I'm not so sure. They're all really great, with the 1966 and 1967 being the longest

1964 Lincoln Sedan (3)

In Nashville, in the early to mid-1970s, (as now) if you wanted to find some cool cars, the place to go was east Nashville. Car lots were literally located all the way up and down both Gallatin and Dickerson Roads. My friend Bard Selden of Tunica, Mississippi used to come to Nashville and we'd drive around hitting junk shops and looking for old cars. Neither of us had any money to speak of then, but we'd ride around. On one excursion to east Nashville, one Saturday, we saw three rare Cadillac Eldorado convertibles, a 1956, 1957, and 1958, the latter of which was for sale for $3,500 at a yard sale. There were also a couple of Jaguar XK 120s parked in garages which were visible from the street.

Shortly thereafter our mutual friend Albert Marlowe, bought a 1958 Eldorado convertible which he kept for 41 years, driving it literally all over the country. Albert also had another 58 Eldorado Biarritz which he kept in California but eventually sold, as well as a gold Rolls Silver Cloud 1 which he kept for 25 or 30 years. Today, Albert retains a 1965 Eldorado convertible.

Albert Marlowe and his `58 Eldorado.

Since most of the cool cars were in east Nashville then, literally the Saturday after my 1964 Lincoln sedan had been destroyed, my future wife and I headed across the river to east Nashville. My intention was to zig zag, taking side streets off of Gallatin Rd. in search of another 1964 Lincoln. We hadn't even been across the river for ten minutes before I espied a 1964 Lincoln sedan in back of a house. I pulled into the back yard from an alley, looked the car over, knocked on the door and was greeted by an elderly woman. I asked her about the car and she said that she used to drive it but that it hadn't been run in a while and used too much gas. She said that I was free to look at it if I wanted.

It was a beautiful dark, royal blue with the original paint in very good, but dirty condition. There was no rust anywhere, no dents, and the chrome was bright and shiny. The leather seats, a light metallic blue, of course, as with my previous two 1964 Lincolns. Even though the car had been sitting for some time, it started right up and we went for a test drive. The car ran fine and everything worked as it should, including the heat and air conditioning. There was only one problem, none of the windows worked. By this time, I'd learned a little about electric windows, so I listened to each of them when I toggled the switches back and forth. There was a noise within each door, responding to the motion of the switches when pushed in either direction, suggesting that they were all 'getting juice' as they say. I'd encountered circumstances in which none of the windows worked, likely indicating a blown fuse. I'd seen other situations where one or more windows didn't work, which usually suggested a switch didn't work, or a window had come off track.

The woman said that she'd sell me the car for $350. I borrowed the money from my future wife and arranged to pick up the car the following weekend. It was wonderful in every way, and the nicest car I'd owned up to this point. As soon as I got the car back to my place, I washed and polished it, and it literally looked almost as good as new. I decided that if the windows were to be fixed, I'd have to do it myself. It was a daunting task, but there was nothing to do but get started. I'd never been inside a car door of any kind before, but I imagined that what I was about to encounter was logically designed, and therefore something I could probably fix, if my initial diagnosis had been accurate. I disconnected the battery and started with the driver's door. I removed the window master switch panel from the arm rest, disconnected each of the individual switches, then unscrewed the door pull, and all of the screws around the perimeter. I unscrewed the door lock button, laid it aside, and then gently lifted the door panel up and away from the inside surface of the door. I found myself facing a full panel covered with what looked like a grocery sack. I knew that this entire paper panel would have to be removed to get inside the door. Its presence indicated that this door had never been previously tampered with. I tried to gently remove the paper so that it could be reinstalled, but it was dry and brittle and tore immediately, so that it all had to be removed in torn sheets.

Once inside the door I could see where everything was placed. It seemed logical to me that the first thing to do was remove the electric motor from the regulator frame and see if it worked apart from the mechanism. I did this, reconnected the battery, and the motor worked fine from the switch, spinning freely in both directions as it should. I oiled it, set it aside, again disconnected the battery, and then rolled the window up and down by hand, lubricating it with a light oil as I did so. I reattached the window motor, and tested it. The window raised and lowered perfectly. I went through the same procedure three more times and all of my windows worked properly. I'd figured it out myself and fixed them without help from anyone.

It was without doubt the most beautiful car I'd had to date, but then, I saw this red 1961 XKE roadster parked in front of some dump of a duplex over near Music Row. The front door of the house was always open. No screen, just an open door. One day I stopped by, talked to its owner, who was someone about my age. To make a long story short, I traded him my beautiful 1964 Lincoln sedan, for my first Jaguar E-Type, a 1961 roadster (see above). Again, it was summer and I needed a convertible.

1964 Lincoln Sedan (4)

I believe this was the fourth 1964 Lincoln sedan I owned. I'd seen it over at an apartment building off Nolensville Rd. Like all three of my previous `64s, it was metallic blue with metallic blue leather interior. It was beginning to appear that nearly every 1964 Lincoln left in Nashville was the same color. Actually it was a beautiful color, although metallic colors on almost every car regardless of make or model were subject to a dull fading back then. The leather interior was perfect. I didn't know who it belonged to so I left a note under the windshield wiper. Shortly thereafter I received a call from John L. Bradley, the car's owner. I don't remember where he said he got it, just that it ran fine, was rust free, and was not used as a daily driver. John L. Bradley was a full-blooded Cherokee Indian, smoked high end cigars (as I did at the time), and also played chess. He worked fairly near Music Row and we became friends. We'd have lunch together from time to time, and sometimes he'd come to my office and play chess with me on slow afternoons. I don't remember the deal we made, but I ended up with the car. It ran great and I used it occasionally.

Another fairly new friend of mine, Scotty Turner, who'd been an L.A. music producer called me one day and said that his new Maserati Merak had run over a parking curb, and punctured the radiator and all of the oil had run out and that it was somewhere being repaired. He wanted to know if I had a car he could use for a couple of days. I let him borrow the 1964 Lincoln. Scotty, whose real name was Graham Turnbull, was originally from Canada. He'd come to Nashville from L.A. but his musical roots were deeper. He'd produced Fats Domino for Imperial Records, Aaron Neville's first LP for a major record label (United Artists), among others, and had been friends with Buddy Holly in Lubbock, Texas and had co-written with him. When I met him he was living in Bellevue and surrounded by significant trophies of his past, the first Fender Stratocaster ever made, a coat James Dean wore in the movie `Giant', awards presented to Fats Domino, etc. He was also best friends with Audie Murphy, the most highly decorated soldier of World War II, an author, and movie star. Murphy had a silver Detomaso Mangusta, a strange looking predecessor to the more popular and better looking Pantera. Audie Murphy had written his biography 'To Hell and Back' about his experiences in the war. Together they had co-written a country classic song called 'Shutters and Boards.'

Scotty returned the Lincoln a couple of weeks later saying that it had accelerated suddenly of its own accord and wouldn't slow down. He told me he was lucky to have been able to stop it. I'd never had any problem with it and was surprised by his experience. That was the last time I ever let him borrow a car and was glad to have it back. Scotty Turner was a strange guy to put it mildly. With the car back in my possession I decided to change the oil, something I'd never actually done myself. I got some sort of container for the old oil, crawled under the car and let the oil drain. While it was draining I forgot all about it and went about my business. A week or so later I remembered it and finished the job. What I hadn't known was that I shouldn't have left the plug out of the oil pan. Moisture had coated, and rusted the inside of the engine, and now the engine wouldn't even turn over. That was that, I'd ruined a perfectly good car. It wasn't the last time this would happen, but it was the last time it would happen this way. In retrospect, perhaps if I'd just reinserted the drain plug and refilled the engine with oil, and let it sit for a few days, it might have ultimately been fine.

1963 Lincoln Sedan

I'd sometimes take back roads around Green Hills rather than getting stuck on Hillsboro Road, or as a short cut to the flea market. For several months I'd passed a nice one-story house on some side road and happened to notice a silver 1963 Lincoln sitting on the driveway behind the house. One day there was a man sitting at a table on the patio as I passed, and I stopped and talked to him about the car. His name was Lee Hunt, and he'd bought the car new from the Lincoln dealer when the dealership had been on West End. He showed me the rear quarter panel which had been severely dented, but not to the extent that it interfered with the operation of the starboard rear door, or the trunk. It was just that one panel. He'd even bought a panel off of a wrecked one so that he could have it fixed, he just never got around to it, and in the meantime, he'd bought a new car and really didn't care anymore. Except for that dented panel, there was nothing wrong with it, he said. The paint was oxidized as all metallic paints of the era were on all cars of the era after a couple of years, both foreign and domestic. The engine looked good visually, and the leather was all black, not the black and white of earlier Lincolns, and it was literally in as new condition. He wanted either $400 or $600 dollars for it. Whatever the amount, I could afford it, so I bought it even though it didn't run when I bought it. I had Lawson & Son Mobil pick it up and tow it to the house I was then renting on Leake Ave. I think I was 25 years old at the time.

Anyway, I called my friend Tom Crockett, and he came over. We dropped a battery in it and it turned over. This was a very good sign. I bought a new set of points, and remembering what I'd learned from Tom Strickland, put some fresh gas in the tank, a little in the carburetor, and it fired right up but immediately conked out as soon as the gas in the carburetor had burned. I primed the carburetor a couple of times more and went through the same sequence until it fired up and stayed running. A bit of smoke exited its dual exhausts and then went away. I let it idle a few minutes to make sure it wasn't likely to stall out, we hopped in, and off we went. Everything that needed to work, worked, including the windows, horn, wipers, and radio. It was truly a beautiful iron. We drove it around Belle Meade all afternoon accurately concluding that we would be less likely to be stopped by a Belle Meade cop than one from Metro. It was a memorable day for me in that it had been sitting for five years and was the first non-running car that I'd ever managed to get going all by myself. It was similar in appearance to the 1964, but four inches shorter overall, and it had more of a Thunderbird era dashboard. Although the 1964 was still my favorite Lincoln of the so-called `suicide door' Lincolns, this car, especially with its black leather seats and black headliner had a more intimate feel, for lack of a better word. Like the 1960 MK V, it had 950 x 14" wheels, as opposed to the 15" wheels which were in use beginning in 1964, the 15s being a decided improvement in my opinion.

I sometimes kept some of my Lincolns parked next door to my office. I kept it for about six months, through the winter, and used it as a snow car, even though the heater didn't work. It was heavy, and had excellent traction and plenty of torque, and it never conked out anywhere, or overheated, or wouldn't start. I really loved that car but I didn't know anyone at any body shop then, and it was time to start thinking about buying a house rather than renting one, which I subsequently did.

I'd wanted a Lincoln convertible as long as I could remember but I'd never had one. My friend Bard Selden in Mississippi had a 1964 and called me at my office one day and asked me if I wanted to buy it. He wanted $3,500 for it. He'd had it for several years, in addition to a couple of other cars, and needed to pay his taxes. I asked him some questions about it, and bought it from him over the phone, though I'd never actually seen it at that point.

1964 Lincoln Convertible

His desire to sell it occurred at an opportune time for both of us. Dick Blake had been recently bitching about the incessant maintenance of my second company car, the 1965 Jaguar XK-E (see above). This was as good a time as any to make another deal with him. I casually mentioned the Lincoln convertible. "Maybe this would be a better company car than the Jaguar," I suggested. He was suckered by the $3,500 price tag and said "It will have to be registered to the company." This was good for me because he would have to pay the insurance and maintenance. "Yes, of course," I answered. He buzzed Linda and told her to `write me a check.' I had no intention whatsoever of relinquishing the Jaguar or paying for its insurance and maintenance, but possession is nine tenths of the law. I'd cross that bridge when I came to it. Dick Blake is mentioned several times in this book, and it might sound like I got the better of him in every deal we made concerning cars. We did fight at times over the Jaguar, and bitterly, but I was making him so much money that he couldn't afford to really piss me off. Almost equally important to him as the money all of us were making him, was the fact that by giving us all company cars, he could deduct the expenses and beat the government out of some money. He truly hated the IRS. That, and the fact that in retrospect, I think he respected me for having the guts and confidence to stand up to him when nobody else would.

A week or so later, I flew to Memphis where Bard and his brother Chad picked me up at the airport. I spent the weekend at Bard's. He was sorry to see it go so we drove around with the top down on Saturday night in pre-casino Tunica with him at the wheel. The sound of the summer night was magical. "Stick your arm out over the door," he told me casually, as we drove along a dirt road between some rice fields. As I did so, I felt what seemed like hundreds of harmless needles striking my outstretched arm. "Those are mosquitoes," he said. And indeed they were.

I drove the car home from Tunica to Nashville without incident, and for nearly two years had no trouble with anything. I treated this Lincoln convertible just like I would a Cadillac convertible, meaning that when I arose in the morning, I'd lower the top, and raise it when I reached my office. I'd then lower it when I went to lunch, raise it when I went in the restaurant, lower it when I exited. Then I'd raise it again so the sun wouldn't bake the leather, when I returned to my office. This was probably naïve on my part, given the complexity of its operation and all of the components involved. To lower the top it was necessary to depress a small lever-like switch on the lower port side dash. When this was done, several things began happening: The heavy screws which secured the trunk lid to the body unscrewed simultaneously, one on each side, directly above each rear wheel. Then the entire trunk lid tilted all the way back from front to rear. When it was fully upright, a previously unseen metal panel folded from beneath its leading edge and locked into place. Then, twin electric motors, concealed within the top of the windshield frame, one on each side, simultaneously unfastened the heavy convertible top from the windshield frame. At this point, the top was raised in one piece and lifted from the windshield. As it moved rearward toward the open trunk lid, it would slowly begin to fold absolutely backward after it had become nearly vertical. Instead of folding in upon itself and layering, that is, stacking itself in a well behind the rear seatback, it began to fold in upon itself when it was upside down. As a result, of this unnecessarily complex mechanism, the lowered top occupied nearly all of what would otherwise be a very large trunk. When the top had basically folded itself backwards and fully into the trunk, the trunk lid slowly closed into its original position, and then screwed itself shut.

To raise the top, the entire sequence transpired in reverse order with the same toggle switch delicately raised. The procedure could be stopped at any point while raising or lowering of the top by merely releasing the button. In the same manner, to open or close the trunk without activating the top, it was necessary to start the procedure, raise the trunk lid, remove your finger from the top switch, for as long as required, and then close it again with the switch whenever you were ready. The purpose of all of this was to give the sedan and convertible the exact profile with the top raised, which it did. Of course with any convertible, there is a great loss of the structural strength and rigidity due to the absence of the steel roof. To compensate for this loss, there are extra measures taken by manufacturers to reinforce the body and or frame. In the case of the Lincoln convertibles, there were cylindrical weights placed ahead of each front wheel for balance.

The problem for any owner of a 1960s Lincoln convertible at any time was the inherent possibility that the top might not raise or lower as needed, without notice, or it might stop mid-cycle, as I'm about to relate. One hot summer day I decided to drive to the nearby Vanderbilt University track where I ran pretty much every day, as usual. I left my office in running shorts and a tee shirt and stepped into my Lincoln convertible, hit the top switch, and the process of lowering the top commenced. The trunk lid unscrewed, tilted back, and the flap beneath it folded out and locked into place. Then the two motors in the upper windshield frame unlocked and the top began to raise, as usual. At the very top of its cycle the trunk unexpectedly closed forward on the fully erect top, stopping its rearward progress. Hmm! I flipped the top switch in both directions and nothing happened. I called the only person in town who could even address the situation, explained what happened and he told me to come on over. So much for my noontime four mile run. So, off I went down the interstate in the slow lane with the white top standing upright and held in place against the wind by the trunk lid, looking very much, I imagine like the Mayflower. I received many looks of astonishment as if I generally drove at full sail. Anyway, as fate would have it, when I arrived at this run down former gas station on Thompson Lane fairly close to Murfreesboro Rd., the man I'd come to see had gone to lunch. Inasmuch as I knew the owner, Bill Smith, and there were probably twenty or more old cars in a field in back of the place I asked Bill if I could go have a look at them. "Sure, just beware of the dog," I was aware of the dog and didn't even bother to stay beyond the length of his chain, instead fixing him with the 'Madman Stare,' my eyes burning directly into his until I was safely past him, and out of reach. There were several interesting cars back there, including an early 1950s DeSoto limousine, in fact, the only one I've ever seen. Much to my surprise, however, was the sight of my second Lincoln MK V Coupe, the pink one, which I hadn't seen in more than ten years. It looked just like it did the last time I'd seen it more than a decade earlier, and I determined to have it back (see 1960 Lincoln MK V Coupe 2) above. Suddenly my musings were interrupted by someone shouting at me from the side of the former gas station. It was the man I'd come to see. I immediately started back, having forgotten all about the dog, and the time worn expression 'meaner than a junkyard dog.' The dog, however had not forgotten me, and emboldened by the familiar sound of his master's voice caught me unawares, latching on to the top of my thigh, nearly shredding my thin shorts and puncturing my thigh. So, in a sense, I did get a run in after all, albeit an unexpected one. I didn't blame the dog.

Anyway after I'd cleaned off some of the blood and washed my wound as much as possible, I emerged and explained what had happened. My host needed no explanation, he could see for himself. "Get in and start the car," he said. He positioned himself somehow in such a fashion that he was able to insert a flathead screwdriver between two contacts of some sort. He directed me to hit the switch to raise the top. Immediately the trunk lid returned to its proper place. "Now lower the top as usual," he directed. He had me raise and lower the top fully a couple of times and everything worked as it should. I asked him what caused the problem and if the problem was likely to repeat itself. I didn't really grasp his explanation, but he said it was unlikely to happen again, and it didn't as long as I had the car. I did, however exercise more restraint, by parking the car in the garage with the top down rather than raising it, and only doing either when absolutely necessary.

It seems like I'd had the car for a couple of years when it met its Waterloo. I'd driven it to Tunica and Memphis before without incident and intended to do so again. During the week leading up to my weekend trip, I had the front seat leather replaced by Stevens Brothers in Nashville in its original leather and pattern, which they'd duplicated with the black hides which I'd found at the Nashville flea market. The Lincoln also had new rear tires. I had booked our client Ronnie Milsap at the Mud Island Amphitheatre on a hot summer night. It is one of the best open air venues I've ever seen, and while it can be hot if the air is stagnant, on this night it was perfect as there was a pleasant breeze. It was truly a perfect night. After the show Bard and I drove back to Tunica with the top lowered, down the two-lane road leading south from Memphis. No casinos, no lights, just stars.

Then, there occurred the first of a series of events which placed me well within the realm of the 'Twilight Zone.' Fifteen years or so earlier, Bard

Selden had started a restaurant/tavern known as The Hollywood, by this time known far and wide as a delta favorite. It was literally across the railroad tracks in an old one-story building owned by his family. When we passed it on this hot Saturday night at around midnight, the joint was jumping with cars filling its parking lot and music blasting from inside. We were both tired and went to bed quickly, with him sleeping on the screened porch as he does year round. I, on the other hand went inside the house to the first floor room where I always stay when visiting. It was hot as hell and there was no air conditioning, but there was a large black cast iron Hunter fan which buzzed and hummed loudly as it spun overhead. I was just about asleep when I was awakened by the sudden absence of the fan's distinctive drone. I immediately suspected an electrical short somewhere and possibly a fire in this very old cypress frame house. I quickly walked through the house and onto the back porch. Bard's fan was off as well. I heard men talking outside and stepped around to the side, still within the porch. As I glanced up, I noticed that wires leading to the house were on fire, and burning, inching their way toward the house. As it turned out, the famous Hollywood had caught on fire and burned absolutely to the ground in less than twenty minutes after we'd passed it. I woke Bard, grabbed my Nikon FG and rushed over there. All that remained was a still burning outline of where the Hollywood had once been.

The next morning we ate breakfast at the Blue & White in Tunica, then returned to Bard's house. I loaded the car, lowered the top and was on my way back to Nashville, up Highway 61, then around south Memphis and over to I-40. It was as hot a day as I can remember. I kept moving, feeling the wind in my hair and exceeding the speed limit whenever I felt it was safe to do so. There was a large wooden airplane propeller hanging out the back of the car which Bard's brother, Chad had given me. There were my briefcase, camera case, ever-present Walther P-38, and a suitcase with my weekend clothes in the back seat. Around seventy miles from Nashville, the car started running roughly, hesitating now and then and gradually losing power. The eighty miles an hour I'd traveled most of the way had diminished to around fifty at full throttle. There was clearly something wrong. I just hoped I could make it home. If I could make it back to Nashville I could have my car towed to my mechanic and have it fixed. If I could just make it home.

The next interstate exit was Cuba Landing, a small stop on the way home. I decided to stop there and see if I could determine what was wrong. Hopefully it was something minor. Perhaps a plug wire had come loose. Road signs along the highway advertised two gas stations and a hotel at the next stop, about fifteen miles ahead at Cuba Landing. When I pulled onto the exit ramp I ascended a slight hill, and then down a slight decline toward a stop sign. When I applied the brakes, there were none. I hoped like hell that I wouldn't be broadsided, and that I could make the 90 degree turn to the right. As soon as I'd applied the brakes there was a puff of smoke, and then burning drops of melting rubber or plastic immediately began dropping around my feet. I quickly pulled the gearshift lever down to D-1 which slowed the car enough to make the turn. I must say, I'd kept my wits about me given the circumstances. Well, all I had to do was make it to the first of two gas stations, grab an extinguisher and put out the fire. As I sped through the stop sign I suddenly realized why I hadn't been broadsided.

What greeted me was a scene from some strange otherworldly movie. Everything that had been advertised on the billboards for the last fifteen miles was there all right, it was just burned to a crisp, abandoned, and had obviously been so for quite some time. There was nothing to do but stop the car and see if I could extinguish the fire, wherever its source. I turned off the car and coasted around in a wide circle until it stopped. I always carried a fire extinguisher, but on this one occasion, I'd forgotten it. I had four of those tiny little bottles of Perrier, but no bottle opener. I opened the hood and threw them against the firewall, but to no avail. Whatever the source of the fire, it was not visible. I actually jumped upon the top of the car and peed into the vent located between the windshield wipers, just ahead of the windshield, but to no effect. Realizing the futility of the situation, and that the fire was actually starting to spread, I slammed the hood shut, grabbed my belongings as quickly as I could and raced back and forth to the now really burning car, making several trips before I had everything including myself at a safe distance from the car. I then began taking pictures of this very strange event, expecting the obligatory explosion, a result of having seen so many cars explode on television and in movies. It was truly a surreal occurrence in that it had happened at all, that everything that was supposed to be there had been destroyed by fire, and that now, I was the only witness to these oddly synchronistic events. And then the starboard rear window which had always been temperamental raised of its own volition. Then, as if to bid me farewell, the horn honked. I snapped briskly to attention, and saluted respectfully, as the horn blasted briefly at full volume, before slowly becoming inaudible.

Sadly, I was unable to halt the spread of the fire through `natural' means.

I bid the car `fondue' as they say in these parts, and made several trips back and forth from the parking lot to the Interstate, finally standing there with my thumb extended, a dark, hot cloud of black smoke rising quickly in the distance. Eventually two rustic-looking guys picked me up in a really beat-up pick-up truck with no back or side windows. My faithful P-38 pistol was in my briefcase. I threw all of my stuff in the truck bed, fairly secure in the knowledge that no weapons known to man would be of any use in this, the actual Twilight Zone. As it turned out, they were kind enough to take all the way to Nashville, to my front door in fact. I wrote them a check for sixty or seventy dollars and thanked them profusely.

Aftermath. I actually thought it could be rebuilt.

1964 Lincoln Convertible (2) Next!

I immediately called Bard in Mississippi and told him what had happened. Then I jumped into another car and drove to the Belle Meade one hour photo place and had my pictures of the burning ring of fire which had been the Hollywood developed along with the images of my Lincoln's sad demise. Then I bought the latest edition of `*Wheels and Deals*,' where, believe it or not, there was another 1964 Lincoln convertible for sale. It was one with which I was already familiar, having been for sale in the back lot of Preston Lincoln-Mercury a decade earlier for $1,500. Now it was $5,000. I went to have a look at it and it was very nice. It needed a new top and had lost its original wheels and hubcaps to turbine wheels from a 1970s Lincoln sedan. This was a negative to me, but not a deal breaker. The original leather seats had been recently replaced by some hideous black swirled vinyl like James Brown had covered his Hammond B-3 organ with, albeit in the correct original pattern with the proper stitching. It had been an expensive undertaking no doubt, and properly done, but it wasn't going to work for me. It has always seemed strange to me that somebody would go to the considerable expense of replacing seats in the correct original pattern and stitching, only to defeat the intended purpose altogether by using vinyl instead of leather. I already knew where I could get a perfect set of black leather seats from a dead 1965 Lincoln sedan owned by Bill Smith, that is, if they would fit. The car had also been repainted in its original color and looked good. I decided to buy this one myself and let Blake buy me something else later to replace the one which had just burned up. I bought it, ordered a new top from somebody in Hemmings and had Stevens Brothers put it on. After that I got the perfect black leather seats from the dead `65 sedan and was good to go.

I really enjoyed this car and had no problem with it for the seven or so years I owned it, but during that time alternated it with other convertibles depending on my mood. I forgot to mention that nearly every 1964 Lincoln that I ever had, convertible or sedan, was afflicted with the same peculiar idiosyncrasy, specifically, that upon crossing any railroad track, the windshield wipers were likely to undertake one sweep across the windshield and back without provocation. My godfather had observed the same curious phenomenon with bewilderment in his new `64 Lincoln sedan. To me it was an interesting quirk. I enjoyed this car but one day traded it along with a 1969 Cadillac convertible (see below) for a 1958 Bentley S-1.

My 2nd `64 Lincoln Convertible.

1962 Lincoln Convertible

Late one cold winter night with snow on the ground, I had somebody from my office drive me out the old highway toward Murfreesboro, TN, twenty or so miles from Nashville. With $2000 cash in my pocket, I intended to buy a 1962 Lincoln convertible that I'd seen that day advertised in some local paper. I hadn't actually seen it since the ad had no photo, but was told that it had belonged to Liz Anderson, mother of late country singer Lynn Anderson. That meant nothing to me. All I was concerned with was that it ran well, had a good top and didn't have any rust. When I arrived, it was as described, a faded light blue with blue leather. It looked presentable in the semidarkness, and ran well. When I was convinced that it wasn't going to overheat or conk out, I paid the woman, got a signed bill of sale and a Tennessee title, and was on my way. I really liked this car and it was as a result if fooling with it that I learned how to manually operate the top, since it wasn't working. What did work, however, was the trunk lid, which raised and lowered with the top switch as designed. Since it was winter, it would be several months before I fooled with the top at all. In the meantime, I had it properly licensed and insured. It sounded like a formation of B-17s, and when I drove it down my quiet residential street its loud exhaust noises would bounce and reverberate off the fronts of the neighbor's houses as I'd pass.

1962 Lincoln Convertible

I really enjoyed this car and drove it often. It required several people to lower or raise the top given the weight of the frame and the awkwardness of having to lay it back almost upside down in the trunk. There isn't much to say about it other than that I drove it regularly in warmer months, and sometimes even on warmer winter days since the heater didn't work at all. I liked it because it was in original unrestored condition. I'd intended to fix it up as new, but I already had a really nice 1964 Lincoln convertible, and soon, unexpectedly ended up with another 1962 Lincoln convertible as I shall describe below. About the only thing I did apart from working on the leather and changing the oil was replacing its 950 x 14 wheels with 15" wheels from a 1964. I kept this car five or six years before I sold it on a whim to someone in Chattanooga. Like most cars I've had, I sometimes wish I still had it.

1962 Lincoln Convertible (2)

This car sort of came out of the blue. My friend Bard Selden, from whom I'd bought my first Lincoln convertible, the late 1964 which died in a blaze of glory, called me one day and asked me if I'd be interested in another Lincoln convertible. It was a 1962, he told me which had belonged to a friend of his who'd recently died. The car was well known to him and although the red leather seats were in good condition, there was another complete set of basically new original seats in boxes, which were included with the car. I flew to Memphis on the way back from St. Louis a week or so later and looked at the car. It was a creamy white color with a white top, and was in very good condition.

The seats were certainly passable and although a bit dry looking in appearance, were not shrunken or drawn up, but were actually fairly soft and supple. I determined that if I bought the car, I'd keep the existing seats since I'd have the top down most of the time anyway. I took a number of pictures of the car inside and out and determined to buy it if I could work it out financially, which I was able to do as soon as I got back to my office. I called the owner's mother and committed to buy it the following weekend.

I didn't really need another Lincoln convertible, and yet another one, this one really beautiful, had unexpectedly come seemingly out of nowhere. I'd always preferred the 1964, since that was the first of the so-called suicide-door Lincolns I'd been exposed to. Now, however, the upwardly curving windows, lower roofline, and shorter wheelbase of the 1961-1963 Lincolns really appeal to me.

I flew to Memphis again and spent the night at Bard's house in pre-casino Tunica. The next morning he drove me to Memphis, and over to get the car. I paid for it and we loaded some of the extra seats and parts, putting some of them in the Lincoln and some into his car. He suggested I get the oil changed so I dropped off the car while we got lunch. The 9.50 x 14" tires looked fine, but given the disaster of my last drive from Tunica, Mississippi in a more than twenty year old Lincoln convertible, I'd probably be sweating blood the whole way home. My biggest concern with any old car is always overheating, especially on a long drive in a car I've never driven before.

Bright and early the next morning I hit the road back to Nashville, allowing  myself a full day in case there was maybe a problem. The interior of this beautiful car was stuffed with spare parts. Not only did the car have no problems at all, it ran so well that I drove it most of the way at speeds hovering in the low 80 mph range. This was probably a mistake since I think my recklessness damaged the engine. I should have kept it at around seventy mph instead, because by the time I reached home, a slight valve noise had developed which remained for the fifteen years or so that I kept the car. Having observed the speed limit for two hundred and fifty miles might not have prevented the valve damage, but it might have. It didn't occur to me until now, 2021 that Tony Sansone, who'd owned the car, had probably never driven it outside of Memphis during the time he owned it.

At the first opportunity, I traded the tires and wheels from this `62 convertible for a set of 15" wheels and hubcaps with Bill Smith from whom I'd gotten the seats for the 1964 sedan from his deceased `65. The 15" wheels needed new tires so I got a new set and was good to go.

The top raised and lowered as it should for the nearly all of the fifteen years I owned it, which bordered upon the miraculous. But I'd learned my lesson with my first 1964 Lincoln convertible, which was, `don't raise and lower the top eight or ten times a day.' I'd learned to carry a large sheet with which I'd cover the seats if it was hot and sunny and I'd leave the top down for days and sometimes even weeks on end since I'd keep the car garaged when not in use.

I'd enjoyed this car for a long time, and just looking at it brought many fond memories of numerous girls in various states of undress over the years, and long drives on summer nights with the top down. The fact was however, that the engine was worn out. It had become difficult to start and had lost power

over the years, and it began smoking. The biggest problem though was that I couldn't find anybody I considered competent enough to rebuild it, so I basically stopped driving it and it remained in the garage with the top up. I'd start it every once in awhile and then put it back where it would remain immobile for a few months. The unpleasant experiences of having the engine `rebuilt' on my first car, the 1960 Lincoln MK V coupe were still fresh in my mind.

One night I'd gone outside to get a bag of dog pellets which I'd left in the garage on the floor. I noticed then that some critter had been helping itself, so I put what I needed in a bowl and opened the rear door of the Lincoln and set the bag on the back seat surface. The next morning I noticed that some creature had sliced the port side C pillar of the otherwise fine convertible top in a perfect `L' shape.

Eventually, I decided to sell the car. Some young guy, about the age I was when I bought it, purchased it off of ebay. He decided to come pick it up from Kentucky, sight unseen one Saturday when I had to be somewhere else at an estate auction. I had the car already out of the garage waiting for him. By the time I arrived home, there was a flatbed wrecker parked on the street in front of my house, and several people standing around the car. The purchaser  introduced himself and said that he'd wanted one of these all of his life and was happy to be getting it. I hoped he wouldn't change his mind after he heard it and drove it. If he had, I wouldn't have forced him to complete the purchase. The battery was low when I'd removed the car from my garage the previous day, and I hoped it would start. I got in the car, turned the key, and the engine turned over very slowly once or twice. Great! I tried again and suddenly the engine jumped to life. I asked him if he wanted to go for a ride, and to my surprise, he declined, saying he needed to get back to Kentucky. He was impatient, and reminded me of myself fifteen years earlier. The engine ran strongly, not smoking, and made no valve noise at all. For a moment I regretted selling it, but drove it down the driveway and onto the now tilted flatbed truck, then watched as they secured it improperly, pulling the front bumper too tightly, separating it by at least an inch from the leading edge bottom of the front fender.

I then gave its new owner an original shop manual, a perfect set of red door panels and armrests, a perfect original dash and instrument panel, an extra matching steering column with attached steering wheel, and some assorted switches and other electrical parts, a veritable treasure trove of expensive and hard to find parts. I watched it being hauled away until it was out of sight, my fifth Lincoln four-door convertible, and silently bid it a fond adieu. I knew it would be the last Lincoln convertible I'd ever own, and so ended a long and pleasant chapter in my life. I'd loved all of them, and except for the unfortunate fire with my first `64, my experiences with all of them had been positive. But there were still, many other cars I'd yet to experience.

Late country singer Marty Robbins and I were talking in my office one day and he told me the story of his first, and probably only Lincoln 4-door convertible. He'd bought one when they were first available and drove it all the way to some concert up north and met his tour bus at the venue. The next day it began raining and he had to drive it back to Nashville. The top not only wouldn't raise, the top switch wouldn't get it to do anything. The dealership was closed and Marty Robbins wasn't then type of guy to wait around very long for anything. He drove it to a gas station, got a welder to cut up the trunk open so they could figure out how to manually raise the top. The following Monday morning he returned it to the Lincoln dealer in Nashville and wanted his money back. There was some hesitation at first, he told me since the back had been cut up with a welding torch, but he replied that it was a new car and was supposed to work as deigned, and that he had no intention of driving all the way back home in the rain. His money was refunded, probably because the Lincoln dealer, Preston Lincoln-Mercury, didn't want any bad publicity. I recently asked Kirk Preston whose father owned the dealership, if his father might have ever mentioned the subject at the dinner table, and he said he'd never heard anything about it, but then, he'd have been 10 or 11 years old at the time.

There is one more thing I ought to mention with regard to the 1960s Lincolns in general, just because I found it peculiar at the time. I include it below from my book 'Vignettes from the Modern Era':

BOSS MAN AIN'T GONNA LIKE 'AT

When I moved to the country 40 miles west of Nashville, I was bored…at first, but there was a 1969 or 1970 Lincoln MK III which had formerly been bought new by the father of a former girlfriend. Over time, it had found its way to the so-called Lincoln dealer, T & A Motors. I thought I might buy it, as I'd had Lincolns all of my adult life, among other cars, but had never had a MK III. When the two door coupe first debuted in 1969, it was Ford's answer to the 1967 Cadillac Eldorado, a successful two-door coupe which had redefined the American luxury car, and had been touted as a 'personal luxury car,' that is, a very large, elegant two-door coupe with a powerful engine and visually striking lines.

This particular MK III had seen better days but still looked presentable in its original light cream color with nice tan leather. It was an impressive car even now, 25 years later. I called the Lincoln dealer and spoke with the man in charge and told him that I'd possibly be interested in the car, and asked if it was ready to go? He replied that he thought the battery probably needed charging, and to give him a couple of hours. We set a time, and I arrived precisely at the appointed hour only to find that somebody was washing the car. This wasn't Jamaica. To me an appointment at an agreed upon time means precisely that, not some vague, but later hour.

But before I proceed with my tale, let me describe the dealership. It was something from the Andy Griffith Show. There were a couple of new Lincoln sedans and a few new Ford Explorers and a couple of new Taurus wagons, not much of an inventory. They were haphazardly arrayed on sort of a semi-paved gravel and grass parking lot in front of the, uh...showroom? It was nothing to me one way or the other, just curious. Maybe there wasn't that much business in that part of the county. But when I opened the front door, I literally had to step over a large sleeping hound, and then walk around another one. Where were the bales of hay? I felt as if I'd mistakenly wandered into the Twilight Zone set of `Hee Haw.' I didn't mind and I like dogs anyway, it just seemed strange.

No salesmen rushed to greet me, instead I was directed as follows by a janitor: "You've got to see Mad Dog. That's who you've got to see. You've got to see Mad Dog. He's the salesman." I inquired as to where I might find `Mad Dog,' and was told that he was on the premises and would be around `directly.' I imagined the arrival of a large stocky ex-marine of the Viet Nam era with a flat top haircut and the stub of a smoldering cigar hanging out of his clenched teeth, somebody who looked like General Patton. By and by Mad Dog sauntered into the room, a tall, gangly wisp of a fellow with thinning blonde hair topped with a large straw hat, not a panama, or an optimo, but something one would use when cutting the yard. He was fashionably attired in a white polyester suit with matching vest and trousers. This was his domain and he was clearly comfortable therein. He explained proudly that the car was outside, and indeed ready to go.

He motioned me to the driver's side with a graceful wave of his arm, and settled suavely into the passenger seat. I turned the ignition key and was greeted by a very loud grinding sound as the starter engaged the flywheel. "It kind of sticks sometimes," he said casually. "Try it again." I did, and the big 460 V8 roared to life. I noticed the fuel gauge was pegged all the way to the left, indicating that we'd be lucky to get out of the parking lot.

"Oh it's all right," he said, casually dismissing my concerns, so I started out of the parking lot and down the highway toward town. Immediately the car began hesitating and sputtering, and I knew that it was absolutely out of gas. I managed to coast to the side of a pump at the Exxon station. It took Mad Dog, myself, and a couple of gas station employees to push the nearly three ton car the remaining six feet or so distance to the gas pump.

Mad Dog bought $3.00 worth of gas and we both got into the car again, none the worse for the experience. The car wouldn't start at all this time. He got out of the car, opened the hood and shouted some instructions. With the hood all the way open, I couldn't see him or hear him, so I opened the driver's door and leaned around, with my left foot on the ground, my left hand on the steering wheel, my right foot on the gas pedal and my right hand poised to turn the ignition key.

"All right," he shouted, "try her now!" Nothing. Some banging and clanging followed as he smacked something under the hood with a hammer, something I couldn't see at all. "All right, try her again, but this time put her in neutral," which I did.

As soon as I turned the key the engine roared to life and the car immediately, and without warning, jumped into reverse of its own accord. When it did, the open driver's door struck a lamp post in between the two gas pumps bending the door all the way forward, parallel to the front fender before I was able to stop the car's rearward movement. I was lucky as hell that my leg hadn't literally been torn off, so I was understandably pissed off by what I correctly perceived to be 'Mad Dog's' bland nonchalance and colossal incompetence.

He shut the hood, pushed his farmer's hat toward the back of his head and surveyed the damage, stating as he scratched his head perplexedly "Boss man ain't gonna like 'at," to which I replied with some irritation, "Boss Man should've had a mechanic replace the starter to begin with, and Boss Man should have had enough gas put in the car for a test drive before I arrived. And what kind of factory authorized Lincoln dealership doesn't have its own gas pump on the premises?" I got out of the car, and myself, Mad Dog, and a couple of the gas station employees managed to at least force the door back in the direction it needed to be, but there was no possibility it was ever going to close again without major surgery.

I saw the once beautiful car parked forlornly behind the dealership several times over the course of the next few months, unrepaired, unmourned, and abandoned. Then, one day, it just wasn't there. I didn't see it again for several years and hoped that someone had bought and repaired it. Such, however, was not the case. One day as I drove down the airport road to take off the trash, I saw it parked next to a large abandoned former factory, awaiting one final ride, its transportation to the scrapyard one county over to the west. I stopped and looked at it and was saddened by the state into which it had now fallen. Not only had the door never been fixed, but the once beautiful tan leather had baked and cracked from exposure to sun and water, and its vinyl top was shredded into strips, and the metal beneath rusted. The rest of the car was mostly either covered with mildew or eaten away by rust. I took some pictures, and that was that. Two days later as I passed, it was no longer there, a truly tragic end for such a once magnificent car.

My son, Scotty

Eight year old Scotty with my `58 Bentley.

X.

The Big Lincolns 1977-1979

The last of what I regard as the `real Lincolns' was the 1979. This is a 1978, the last car which came stock from the factory with the famed 460 C.I. engine.

My first 1979 Town Car

The last real Lincolns in the proud history of this exceptional American brand were the 1978 and 1979 Lincoln Continentals and Town Cars. Even though these cars continued through 1979, the engine size was diminished in its final year, to the detriment of the final `Collector Series' cars. I'd always been impressed by these giant cars. They were larger than any other cars on the road, a final exercise in American automotive excess before Lincolns ceased to have any relevance at all as passenger cars.

Cadillac had lost its cache beginning with the 1977 models and continued downhill from there, reaching their lowest point with the so-called Cadillac Cateras, Cimarrons, and Fleetwoods, of the 1980s, which should never have even been imagined, let alone manufactured. Lincoln continued to make better cars than Cadillac through 2012, at which time Lincoln sedans became in my opinion, worthless, burdened with front wheel drive and bodies shared with other generic Ford offerings. Cadillac had however, continued to make one `big' car through 1977 with its Eldorado, which for its final year as a real Eldorado, or even a Cadillac for that matter, had lost its magnificent 500 CI engine in favor of something smaller, and more fuel efficient.

Even though my first car, my 1960 Lincoln MK V had been big, it wasn't as large as my first `big' Lincoln, a 1979. I don't remember where I got it, from whom, or what the circumstances were, somebody in Nashville. It was cheap enough, as I remember, as in the 1990s these cars were considered dinosaurs. It had the smaller V-8 although I didn't notice, as it was fast enough, albeit thirsty. But…if you like cars, they must be fed.

My 1979 was a light metallic blue four-door with a matching light blue interior with tufted leather seat backs and cushions. It was definitely `overdone' compared to the more restrained leather seats of the 1960s Lincolns, but beautiful nonetheless. This beast also had a matching metallic blue vinyl half top with opera windows, a nod to those appearing with the exotic 1972 Lincoln MK IV. My car also had the open rear wheel wells which I preferred over the larger fender skirts. The open wheel wells also had fender skirts but these were minimal. There were also attractive 15" finned aluminum `turbine' wheels which added to the car's appearance. Last but not least, it had the peculiar power vent windows, a feature which was appealing in theory but would probably become a problem eventually, as it did in my case. Those vent windows were interesting technically in that whenever one wanted to lower either of the front windows as soon as you hit the window down switch the vent window lowered all the way first, after which the main window could be lowered as desired. The same switch pressed forward raised the window. As soon as it reached the top of its cycle, continued pressing of the up switch would raise the vent window as well. Its operation allowed the vent window to be raised or lowered to allow some ventilation without having to raise or lower the main window. However, to lower the main window at all, the vent window must be lowered all the way first. While this was good in theory, unless there was a breeze, or rather a strong wind from either side of the car, the vent windows didn't really introduce much air into the car's interior. These curious vent windows continued with the post 1977-1979 cars, but as I recollect, were gone by 1998, and probably earlier.

I really liked this car but it wasn't as nice an example as I would have liked. It was presentable, but that was it. I'd bought it on a whim and decided that if I liked it, I'd find a nicer one later. I'd enjoyed it immensely especially on a winding country road. It was truly a beast, with its expansive hood and Lincoln emblem resembling a gun sight in the distance, it was really fun to drive. The passenger side vent window would sometime get stuck and I'd have to put the car in park, slide over to the passenger seat and play with the window switch as I attempted to get the vent back into position where it could be raised or lowered the rest of the way. This didn't happen all the time, but enough that it was an annoyance. Once, I stopped to get something from a convenience store and attempted to raise the vent window, but it refused to raise all the way, so I lowered it and attempted to raise it again from the driver's seat without having to manually align it. I was in a hurry and tried to force it using the window switch. I heard a `pop' and that was that, the vent glass had shattered. I kept the car for a couple of weeks after that incident, and called my automotive pal Harrison Peyton and gave the car to him. What had happened with the vent window had been my fault, the result of my impatience. Hopefully, I'd learned my lesson. Once again, "If it doesn't fit, don't force it," as my father used to say.

1977 Lincoln Town Car

The paint was a pale `battleship gray' a color of which I'd seen too much of in the navy. Still, this car was a beast.

My next `big' Lincoln was a grey 1977 Town Car. I'd espied it on a small car lot on Columbia Highway within two miles of the square in Franklin, TN. When I'd been an agent at the Lavender-Blake agency in the mid-1970s, one of our clients had been country singer George Jones. He'd had a big grey four-door sedan exactly like this one which had grey leather cushioned seats. His, like this one, had been equipped from the factory with a grey vinyl half roof and opera windows. His, like this one, also had a very rare glass or Plexiglass (I'll just say glass) roof in front of the vinyl half top, somewhat reminiscent of some roofs on some 1950s Ford `Victorias.' It wasn't a glass sunroof, it was a glass roof, meaning that the entire front half of the roof, the part which covered the driver and front passenger was made of glass. It might have been

Plexiglass, I'm not sure. There was a rigid headliner beneath the glass on the inside which housed a large manually sliding panel which could, with some effort, be slid backward so one could see the sky, tall buildings, or whatever. The roof itself was fixed in place and couldn't be opened at all.

Hillbilly singer George Jones used to drop by the office frequently in an inebriated state and literally drive his giant Lincoln as far up the front steps as he could get it. It was not unusual to see it `parked' this way. Sometimes he would get mad and drive away after awhile. At others, he'd have to have the car towed off the steps because he couldn't dislodge it. At other times Shorty Lavender would call the police who would escort him off of the property. I'm pretty sure the car which I bought was the singer's. Personally I couldn't care less, since he'd caused me a lot of time and trouble skipping concerts which I'd arranged. In any case, I really liked the car and enjoyed it and had no trouble with it during the time I owned it. I wasn't especially thrilled with its battleship grey exterior but could live with it. The grey leather would have been fine with a royal blue or black body color but with the grey outside and grey seats, it looked bland.

At about this time, I met Nashville artist Jack Kershaw who lived over by David Lipscomb College in a house which had been built as the `Oriental Country Club' clubhouse in the early 1900s. Jack and I became good friends and I helped him find cars, not that he should have been driving. I don't remember what he'd been driving when we were introduced by a mutual friend. At the time, however Jack had a dead 1960 Imperial sedan in the back yard as well as a 1967 Camaro SS convertible which was buried up to its wheels in dirt. Jack was extremely interesting. He'd graduated from Nashville's Montgomery Bell Academy in 1936, making him likely MBA's oldest living graduate. He'd also attended Vanderbilt, earned a law degree at some point, and married into a prominent Nashville family and lived an interesting existence. He was both an artist and sculptor, and his late wife had been an incredible photographer. Jack had been involved in the WPA arts project and had been responsible for the art gallery which still exists in the basement of the Parthenon at Centennial Park. Jack also had assisted sculptor William Edmondson and brought him into the WPA arts program. Kershaw had also been one of the attorneys representing accused Martin Luther King assassin James Earl Ray, and had a number of audio tapes of him interviewing James Earl Ray and swore that Ray was innocent.

We'd remain friends until his death fifteen years later. Jack could have been a commercially successful artist and had been paid for portraits and other paintings. Generally, however, he kept most of his work. While some of his paintings bordered on the surreal, his portraits were as good as those of any of the great masters. Many of his subjects actually appeared to be alive, so great was his skill at painting the human form. I fell in love with a fanciful painting of Nashvillian Eve Zibart before she was married. This painting depicted her on an ice skating rink and was done in 1947. I had to have this painting and he wouldn't sell any of his works, but, he loved cars so I traded him my grey 1977 Lincoln for the painting which I still have. I kept the car for several years and had no problems of any kind. As I recollect, the only issue I had was that there was no specific blower fan speed control, a defect which was corrected the following year. Let me say, this car, in fact all of these 1977-1979 cars, were truly gigantic in proportion, and interestingly enough, their side profile, except for their battering ram front and rear bumpers, was a logical evolutionary stylistic continuation of the 1961's revolutionary profile. The large grill had obviously been influenced by Rolls-Royce, but not to the extent that Ford could be accused of trademark infringement. It took some getting used to for those familiar with the 1961-1967 so-called `suicide door' Lincolns, all of which had purely horizontal grills. Be that as it may, these were remarkable cars.

1979 Collector's Series

The 1979 Lincoln was the last of a great line of incredible cars. This was my next big Lincoln, a 1979 Collectors Series, considered by most people interested in such matters, to be the best of the last large Lincolns, which in many ways it was. As I remember, the Collector's Series cars were only available in two colors, a dark navy blue, and white. To the best of my recollection, all of them only had velour interiors, that is, no leather, but I'm not certain. They also lacked the opera windows which had made such a significant style statement when they debuted on the 1972 Lincoln MK IV.

1979 Lincoln Collector's Series

Back when old cars were still advertised in the local newspaper, I found this one, listed with several other interesting cars, including the most beautiful 1976 Cadillac Fleetwood I'd ever seen, a deceased but complete 1949 Cadillac Fleetwood, and a few other cars which didn't interest me. The woman selling these cars had them all sitting in a field off the interstate somewhere in Donelson, near the home of President Andrew Jackson. I called about them and drove out to see them. Her husband had died and she didn't want any of them. She wanted $5,000 for the Lincoln, which only had 24,000 original miles and had been garage kept all of its life. It looked brand new inside and out.

The 1976 Cadillac Fleetwood was, like the 1979 Lincoln, the last of the large American luxury sedans (from Cadillac). This Fleetwood Brougham was a beautiful original robin's egg blue with matching vinyl top and leather seats. It had less than 3,000 original miles and was unbelievably elegant, and I'd never seen that color before or since on any car. It had the magnificent 500 cubic Engine and ran like a top. There was, however, one problem which was a deal breaker for me. The entire car was literally saturated throughout with rust despite the fact that it ran like new. I probably could have bought it for $1000 but it was too far gone, despite its beautiful color. I offered $4,000 for the 1979 Lincoln and my offer was accepted. It made it home, but that was about all, despite its low mileage.

As it turned out, the fuel tank was full of rust. I was able to drive the car by keeping several fuel filters in the glovebox. They were easy to install and literally screwed into the side of the carburetor. I had a new car and I wanted to drive it. Changing the metal fuel filter would carry me for awhile, but the only real solution was a new fuel tank, which I was able to order from one of the main chain parts stores. After the new tank had replaced the original, the car ran as new. If the smaller 400 CI engine lacked power, I didn't notice. This Lincoln was huge and it was fun to drive. I got used to the dark blue velour interior although I preferred leather. One thing I didn't like about it was the fact that any movement across the seats generated static electricity. The power operated sunroof was huge and I enjoyed it, and the power vent windows worked perfectly every time without any issues. Like I said, it was basically a new car.

One summer day I was parked in front of Rhino Books on Granny White Pike and happened to see my friend Nashville artist Jack Kershaw. Actually, he saw me as he exited a restaurant in the same block. He saw me in the car and said that he had to have it. He offered me $5,000 for it, and after several days thinking about it, I agreed to sell it to him. I'd had it for several months and enjoyed it, but if I was going to buy one to keep, I might as well have the durable, more powerful 460 CI engine and the formal padded half top, which I preferred, and a full leather interior.

This beautiful machine, the last of the real Lincoln sedans, met its unfortunate demise prematurely at the hands of Jack Kershaw. First of all, he backed another car into the driver's door severely denting it needlessly. Basically, his method of backing any car consisted of stopping just as soon as he hit whatever car or object happened to be behind him. It wasn't this incident that destroyed the car however, it was letting his next door neighbor's teen age son drive the car to Atlanta for the weekend. On the way home one of the car's radiator hoses ruptured while the car was on the Interstate, and instead of pulling the car off the side of the road, the kid kept driving it. Perhaps, in his defense, there was no immediate place to pull over. The bottom line was that the car's engine was completely destroyed. Jack should have had the belts and hoses replaced before doing anything other than driving around town, or at the very least checked them for dry rot, cracks, or bulges.

Jack's next door neighbor was a pretty capable mechanic. He felt bad about what had happened and said that if I could find another engine for Jack he would replace the dead one. I immediately began a search for another giant Lincoln sedan and found one sitting outside a business office of some sort in Smyrna, twenty or so miles southeast of Nashville. It looked like it had been parked there for awhile, and it had. The car's owner said that it had run when parked but that he'd just stopped driving it so it hadn't moved in the last three years. I walked over and had a closer look. It looked OK, just dirty. There were also a bunch of old clothes which someone had thrown in the back seat. I offered the owner $300, and he accepted my offer. I was fooling with all of this as a favor to Jack because he was one of my best friends, and also because he was in his 80s. A couple of days later I found a wrecker and rode out to Smyrna with him to get the car. As he was hooking it to the wrecker I reached in the back seat and began removing those old clothes. As soon as I removed the last handful from the back seat I saw a large snake of some sort which immediately attempted to duck into the space between the rear of the seat bottom and the lower edge of the seat back. There wasn't time to examine the serpent to determine what it was. I just grabbed it quickly with my right hand, extracted it as fast as possible, and threw it outside of the car before it could strike at me. The wrecker operator had witnessed the incident with bewilderment as it had indeed happened quickly. When the snake hit the ground it took off somewhere. It was moving deliberately but not, it seemed to me, in any particular haste. It was thick and a bit over a yard long. All I knew was that it wasn't a rattlesnake and it hadn't bitten me. That was enough.

This `new' giant Lincoln was towed to Jack's house where it rested in blissful repose along with a copper colored 1973 Cadillac Sedan De Ville I'd found for Jack a year or so earlier, which had died in place with 43,000 miles on its odometer. Jack's next door neighbor, Bobby Phillips, managed to successfully remove the dead engine from the 1979 and replace it with the engine from the donor car, but after several months, it still wasn't operational. Jack was certain that he would be back on the road any day. In the meantime, I'd take him to the store or to lunch usually once a week and he had other friends who would take him somewhere if he wanted to go.

One day, several months later, I stopped by Jack's house unannounced, as usual. The `new' $300 Lincoln, was gone, and the formerly beautiful white 1979 Collectors Series Lincoln was getting ready to be loaded on a flatbed and hauled off to the junkyard. It still had its beautiful turbine wheels. I think Jack said something about a codes violation. In any event I quickly asked if I could have the wheels from the `79. The guys hauling it away said they'd bring them back to me after they dropped the car off when they came for the remaining car, the beautiful but deceased copper 1973 Cadillac Sedan De Ville. When the guys returned for the Cadillac, they brought me the wheels as promised. These same wheels, with different hubcaps, were used during the late 1970s as options for both Ford and Mercury sedans. As I recollect, the spaces between the turbine spokes were painted a dull grey on the Lincoln, while unpainted when used on the other cars, which, in my opinion gave them a cleaner appearance.

The sad and premature death of the 1979 Lincoln Collectors Series had been a needless, pointless tragedy. Once again Jack Kershaw wanted to start over with another giant Lincoln, so I found him a really nice burgundy 1978 sedan with a matching velour interior. Hopefully, he'd take care of this one. He'd already been personally responsible for the untimely and needless demise of several cars before I'd met him, including a 1929 or 1930 Packard dual cowl Phaeton which he'd inherited and cut up and turned into a pickup truck, a cruel and senseless act. One of its giant wire wheels along with the removable second windshield assembly remained in a shed on his property. This next 1978 Lincoln ultimately suffered the same sad fate as all of his other cars.

1978 Lincoln Town Car

Well, I wanted another big Lincoln sedan. For some reason I'd always preferred them over the 1970s MK IV and V Coupes, although those were wonderful cars. I think that I just preferred the larger overall size of the giant sedans. Anyway, one day in Centerville, there spontaneously appeared a temporary used car lot, meaning one which wouldn't likely last for more than a month, which it didn't. In addition to the usual crappy, generic, and beat up 1980s Honda 'Accordians', Toyotas named after cigars (Corona, Corolla), and Ford Tauruses, there was a 1978 Lincoln Town Car. It was a beautiful burgundy with a matching full leather interior and turbine wheels. It lacked the preferred half top, but was instead adorned by a full but tattered and shredded matching burgundy vinyl top. It was priced at $250. Plus a 'doc' fee of $50. I was understandably offended by the so-called 'doc' fee as I'd never heard of such a thing before, and considered it to be nothing more than some arbitrary fabrication by the dealer in an attempt to extort extra money from potentially dimwitted motorists who wouldn't know the difference. I'd been at sea in the US Navy and had never heard of a dock fee, although such an expense in that instance seemed reasonable in theory, and therefore at least potentially justifiable. A call to Bard Selden confirmed my suspicions, that the so-called `doc' fee was an arbitrary `document' fee, indeed something made up to extract additional money from the customer. I did not object to the $50. If that amount had been part of the cost of the car I wouldn't have minded. What I minded was any additional, arbitrary, and artificial fee which previously didn't exist, and only did so now as the result of collusion among so-called dealers. Sort of like `closing costs' on a residence or commercial building. $300 for a nice example of the last great American Lincoln? Hell yes! Of course it needed tires, which it got. I didn't know what to do about the top, since, generally speaking, I consider vinyl tops nothing more than rust traps.

Everything worked, including the troublesome vent windows. It was worth more than that as scrap. I bought it on the spot. I had no idea what I would do with it, but it was a really nice car, except for the shredded vinyl roof. New tires, an oil change, and a new battery made it road ready. By this time I was living at my girlfriend's house in the country outside of Nashville. My house was still in town and I'd drive there and work writing books, meet friends for lunch, and go running on the horse trails in Percy Warner Park near my house. I had a couple of cars in the garage at my crib in Nashville but often drove this Lincoln around town for errands. Most of my friends knew that I was nuts as far as cars were concerned, so were never surprised by anything I ever drove. Some of my former music business contemporaries weren't so sure, and no doubt imagined I'd fallen on hard times. The reaction by motorists in general however, was decidedly reminiscent of that caused by my first car, my 1960 Lincoln MK V coupe. I was always given wide berth by motorists in newer, more expensive, but not necessarily `better' cars. I imagine they surmised that anyone driving something `like that' obviously had nothing to lose, was most likely uninsured, and probably insane.

Obviously inspired by Rolls-Royce, but not close enough to justify a trademark infringement suit against Ford from a less powerful, financially strong company.

The truth is, there is nothing quite like driving one of these gigantic beasts. When you overtake lesser cars, you do so in sections. Your front fender passes the adjacent car, followed by your two doors, and then the rear quarter. The long view down the hood is incomparable, it seems to go on forever. Your left shoulder seems about a foot from the inside door panel and you are surrounded by steel…not rubber, plastic, or fiberglass. It's a true American iron and there will never again be anything like it manufactured by Detroit, or anywhere else ever again. The 1978 Lincoln represents the zenith of the American automobile. It is unapologetically large, ostentatious, and excessive, and says basically `I really don't care what you think…about anything.'

I never got the top repaired because I considered the car expendable and didn't think I'd have it that long, but I ended up driving it frequently during the two and a half or so years I had it before it met its `Waterloo.' Its end came one morning when I turned a bit prematurely and ran over a curb, essentially destroying the transmission linkage. I immediately had it repaired but the fix only lasted another two weeks before it no longer worked. I returned the car to the transmission shop and was told that everything was so bent that it would all have to be replaced with original parts, which were unavailable except possibly from a junkyard somewhere. This was in the days before self-serve junkyards like Pull-A-Part, and the internet. If you've ever looked at a diagram of steering column gear shift linkage to an automatic transmission, you'd be surprised that it works at all, given that it's so convoluted. A floor mounted automatic transmission shifter is much simpler and makes a lot more sense. It was possibly an option that would have saved this car for me but the alteration would require cutting a hole in the floor, but even then, the presence of the very large front seats would not allow its movement.

There was one minor incident of a mechanical nature which I addressed myself. The alternator light came on one cold winter day. I had it checked, and did indeed need a new alternator. Replacing an alternator on a Cadillac Fleetwood, for instance was easily accomplished in fifteen minutes or less. With this Lincoln, it was located almost beneath the car. I had to wedge myself underneath the car like a lizard. The alternator was huge, and it was an awkward procedure, but after an hour or so, the replacement was accomplished. I subsequently gave the car to a friend who could pretty much fix anything on any car and I never saw it again, but I remember it fondly, even now. It was one of my favorite cars ever.

1977 Lincoln Continental

My 1977 Lincoln Continental was almost larger than this church.

I had to go to the Opryland Hotel for music business related meetings or functions from time to time, and then, as now, my eyes were/are always roving, looking for interesting cars in driveways or backyards. On one occasion I spied a white 1977 Lincoln sedan from Briley Parkway on the way to the Opryland Hotel. I noticed it several times before I actually stopped to look at it. I knocked on the door, a man answered and I asked him about the car. It wasn't for sale per se, but he would sell it if somebody wanted to buy it.

It was white, which I don't like as a rule, and it had white leather, which is even worse. I like the color itself, it's just really hard to keep clean. The car had been garage kept and the leather was perfect as was the original paint, and the banded vinyl half top. It was a Continental as opposed to the more expensive Town Car. Consequently, it lacked the troublesome power vent windows and instead, had one-piece front windows, which I preferred. The white leather seats were similar to those of a so-called 1960s `suicide door' Lincolns and lacked the individual seat cushions of the more expensive leather seating option. I considered this to be a plus. I hadn't known that single windows without vents or full leather seats minus cushions were even available. It also had the signature `opera windows' which debuted with the 1972 Lincoln MK IV coupe. While these lengthwise ovals were considered hideous and excessive to most motorists by the mid-1990s, I liked them precisely for those very reasons.

The owner told me the amount he wanted for the car. I don't remember what it was but I considered it to be good deal for me. At this time these were considered `old cars' and nothing more. He apparently believed this illusion as well. I agreed to his price and picked up the car later in the week and was happy with my purchase.

I always preferred open rear wheel wells over fender skirts and concluded that I should be able to replace the full fender skirts of the 1977 with those minimal skirts from a junked or wrecked 1978, which I was able to do with little inconvenience. Apart from this, my only problems with the 1977 were its heating and air conditioning controls. The 1977 did not have a specific speed control for the climate control's fan. Instead there was some lever which was moved from port to starboard which meant under most circumstances the fan was all the way on or hardly blowing at all, so one was constantly sliding it from side to side. This was remedied for 1978 with a manual blower control.

I preferred the leather of the Continental in that it was a bit cleaner, that is, more reminiscent of the 1961-1965 cars. The more expensive pillowed seats of the Town Car were more common and were available in fabric or leather.

I really liked this car but couldn't decide whether I preferred turbine wheels or the deep dish wheels, both of which were options. Since both wheels were 15" in diameter and used the same size tire, I decided to have both simultaneously and put the dish wheels on one side and the turbine wheels on the other. Since anybody looking at the car could only see one side at a time, nobody noticed the difference. I kept this car for nearly a decade and enjoyed it immensely. I would probably have it now except that one day I received a call from someone about an ice blue 1976 Cadillac Fleetwood I'd seen once nearly a decade earlier. When I bought the Fleetwood (see below), I knew my girlfriend wasn't going to go for me bringing yet another car to her formerly tranquil house, so I sold it to a friend on the day I bought the Fleetwood. In other words, I'd left the house in the morning in the Lincoln, and returned in the Fleetwood that evening. We sort of have a deal. She tolerates my numerous cars while I put up with her useless, ungrateful, constantly howling cat. I think she got the better of me on that deal, hands down.

XI.

2000 Lincoln Town Car

One day my Mom called me and asked me if I wanted their Lincoln Town Car. My father still had shrapnel in his knee from World War II and found it very difficult to get in and out of the car despite its large (by modern standards) size. Mom wanted to get some sort of Volkswagen sedan which she thought would be easier for him to get in and out of. Yes indeed! The Lincoln had traveled a mere 34,000 miles and was only two or three years old. I drove them over to pick up the VW and left in the Lincoln. It was a strange looking car to me in that, like a Porsche 928, it seemed to look different from every angle. Sometimes it resembled a large turtle, while at other times I compared it to a piranha, with its toothy grill and extended mandible. At other times it looked quite attractive. One thing for sure, it wasn't like any Lincoln I'd ever had, other than an excellent 1993 Town Car, and that was only due to the presence in both cars of rear suspension air bags. As I might have mentioned elsewhere, I think air bags in terms of suspension components or their derivatives are pointless, potentially dangerous, and generally undesirable.

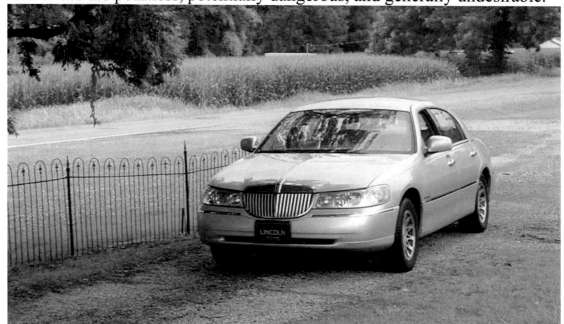

Despite these seemingly negative observations, I really appreciated the unexpected gift of this car, and really grew to like it. It was comfortable, low to the ground, and handled very well, for what it was. It had nice leather seats and was very comfortable. It was an excellent passenger car with many features which I'd never had before in any car. I liked its onboard digital compass, dual trip odometer, and especially the feature that indicated how many miles were available for the amount of fuel on board. In terms of performance it was `slow' off the line although it cruised well at higher speeds. If it became necessary to accelerate suddenly from any speed there was a very big lag time between the time you stomped the accelerator and anything happened other than the probable use of a gallon or more of gasoline.

The body was interesting in that it was shamelessly adorned with rubber, plastic, or some other similar material. Both bumpers, front and rear, for example, wrapped all the way around the sides of the car to their respective wheel wells, and in comparison to the heavy steel bumpers of a 1979 Town Car, were basically weightless. The valve covers were also made of something other than steel, most likely fiberglass. Additionally, there was a large open space perhaps a foot or more, between the front of the radiator, and the back of the front bumper. As I discovered this, I hoped I was never in this car in any kind of accident.

I never looked at this car and considered it beautiful, but I grew to appreciate its looks nonetheless and definitely enjoyed it, putting more than a hundred thousand miles on it before it unexpectedly met its `Waterloo.' This occurred in an ill-conceived trip through Memphis to New Orleans. I knew that it was going to snow but figured that I could make it to Memphis before the weather became a problem. I've driven comfortably and without terror in all kinds of cars in all kinds of weather, all of my life. Beyond Jackson, Tennessee, west toward Memphis, it was really snowing heavily, a powdery but heavy snow. It wasn't even sticking to the windshield, just basically dust. I didn't even need my wipers. The road surface looked clear and traffic was moving rapidly in both directions. I looked at my instruments and noticed the outside temperature was 23 degrees, and I slowed down to around fifty mph and moved to the slow lanes as trucks and other cars blew passed me. Traffic had been heavy and suddenly the snow began sticking quickly. No big deal, I only had another fifty miles to Memphis. In another five minutes or so, and without any notice, the car started spinning around in circles in the middle of the interstate as it continued to move forward. I had absolutely no control at all over what it was doing. In mere seconds it straightened up and was again heading nose first, this time leaving the road to the right and onto the shoulder down into a slight ditch, then ascending a fairly steep bank, before ceasing its forward progress after running through some heavy brush and striking a tree. All I could do was hold on.

As soon as Lincoln stopped I made certain that neither of us were hurt. The inside of the car smelled like something was burning, which I concluded was the residue from the activation of the air bags. This was my first experience with air bags and they'd worked exactly as they were supposed to and neither of us were injured. My girlfriend had more presence of mind than I did, and retrieved my pistol and cell phone. By this time the snow was heavy and sticking fast as the temperature continued to drop. I knew that the car couldn't be seen from the road and that if we didn't get to the side of the Interstate and get picked up soon, we'd literally freeze to death. I called 911 and explained where we were. An ambulance was already nearby looking for other cars and soon picked us up, and within fifteen minutes dropped us at a hotel at the Brownsville exit. Fortunately, this had all happened mid- to late afternoon on a week day, so as soon as we were checked into the hotel we contacted State Farm and arranged for a rental car and to have the Lincoln removed from the Interstate and towed somewhere nearby.

The next morning, Ivy Delk's son picked us up at the hotel and took us back to the lot to get whatever we needed out of the car, before taking us to the car rental agency in Jackson, Tennessee. It was the last time we'd see the car. I took pictures of it and thanked it for holding up so well in the accident. At the rental agency we ended up with some small GM Malibu. We got lunch and returned home to Centerville, none the worse for the experience. The roads were clear all the way back home. We were lucky to be alive under the circumstances. I considered that my car sacrificed its life in saving ours and was a bit sentimental about it. That car had taken us all over the South, had never conked out, never left us stranded or had to be towed anywhere until last night. This was absolutely my fault. All I had to do was wait a day. If we'd left for New Orleans a day later, we could've spent the night in Memphis, had a pleasant dinner and then leisurely driven to New Orleans the following day. Or we could have driven Southwest through Birmingham and avoided the snow altogether. It was a pointless waste of a really good car.

Silver Lincolns of that vintage were as common as flies on a summer day and I determined to buy another one ASAP. I began looking but could scarcely find one for less than $10,000 and all of them had covered at least a hundred thousand miles or more. I'm willing to pay whatever amount necessary for what I want with one stipulation; that being there is a fair exchange between buyer and seller. I could do better. In the meantime, I was without a trip car. This was resolved with a Mercedes S 420 a couple of months later.

2008 Lincoln Town Car

Fast forward eight years. And then, once again, I went to unlock the door of my gold 1999 S 420 and the key turned, but the door wouldn't open. There ought to be a mechanical lock. Is there? There's one in the trunk so the battery is accessible. I called Alex Davidoff in Nashville and he said, "I can't tell you what's wrong with it without looking at it." True enough. I debated what to do for a week. I couldn't get into the car, and in order to have it towed, since the transmission was locked in park, I was given a towing quote of nearly $800 because some special dolly which cradled the rear wheels would be required. $800 to tow a car 45 miles? What world do these people inhabit?

As a result of this occurrence, and since it had already happened once in Memphis, I realized that it might perhaps be foolish to drive any of these high-maintenance late 1990s Mercedes sedans beyond a distance of 200 miles each way. Although I'd driven my 1999 S 420 both to Savannah, Georgia, and New Orleans numerous times, the reality was that I could no longer count on being able to get into my own car. At best I might have to call a locksmith, or worse, I might have to have the car towed back to Nashville, rent a car, or deal with everything at once in the middle of the night several hundred miles from home. There might not be a Mercedes dealer within a hundred miles. This was beginning to be more than I wanted to deal with.

I called a local locksmith who worked vainly attempting to lift the door lock buttons for more than 40 minutes. He finally called me in the house and said he couldn't get the door unlocked. I'd told him upon his arrival that he needed to hook a loop around the driver's door handle, but he hadn't done that. After I guided him through the procedure, the door was open in less than five minutes. I got in the car and it started right up and ran fine. I drove it to Alex in Nashville and it was ready the next day. He'd used a parts car I had there so the pump motor and labor was $200 instead of the $1100 it had been the last time. This is why parts cars are a necessity. I have no intention of disposing the three big 1990s Mercedes S sedans.....BUT. It was now time to return to a domestic car for US trips in excess of 200 miles each way.

There were no new cars that I even wanted. The new Lincolns were merely rebadged Fords. Anything with front-wheel drive was out. All wheel drive was a possibility in theory, but not available in any car that I'd want. Cadillac? No thanks. A large truck was a possibility as I like them, but I really don't want to have unusable space, which the truck bed would be for me most of the time. My sister and her husband have an Escalade but I want a large car, not another SUV. I'd get another Ford Explorer, but they are (or were for a few years) front-wheel drive or all-wheel drive. On the Interstate I want something that can maneuver quickly at fairly high speed without overturning.

That basically removes any SUV from consideration. That 2000 Lincoln Town Car was nice before I wrecked it in the ice. A Lincoln Town Car from 2005 through 2012 (its last production year) seemed like the most desirable, as well as the only option available. There are plenty of them around, they hold up very well, and they frequently have odometer readings in excess of 200,000 miles and still look brand new and run great with all systems working. They have had consistent five-star crash ratings for years, and while lacking the speed, power, handling, or looks of a large Mercedes sedan, they're comfortable, familiar, and most importantly, can be fixed at any Ford dealership if necessary. Many of their parts are available at Auto Zone and other similar places. Bard Selden had bought one which he drove to Hot Springs a couple of years ago and I liked its looks.

I began checking Nashville Craigslist and soon found a nice looking 2008 silver Lincoln (most of them are silver) with grey leather. It had 80,000 miles and was located in Shelbyville, Tennessee, known as the home of the Tennessee Walking Horse Celebration. I rode over there with my sister and her husband as they were both sort of in the market for one themselves. They'd bought a new one in 1998 when that body style had debuted, and had liked it. My other sister subsequently bought a dark green one, and my mother had bought a silver one, which she gave to me, and then a white one, which she gave to my other sister.

At this point, these 2004-2011 Lincolns are almost becoming clique cars, like the 1990s Mercedes S Class sedans. That is, we are members of an unofficial fraternity of the automotive cognoscenti. Almost anybody still driving either of these cars has specifically sought them out for particular reasons unknown to the general public consumer. These so-called 'big' Lincolns are probably the last 'real' Lincolns, that is, 'big' for their era, rear-wheel drive sedans. It's doubtful that Lincoln will ever again be 'America's Car of State' but merely generic rebadged Ford products and ultimately disposable, like most every other car made for the population at large.

The car for sale literally looked brand new. It didn't quite resemble a giant Galapagos tortoise as much as the pre-2004 Town Car, which was a plus. There was no wear anywhere on anything. I drove it and it ran fine, with everything working as it was supposed to. The two questions which (among others) I always want answered to my satisfaction are: How long have you owned the car, and why are you selling it? He'd owned  the car less than a year and had borrowed the money to pay for it at a local credit union. He was basically a hot-rodder with a couple of projects underway, as well as a tricked out mid-1960s pick-up truck which was his daily driver. The Lincoln was really a bit too sluggish and imprecise in its handling for him. His assessment of its performance was correct. Most importantly, however, his father was giving him a low mileage Chrysler 300 Hemi, a much hotter car.

There was one minor problem. The credit union had the title and wouldn't release it until the loan was paid in full. More specifically, the title was at a location in another state. He owed $7,000. I got a cashier's check in that amount, payable from myself to the credit union, drew up an agreement between ourselves, which he signed, and then I followed him to the credit union in the Lincoln, paid off his loan and drove the Lincoln back home. The credit union had agreed to send the title to him overnight, which it did. The seller received it and met me in Columbia, Tennessee the following day, as agreed, driving his Chrysler 300 with his father in the passenger seat. He signed the title in my presence, we shook hands and went our separate ways, both satisfied with our transaction.

Wasn't there a risk involved in basically paying cash for a car and not getting a title at the same time? Or paying off a loan in someone else's name? Yes, but I'm a good judge of character. The seller was a long-time resident of Shelbyville, and the jurisdiction for any legal problems would be the state of Tennessee. We were both car people and understood each other. The car had an up to date Carfax report and a legitimate paper trail. I was able to get the car because I was willing to make the drive to Shelbyville.

We drove it To Holly Springs, up to and around Memphis, and back home, around 500 miles in all. I'm not especially concerned with the price of fuel, as I've mentioned. The lower the better, obviously, and I generally buy gas at Fairview on the way home from Nashville, where 93 octane is .40 cents less per gallon than in Belle Meade. This Lincoln averaged 21.1 miles per gallon. It's the only car I've ever owned which can use 87 octane fuel without choking and sputtering. Anyway, I've had the car over two years and am happy with it.

These 1998-2012 so-called `big' Lincolns are the last Lincolns. Another so-called `new' Lincoln Continental debuted several years ago with much fanfare and turned out to be just another generic Ford front-wheel drive box. It seems to me that Ford ran the brand into the ground almost intentionally, as if looking for a reason to stop making cars altogether. The common refrain seems to be that `nobody wants cars anymore.' I think it's more accurate to say nobody wants small, generic looking cars at a luxury car price. Ford must have sold millions of these Town Cars, and something of that size, with rear wheel drive, would do well today. Regarding the last of the so-called Lincoln Continentals, as the late country singer Ray Price once told me "You can't polish a turd."

184

XII.

The 1967 & 1968 Cadillac Eldorados

1967 Eldorado

I'd always been in love with the 1967 Cadillac Eldorado since I first saw it at age 16. What was not to love? It had a big V-8, a long nose, disappearing headlights, and the best looking hub caps I'd ever seen on any car. It was, despite being a two-door coupe, a large, heavy car. Its exotic lines and sculptured stern belied its heft. It was a beast. I remember being on the way to Ft. Lauderdale for spring break the day Martin Luther King was shot. We spent the night at the Atlanta Towers in an apartment owned by Fleet Transport. As we drove beneath the building into its parking garage, there were at least five or six Cadillac Eldorados, all 1967s or 1968s, with their sterns sticking out. While I'd liked the 1950s Eldorados, and later the 1964 Eldorado convertible with its open rear wheels, I'd never seen a Cadillac, or anything else, for that matter, as exotic as the 1967 Eldorado. I knew what front-wheel drive was because I knew of two people in my neighborhood who had 1930s Cords, and when the Olds Toronado had debuted in 1966, there had been many comparisons to the Cord in the car magazines of the time. As far as front-wheel drive was concerned, I had no experience with it and therefore had no opinion regarding it one way or the other.

The new Eldorado was described as follows in the showroom brochure:

"Eldorado…dramatic blend of the best of two motoring worlds! For this brilliant new Cadillac combines the spirit and action of a true performance car with the comfort and five-passenger spaciousness of a true luxury car. It represents a whole new luxury car concept-yet its Cadillac identity is dramatically evident in a grille of striking simplicity and its overall look of dignity and distinction. Eldorado seems poised and ready to go, with its long spectacular hood, its daring roof lines and its sweeping rear deck styling. Eldorado is the first motor car in the world to combine the precision of front wheel drive with the maneuverability of variable ratio power steering and the balance of automatic level control. Here is the car for those who want new spirit and action in their luxury cars. Fleetwood Eldorado…the one car that must be seen to be believed, driven to be appreciated, and owned to be totally enjoyed."

Of course, that was advertising mumbo-jumbo. What I did know was that it was really, one of the most beautiful cars I'd ever seen. The 1967 Eldorado also had an eight-cylinder, 340 HP, overhead valve 429 cubic inch engine. Its dimensions were also desirable. It was long low, and unapologetically large.

I also knew was that one day I would have one or more. In the meantime, what little I knew about them, was all based on strictly visual considerations. I specifically wanted a 1967 rather than a 1968-1970 (after which the body style changed). First of all, I preferred the uncluttered styling of the front end as opposed to the rearrangement of the front fenders' leading edges, as on subsequent cars with the same body style. For 1969, 1970, and forward, the retractable headlight covers had been abandoned in favor of fixed dual-headlight clusters, a stylistic error in my opinion, at the time. Also for 1969, the spectacular hubcaps of the 1967, which had been carried over into 1968 were gone, and by `69 the windows had been outlined with trim and the roof had thus been slightly altered. However, the leather seats of the 1969 and 1970 cars were of a much different, and in my estimation, superior design.

At age 25, I decided that I could afford to buy an Eldorado. One came to my attention that was owned by a local big bandleader named Brown. It was a metallic green with black perforated leather and what the catalog described as `Strato-bucket' seats. Everything worked including the heat and air conditioning. It was a light metallic green and had a padded black vinyl top and was really beautiful. I bought it, I think for $1,800, pretty much the going rate at the time. It ran great and was fairly fast given its large size. Back then in the music business in Nashville, everybody who was anybody had a big Lincoln or Cadillac, but they'd largely abandoned the 1967 and 1968

Eldorados in favor of newer models like the 1971, 1972, and 1973, Cadillacs of all types. I didn't need a new car to be cool. I knew that the 1967 Eldorado was timeless in its elegance. New Cadillacs were a dime a dozen, but 1967 Eldorados weren't. I was happy to have it. It was also the first Cadillac I'd ever owned and I appreciated its other features like its tilt-telescopic steering wheel, automatic climate control, and sentinel lights which remained illuminated long enough to allow you to exit the car and walk to your house. The cornering lights were a Cadillac feature which activated when the turn signal lever was moved. Casting a light to the curb from a lens in the lower leading edge of each front fender, just in front of the wheel.

I was married at the time and was going to be forced to go to Miami for my brother-in-law's wedding. It was nothing I had any desire to do. My wife wanted us to ride in a caravan of cars with some of her relatives. That wasn't going to happen. I said, "No, I'll drive us, but I don't want to have to fool with anybody else." We should've flown, but I rather liked the idea of driving my Eldorado to Florida. On the day of our departure we headed down I-24 to Chattanooga, and over to I-75 South, around and through Atlanta. We made it to Florida down to the middle of the state and then the car started running roughly, I mean really roughly with inadequate power. Given our location, I thought it would be best to cut over to Daytona, a place I knew well. Bottom line, the car made it to the Daytona Cadillac dealer, but barely. A couple of tests were performed and I was told that it needed a valve job on one side. "Shouldn't both heads be done at the same time?" Technically, yes. I told them to go ahead. I thought we'd still make the wedding which was a couple of days in the future. That didn't happen. We checked into a hotel on the beach and got the car back four days later. It was again running like it should. Regrettably (not really), we'd missed the wedding. "That's Life," as Ray Charles sang.

One day, on the way home from my office the car began running hot. Apparently there was some problem with the radiator. I took it to the Mobil station in Belle Meade where I had any automotive work done at the time. They removed the radiator, sent it somewhere and had it fixed. Somebody there, rather than unscrewing the tubes from the transmission to the radiator had instead cut them, and joined the two ends with a piece of rubber hose. When I discovered this I was irate, but the damage had already been done. Now, I'd learned a new lesson. It was necessary to instruct a mechanic not to cut steel, brass, or copper lines. Instead, unscrew them carefully.

Winky! Although this is a 1968, it came from the factory without a vinyl top. Any Cadillac Fleetwood or Eldorado of the 1960s (other than a convertible) without a vinyl top was a rarity.

I kept the `67 Eldorado for several years, and bought a couple of others from car lots over on Jefferson Street. I paid a hundred dollars for one which was in good shape physically, but didn't run. I had it towed over to my house and stuck under the carport. It was a flat metallic green and minus the ever present vinyl top. It had come this way from the factory, as evidenced by the chrome trim surrounding the rear windshield. It was the only one I've ever seen or owned that came from the factory without a vinyl top. I considered it work of art, a metallic sculpture, and bought it as such.

My first Eldorado had been a fun car and I was by no means through with Cadillacs or Eldorados, but I had learned a bit about front wheel drive, especially when I'd had been forced to pay $1,100 to the Cadillac dealer to have one of the front axles replaced. Now, these axles can be ordered fairly inexpensively from most of the national auto parts chain stores. I ended up selling it to some guy on Music Row who had several of them so that I could buy my first Cadillac convertible.

1968 Eldorado

In the meantime, I bought a 1968 Eldorado from a Nashville songwriter who had an office in the United Artists Tower building where I worked for a few months. It was a beautiful royal blue with matching dark blue leather seats. It ran great but the vinyl top wasn't in the best of shape. I drove it around for a couple of months and sold it to some guy who drove it back to Lubbock, Texas without issue. It was the prettiest color Eldorado I'd ever seen, but I still really wasn't making any money yet and couldn't afford to have the white vinyl top replaced.

1968 Eldorado (2)

I never thought that I'd get another 1967 or 1968 Eldorado. My first Eldorado had been a 1967, as noted above, which I'd at first preferred. The `67 was the first of the front wheel drive Cadillacs and the first with that exotic body, but over time, I preferred the 1968 over the 1967. For one thing, I'd come to like the running lights in the leading edge of the front fenders, something I definitely didn't like originally. Also, new for 1968, was a much larger, more powerful engine, the 472 C.I. (actually 471.7) or 7.7 liters, given current engine displacement terms. It produced 375 horsepower, an incredible amount for the era, especially from something seemingly as unlikely as a Cadillac. In actuality, Cadillac had a long history of high performance cars including V-12 and V-16 engines in the 1930s and early `40s. Even more recently, Cadillac Eldorados in the 1950s had two four-barrel carburetors, and by 1959, had switched to three two-barrels, well ahead of the high-performance Pontiac GTO (1964) Tri-Power three carb configuration. For 1969, the Eldorado offered a 500 cubic inch (8.2 liter) engine, which would be the standard for all Cadillacs during the 1975 and 1976 model years.

It's wasn't that I didn't want another 1967 or 1968 Eldorado, per se, it's just that I'd had the experience and didn't necessarily need to repeat it. My `67 had been a wonderful car but the floor on the driver's side had rusted through beneath the carpet. When I'd taken it to the Cadillac dealer to get it fixed, I'd assumed that a new piece would have been welded in. Such, however had not been the case, they'd merely stuck a thin piece of metal under the carpet. Anyway, it had been 20 years or so since I'd had an Eldorado of that era. The ensuing cars, including the 1976 Eldorado Convertible that I still had, absolutely lacked the grace and elegance of the revolutionary 1967 and `68 Eldorados. Most people prefer the 1967 over the 1968, since 1967 was the first year for the front wheel drive model. The `68 also lacked the water and rust trap behind the rear windshield, which although not a problem for me with my first `67 was probably a problem for almost any `67 by this time.

Anyway, I read Nashville's weekly `*Trader's Post'* and found a 1968 Eldorado listed for $2,000. I'd driven my 450 SL for more than a year, and sold it for $2,000 more than I paid for it. Having sold the Mercedes, I felt that my fleet was down a car. I'd seen the Eldorado listed for several months. At this point, these were just `old cars' and nobody really wanted them other than people who'd already had one, or the now fewer number who'd always wanted one. Anyway, I called the person who had the car listed, and drove over to a nice section of fashionable Brentwood to examine the car. It was black, with a nice beige leather interior and factory bucket seats. The owner said he'd gotten it from his brother and didn't need it, or particularly want it. The fact of the matter is that I was the only person who'd come by to see it.

I started it and it smoked a bit at first. He said it had been sitting awhile, and sure enough the smoke went away fairly quickly and the car ran smoothly. I told him that I'd take the car for the price offered and that I'd be back to pick it up the next day. I was excited about it, thrilled actually, like I used to be

190

when I was about to get an old XK-E in a few days. It was a big, beautiful car, long, low and rakish, much larger, in fact than it looked. I would have preferred that it didn't have the black vinyl top, as it interrupted the car's fluid lines, but the top was in good shape, so I didn't especially mind. The car was rust free, and the doors, trunk, and hood all lined up properly, and the black paint was shiny and reflective. It was the only one I'd ever seen with factory bucket seats, and after I bought it, became the only 1967/1968 Eldorado in regular use in Nashville. It made a hell of a statement, and suited my personality.

I didn't drive it that often as I had other cars again, including the 1970 De Ville convertible. When I did drive it, however, I enjoyed it, but, and this is the reason I don't like front wheel drive, there was simply too much going on

up front. Too much weight on top of the two drive shafts, and steering, drivetrain, and brakes intertwined, a bad idea under any circumstances, a worse idea on a car that heavy. The thing always moaned, groaned, and clanked whenever I had to stop it. It probably needed the front end rebuilt but as little as I drove it, it wasn't worth the expense. And besides, the car was nearly thirty years old, and what mechanic in town still working actually had any experience with these cars?

191

1968 Cadillac Eldorado

Before I proceed, let me tell you what happened with my friend Crockett's 1968 Eldorado. It was a truly beautiful car, black with red leather seats. One Saturday afternoon we were in East Nashville looking for old cars and old records at junk stores. We were backing out of the parking lot at some junk store when all of a sudden the earth unexpectedly shook as if there had been an earthquake. This was accompanied by a loud crash as the starboard, that is, the passenger side front of the car hit the asphalt surface. What had happened was that the upper control arm had literally broken in half causing the front end to drop to the ground. We'd been driving 70 mph on the interstate shortly before this incident. I hate to think what might've happened had this occurred while we were driving at that speed. I figured that was the end of that car forever, but he had it fixed and drove it successfully all the way to Los Angeles, where he subsequently moved. In any case, I never forgot the experience and knew that such an occurrence was at least in theory, a latent possibility with any front wheel drive car, especially a heavy Cadillac.

I had to have $1,000 worth of work on the transmission at some point during the first year or two, but other than that, it was fine. Then late one warm fall Saturday afternoon I was out driving the Belle Meade Blvd. loop, taking it for a spin as I was wont to do, when suddenly the car stopped moving under its own power. It was coasting as I quickly turned into the parking lot at the tennis courts at Belle Meade Country Club. I turned the engine off and checked the transmission fluid level. It was low. I jogged the mile and a half home, got another car, drove to the store and got several quarts of transmission fluid, put them in the Eldorado, started it and put it in gear. It still wouldn't move. I left it there, drove home quickly, called Hillwood Wrecker Service and had them drop it at the Shell Station on Harding Rd. as I knew the owner there and he actually still worked on cars.

The following Monday I stopped by the station and he told me that he didn't want to fool with it, that it was just too much work. I had it towed home and stuck into the garage with the front pointing out. I didn't know what to do with it, so it sat there for seven or eight years until I sold my house, at which time I had it towed to the garage of my girlfriend's house outside of Nashville. Unlike my previous experience with the driveshafts on my `67, I was able to buy everything I needed from one of the chain auto parts stores in Nashville, as well as a new carburetor and front disc brake calipers. By this time, I'd found an old school mechanic, a young guy out in the country, who could fix anything. I had both shafts replaced, a new carburetor, and new brake calipers on both sides. It ran great and had plenty of power, but by this time I didn't care anymore. I kept it another couple of years and sold it on ebay to some guy in California who deposited the purchase amount in my bank's branch out there. As soon as the money showed up in my account, here, I called him and told him to send a truck, which he did. It remains one of the most beautiful cars I've ever had, but I hate front wheel drive, and that's the big drawback for that car, for me, at least. It still groaned under its own weight every time it started or stopped. I still look at them on ebay from time to time, and think about getting another one, but doubt that I will, despite the fact that I consider it to be one of the most beautiful cars of all time. If it had been manufactured with rear wheel drive, as it should've been, I'd still have it today. As it was, I kept for fifteen years and passed it along to its next owner with all major mechanical work having been accomplished. There was one significant lesson I learned with this car. Never, that is, never wash any car with dishwashing liquid as it immediately dulls the paint by removing the shine.

XIII.

The DeVille Convertibles, and a slight detour with a 1959 Coupe.

1969 DeVille Convertible

There weren't that many DeVille convertibles in Nashville in 1969, at least, as far as I remember, because during that period I was in the navy. There were several however that managed to stay around until I could find one I could afford.

My high school friend Tom Crockett had moved back to Nashville, rented a duplex on West Brookfield in Belle Meade, near the house in which he'd been raised, and arrived in a black 1970 Cadillac DeVille convertible. I'd never had a Cadillac convertible at that point but decided that I wanted one.

My first was this faded blue 1969 DeVille convertible which I bought for $600 from a car lot on Gallatin or Dickerson Road in East Nashville. It was a heap, with a bad top and worn paint, but it ran, and it was a convertible. It was all of the money I could come up with at the time. I'd sold my 1967 Cadillac Eldorado for the $600 I needed to buy the convertible. I'd sold it at a loss, but I wanted a convertible, and back then I still wasn't making any money, although that was about to change.

My first convertible had a worn interior, which might have been white

leather. The heat and air conditioning didn't work, and as to the tires, I'd seen more tread on a Trojan rubber. I was however, able to come up with enough money to have a new top put on it at Steven's Brothers, and was good to go. I enjoyed it all that summer during the late 1970s although it experienced some interesting circumstances during the period in which I owned it. The top didn't work and had to be raised and lowered by hand. This meant initially disconnecting the top from the two hydraulic cylinders (one at each side) behind the back seat. Raising or lowering the top was generally a two-man operation and not difficult with two people, although I frequently did this by myself.

One day I was standing in front of the office where I worked on Music Row in an old dump known as the Fender Building, working for a company which didn't last long as a talent agency. Anyway, it was summer and I had just put the top down, by hand and was standing there when I was approached by a tourist, some nosey woman from somewhere up north, judging from her accent. She apparently didn't like my car and had stopped to express her disapproval. "I bet that thing uses a lot of gasoline," she observed, with some sarcasm. I stopped what I was doing and turned to look at her. She wasn't particularly attractive, and was somewhat annoying in her appearance. I can't say what it was, I just didn't like her. "Yes," I replied courteously, "it does use a lot of gasoline, but then, gas is plentiful, and of course, gas is cheaper than blood," meaning that large cars, despite their cost of operation are safer than small cars.

"Well," she replied angrily, "what are you going to do when there isn't any more gas?"

"I don't think that that is of any particular concern in the foreseeable future," I said dryly, confirming my suspicion that I was conversationally engaged with some ignorant leftist busybody.

"We will run out of oil and gas sooner than later," she stated with firm conviction, "and what will you do then?"

"I guess they'll have to grow some more dinosaurs," I laughed, dismissively.

My remark really pissed her off. "I think you're crazy," she said.

"I think you're crazy for talking to me," I said, as she walked off in a huff. "You should mind your own business."

One bright beautiful summer morning, I put the top down and headed off to work. Visibility was 100% and the road was flat and straight. I pulled out of my driveway in the direction of Belle Meade Blvd. less than a quarter mile away. I saw a pickup truck stopped at the end of a driveway ahead, preparing to back out onto the street. My eyes met those of the driver, and then, as I approached, the moron backed out into the street, right in front of me. My right front fender basically tore off the back end of his trunk behind the back wheels, including his tailgate and heavy aftermarket bumper. I stopped my car, and strange as it seems, he considered himself to be the injured party, despite the fact that he'd backed onto the road in front of me at point blank range. He indignantly asked if I had any insurance, to which I replied "Do you have any damn insurance?" At that point, he stuck his finger in my face. The proper response in this case is to grab the person's finger in your fist and slowly bend it upward while forcing him downward, but since he was such an angry old bastard, I figured the police would put him in his place soon enough, which they did. When the policeman arrived I kept my mouth shut while the loud-mouthed asshole raved and tried to make it look like it was my fault. He licd and said that I was speeding, but I'd been doing less than the posted 35 mph. There were no skid marks. When the policeman asked for my side of the story I related it calmly and factually without embellishment. "You can't back out of a driveway into oncoming traffic," he told the offender. The cop then asked me if I wanted him to give the guilty party a ticket I said, "yes, that would be great." If he hadn't been such a lying son of a bitch, I would have declined the cop's offer. Not only had he inconvenienced me and wasted my time, he'd lied about it. To hell with him! His insurance company paid me $600 for my fender and destroyed battery.

1969 DeVille Convertible (2)

I took the insurance money and bought an entire 1969 Cadillac convertible for $110. I'd seen the car out behind a house on Leland Lane the preceding several months, and noticed that it hadn't moved and was covered with leaves and dirt. One day I stopped and knocked on the door to ask about it. The woman invited me into the small house which she shared with her adult son who was clearly 'not right.' The place was filthy, and mice darted across the floor unhindered, but I bought the car. It was a faded metallic gold with a white top and white leather. It wasn't running so I had it towed back to the small house I was renting. At this point, I still knew basically nothing about cars, but was learning as I went along. Now, I probably would've been able to get it running, but at that time, I didn't have a clue. I did, however manage to remove the dented fender from my damaged car and replace it with the fender from the gold car. It was a learning experience for me, but in reality, was not unlike fixing a big model car. I soon sold both of the 1969 Cadillac convertibles to two guys from Louisville, Kentucky, but not before I bought my first Coupe De Ville.

1969 Coupe DeVille

Alas, winter was coming and as the convertible didn't have a functioning heater or defroster, I realized I was going to have to make some other arrangements before the cold weather set in. With that in mind, I went on an excursion to the used car lots in the less desirable parts of town such as Nolensville Rd., Murfreesboro Rd., Gallatin, and Dickerson Roads. These, at the time were always the best places to find old Cadillacs or Lincolns, the only cars in which I was then interested. It didn't take long. Within half an hour or so, I found a gold 1969 Cadillac Coupe De Ville at some dump on Nolensville Rd. It had fairly good paint, a black vinyl top, and a gold brocade interior. It was quite presentable, ran well, and everything worked, including the heater and defroster. It was priced at $400 or thereabouts. I haggled the guy down to $325 paid for it with my credit card, and was happily on my way.

The interior was nice enough, but it was fabric, and the driver's seat looked sort of ragged. I located a wrecked 1969 Cadillac coupe which had been sitting in front of some place on Murfreesboro Rd. for months with its front smashed in. I used my AAA card and had Lawson & Son Mobile station pick up the car and tow it to Crockett's house a couple of miles away. There, I performed my first successful interior replacement surgery, successfully removing the nice leather seats and door panels from the wrecked car and putting them in my Coupe De Ville. The leather didn't match the gold exterior of my new car, but it worked. My friend and I also replaced the dash and some other parts, stripped the car and had the hulk towed to Sam Knight's junkyard on Charlotte. The car lasted all winter and was running fine when I got my first company car and no longer needed it. I traded my first Coupe De Ville to Dr. Glenn Hall for a Mk VII Jaguar sedan. It was all there but in rough shape and never ran again, at least not on my watch. It was towed to the barn at my parents' farm in Leiper's Fork, Tennessee and remained there until I got rid of it. It was more or less a sculpture which I enjoyed looking at when I visited them. My mentor Tom Strickland, asked me if he could have the camshafts, which he replaced with others, which was fine with me as I wasn't going to restore the car or use it for parts.

1968 Cadillac DeVille Convertible

By now, I was working for Dick Blake International, and finally earning

more money than ever. Summer was coming, again, and I bought this 1968 Cadillac Convertible. This picture was taken with a Minox B spy camera, thus the grainy image, which doesn't do the car justice. It was in really nice condition and was white with red leather seats, and rust free. What looks like rust above the grill are shadows from nearby trees. The 1967s and 1968s are two of my all-time favorite Cadillacs. It had a 472 CI engine which ran well, but drum brakes. The red leather seats were excellent.

It lasted me all summer and then I traded it to Jim Reed, the local Chevrolet dealer for either this MK IX Jaguar or a dead but complete red Jaguar XK 120

Roadster with right hand drive. I realized that the MK IX Jaguar, while complete, was way beyond my skill level. Maybe I took the XK 120 instead.

I don't remember. Jim already had an aluminum bodied XK 120, a 1954 Eldorado, and a 1930s Rolls Phantom and really didn't need either car. I think the right-hand drive XK-120 roadster ended up with Glen Hall, who by this time was no longer in medical school in Memphis, and was living in Cookeville, TN. and working as a pathologist.

I knew this was never going to run again as soon as I saw it, at least under my watch. Be that as it may, I enjoyed seeing it in the barn when I visited my folks.

198

1967 DeVille Convertible

I live for summer, and always have. In my late twenties I tolerated the winter but when spring arrived I had to have a Cadillac convertible, no matter what other car or cars I might own. I was working for Dick Blake, a talent agency in Nashville and the company was making a lot of money, a large portion of which I was generating. I always wanted a raise based upon my sales, but Blake was tight with a dollar. He did, however, like equipment and had two company airplanes, a sound and light company, several buses and sound trucks and many minions. One day as I was pressing him for more money, he suggested that he give me a loan to buy one or more cars, since I liked cars so much. It wasn't really a loan, per se, in that it would be hidden in the books somehow, though technically, it would be a loan. Wink. Wink. All I knew was that it was a `right now money blessing' as Rev. Ike would say. I got a check, cashed it, and began a search in east Nashville, where I always went when looking for old cars worth having. Within fifteen minutes of leaving my office I located a beautiful 1967 Cadillac De Ville convertible. It was a copper/bronze color with its original paint in very good condition, dark brown leather, also excellent, and a black top. It had just had a new transmission, and was a really beautiful car. I'd never had a `67 Cadillac of any kind other than Eldorados. The crisp razor edge styling had always appealed to me. I took the car for a test drive and since everything worked and the engine ran smoothly with plenty of power. I agreed to buy the car for the asking price of $1,700, and picked it up a few days later. I told my boss that I'd bought it and he said, something like `That's good.' He didn't care one way or the other and never mentioned it again or asked what I did with the rest of the money. He probably surmised that this would keep me quiet for awhile, which it did. It was a really wonderful car and I enjoyed it.

1959 Cadillac Coupe

One day, I was driving around in Nashville's famed Bordeaux wine district during lunch time, or rather I should say the `wino' district, out around Clarksville Highway. I took a side road and saw a 1959 Cadillac coupe with a for sale sign in the window. It was parked in the front yard of a small house. It wasn't a Coupe DeVille, but I didn't care. It was completely original, hadn't been repainted or altered in any way. It may have even had roll-up windows. I don't recall. The interior and seats were original and perfect as well, some sort of black brocade fabric seats with white leather bolsters. The car was a rare survivor in that it hadn't been worn out. What `59 Cadillacs still survived in the late 1970s had usually changed hands many times, always downward, and most had minimal, if any maintenance as time progressed. Most of Nashville's fleet had reached the various junkyards around town by this point or were rusting in peace in backyards in east Nashville by 1980.

I'd never had a `59, but always sort of wanted one, but never really gone out of my way to find one. I knew that they were good cars mechanically because there were still some in daily use in town even through the mid-1970s, by which time the `59 and `60 Lincolns were long gone. Anyway, I called the owner who'd somehow ended up with it and didn't especially want it. I met him the next Saturday and took it for a spin. It was every bit as solid as it looked. No rattles, no smoke, no loud mufflers, and plenty of power. It even had new tires. There was one problem however, the fuel gauge didn't work. That was, in this instance, the equivalent of an airplane without an altimeter.

The owner admired my `67 Cadillac convertible and before I left him, we'd agreed to an even trade. A few days later we traded titles and I was on my way. I was now short a Cadillac convertible, actually a convertible of any kind, but I knew I'd have another one soon enough. Up until now, the 1967 convertible was the best convertible I'd ever had, apart from a Jaguar, and I'd really enjoyed it, and the `59 Cadillac was, in my estimation, the most exotic production car ever designed. When you look at one now, not that you're likely to see one on the street, you know that nothing that visually exotic will ever exist again, anywhere as a mainstream production car. When the Cadillac division of General Motors put forth the 1959 Cadillac, it was the focus of their entire line of cars for the whole year. It wasn't like now, when Cadillac has several different cars out every year at the same time.

I loved the 1959, had no trouble with it, and only ran out of gas once, despite its non-working fuel gauge. Like most cars that I ever sold, it was something done on impulse without much forethought. Such was the case in this instance. There was no good reason for selling it at all except that by this time I had a 1974 Fleetwood Talisman, as a company car and a 1967 Jaguar E-Type Coupe. I'm sorry I sold it and wish I had that 1959 now. It was more unique than any so-called exotic insect-looking wedge of today, an exercise in pure excess without apology.

Except for the very rare Eldorado Brougham, every one of the `59s had essentially the same face and stern, all with the giant fins, even though the bodies were different. For 1959, in addition to the basic two-door bubble top coupe, there was an Eldorado coupe, a Coupe DeVille, both Eldorado and DeVille convertibles, two different sedan DeVilles, a long wheelbase limousine, and a Fleetwood, which truly resembled a spaceship. It was, in my opinion, more exotic than the very rare 1959 Eldorado Brougham, which to me at least from the stern sort of resembled a 1961 or 1962 DeVille. The Eldorado Broughams of 1959 and 1960 were designed by Pininfarina, and were made in very low numbers about 100 each year. Strangely enough, as I wrote this, there was a rare 1960 Eldorado Brougham, (one of a total of one hundred and one produced that year) for sale on Nashville craigslist with an asking price of $55,000. I include a picture of it, courtesy of Nashville craigslist. It eventually sold to somebody after six months or more, and I doubt for that price as the ad said it needed `complete restoration.' Still, be that as it may, it remains one of the rarest Cadillacs in existence.

1960 Eldorado Brougham

1969 DeVille Convertible 3

OK, so I had another 1964 Lincoln convertible (see 1964 Lincoln convertible 1), and that was a good thing, but that left me with only one company car, my `65 Jaguar E-Type roadster. I wasn't about to take a step backwards. I was making Dick Blake so much money that I didn't think he'd care if I got another company car. To both of our minds, they were cheap enough. I went to him and said, "That was a terrible tragedy, what happened with my Lincoln convertible last week. I barely escaped with my life. I think I need another company car. He knew that my Jaguar was not to be mentioned. We'd already had a showdown over it, which he'd lost at a personal cost of several hundred thousand dollars a couple of years earlier, the upshot of which was that I still had my E-Type as a company car and he still had me working there.

He asked me what I wanted and what it would cost, not that he especially cared at this point. It was all tax deductible for him and he hated the IRS, as I've mentioned. I told him about a 1969 Cadillac DeVille convertible I'd found and that its owner wanted $4,000. He told me that it would have to be listed as company property. That was fine with me because if it was a company car I didn't have to pay insurance, fuel, or maintenance, and if I wanted it in my name at any point in the future, I could probably talk him into it if for no other reason than by that time, whenever it might be, he'd be tired of the fuel bill as he'd been with my first company car, the 1974 Cadillac Fleetwood Talisman.. "Tell Linda to get you a check," he said, and that was that.

This was the nicest 1969 DeVille convertible I'd had yet. That first one had been ugly with its faded metallic blue paint, and gold hood and fender after it had been rammed. This one looked almost brand new with nice silver paint, near perfect original ostrich-grained black leather and a top which could pass for new. The car was smooth and quiet, didn't rattle or shake, and everything worked perfectly, including ice cold air conditioning. My motoring fleet at this time consisted of my 1974 Talisman, the 1965 E-Type roadster, a 1964 Lincoln convertible, and now, a 1969 Cadillac DeVille convertible, all in most excellent condition and used regularly.

1969 DeVille Convertibles 4 & 5

When my boss Dick Blake died in October, 1983, I turned in both of my company cars to his estate, as mentioned elsewhere, including the 1969 beautiful silver DeVille convertible mentioned directly above this. I finally decided on another 1969 DeVille convertible. The 1969 was my favorite of what I considered at the time to be the modern cars, and was preferable to the 1967 and 1968 DeVilles I'd already owned. Actually, the aforementioned models were, in my estimation, more desirable cars. Their lines were crisper and less bulbous, and their dash and interior fittings were more detailed and well-crafted than those of the 1969 and its sister ship, the 1970. In fact, the door panels and dashboards of the `69s and `70s were basically plastic covered foam, not even remotely attractive even with their blatantly fake, faux (or `fox' as we say in these parts) wood inserts. Be that as it may, the `68, `69, and `70 convertibles were equipped with 472 cubic inch displacement engines, which in practical application, delivered plenty of torque and acceleration.

I found two 1969 Cadillac convertibles. Both of them were for sale locally in Nashville at the same time, both were white, both had black leather, and black tops. As I recollect, both of them had stereo dash covers, that is, with a speaker on each side at the base of the A-pillars. I drove each of them regularly, and was fortunate at the time in that close to my house, there was a high school friend who had a garage on nearby Highway 100. He'd been maintaining my American cars for several years. I had him check both of the Cadillacs out and asked him to analyze the merits and demerits of each, and recommend which one I should keep. The best one was taken to some paint shop over near the fairgrounds which my friend Bruce Shelton had discovered. The guy who ran it had done a good job with one of Bruce's cars. Given my good luck with the Cadillac dealership's taking my last E-Type to the bare metal and repainting it red, I was ready to do the same with my new acquisition. It was going to require the removal of all of the chrome, including both bumpers. I discussed the color with the proprietor and told him that I wanted a `fire engine red,' one of my favorite colors. The one thing I specified was that I wanted no `orange' at all, that is, nothing even approaching red-orange. He gave me a price to which I agreed (whatever it was). "When can we do it?" I asked. "Just check back with me." After being delayed for a month or so by his previous commitments, he finally took my car in to be painted.

I'd checked on its progress once or twice a week. In about three weeks it was ready, and so was I. Summer time was calling me, and I was eager to answer. When I got the car back, it looked great. I then had a new black convertible top fitted by Stevens Brothers. The air conditioning was brought to working order by Mayo and Shrum, and I was ready to go.

While the black leather was in good condition, and I seldom left the top down very long, black absorbs heat and that eventually began affecting the leather. It wasn't bad, but with the rest of the car looking great, I wanted the leather to match.

The mid-eighties were good times for finding cool cars just sitting around in people's yards, beside gas stations, or simply abandoned where they died, since portable car crushers either didn't yet exist, or were in limited use. Eventually, however, portable crushers became widely used and could be attached to a semi and hauled anywhere they were needed. In this way many rurally located treasure troves of old cars were flattened, stacked on trailers, and hauled to giant recycling scrapyards in nearby cities. In the case of middle Tennessee, this meant Nashville's Steiner-Liff, which was located across the Cumberland River.

One day as I was riding around after lunch with friends from my office, we espied a 1969 Coupe DeVille in quiet repose at the bottom of a driveway somewhere near Belmont Blvd. It didn't look like it had moved in awhile. We'd pass the house frequently when in the area as it was located on a main road. I'd always check to see if it had moved, or if it was even still there. One day on impulse we stopped and I quickly looked at the car while one of my friends knocked on the door. There was no answer, but the car had a perfect black leather interior. I kept checking back whenever I was in the neighborhood but nobody was ever home. One day there was a man home and he told me the car belonged to his son. He wouldn't give me his son's name or phone number even though I clearly explained to him what I wanted. I checked back later and found the man at home again and this time he gave me his son's phone number. I called the son, who was probably around my age at the time, that is, mid-thirties and asked him if he'd sell me the front seat. He thought about it for a minute and then gave me a price, which, as I recollect, was what I had in mind at the time, whatever it may have been. A week or so later, I went over on a Saturday, paid his father, and, with the help of Jeff Nunnally, switched front seats with the Coupe DeVille in the driveway, and was good to go.

Believe it or not, people often used to challenge me to spontaneous street races regardless of what I might be driving, although I don't know why. Why would anyone in a sports car feel a need to challenge any large Cadillac to a street race? And a Mazda RX-7 challenged my 1969 DeVille to a duel in front of St. Thomas Hospital late one night, racing his engine and looking over at me. When that light changed to green, we both hit it and I smoked him like a cheap cigar. When he saw the way it was going to turn out he backed off fairly quickly, obviously surprised by my unexpected acceleration. I don't recommend or approve of street racing ever, and can only recollect three instances in my entire automotive history, all of which I won. But youth is reckless, and if one is stupid enough to race in town, in front of a hospital is probably the best place to do it. These days what I'm likely to be driving probably won't outrun whoever might wish to test me, besides, what's the point? Many new cars now have horsepower and torque which were unimaginable in the so-called 'muscle car' era.

As with my Jaguar roadsters, I'd often drive it around the Belle Meade Blvd.-Chickering-Old Hickory loop in Nashville on warm nights with the top down. On one hot, dark summer night I was driving down Chickering toward Old Hickory. The top was down and I was having a great time chatting with my new girlfriend, just enjoying the night. As I approached Old Hickory, where I intended to make a right turn, I noticed an ambulance in the field about a hundred yards in the distance. I remarked that this was strange in that there was nothing out there, just a large mowed field. Perhaps somebody had been going too fast and had run the stop sign and ended up way out there. But if that had happened they'd have had to have hit the guard rail broadside and either gone through it, over it, or under it, and it was in place and appeared undisturbed. It was so dark that night that all we saw was an ambulance in a field with its lights flashing.

The following Monday I was at Jag Cars Ltd. Visiting Joe Robinson, who'd maintained my E-Types. There was a framed letter on the wall thanking Joe by somebody whose name I didn't recognize, which read "Joe, thank you for maintaining my 1967 Jaguar XK-E. If it weren't for you, I wouldn't be able to drive and enjoy a car like this in Nashville." This was true enough. In the 1970s and 1980s people I knew who had brand new Jaguars would have their cars serviced and maintained by Joe, even knowing that to do so would potentially void the factory warranty. He was that good, and the Jaguar dealership at the time, was that bad. Joe Robinson's garage, was by this time, near Ft. Negley, and always populated by whatever E-Types, 120s, and other XKs were remained in Nashville then. There was a photograph of the British racing green roadster beneath the letter. I was familiar with the car, and it was nicer (though just barely) than the red 1965 roadster which had been my last E-Type.

"Whatever happened to that car?" I asked Joe since I hadn't seen it in awhile.

"You haven't heard?" he asked with surprise. "He was killed last Saturday night. He went under a guardrail and was essentially decapitated."

"Where?"

"Where Chickering dead ends into Old Hickory. The car was brought here and I spent all day yesterday cleaning it out. It was full of blood, a horrible thing."

I told him what I'd seen that night, and that I'd driven by shortly after it had happened and had wondered how anyone had ended up way out in a field that far from the road.

I didn't care to look inside the car as he pointed it out to me from the office, but sure enough, there it was draped with a loose cover. The Jag's nose was very low, and instead of hitting the guard rail, had passed beneath it. The top had been down and the guard rail scratched the hood and then removed the A-pillars, that is, the front windshield and its supporting structures. Other than that rather minimal damage, the car was fully drivable even now. As I looked at it now, I remembered how I used to be afraid of my own E-Types, given their small size, front strut architecture, and my own propensity for speed on the open road. I was glad now that I hadn't had Blake sign it over to me and that I hadn't bought it from his family. I remembered something country singer Ray Price had told me about his Lear Jet barely being restarted in the middle of a high speed stall. "I promised myself that if this thing landed safely I'd never get on another plane as long as I live. I'd probably flown a million miles over the years, and like a cat, probably used up eight of my nine lives." And that's the way I considered my E-Types. I'd had ten or eleven of them over a ten year period and done my time. I remembered smoking some guy in a Saab Turbo on Highway 100, my Jaguar hitting almost 130 mph as I passed the exact spot where a friend of mine had been burned alive a few years earlier when someone had pulled out from a side street when he'd been going way too fast. This is insane! I'd thought as I looked at the speedometer. I'd loved them all and was thankful for my experiences, but now I intended to explore larger open top cars in greater detail. Still, I feel nostalgically wistful when I think of them, like remembering a lost love.

I enjoyed this red 1969 DeVille convertible more than any large convertible I'd had so far. With the Lincolns there was always the possibility that the top might or might not work with no advance notice. The DeVille's top always worked, and I was armed with the knowledge that in the event it stopped working anywhere unexpectedly, all I had to do was disconnect the top mechanism from the rear cylinders at each side, and the top could be raised or lowered by hand. I had no hesitation driving this car anywhere out of town and often did.

Like all cars, the 1969 Cadillacs had certain eccentricities, two of which readily come to mind. The first was its horn button. Actually it wasn't a button, but an entire circle, an inner rubber ring which was a part of the steering wheel, and in theory, could be conveniently activated anywhere by merely pushing any part of the inner ring with one's thumb. It worked well for the most part, although once in awhile, always at night, the horn would blast without notice until I got out of bed and disconnected the battery. Thinking about these cars at just this moment, makes me want to go buy one now, I mean right now, today.

I kept this wonderful car from 1983 through the summer of 1987, at which time I traded it and my 1964 Lincoln convertible for a 1958 Bentley. After that I saw it once or twice a couple of years later parked at Belmont University, and really missed it, and the fond memories it sparked, but by this time I had my `76 Eldorado convertible. The last time I saw my beautiful red `69 Cadillac convertible, it was sinking into the dirt next to some dump of a beer joint on Lebanon Road a couple of miles away from downtown Nashville. I recognized it immediately and stopped, looked at it, and asked about it. Some rustic (I'm being kind) hick of a waitress told me that it wasn't for sale. I wistfully remembered the words of John Lee Hooker's classic `Don't Look Back,' and realized that part of my life and what it represented was over, and though it had been fun, I didn't wish to return to it.

1970 DeVille Convertible & Two More `69s

My first book, 'Music City Babylon' (the publisher's title, not mine) was released in late November 1992. When spring arrived, a man's thoughts turn to summer, and there appeared a 1970 DeVille convertible for sale in a Nashville paper. It was a metallic red with a white leather interior and a white top, both of which were in good condition. At this point I had a 1962 Lincoln convertible and a 1976 Eldorado convertible, so I didn't really need another car…but, my girlfriend decided to buy it, which she did. The very next day we took off on a trip down the Natchez Trace to Natchez, then to New Orleans, back through Natchez, up Old Highway 61 to Tunica, Memphis, and back to Nashville. By the time we returned we'd covered more than 1,200 miles in a car we'd known absolutely nothing about prior to our departure, other than what its owner had told us. It had been a really fun trip although the Natchez Trace was frightening in terms of fuel considerations. There'd be a sign saying 'such and such' town with an arrow to either the right or left, leading off the Trace, but absolutely no mention of distance. In other words, it appeared that we were running out of gas, and there was no mention when or even if there was a gas station on the Natchez Trace, so did we drive on and hope for the best, or risk leaving the Trace for a city which could be six miles away, or maybe sixty? At this point, all I knew was that the car was very thirsty. Eventually, there was a gas station on the trace and we filled up again. Other than that, the car ran flawlessly and we really had a wonderful time.

The 1970 was the last rear wheel drive Cadillac convertible, the end of a tradition dating back to the very first Cadillac, itself an open car. The 1970 was equipped with the venerable 472 CI engine, although it would be the last model year to have that powerplant. Already, for 1970, the Eldorado Coupe was fitted with an even better and more powerful 500 CI which would become standard issue in all Cadillacs through 1976, starting with the 1971 model year. This '70 DeVille was fast, agile, comfortable, and dependable. These cars were basically trouble free from their inception, and this one was no exception. About the only thing I didn't like about the 1969 and 1970 DeVille convertibles in comparison to their 1967 and 1968 predecessors was that the ass end of the 1969 and 1970 models seemed to be a bit higher off the ground than necessary. In thinking about it now, it's probably that Cadillac changed from leaf springs to coil springs at the rear during this period, but I'm not sure.

The 1970 was also remarkable in that it was the last Cadillac convertible to have a 'normal' top, that is, one which simply folded straight back without foolishly designed wires, floating bars, and unnecessary hinges (see 1976 Eldorado Convertible below).

There was one curious occurrence worth mentioning. One day, seemingly out of nowhere, this usually fast car, suddenly seemed to lack power, as if it had a clogged catalytic converter, even though I knew these cars never had them. It acted a lot like a Jaguar XK 120 I'd once fooled with which had a blown head gasket. At length, after attempting my own diagnostic solutions, I hobbled over to the Midas muffler shop on Charlotte where my former Hillsboro High Schoolmate, Dainey Canfield, had ended up after he'd lost the lease at his long-standing repair shop on Hwy 100. He could fix anything. I'd specifically sought him out since he'd maintained my domestic cars for nearly a decade before his shop closed. He asked me some questions, then put the car on a lift, took a wrench, and began banging around on the exhaust pipes. I wondered why he was banging on the exhaust system since it wasn't rusty, dented, or anything else. What did this have to do with my engine?

I replaced the 1970 grill with one from a 1969 for a bit.

209

After a few minutes, he said, "These cars originally had concentric exhaust pipes from the factory, and given the overall original condition of this car, I suspect that the inside pipe has collapsed. We'll have to cut it off with a saw to make sure. I can't guarantee this is the problem, but it's a chance you'll have to take." By this time, I no longer needed a translation. What he meant was that I'd immediately be buying a new exhaust system right now, whether or not this fixed the problem. Believe it or not, after he cut a section out of the pipe, I could see that there was indeed a collapsed interior pipe within the outside pipe, which looked fine to the naked eye. I'd never heard of concentric exhaust pipes, that is, one pipe within another one. I could clearly see that it was nearly impossible for exhaust from a big engine to blow through such a small space. But the physics still didn't make sense to me. How could, or why would an interior pipe collapse with exhaust flowing through it. I could theoretically grasp the concept that outside pressure might collapse a pipe, but given the volume of really hot exhaust flowing through the pipe it would be more likely to expand than contract. As it turned out, this was indeed the problem, and I just had to replace this one section, given his diagnostic tapping on the rest of the pipes. When the car was back on the ground, it again ran like new and was once again fast as hell, though not quite as thirsty. This incident again stresses the value of a true mechanic. Specialized knowledge to this extent is only available through experience.

Once again, on a clear sunny day with 100% visibility, I was nearly rammed from behind as I prepared to turn left onto my street, a disaster averted at the last possible moment as the driver awakened from her trance, with much screeching of brakes and swerving, merely scraping the starboard rear bumper with the side of her car. It seems strange that the frequent times I've been rammed by unobservant motorists, have generally occurred on sunny days.

I kept the car at my girlfriend's garage in the country during the winter and would retrieve it in the spring. The 1970 DeVille was essentially the same car as the 1969 which had originally been my preference, and maybe, still is. On the other hand, the grill of the 1970, was somehow `cleaner' for lack of a better word, and gave the car a crisper appearance. Although the body and the interior were essentially the same as that of the 1969 DeVille convertible, I preferred the 1969 grill and hubcaps, and exchanged them, but eventually replaced the 1970 grill. One cold winter day on a visit to her house (we'd been living at mine in Nashville), I opened the garage door to have a look at the convertible, and to my surprise it had a very low tire on the front passenger side. It was cold as hell, and I'm a bit like an alligator or a snake. If it's 20 degrees outside, I'm 20 degrees. Anyway, not wanting to have to deal with it in the freezing cold, I removed the jack from the car and placed as it required beneath the front bumper, jacked it up so that there was no pressure on the nearly flat tire, and left it that way until spring. That turned out to have been a mistake in that when I returned in the spring, the weight of the engine and front end upon the jack, over time had gradually dented the bumper and pushed it up a bit. It wasn't horrible, but it was noticeable to me, and that was enough. Lesson learned.

On another occasion, with the car back at my house in town for the summer, we exited the house preparing to get into another car when suddenly, the unexpected sound of a large caliber gun assailed our ears. A perfectly good (or so I imagined) Michelin tire suddenly exploded, without provocation while the car was just parked in the driveway. Oh well.

At about this same time, my pal Bruce (see `Ramblers' below) had bought a beautiful metallic mint green 1970 DeVille convertible from `Dr. FenFen' as he was known locally, an M.D. who'd been prescribing some hazardous diet drug which has since been taken off the market. Anyway, Bruce's car was really nice, and one day I noticed that one of his hubcaps was missing. He's one of my very best friends, someone I've known since I was seven years old. Anyway, our relationship has at times, been a bit like that of *Mad Magazine's* Spy vs Spy.' Since what happened with his hubcap was sort of funny, I include herein the story from my book `Vignettes from the Modern Era':

In my own defense, I can't say with absolute certainty that it was actually `his' hubcap in the first place, although his 1970 Cadillac convertible was missing a hubcap identical to this one, and we both lived nearby. I was driving down Harding Road and saw it lying there off to the side of the road across the street from Belle Meade Mansion. I recognized it as belonging to a 1970 Cadillac like the one I was driving. I turned around pulled over to the side of the road, and picked it up.

I saw Bruce a few days later and said, "It looks like you're missing a hubcap."

"I don't know where the son of a bitch is," he replied.

"Well, I happen to have an extra one which I'd sell you for $25." He agreed to my price, so I reached into the trunk, withdrew the hubcap, and he paid me for it. If he'd bitched about my price or anything else, I'd have probably just given it to him since it was most likely his anyway, and had probably rolled off while he was driving down the street. But it was just much more fun this way, for me at least. I honestly don't know whether it was the same hubcap as he'd lost, but it probably was. I took the $25 and bought an entire set of 1969 Cadillac hubcaps, which I liked better, anyway.

Another `69 DeVille Convertible

In the meantime, my girlfriend, having been thrilled with her purchase of this convertible bought two more, a gold 1969 which I'd found in Waverly, Tennessee, which I'd counseled her against, and another 1969, again sight unseen, which I bought over the phone from Florida, once again figuring that if it made it all the way to Nashville, it would be ok. It did, and it was, but by this time the red 1970 was all we needed, since I had the 1976 Eldorado convertible (see below) and my 1962 Lincoln convertible. In some freak ice storm, a pine tree crushed the carport behind her garage, and flattened the windshield of the gold 1969. Pine trees should never been with striking distance of one's house, garage, or any other out buildings.

The brown `69 at its previous home in Florida, attired with Eldorado hubcaps and a 1970 grill. "I'll take it if it makes it."

State Farm paid her for the shed which my girlfriend wanted replaced. I advised against doing so until all of those nearby giant trees were removed. I gave the `69 to my pal Harrison Peyton who drove it back to Nashville. The `76 Fleetwood was not damaged.

We kept this 1970 Cadillac for nearly twenty years, but the last five or so years of its time with us had been spent in a storage unit several miles away after we'd moved to the country when I sold my house in Nashville. Finally, realizing that I was never going to drive it again, I sold it to somebody on craigslist and he came to pick it up. I called him a couple of weeks later, and was glad to hear he had it up and running.

XIV.

The 1975 and 1976 Eldorado Convertibles

Before I relate my wonderful experiences with the 1976 Eldorado, I should mention a bit about those cars in general. The Carter administration had stupidly lowered the national speed limit to 55 mph and had succeeded in scaring both the public and the auto manufacturers to the extent that the convertible, as an American icon of the open road was to cease to exist, once and for all. Although the Cadillac Eldorado would continue in its large body style for another year or so, much was made of the so-called `last Cadillac convertible.' There were articles in almost every national newspaper of the time about the 1976 Eldorado convertible, and its sad demise. Many speculators bought them and would attempt to re-sell them at triple their purchase price. I remember regularly seeing them priced at $40,000, and sometimes higher in the *Wall Street Journal*, and elsewhere. Some bought them with no intention other than that of having one of the last Cadillac convertibles. Others bought them for their sometimes infant grandchildren, so they could see what American cars used to be. The result of this conservation, regardless of its initial motives was that many of the 1976 Eldorados were very well taken care of, and consequently fairly plentiful. When car manufacturers like Chrysler and others began making convertibles again, the bubble deflated.

1976 Eldorado Convertible

The 1976 was to some buyers, the best of the front wheel drive Cadillac convertibles, and it probably was, although it was almost identical in every way to the 1975 Eldorado. The tried and true 500 ci (8.2 liter) 400 hp engine which was new for the Eldorado in 1970, replaced the venerable 472 ci (itself an excellent engine) which had debuted in 1968.

The 1970 DeVille convertible marked the last of the rear wheel drive Cadillac convertibles, and the first front wheel drive Cadillac convertibles showed up for 1971, a complete departure from the 1967-1970 Eldorados, none of which had been offered as a convertible, although there were often homemade attempts at producing one, usually with unsatisfactory results. The new Eldorados, both coupes and convertibles, were long, low, and powerful. Their rear fender skirts continued the unbroken body line and made them appear even longer and more rakish than they really were. Actually the 1971s were only a bit over 6 inches longer than the 1970s. I like all of the front wheel drive convertibles, despite their front wheel drive. They were all similar in appearance, all had an 8.2 liter engine, and all had similar bodies. The '71s and '72s seemed to me to have crisper lines, given their bumpers which were still incorporated within the fenders as opposed to sticking out as required by US regulations beginning in 1973.

One spring day in 1988, my friend Bruce and I stopped by a high end car dealership located in a building off of Franklin Road, close to downtown Nashville. There, among their offering of cars for sale was a royal blue 1976 Cadillac Eldorado convertible, with just 33,110 original miles. It occurred to me that since I'd traded one of my Lincoln convertibles and my wonderful red 1969 Cadillac De Ville convertible for a 1958 Bentley, I really no longer had a convertible which I could drive out of town. After my first 1964 Lincoln convertible had met its sad end as related elsewhere, I really didn't feel comfortable driving my 1962 Lincoln convertible, mainly because one could never be absolutely sure that the top would always work, and even though it always had, it might not work the one time I'd needed it to. Besides that, when the top was down (since it folded backward), it took almost all of the room in the trunk, so that it was difficult to store anything any larger there than a briefcase. I should never have traded those two cars for the Bentley, but I'd never had a Bentley before, and wanted the experience (see below). By now, after five years, I was tired of the 1948 Rolls, and given my experiences with the Bentley, would actually prefer a modern convertible which I could actually use.

I already had too many cars, so I traded the dealer my 1948 Rolls Wraith, my '58 Bentley, and my really great 1962 Lincoln convertible as an even swap. I know it was insane, but. The Eldorado was front wheel drive, something which I detested by this time as a result of my aforementioned troubles with my '67 Eldorado. I was willing to overlook the inherent problems of front wheel drive in this case, due to the wonderful condition of the car. The white convertible top was perfect, as was the soft tan leather. The steering wheel wasn't cracked like that of most 1975 and '76 Cadillacs, and I liked the open wheel wells of the '75s and '76s. More importantly, everything worked exactly as new. And to top it all off, the 500 cubic inch engine had fuel injection. It was the first car I'd ever had up to that point with fuel injection. The engine had more than enough torque, and would haul ass off the starting line.

There were a couple of things which I didn't like about the car, including the rubber fender extensions, front and rear, and poorly and stupidly designed folding convertible top. I was willing to overlook these, and other pointless features in this case, because the car was basically new. The 1971-1974 Cadillac Eldorados, the first of the front wheel drive models which included convertibles as well as coupes, had full metal front and rear fenders, although by 1974, there were non-metal `bumper extensions' on the rear. By 1975 and 1976, they were also on the front fenders. Although I didn't like the rear bumper extensions, I could live with them. The main problem back then was that these rubber, or whatever they were, pieces frequently froze and became brittle and broke, leaving an unsightly space of several inches extending all the way from the top to the bottom of each fender. On top of that, they were expensive to replace. Not only that, the replacements had to be painted to match the body, and the replacements were subject to the same rapid deterioration as the originals. More annoying than these considerations was the fact that they interrupted the otherwise beautiful lines of the fenders with what were clearly poorly fitted and ill-considered hunks of rubber, soft plastic, or whatever. The eye of the beholder was immediately drawn to these unsightly hunks of rubber.

That being said, I was driving up an alley off of Nashville's Music Row, one day and stopped before pulling out onto a side street. I was stopped, but that didn't prevent some moron in a white van from backing down the street the wrong way and hitting my front fender. He just happened to hit my bumper end broadside, and it performed as designed. I bought another one from the Cadillac dealer, installed it myself and had a body shop match the paint. The incident was the other driver's fault and he paid for it. Because of the bumper end, the entire fender didn't have to be replaced, just the end. I still would have preferred a solid steel fender.

Another thing I didn't like was the spare tire. It was a full size wheel with some sort of small tire which was supposed to be inflated with the no doubt highly flammable contents of some aerosol can which by now probably no longer had enough pressure to blow up a birthday balloon. I bought a regular size Eldorado wheel with a good tire from a junkyard and disposed of the useless spare which had been provided with the car, thus lessening my already fairly minimal trunk space.

Now, as to the convertible top. This was a foolish and pointless attempt to expand the width of the rear seat by a couple of inches on each end by doing away with the housings at each side of the back seat for the folding top mechanism. I think the logic was that the rear seat of the convertible would then be the same size as that of the coupe, as if somehow that mattered. To accomplish this feat of questionable utility, the top was completely redesigned inside and out. With few notable exceptions, convertible tops historically detached at both sides of the front windshield, and then, hinged in one or more places, easily folded straight to the rear where they reposed in a well behind the back seat. The principle was the same whether the car was a one or two seat car. Now, parallel side rails of the top frame, instead of simply folding back, collapsed toward the center of the top in a complicated series of unnecessary mechanical maneuvers augmented by a series of moving cables.

To make matters worse, the top was now hinged six or seven inches behind the front windshield as well, so that when the 'top down' switch was pulled, after the top had been manually disconnected from the windshield frame, not only did the top frame rails begin to collapse toward the center, but the front several inches of the top folded up from the top of the windshield frame and back at the same time. All of this uselessness was operated by mechanical gears and cables powered by a shaft emanating from each end of a single electric motor centered on the upper back side of the rear seat.

In practical terms, this meant that after very little use, the cables stretched, as they are known to do, and there was no longer a really tight seal between the top of the windshield and the convertible top in its raised position, which is where it spends most of its time. Consequently, with the top raised, air and sometimes water enter the car between the top of the windshield and the underside of the convertible top. This almost never happens with GM convertibles with the older top mechanism which was discontinued after the 1970 model year. But, it gets worse, as I was soon to find out.

Since my top was basically new, it worked, for the most part as designed…at first. One day I took my son to an afternoon movie. We'd been riding around with the top down and I pushed the button to raise it before we went inside. It started to lift up and fold in toward the center, then suddenly one of the cross bars with pivoting ends went sideways and ripped itself loose from the fabric seam which held it to the underside of the top. It jutted a couple of inches out toward the side of the top, away from where it was supposed to be. It was never right after that, although after the top was up, I could physically move it back into position, but not upright like it was supposed to be, giving the top a sagging appearance in the center. Thanks a pantload.

And then one day, the top simply wouldn't raise. I drove to Stevens Bros. Nashville's convertible top experts at the time. It took four of us to forcibly raise the top. Apparently either the top motor or relay had just stopped working. A new motor and relay were bought and I fixed the problem myself. Now, however, the left side and the right side of the top mechanisms were not operating at the same time. A look at the place where the top frame and mechanism attached to the body indicated the reason. The gears had come loose on both sides from their housings. What a piece of crap. The top still went up and down, but preferably with the help of at least one other person so that it wouldn't damage itself any further. At this point I used the top as little as possible. I kept the car in the garage, so if it was summer, it was down, and in winter it was raised. I could lower or raise it, with help, if I had to, but now for the most part kept it either up or down.

One day a couple of friends and myself decided to ride to Chattanooga and spend the night. One of them stuffed his suitcase into the trunk as far as it would go, and then the other luggage was added and the shallow trunk closed. When we were getting into the car, I decided to lower the top. As it completed its complex decent, there was a pop. Yes, a muffled pop. When the top went all the way down the glass window struck the suitcase and shattered. Thanks again. What this meant was that I could no longer drive the car in cold weather. I ordered a new back window but never had it put it in, since the car was always garaged.

I don't actually know when GM decided to start using this foolishly designed top. It must have been in 1971, since my 1970 DeVille convertible hadn't had it. This convertible top was applied not only to Cadillacs, but to Chevrolets, Buicks, Oldsmobiles, and Pontiacs as well.

And then there was the problem with the idle speed, from the moment I got the car. It idled way too fast so that I had to literally keep my foot on the brake hard at every stop sign or light, or in traffic because otherwise it would take off with a lurch. I took it in to have the problem corrected and was told that there was no adjustment for idle speed. I got used to this because it's just the way it was.

One morning I walked out to the garage and got into the car. The top was down and I was ready for a great day of motoring. When I started the car, it barely ran. It was coughing and sputtering and wouldn't run fast enough long enough to get out of the garage. It felt like the problem was a blown head gasket. I had it towed to the Cadillac dealer in Brentwood. A day or so later they called and said that the problem was that it needed a new computer?

Computer? What computer? Well, they told me, the fuel injection was controlled by a computer. This was news to me. There was worse news yet. A new one was around $1,200, and they didn't have one and didn't think they could get one. I had it towed back home and stuck in the garage while I thought about what to do next. I turned to the back of *Hemmings Motor News,* and after making several calls located one for $400 with no guarantee that it would work. I made a few more calls, and found a used one for $600 or thereabouts, disconnected the battery, unplugged the dead one and installed the new one easily myself. I reconnected the battery and the car started as normal, as if nothing had happened at all.

After another year or so, the computer expired again, and I sold the car to my elderly friend Jack Kershaw. He had the computer replaced and the car professionally repainted in black, a color which he preferred. He had it over a year before it met its waterloo. One pleasant afternoon he was driving innocently around Nashville's Green Hills when the car backfired somehow under the hood and caught on fire. My friend couldn't get the hood open and the fire department around the corner came quickly axed the hood and extinguished the fire. The car was towed to a wrecker yard near Donelson, a Nashville suburb. Like most people who are car crazy, I go through different phases. By the time I sold this car I'd had the Cadillac experience, having had the best of the cars I'd wanted, including the 1967 and 1968 Eldorados, the, the 1967-1970 DeVille convertibles, the 1974-1976 Fleetwood Broughams and Talismans, and the 1975-1976 Eldorado convertibles.

One day I stopped by his house and noticed the car was gone. I asked him where it was and he told me what had happened. "When was this?" I asked. "About six weeks ago," he replied casually. I told him we'd better check on it right now, which we did. I called out there and was told that it had been crushed and sent for scrap a week or so earlier. The office manager told me that she'd sent several letters to my friend asking him to come pick the car up, and he had failed to do so, so it was crushed. At this time, the car still had less than seventy thousand miles on it. And that was that. Jack kills another one!

This had been my first front wheel drive Eldorado convertible and had been expensive in that I'd traded a Bentley, a Rolls-Royce, and a Lincoln convertible for it, although I soon bought the Lincoln back. As luck would have it, the prices of 1940s Wraiths and `50s Bentleys began rising steadily, not that it especially mattered at this point. I'd always wanted an aluminum bodied Phantom or Wraith and a Rolls or Bentley Cloud. I'd had the experience and enjoyed them both, but for the moment at least, I wanted every subsequent car to be faster, and the Eldorado had been. During the time I owned it, it was fun to drive, beautiful and elegant. Above all, it lacked the front end groans and clanking I'd always experienced with the 1967 and 1968 Eldorado coupes.

Even though this car met a tragic end, it had been one of the most important cars I've ever owned from a purely personal standpoint. I'd basically acquired it with the intention of taking an out of town girlfriend on a weekend trip, which I did. The trip had been to Memphis and pre-casino Tunica, Mississippi, and in that regard, was well worth whatever the car cost or might have ever cost. I remember it very well even now, more than thirty years later, us riding in the back seat with the top down, my head in her lap, with my pal Bard at the wheel, fireflies everywhere and the night sky punctuated by shooting stars. I'd kept it from 1988 to about 1997. Prior to getting rid of it, I'd been content having it, my 1975 Fleetwood Brougham, and my 1962 Lincoln Convertible, a period of automotive calm which lasted until April 1993 when my new, and now long term girlfriend bought the wine red 1970 DeVille convertible which I've detailed above.

Heading north from Hollywood…Mississippi, that is.

As regards to my 1976 Eldorado convertible, I'm inserting a short tale from my book `Vignettes from the Modern Era.' This story is about a so-called singer I used to represent who never `made it' despite his incredible talent. Perhaps his actions pertaining to his 1976 Eldorado convertible might give a glimpse as to why he never succeeded, since as it has been said, "The way you do anything is the way you do everything." Truer words have never been spoken.

`WHAT GOES AROUND'

David was an aspiring singer, and probably the worst person I've ever known. He didn't actually kill anybody. Instead he fed off their energy. He was horrible. Of the people in his immediate circle during the year and a half I wasted fooling with him, one had a heart attack and died. Another had a heart attack, but survived. Another was fired from his job, and his wife got cancer and died. Another man got a divorce and lost his business.

Another woman lost her job of twelve years. Additionally, he had the truly unique ability to bring out the absolute worst in everyone he ever met, myself included. Anyway, I had a Cadillac convertible, a big, dark blue 1976 Eldorado, the last of the real Cadillacs. Well, it wouldn't do but that he had to have one too, and it had to be better than mine. Sure enough, he got one from his home town, someplace in New Jersey, and had it shipped down to Nashville on a truck by some insured transport company. He called me as soon as it arrived and I went over to his apartment to see it. It was black with red leather and a white top. The paint was original and in perfect condition. So was the leather and the top. It was definitely` better' than mine, which is what he wanted, not that I particularly cared. In transit however, there must have been a car on the hauler above his, because some oil or transmission fluid had dripped onto the trunk lid of his car and slightly discolored the paint. It was noticeable, but just barely. The damaged area was about the size of a quarter.

He was furious and vowed to make somebody pay. In retrospect I believe now that he was working himself into a state of self-induced righteous indignation to justify the con game he was about to perpetrate on the carrier's insurance company. He raved about how his original car would never be the same now that this damage had been done by the negligent car transporter. I assured him that it was no big deal. "Just get the trunk lid repainted," I said. "It won't cost more than a hundred dollars at most, and they'll probably pay for it."

But he'd already hatched a plan that he would demand $5,000 because the entire car would have to be stripped, taken down to the bare metal. Otherwise, he reasoned, the paint on the trunk would not match that on the rest of the car. It was more than that, he explained indignantly. They had also somehow punctured the top as the result of their carelessness. Well, actually he had punctured the top himself, he explained. It wasn't much of a puncture, like maybe an ice pick would do, but he wanted that money, and had worked himself up to the degree that he wasn't committing fraud, he was just getting what he had coming as a result of the damage `they' had done to his car and the stress and inconvenience this had caused him. "It was like they did this to me intentionally," he told me. It's not a lie if you believe it, and he believed it now, having twisted it around in his cunningly dishonest mind.

I told him that what he was contemplating was not merely illegal but unethical. Since he literally had absolutely no sense of right or wrong, he actually did not understand my misguided advice, my attempt to dissuade him from his plans. It was like I was somehow against him too. I stood my ground, but he went ahead, nevertheless. He browbeat, harassed, threatened, and intimidated the insurance adjuster so thoroughly that to my surprise, they sent him a check for five thousand dollars. The car was not worth more than $7,500 at the time. He felt vindicated. His car would never be right, of course, but at least he'd managed to stop the transport company from 'putting one over on him.' He'd done nothing other than protect himself from one of those 'greedy corporations.'

What he did was pocket the money and find somebody out in the sticks who agreed to take the car down to the bare metal and refinish it better than new for $1,500. In other words, in his greedy self-absorbed mind, he figured that he was getting paid $3,500 to have his car repainted. He'd pocket the extra $3,500. But as they say, what goes around comes around. Things didn't turn out quite like he'd intended. He'd paid the body shop owner a $500 down payment but work had not proceeded as expected. The car had had all of its chrome removed, the side strips, the front and rear bumpers, and the door handles. The body had been stripped of all of its paint and covered in flat gray primer. It was a mess. To make matters worse, the car, which was supposed to have been kept inside the shop, out of the weather, had instead been unceremoniously left in the gravel driveway area outside the corrugated metal building, exposed to the elements.

It was at this point that my client asked me, as a Southerner, and a hick, to intercede in his behalf with the shop owner to see if I could persuade him to finish the job. I discovered that my client had promised the body shop owner that in exchange for a lower price, he would help do much of the work himself, using the grinder and sander in the laborious job of removing the old paint. He'd actually worked for about three hours the first day and that was it. Of course he neglected to tell me that he'd agreed to all of this at the outset. He'd failed to mention any of this. I visited the shop owner on his behalf and got the entire story.

At this point the shop owner was willing to start to work again, as soon as David paid him another $500 as originally agreed, since the money was to be paid incrementally as work progressed. The other thing, the shop owner said, was that the car's owner would have to come back and work, as agreed, that meant physical labor, not standing around watching while somebody else did the work.

Though David had, in fact, agreed to do the majority of the work himself, he balked at doing anything additional, having experienced a few hours of real work for the first time in his life. He didn't intend to pay the shop owner any further money for 'ruining his car.' He'd get a lawyer and sue the shop owner for substantial damages. So he sought several lawyers, seeking to find one who would work for nothing other than the honor of representing him. In the meantime, David had been brave from a safe distance, calling and harassing the shop owner several times a day, but the fact was, David was scared of the shop owner, who was tough, skinny, and fearless. By the time I paid the shop owner a second visit his attitude had changed much for the worse. "I'm not going to finish the car for any amount of money, and

I'm not going to release it until he pays me for the work I've already done. I hate that son of a bitch and if I see him again he might have an accident. All those pumped up gym muscles don't mean shit to me. He's never done a real day's work in his life. If he calls me again I'm going to fuck him up. I hate that yankee piece of shit."

I agreed with him, because he was right. I'd come to hate the son of a bitch myself for being who and what he was. I personally hoped the shop owner would ruin the car.

Three weeks later, after telling me about the situation several times a day, David decided that the best thing to do was to get the car out of that place as soon as possible. He'd been unable to find a lawyer who was willing to work for nothing. I agreed to let him store the car in the driveway behind my house for a couple of weeks until he decided what to do with it. Of course he had to pay the shop owner an arbitrary 'storage fee' since the shop was no longer working on the car. It ended up costing David another $1,000 to get the car back, $1,500 in all. What a shame. I asked David if he might see some connection between what had happened to him and the fact that he had basically stolen $5,000 from an innocent party through a false insurance claim. He saw no connection at all and was angry that I would even suggest that he'd done anything unethical. "That's not the kind of person I am. I was just seeking a fair compensation for the damage to my car. C'mon man, you saw the damage that transporter did to my car."

In the three week interval that the car remained at my house, he found another body shop willing to take the car, who would fix it as good as new for $2,500. The car was towed from my house and the next time I saw it, it looked almost as nice as it had the first time I saw it, only now, of course, the paint was no longer original, thus reducing the car's value. It had turned out fine after all, David reasoned. The car would have had to have been stripped down anyway. Since that had already been done, the new body shop was charging him less that it would have if it had been necessary to start from scratch. He'd still managed to pocket a grand for his trouble, and still have the car repainted.

In the meantime, he continued working against me, seeking to undermine the work I had been doing on his behalf, as his manager. He was driving me crazy and not making me any money. I went to a friend of mine for advice, the manager of one of the most successful and enduring acts in country music. He asked me if I seriously thought David was going to make it, to become a star. I told him that the singer was probably the most talented act I'd ever represented, even though I had represented some of the most successful acts in American music, a fact of which he was well aware. I mentioned that I had him under contract. My friend advised me to drop him as a client immediately and not to look back. "If he is as bad as you've described him, it's unlikely that he'll ever make it anyway, and even if he docs, imagine what he'll be like then. You're better off without him, even if he does make it. You've had many acts, you'll have many more, but ultimately you can't make a good deal with a bad person."

I weighed his words carefully and released David from his contract with me. It turned out to have been a wise decision on my part. He never made it as a singer, despite his incredible talent, because of his self-destructive nature. He actively attempted to cheat everyone who worked in his behalf, even before there was any reason to do so. Everyone who knew him for more than two weeks actively hated him. He was that bad. His actions behind the scenes reminded me someone deciding to steal the silverware as the Titanic was sinking. He's the only person I've ever actually fantasized about killing.

As to the car, it was fixed again as I related, but then, one day downtown, David had illegally parked it, since the law did not apply to him, and a city bus came flying around the corner and destroyed it, crashing the back bumper all the way to the back seat. He still didn't see any connection between his thievery and its immediate consequences, but as they say, what goes around comes around. It really couldn't have happened to a nicer person. And he never did make it as an entertainer. Ah, sweet mystery of life!

1975 Eldorado Convertible

My 1976 Eldorado convertible had needlessly met its demise, and I still had a 1970 DeVille convertible so I wasn't looking for another Cadillac convertible, per se. My friend Bard Selden had made a rare visit to Nashville one weekend, so off we went to East Nashville looking for cars and junk stores, just like we did in our twenties. I didn't need any more cars and neither did he, but it's always fun to look. We hadn't been long on Dickerson Rd. before I espied a `75 or `76 Eldorado convertible at one of many nondescript car lots. We turned around and I went back to have a look. It was the only decent car on this otherwise low end used car lot. It was a `75 with a beautiful metallic desert rose color with a nice white convertible top and a perfect white leather interior. I believe the dealer was asking $3500 or thereabouts for the car. I was told that all it needed were brakes.

Bard and I attempted to take it for a spin but it was so out of gas that it barely managed to coast into the nearest `horse piss' gas station. I put in $5.00 worth of gas and we were on our way. It was more than `just needing brakes.' It had no brakes to speak of at all, so it wasn't much of a drive. OK, I didn't need it, I'm not fond of front wheel drive, but I'd loved the 500 cubic inch engine of my `76 Eldorado convertible and this one ran fine, without the hard to control acceleration of the `76's nonadjustable fuel injection's racing idle speed, since it had a carburetor.

I thought about it over what remained of the weekend and called the car lot's owner the following Monday. My parents had kindly given my son a 1992 Buick (also pronounced `Burick' or `Buiss' in some circles). It was a very thoughtful gesture on their part but I had no intention of sending my son off to college in something that weird or small. I think this particular Buick was a 1992, with the once significant `Park Avenue' name having been resurrected. It was considered `full size' Ha! It was front wheel drive and the hood opened strangely as on an early BMW 2002, that is, it was necessary to unlatch the hood from inside the car, then lift it upward just in front of the front windshield, push it forward on rollers, and then finally open it forward the rest of the way by lifting it completely. Strike two! To make matters worse, the seatbelt wasn't anchored at the base of the floor as it should be, instead it was attached only to the door frame which meant that should the passenger of driver door open in an impact, the passenger or driver would likely be dumped on the street or thrown from the car. Strike three!

Be that as it may, I thought I might be able to trade the Buick for the Eldorado, since that type of car was more in line with the rest of the cars the dealer had for sale. I told him about it over the phone and that everything worked and that it was in good condition with nice paint and a perfect fabric interior. There was one problem which I told him about: the `check engine' light was on. He said that didn't matter, and if the car was as nice as I'd described, he'd take the car and $1200 for the Eldorado. This sounded good.

On the day I acquired the car, I drove the Buick to the car lot, afraid that he might change his mind, but at the same time grateful to my parents' desire to provide my son a car for college. So I was stealing my son's car so I could get another car that I didn't need? No. He was upgraded to a black 1976 Cadillac Fleetwood Brougham whose original owner had been known to me. He was happy, and so was I.

I drove the Cadillac convertible home (holding my nuts all the way, as usual), since it basically had no brakes, and arrived without incident. I had the car's brakes fixed immediately and kept the car for around two years, but didn't use it much and finally sold it on ebay. It was a beautiful car with perfect white leather and in a rare exterior color. I miss it now. The 1975 and 1976 Cadillacs were the last of a long line of iconic American cars which were since their inception, admired and desired worldwide. Today Cadillacs are more efficient, and in a sense 'better' but sadly, like most American offerings from the big 3, now, merely generic. Every once in awhile I think about getting rid of all of my cars and letting my fleet consist of a perfect 1975 or 1976 Fleetwood and some sort of late 1960s DeVille convertible, cars I know and love, but there are just too many cars out there I've yet to experience. The majority of motorists are content with one or two nice cars, and I envy that state of mind, and the contentment it produces, but so far, it just hasn't worked for me.

XV.

1974-1976 Fleetwood Broughams & Talismans

When The 1971 Cadillacs debuted they were a complete departure from the 1969-1970 models, especially in terms of the Fleetwoods, which now had a very formal roofline with rounded edges at the tops of all four side windows. It was not the first formal C-pillar roof line of late. The 1961 Fleetwood, in fact all of the Fleetwoods, beginning with 1961, had formal roofs. The 1971 however, ushered in a new era of perceived exterior luxury. I say perceived because the 1964, as an example, had many real wood accents, both on the doors and behind the front seat. The 1971 Brougham looked longer, lower, and wider than its 1970 predecessor, but lacked the interior refinements of earlier cars. The appearance of the coach lights just behind an already formal rear window, only accented the perception of formality, privacy, and power.

The new Fleetwood made a statement with which Lincoln could no longer compete. This would of course change in 1972 when the MK IV debuted with its c-pillar opera windows. My roommate, Mike Cofer at Chattanooga had an elderly grandfather who bought a black 1971 Fleetwood Brougham. I loved its look. From time to time we'd eat dinner at his parents' house and the grandparents would join us. That car was a sight to see, given its new and unique styling and mirror finish. This roofline and window treatment would continue through 1976.

Dick Blake, president of Dick Blake International was tired of his agents constantly demanding more money, especially me. But we were getting our client Barbara Mandrell $70,000 a night in early 1980s money. We also were the exclusive agents for Ronnie Milsap, Merle Haggard, Brenda Lee, Ricky Skaggs, and others, all of whom were at the top of their income potential. None of us were receiving commissions. It's true that we were making money, but not enough in proportion to the revenue we were generating.

Blake devised a plan to cheat the government out of some money while getting all of us off his back. He would give each one of us a company car, pay our insurance, fuel, and maintenance, and deduct all of it as a legitimate business expense. It sounded good to me. My friend Bard Selden in Tunica, Mississippi had a copper-colored 1974 Fleetwood Talisman, which he still has all these years later. We were told that we had around $16,000 each to pick out a car. This was in 1978 or 1979, I really don't remember. One of the agents selected a new Toronado, another decided on a new Buick Riviera. I wasn't interested in any of these cars. As far as I was concerned, they were the same cars with different badging, and they were both front wheel drive. I was thinking about something better. I found a 1974 Fleetwood Talisman in the paper for sale for $3,400 which had approximately 34,000 original miles on its odometer. I told Blake that I wanted the Talisman as opposed to a new car. It was saving him at least $12,000 right off the bat. He pretended to hem and haw a bit but I already knew it was a done deal, which it was. I drove out to Fairview to look at it, and recognized the seller who'd owned a market on Elliston Place in the university district of Nashville, back when I was fifteen years old. I remembered him and that he'd had a Rolls-Royce Silver Cloud at the time. Now he owned the only Liquor store in Fairview, located about twenty miles or so southwest of Nashville.

The Talisman was magnificent, a pale yellow with caramel-colored bucket seats front and rear. This was not a color to be found on any car in Nashville at the time. It reminded me of a late 1920s Packard paint and upholstery catalog I'd once seen, which featured a similar color. I took the car for a spin and everything worked as it was supposed to. There was a locking console/arm rest between the two cloth front seats which featured a flip-up writing tablet in addition to a large storage space. The rear also featured bucket seats and a large locking center console, making the limited edition Fleetwood Talisman a rare car indeed. As I recollect, there were around a thousand or so made during the 1974 model year. The Talisman also had a padded vinyl top which made it appear even more formal than a regular Fleetwood Brougham. I told the seller I'd take it and we arranged that I would pick it up a couple of days later in Nashville and pay him then.

Man, was I excited! The first thing I did when I returned to the office was to call my pal Bard Selden in Mississippi, who was the person who first made me aware of the Fleetwood Talisman. I told him all about it and he was happy for me. I had somebody drop me off at the Frosty Root Beer distributor off of Jefferson Street where I met the owner, paid him, got the title and returned to my office. The car was every bit as magnificent as it appeared at first sight. The AC compressor conked almost immediately but I had it replaced and was good to go. The interior seating was comfortable and surprisingly durable, and

wasn't as likely to shock you with a big jolt of static electricity as the so-called velour interiors of the large '70s Lincolns. For 1975, the individual rear seats and rear console were replaced by a single rear bench seat for the remaining two years of the Fleetwood Talisman's manufacture, a mistake I thought. On the other hand, perhaps G.M. thought a car that large should be able to seat more than four adults.

Unfortunately someone ran a red light and turned in front of me at Demonbreun Street in broad daylight. The port fender and hood were replaced by the Cadillac dealer and it looked as good as new, but it was no longer original. Then my car was rammed one Sunday morning at the intersection of Woodlawn and Bowling, by some old lady who wasn't paying attention. This time it was the starboard front fender that got it. Back to the Cadillac dealer for another fix. A few years later, on a perfectly clear and sunny day, my 1962 Lincoln convertible would be whacked behind the back wheel by another inattentive driver at the exact same place on Demonbreun, in exactly the same manor, also on a sunny day with 100% visibility..

Then, one Saturday morning I'd come to my office on Music Row for something and the car ran out of gas. I walked down the street to the Consumer's gas station with a jug, brought a gallon of gas back to the car, and then backed into the parking lot sign, severely damaging the port rear fender with a big gash. Back to the Cadillac dealer, again, which was fortunately close to my office and located on Broadway. Then, I backed the lower edge of the port taillight housing into a curb, pulling it away from the top of the fender. Back to the Cadillac dealer's paint & body shop. By this time, I'd developed a friendly relationship with the head of the body shop who'd been with the Cadillac dealership almost since it had opened. It was then called Ralph Nichols, and was the only Cadillac dealer in Nashville. At some point, after Ralph Nichols died, it became Bunch-Nichols.

During the 1950s and 1960s most of the Nashville car dealerships were located on Broadway, among them were Cumberland Dodge, Beaman Pontiac, Jim Reed Chevrolet, Preston Lincoln-Mercury, Maxwell Smith, Ralph Nichols Cadillac, E. Gray Smith Rolls-Royce & Bentley, Hippodrome Oldsmobile, etc. I especially remember the Cadillac dealer very well because it owned a Harley-Davidson three-wheeler service cycle. It was a beautiful dark red with black wire wheels and gold lettering and sported a hook on the front wheel. When someone's car needed to be serviced the motorcycle would be driven to the owner's residence, and the serviceman would attach the motorcycle to the car's rear bumper and then drive the car, with motorcycle in tow, back to the Cadillac dealership for service. When the car was ready, it would be returned the same way, and then the motorcycle would go pick up or deliver another car. This one man performed this service five days a week and we'd frequently see him en route from one place to another. It was a really beautiful motorcycle with a gear shift lever on the side of its gas tank.

One day in about 1990 my friend Bruce told me that he's seen my former Talisman sitting in a yard off of Granny White in Nashville. He also said that there was a Rolls Silver Shadow which was sitting in the driveway and that neither one of the cars looked like they'd moved in awhile. I took a drive over there and it was indeed my former Talisman, a wonderful car which I'd needlessly sold on an impulse because I'd once mistakenly thought I had 'too many cars.' A lot had happened to this once beautiful car in the five or six years since I'd sold it, none of which had been good. The entire metal strip beneath the rear window which ran across the top of the body between the trunk lid and the bottom of the vinyl top was completely gone, having rusted away entirely. I should have never sold it to that oaf. There was a bit of minor rust around the leading edges of the hood, but otherwise the car was in good shape, but dirty and neglected. It also had a couple of flat tires, of the wrong size. For some reason its current owner had put much smaller tires than the

LR 78 15s it was supposed to have.

My former Talisman in a sad light, now back home, for the moment.

The Rolls was a 1967, silver with red leather, dead at 38,000 miles from neglect. A tree branch had fallen on the roof and dented it. This was another Rolls that would never move again under its own power. The Rolls didn't matter to me, at this point, but I wanted the Talisman back. It held many fond memories for me, having been my first Cadillac Fleetwood, and my first company car. I called the guy I sold it to since I still had his number. He had a new Corvette and didn't care about it one way or the other. It ran when he'd backed it under the large bush. He had the title but didn't know where the keys were.

I bought it back and had it towed to my house. The first thing I did was clean it thoroughly to see what would need to be done to fix it. The interior looked fine, if a bit dusty. Actually those Talisman seats were more durable than the leather was. On some level I felt that its present state was my fault. I would never have sold it if I'd even remotely suspected it would end up in this condition, but the person who bought it from me seemed delighted to have it and said he'd always wanted one, so I thought I was doing him a favor. The good news was that a year or so after I'd sold the car, I found an extra set of the three original keys, the ignition key, the one for the locking front and rear consoles, and the third key for the glove box and trunk. The problem was that now I couldn't find them. I'd seen them within the last year, and they had to be around somewhere. An exhaustive search didn't locate them. I was anxious to get this car properly repaired, so I called a locksmith and told him what I needed. He said the ignition key would cost $45 and he could be over in a couple of hours. I had things to do and told him to come on over even though I wouldn't be there. I'd leave the money in the glovebox. Great! I'd have it on the road almost immediately.

I returned home excited at the prospect. The good news was that I now had an ignition key, the bad news is that the moronic locksmith had destroyed the steering column, it now hung loosely laboring under its own weight. I couldn't believe it. I didn't remember who I'd even spoken with or what company he was from as there were plenty of locksmiths in the phone book. It was my fault for not writing down his name and number, and also for not being there when he arrived. The damage was done and I was sure he wouldn't be able to repair it. It was also my fault for assuming a level of competence not in evidence. It was my fault, but be that as it may, this was the `straw that brought the camel back' as Andy Brown so succinctly observed. I cleaned and washed the car to make it look as good as possible, photographed it, and then called Harrison Peyton who came and drove it away. It was a tragic end for such a magnificent car. Ironically, I subsequently located the three original keys hanging on a hook along with some others where I'd hidden them, and I still have them now.

The Talisman was basically trouble free the five or so years I'd owned it except for a six or seven hour trip I once made from Nashville to Memphis one Friday after work. The alternator was foolishly mounted atop some metal stalk affixed to the side of the engine and resembled some strange one-eyed sea creature. That it would break was more or less inevitable at some point. I just didn't expect it to happen one cold Friday evening. This was in the days before cell phones. The alternator light came on before we were even twenty miles out of town. I should have turned around, but it was still running so, intrepidly foolish as I was at the time, off we went. To make a long story short, we made it to a truck stop, it was repaired while the battery was being charged, which took several hours. It was already long after dark. When it was finally good to go we got back on the interstate and the alternator light came on almost immediately. The mechanic had put on the belt too tightly and it snapped. Back to the truck stop for another hour or so, and back on the road.

The next day Bard had located a replacement alternator mounting bracket at a junkyard somewhere in pre-casino Tunica, the problem was fixed on Saturday and on Sunday afternoon we made it back to Nashville without incident. My first Fleetwood had been a wonderful experience and these would remain my car of choice through the first decade of the new millennium. I just knew I'd have a 1974, 1975, or 1976 Fleetwood Brougham forever. The next one was still a couple of years away, and came to me unexpectedly as many cars have.

1975 Fleetwood Brougham

This new Cadillac was probably the most beautiful car I'd ever seen. I was a young talent agent working upstairs in an old house on Music Row. My two bosses had their offices downstairs and each of them had new 1977 Lincolns. The Lincolns were gigantic, even for the time. But one of their friends from another agency used to drop by from time to time, and he had this 1975 Cadillac Fleetwood Brougham. It was a royal blue, with a finish that was so deep it shimmered. It looked as if you could walk into the surface and simply disappear. The car was long and low, much lower in profile than their two 1977 Lincolns. It had a blue leather interior of a lighter shade than the exterior, and it looked soft and inviting. The roofline, especially the area above the windows at each side was squared off, but sloped gently toward the rear. Its matching vinyl top was punctuated by opera lights at the leading edge of the rear quarter, accenting its formal lines. It didn't have its hub caps for long. 1975 was the first year for the wire wheel discs which actually resembled real wire wheels. Two original sets were stolen and ultimately replaced with some crappy aftermarket `basket-weave' chrome-plated wheels.

I used to pause in front of the downstairs front door for a moment and look at it parked across the street each time it was there, going downstairs on some pretext so that I could admire it. Then one day, it wasn't there. It had been replaced by a new Cadillac Fleetwood Brougham, an all-white 1978 with beautiful tufted red leather seats. The new car wasn't in the same league, however. It was smaller, shorter, and higher, and at the time, totally lacking in comparison. I asked the owner if he had traded his other Fleetwood in on his new one. He replied that he'd kept the other one and that it was at home in the garage. I didn't ask if it was for sale because I couldn't have afforded it anyway.

Then one day, eleven years later, I was driving down Music Row in Nashville, and noticed this same 1975 Fleetwood parked in front of the owner's office. There was a `For Sale' sign in the window. I immediately turned, circled the block, and pulled over next to the curb several cars down the street. The car was just as beautiful as it was the last time I'd seen it, nearly a decade before. I went inside and asked the owner what he wanted for the car. He said $4,000, and encouraged me to take a test drive. I knew that I had to have this car. It wasn't that I needed it, but I knew I had to have it. I paid the asking price, even though I thought it was more than the car was actually worth at the time, and was thrilled to get it.

When I took possession of the car it had exactly 80,412 miles. I kept it from April, 1986 through November 2004 and finally gave it to my girlfriend's yard man who wanted it for his grandson. The car had been sitting behind her garage for several years and was rusted in the fenders behind the rear wheels as well as along the surface of the undercarriage. I knew that I was never going to get around to fixing it up properly. By the time I let it go, I had more or less lost interest in that series Fleetwood, and had moved on to other cars. I charged the battery, aired up a couple of the tires and sprayed some starting fluid into the carburetor. The car started right up and was still as quiet as a whisper with no knocks or tapping, just sheer power. That 500 C.I. engine was one of the best engines ever made for a passenger car, and the car never failed me, not even once during eighteen years. I let it warm up, then drove the car down to the end of the driveway and parked it out of sight from the road and left the key under the mat.

It was still an amazing car, even though the paint had faded on the hood and trunk. The vinyl top was still like new, despite the fact that the car had been sitting outside for years by this time. The arm rests which were prone to cracking, especially the driver's side, were in relatively good shape, as was the leather throughout. The steering wheel had separated in one place with a half an inch crack, a common occurrence for 1974-1976 models, and the dash cover had cracked in several places. The windows all worked and were still almost as fast as a guillotine. I took some pictures of the car from every angle and then walked away from it for the last time. It sat there for a couple of days and, then I came home one afternoon and it was gone. The yardman later told me that it had started right up and he'd driven it the fifteen miles to his house without incident.

I'd sort of expected to see the car on the road soon, but never did. Apparently his grandson had gotten into some kind of trouble at school so he was not given the car after all. I was not surprised. I'd known somehow, somewhere, in the back of my mind that the car would never be fixed up, repainted, or even driven again. It would, however be parked in a large overgrown field in back of the yardman's house where it would rust in peace. This was not the ideal end for a car I had planned to keep forever. I had probably owned it longer than any car I've ever had before or since. But I'd rather have had it restfully residing there forever, than stripped of a few parts at the salvage yard and then rudely crushed and impersonally stacked along with other cars on top of a flatbed and hauled to the smelter. Sadly, unable to locate the keys it was sold to the scrapyard. Hell, I could have done that myself.

I remember feeling warm, secure, and comfortable in the freezing rain with the windshield wipers slowly raking back and forth as the water formed into beads and rolled to the side of the very long hood. I remember flying down a steep snow-covered hill, gathering speed and emerging at the bottom and ascending another hill, even steeper, passing an entire line of sliding, snowbound motorists, bewildered at the sight of this speeding but elegant monster effortlessly passing them as if they did not exist.

I miss the car now, and what it represented to me. I miss being able to read street signs reflected off the hood's liquid mirror finish. I miss its large Cadillac crest at its far end. I miss its long, elegant good looks, and the arrival statement it made. I also miss the girl I loved then, and remember the time we did it in the back seat in the parking lot of the Vanderbilt girl's dorm.

1976 Fleetwood Brougham

Nolensville Road, was, as I've mentioned elsewhere, one of the few places in Nashville where one could reasonably hope to find old cars worth having. It was also one of the best places for ethnic restaurants. Anyway, over the course of several months I noticed this Cadillac Fleetwood parked in the same place beside some transmission shop. I stopped to have a look at it one day. It was in surprisingly nice condition with excellent tan leather, good paint, and a vinyl top which was in good shape as well. I found out that it had been brought in for transmission work, but had never been paid for or picked up. In the meantime, someone had stolen the carburetor. To make a long story short, I bought it for $ 50.00 and had it towed to my house. I figured that it would be a good parts car for my 1975 Fleetwood, which I still had then. The only problem was that I really didn't need any parts, so I stuck it behind the garage. Anyway, I ended up trading the engine to someone I met who had some parts I might need for my 1970 Cadillac convertible.

It was interesting to watch these three guys come over with some chains and a primitive hoist remove this heavy cast iron engine and haul it away. I wondered what they were going to do with it. They didn't even know whether or not it worked. Apparently they didn't care. A month or so later, I heard someone revving an engine loudly in front of my house on this quiet residential street. It was loud, and what the hell was it? I looked out a front window and saw a car which somewhat resembled my old 1974 Chevrolet Nova coupe. The ass end was raised like the tail of a scorpion and there were bigger wheels on the rear than on the front.

I recognized the driver and went out to see what he was up to. It was Harrison Peyton, the guy I'd traded the Cadillac engine to. To my surprise, he'd already managed to install this engine in this Buick 'Nova.' It was a fairly simple process, he told me. All he had to do was cut away some of the firewall to accommodate the larger engine. And he had to affix it to a transmission, and then, it needed a carburetor, and the linkage had to be fabricated. The driveshaft had to be shortened and balanced, and of course new engine mounts had to be created and welded in place. All in a day's work. He'd hoped I'd be home so that he could show me his masterpiece. "Hop in," he chirped. "I call this the 'Bu-Cad!' Hold on!" He stomped the accelerator and the 8 liter plus engine instantly came to life as the tires screeched and smoked, leaving about a fifty foot patch of burned rubber as the super light rear end fishtailed all over the road.

It was a hideous contraption but fascinating nonetheless that somebody was able to do something like this and actually make it work. I soon had a wrecker haul the carcass of the '76 Fleetwood to the junkyard after I'd removed some parts I might someday need. At this point I'd determined that no matter what other cars I might ever own, a 1975 or '76 Cadillac Fleetwood would always be a staple of my automotive fleet. After the removal of this dead 1976 Fleetwood, my operational fleet consisted of my 1975 Fleetwood, a 1970 Cadillac De Ville convertible, my 1962 Lincoln convertible, a 1976 Cadillac Fleetwood Brougham, and a 1976 fuel injected Eldorado convertible all of which were low mileage and in very good condition. I figured I was settled for the time being and had my bases covered. I probably would have remained so for at least a year if I hadn't read an ad in the local newspaper offering a 1976 Fleetwood Talisman for sale.

1976 Fleetwood Talisman

Note the upturn at the bottom of the window. Rolls-Royce would adopt a similar rear window treatment with its coming Silver Spirit and Silver Spur models in 1981.

I was content with my fleet, and even though I had no intention of buying any other cars for awhile, I was still interested in everything, so I read the *'Trader's Post'* weekly as well as ads in the local newspaper. One day, I saw an ad for a 1976 Fleetwood Talisman. I missed my 1974 Talisman, which I'd sold needlessly, but here was another one. The 1976 was the last year for the Talisman, and preferable to the 1974 due to the `76's 500 C.I. engine, one of the best two-valve V-8s ever made for any passenger car. The `76 also had better door pulls, rigid hinged metal as opposed to the flexible door pulls on the 1974. The only drawback for the `75 and `76 Talisman over the 1974 is that they lacked the large rear console of the 1974, as I've mentioned. The ideal situation would be to have the rear seats and console from a `74 and use them in a 1975 or `76 Talisman.

Anyway, this car was located out somewhere near Rivergate Mall, an area I might hit once every two years, if even then. I spoke to the car's owner and he said that it was in very good condition and that it ran great. I agreed to meet him at a certain exit off of I-65 to have a look at the car. It was a nice summer day and I didn't especially mind the half hour drive, and I could probably use a nice Talisman in addition to my 1975 and `76 Fleetwood Broughams. It wasn't like I needed more cars, but it didn't hurt to look.

As I exited the Interstate I espied the car on the side of the road about a hundred feet from a gas station, steam rising from its open hood. I pulled my car to a stop behind it. The car was most definitely not in good condition. Its body was basically rust free except for some serious surface rust over a really bad paint job. I couldn't tell what color it had originally been at first glance. Anyway, the car's owner was standing beside it. I spoke briefly to him and stepped inside the car and into the driver's seat. The $1800 optional Talisman interior was dusty but otherwise in almost new condition, in stark contrast to

239

the car's exterior. As I was seated there examining the dash and instruments, which were also in perfect condition I was distracted by the sound of running water. Its source was the car's owner standing and pissing on the ground between the open front passenger door and the car's body. After looking at the car I decided that I didn't want it at any price. He said that he 'thought I was going to buy it' to which I replied that he'd said that it was in good condition, which it clearly was not. He asked me what I'd give for it. I replied that I really didn't want it. "What about $100?"

I still didn't want it, but with two Fleetwoods already it might be good to have a parts car. After the car had cooled down I could see that the problem was a split radiator hose. He had the title with him. I told him that if the car could make it to the Shell station a hundred yards away under its own power I'd give him a hundred dollars, which it did, and which I did. As it was late Friday afternoon and traffic was getting ready to be heavy, I didn't want to have to fool with having it towed to my house until the next day.

The car arrived via Hillwood Wrecker service the next day. I replaced the hose and drove it around on a couple of nearby streets and it ran quietly and smoothly with plenty of power. The windows worked as they should. Actually, the car was mysterious in the sense that it ran perfectly and its interior was almost like new, while the outside was rusted, and dented in a couple of places, with the factory padded vinyl top having obviously been sliced here and there. I kept the car for a couple of months before I called Harrison Peyton, inventor of the aforementioned 'Bu-Cad.' He was glad to have it, drove it home without incident, and no doubt put its large engine to good use.

1976 Fleetwood Brougham (2)

And while we're still talking about 1974-1976 Fleetwoods, I once had a white 1976 Fleetwood which had a black vinyl top but no coach lights on the rear sides of the roof. It was the only Fleetwood of its era I ever saw without them. This car had some sort of blue tweed fabric covered seats with leather bolsters rather than full leather seats. It also had a manual seat lever rather than power seats, the only Fleetwood I'd ever seen similarly equipped. As I recollect it had around 57,000 original miles. It was in great shape despite its curious lack of options, and it still had climate control, power windows and a 500 CI engine. Somehow it felt lighter than my 1975, but it sat up high and was very fast, with absolutely no hesitation of any kind. Strange to say, I sort of liked its fabric interior, as it was different than the leather, and somehow seemed more suited to this particular car. I kept it for more than a year, and it was truly a wonderful car, but I was again starting to have too many cars again and ultimately traded it for a new Trek 9000 full suspension mountain bike (which I still have). I'm sorry I don't have that white '76 now.

1976 Fleetwood Brougham

Ever since I mistakenly sold my 1974 Fleetwood Talisman one summer, on impulse, I'd regretted not having a really great `74, `75, or `76 Fleetwood. As I mentioned earlier I'd bought a 1975 Fleetwood in mid-1986 and still had it, but during the last 21 years it was looking a bit tired. By 1995, there weren't many large Cadillacs left on the road, at least not in Nashville. One day I saw a 1976 Fleetwood parked illegally in front of the former H.G. Hill store in Green Hills. It was a striking ice blue with a matching ice blue vinyl top, a color combination I'd never seen before. I walked over to have a closer look. It had flawless paint and its white leather literally looked brand new. As I was admiring it, the owner exited the store. I introduced myself and told her that if she ever wanted to sell her car she should give me the first shot. I remembered her name but her phone number and address were unlisted. I left several notes for her at the bank in Green Hills where she did business, but there was never any reply and I never saw the car again until one day in mid-2007, when I received an unexpected phone call from the elderly woman's daughter, saying that the car was for sale if I was still interested, since the owner no longer needed it. I'd never forgotten the car, who would? The odd thing is that I'd hired a private detective to get her address and phone number literally the week before she called me.

By this time, I'd moved to large Lincolns but still wanted a large Fleetwood. I drove to her house and looked the car over. It was as beautiful as I remembered except that it had a minor dent in the starboard front fender. It now had 32,000 miles instead of the 24,000 that it had when I first saw it more than a decade earlier. I took it for a test drive and it absolutely moved like the wind, despite its large size. It had a really powerful carbureted 500 cubic inch engine which was original to the car. It was fast, solid, and elegant, with no rust anywhere. The original paint was nice, but no longer perfect, despite the fact that the car had been garaged all of its life. I had the money, if not an actual need for the car. I offered $3,200 for it, which I considered to be a fair price at the time, and arranged to pick it up in a couple of days. What a magnificent beast!

As I was then living at my girlfriend's house forty miles or so west of Nashville and had already filled her garage and barn with my cars, I knew that she wasn't going to go for me showing up with yet another car, especially something this big. The only way I could get the Cadillac and still preserve domestic tranquility was to drive one car to town and come back with the Cadillac, so that the actual number of cars on hand would not increase.

With that in mind, I called a friend and offered to sell him my 1977 Lincoln Town Car. He could pay me later, so much a month. I knew he'd like to have the car so I sold it to him for $1,000, much less than what I'd paid for it. On the day in question I met him and he drove me to pick up the Cadillac. I paid the owner and was on my way. I had the dent in the front fender fixed a few months later, but didn't drive the car much because I had other cars and didn't want to mess up its perfect original white leather interior. I hate white leather, not because it isn't pretty, but because it doesn't age well. I think that it has to do with the way the leather is dyed, but it seems that with white leather, the color is applied on the surface and doesn't really penetrate the leather. In any event, I knew that if I started using this car regularly, the thirty plus year old leather would quickly crack and become discolored, so I didn't drive it much.

I kept in in the garage for around two years and then sold it so that I would have space for one of my other cars. The 1975 and `76 Cadillac Fleetwoods are in my estimation, the best Cadillacs of the modern era, far better than the pint-sized things that are being produced now. These cars are unapologetically bold, powerful, and elegant. Yes, the new cars are more economical, but so what. They're small and nondescript and make no statement whatsoever upon their arrival other than, `I look pretty much like the rest of the cars here.' I don't honestly see how anyone who ever owned a `real' Cadillac could settle for something which is so much less than what a Cadillac is supposed to be. And front wheel drive? No thanks! I would have kept that car forever if its interior had been any color other than white.

I'm not planning on buying another one, but it's not out of the question. The buyer, from Charlotte, North Carolina, also had a Rolls-Royce Spur and was thrilled with the Cadillac. He subsequently had the original ice blue top replaced with a white one, which I thought was a big mistake, but it was his car to do with as he pleased. And thus ended a very long and pleasant association with the Cadillac 1974-1976 Fleetwood Broughams and Talismans.

As far as the 1977 Lincoln I got rid of to get this Fleetwood is concerned, it had been a wonderful car and I was comfortable driving it anywhere. I should have kept it, miss it now, and may buy another one at some point.

XVI.

Rolls-Royce & Bentley

When I was a teen ager and stuck in military school, in the mid-1960s, I used to cut out pictures of old Rolls-Royces that were listed for sale in the back of car magazines. There were other cars there at the time as well, all cheap enough back then: Cadillac-powered Allards, Mercedes 300 SLs, old Packards, Bugattis and Ferraris. But it was always the Rolls-Royces that I wanted. I didn't know much about the different models, coachbuilders, or anything else back then. But I intended to learn. When I was in my mid-twenties, there was a guy around Belle Meade named Michael Corzine, who owned a jewelry store in Green Hills and had a black Silver Wraith which he drove regularly around town back in the mid to late 1970s. I'd see it upon occasion in my part of town. It was beautiful. One day I didn't see it anymore, and didn't notice that I didn't. By spring 1984, I was the president of In Concert, a Nashville based talent agency. I happened to see a 1948 Silver Wraith in the Nashville edition of *Wheels & Deals*, a weekly publication, which car enthusiasts like me, used to eagerly buy every week. Back then, there were plenty of really great cars that regularly showed up for sale in the Nashville area. The Rolls was priced at $12,500. I called its present owner and inquired about it. He said that it ran fine, but that….Whatever else he might've said, I don't remember, or didn't hear, blinded as I was by my desire to have an old Rolls-Royce, any old Rolls-Royce.

1948 Freestone & Webb Silver Wraith

The car was located somewhere within fifty or sixty miles of Nashville. I drove out there, arriving after dark, not a good time to be looking at any car, especially a black one. I was undeterred. I took it for a test drive by myself, and while it rode rough and bounced around like a jeep, the six-cylinder engine seemed to have adequate power and didn't smoke. I was in love, again. I should mention at this point that I didn't have the money to buy the car. I already had several cars, owed money to the bank for a couple of them, and didn't want to borrow any more money I'd have to repay. I told the car's owner that I'd get back to him. I showed pictures of the Rolls to my friends and they all said I should get it. "OK, where can I get the money for this car without it coming out of my pocket, and without me having to go in debt to get it?" There's always a way to do anything you want to do," Rev. Ike had said, and he was right. I just hadn't figured it out yet.

One night I was at the Barn Dinner Theatre in Nashville, a local institution for nearly 60 years, closed permanently as of this writing, courtesy of the China virus. Back then there were no cell phones, so I asked the owner if I could use a phone somewhere with privacy. He was kind enough to let me use the phone upstairs in his office. With trembling fingers, I called Sherwood Cryer in Pasadena, Texas, owner of the famous Gilley's Club, my business partner at In Concert, and told him about the car. He asked me if I was going to buy it. I replied that I'd like to but didn't have the money. "I was wondering if I might buy it as a company car," I finally said after a bit of hemming and hawing. "Can you afford it?" he asked, meaning could the company afford it. "Yes," I said. "Well, you might look good in a Rolls-Royce," he said. At this point things were moving ahead steadily at In Concert so I was the golden boy, so to speak. I danced down the stairs, hardly able to think of anything else.

A rich sort of a friend of mine at the time, had a 1930s Phantom and a Silver Cloud, among his fleet, and had recently offered me his Cloud for $12,500. He wasn't actively trying to sell it, and certainly didn't need the money. Now that I had the money to buy a Rolls at that price, I began to think that maybe the Cloud might be a better option. It was a more modern car, with an automatic transmission, and would probably be easier to get fixed, not that any Rolls-Royce would ever need anything. After all, they're `the best in the world.'

I might have, and probably would have bought the Cloud, except for its color. It had a nice dark green leather interior, but the outside was a two-tone green, not British racing green, but a putrescent light green, over a slightly darker but equally offensive pea green. Besides, the Wraith was a bigger car, with long sweeping sides, an aluminum body, and giant P-1 headlights, with running lights atop each front fender, and another large center-mounted light in front of its massive grill. I decided on the Wraith.

One thing I generally, though not always insist upon when buying a car, is that it be delivered. After the expensive and troubling experience with the 1970 Olds 442 convertible (see above), I wanted the Rolls delivered by the seller. In this case, I meant driven the fifty or sixty miles to my office at 117 16th Ave. South. I figured that if the car made it without issue, it was probably alright, and if it didn't the deal was off and I could buy the Silver Cloud. I told the owner I'd have a cashier's check waiting for him and that he could cash it at the bank behind my office if he liked.

It was a sunny spring day, and in due course, the car arrived at my office. It was truly a work of art, black with beige leather, British number plates, and even the original owner's manual. I paid the owner, received the title, called my insurance agent and got the car insured. I thought it best that I waited until after work to fool with it. It was beautiful, but pretty is as pretty does. After work, I opened the front door, which opened backwards, like the rear door of a 1960s Lincoln Continental. This design probably wasn't a very good idea, I remember thinking at the time. What if the door opened of its own accord without notice? The car was right hand drive, as most of the Wraiths were, which of course, I already knew. I didn't care. With the door open I got a good look at the shifter which, instead of being in between the two front seats, in the middle of the car, was located between the outside edge of the driver's seat and the inside of the door. The shift lever was situated within a chrome panel, and was supposed to move within specific slots, as with a Ferrari, which meant that there was no play, or additional movement possible, and surprisingly, none needed.

I got in it and looked at my surroundings. The driver's seat needed to be recovered with leather, but that wasn't any big deal. Stevens Brothers could handle that with ease. They'd done a wonderful job on my '64 Lincoln, the one that burned up a few days after they'd replaced the front seat in leather in its original pattern and stitching. While all old Jaguars smell more or less the same, all old Rolls-Royces also have a distinctive fragrance, and this one smelled wonderful. Old wood and old leather. Ah! The instrument panel was burled walnut, and was in really good shape. Matching wood was everywhere it seemed, surrounding each window on the inside of the car, and beautifully scalloped sills beneath each window. This car had much more interior room than a Silver Cloud. It also had a large manually operated aluminum sun roof which was bordered by matching wood around all four sides. It had been built upon chassis WCB7 by coachbuilder Freestone & Webb, which meant that a wooden frame had been constructed for the body structure, with handmade aluminum body panels affixed.

Now familiar with my surroundings, I looked at the instruments, inserted the key, turned it, and pushed the starter button. The engine started right up, and ran smoothly. I put in 1st gear and I took off for a drive. All of the instruments appeared to be working. Everything was beautiful, that is, until I started my return trip up the hill to my office at 16th and Demonbreun. Suddenly, as I changed gears, the car would not go into gear at all, and began coasting backwards. This was my first real time out in this car so I knew nothing about it. Here I was, coasting backwards into oncoming traffic on a Friday afternoon, and picking up speed quickly. For some reason, the brakes weren't doing anything to stop, or even slow the car. There was little visibility out the small back window, and the large size of the rear C pillar roof panels further obscured my sense of where I was going. STARK TERROR! Is the only way I can describe it. Add to the existing scenario the large size of the steering wheel, the inherently loose steering anyway, and the backward motion. The car was also tall, and unwieldy. It seemed like it was about to capsize at any moment. By the grace of God, I somehow miraculously avoiding being hit, and managed to stop the car's backward motion against a tall curb.

The bastard who sold this car to me had probably trailered it to the bottom of the hill, unloaded it, and driven it the quarter mile to my office. Of course, I knew it wasn't his fault. I'm the type of person who makes quick and sometimes 'wrong' decisions, and am always willing to accept the consequences as well as responsibility for my actions. Now, I suddenly had three immediate problems; a car which I'd bought with company money, which didn't work, the probability of an expensive repair, and damage control for having made a bad decision.

Being the foolish optimist that I am, I considered my present circumstances, and decided to attempt to drive it home if I could. I restarted the engine, somehow got the car into 1st gear and headed straight home. I made it almost all of the way and then it died on Harding Place before I made it to Lynwood Blvd. I don't remember what happened, but that was it. I had a wrecker pick the car up and take it to its towing lot.

I was extremely disappointed but not dissuaded. I called Claude who'd worked at E. Gray Smith, Nashville's long term Rolls and Bentley dealer for years before retiring. E. Gray Smith had originally been the Packard dealer in Nashville and had built a beautiful building on West End in 1929, and had also been the Duesenberg, Cord, and Auburn dealership. Though the building remained, the dealership had gone the way of the aforementioned Packards, etc. At some point, probably in the early 1950s. E. Gray Smith had moved next door to Ralph Nichols, Nashville's only Cadillac dealer until the 1980s. The original 1929 building had become a women's clothing store and other things prior to becoming the Nashville home of Tower Records and ultimately being razed. Anyway, Claude would know what to do. I called him, told him who I was, and explained what had happened. He said that I should call so and so in Donelson, a Nashville suburb, mention Claude's name and that he'd said to call. I called the mechanic in Donelson, explained the situation and he said he'd be glad to take a look at it. I asked his address and told him that the car would be delivered Monday.

I called the mechanic on Monday to make sure the car had been delivered and my pal Bruce and I headed out there in the early afternoon. My confidence dropped as soon as I entered the premises. My car was in his shop and was in good, if limited company. There was a fairly new late 1970s Rolls Shadow II or Wraith over in the corner which was covered with a very thick layer of dirt and dust, indicating that it hadn't moved in a long time. "What's wrong with it?" I asked innocently. "There's something wrong with the brakes," he said. "How long has it been there?" I asked.

"It's been there about 5 years?" he sort of laughed, looking around the room, as if seeking confirmation from one of his sidekicks. "Belongs to some Jew doctor from Miamuh."

These words weren't particularly comforting under the circumstances, as one might well imagine. OK, now my car is in the hands of an ignorant, bigoted, and probably really incompetent hick in the wrong part of town. This is just really great. No, I consoled myself, Claude had recommended him. He knows what he's talking about. Surely this mechanic isn't as stupid as he looks. This will turn out alright, I thought, despite the rapidly mounting evidence to the contrary. Bruce and I left, neither of us particularly confident of the outcome.

A few days later I received a call from the mechanic, and answered the phone, hoping that the problem was just a minor adjustment of some sort with the clutch, and that I was good to go. "I've figured out what was wrong," he told me, "come on out here and I'll show you."

Nothing could have prepared me for the sight I was about to behold. My car was literally in pieces. Both front seats were out of the car, as was all of the floor. There was just a big hole where the floor had been. The transmission was missing altogether, and the floor of the garage was littered with gears, screws, and other parts which I didn't recognize. The heavy, greasy driveshaft was resting on the nice leather of the backseat and hanging beyond the window and resting on the beautiful scalloped wood ledge beneath it. Screws, gears, and other parts which should have been clearly labeled and placed in separate plastic bags lay unsorted in pools of grease on the floor of this hick infested craphouse. Jesus, could this be any worse? The damage inflicted upon my car by this moron was clearly irreparable. I was so bewildered as to be almost speechless. He showed me a gear shaft of some sort with gears which were clearly well worn, and useless. I maintained my composure, asked what I owed him, and told him that I didn't have the money to fix anything this major until I saved some money so that I could afford what it might cost to have him fix it. I thanked him and praised his obviously extensive knowledge of cars and told him to box everything up as well as he could, and that I would be out to pay him tomorrow for the destruction…er, work, he'd already done. I had no intention of letting this moron do any further damage.

Actually, I felt like tying him up, stuffing an oily rag down his throat to muffle his screams, cutting off his toes one by, one with wire cutters, and burning him alive in his `shop,' if I may use the word `shop' in relation to that dump, but I'd have to move my car out of there first, and by that time, I would've had time to consider the consequences of my actions. Generally

251

speaking, I'd basically hired a retarded monkey to disassemble a Swiss watch. I was courteous, since being of rustic descent myself, I knew that if I'd told him what I really thought about him and his limited intelligence, half of my parts would have been thrown away. At least now, he might make some minimal effort to see that the majority of the parts were gathered from the floor and tossed haphazardly into a greasy cardboard box.

His diagnosis had been correct, although medically speaking, he'd killed the patient in reaching it. I bought a copy of *Hemmings Motor News* and went to `parts and services' at the end of the Rolls-Royce cars for sale section. After a few calls to different advertisers, I ended up speaking with Tony Handler, a California based Rolls parts guy. To my surprise, he said that, yes, he did in fact have a fully rebuilt and complete gearbox for a 1948 Silver Wraith on hand. It was fully assembled and ready to go. I don't remember what it cost, but I think it was round $2,500 plus core charge and delivery cost. I gave him a credit card number and a shipping address.

Next, I called Joe Robinson at Jag Cars, Ltd., the person I should've called to begin with. He'd kept my E-Types running for several years, and there'd always been a Rolls-Royce or two around his shop, as well as some exotics from time to time. I explained what had happened, and that I had a new gearbox, fully assembled and ready to go. All he'd have to do is install it. I neglected to tell him that the entire inside of the car was in pieces, none of which were labeled, and that some few might actually be absent altogether.

Joe was a bit vexed that I hadn't called him to start with, as well he should've been. All I can say was that I panicked and reacted, rather than thinking about it. And now, it was going to cost more as a result. That is, if he would even agree to do it. I finally persuaded him to do it. $5,000 and a couple of weeks later, I was actually on the road and couldn't have been happier. I eventually had the front seats recovered in matching leather by Stevens Brothers and was good to go.

During the four and a half years I had the car, I really enjoyed it, although a couple of things happened which were rather interesting. One sunny afternoon as I was coming down the hill from Bellevue on Hwy 70, I suddenly heard a loud `whoosh' and instantly felt a change in the air pressure inside the car, and felt like I was about to be sucked through the top. What had happened is that the rather large aluminum sunroof lifted out of its housing in the roof of my car. I looked in the mirrors and saw it spinning about 15 feet up in the air behind me. It looked like Dorothy's house in `The Wizard of Oz.' It was a big piece of metal and I was fortunate that it did not land on one of the many cars in the area. I immediately pulled to the side of the road, turned off the car and sprinted back up the hill to retrieve it from where it had landed. The corners were hopelessly bent and dented, so I had Joe Robinson cut and fit a piece of Plexiglass where it had been, thus giving me a permanent moonroof.

On another occasion, I ran into one of those upright cement filled steel cylinders in front of a 7/11 store and shredded my port side front fender. I called Joe Robinson and he said that it should go to a truck body repair place since it was made of aluminum. After a couple of phone calls, I managed to find a place that repaired UPS aluminum bodied, and other trucks. I drove it over there and left it, and had it back in around two weeks, as good as new.

The Wraith's electrical system was questionable at best, not that it ever caused any problems. I still don't understand the concept of `positive earth.' For me `negative' always means ground. How can ground ever be anything but negative? The Wraith's battery was also located beneath my seat cushion. Since I'd already had a battery explode in one of my 1964 Lincoln convertibles, I always sort of wondered, given English electrics whether my cigar might not at some point, when I least expected it, ignite some errant battery fumes and launch me a la James Bond style through the roof, relieving me of my manhood and setting my hindquarters on fire in the process.

One summer Saturday night I'd made a couple of loops and then suddenly got a flat tire. Normally, a Belle Meade police officer would have come by in ten minutes or less. I wouldn't have cared one way or the other except, that the rear fender was so close to the ground with the tire flat, that I was literally unable to get the jack under the frame. There was a party going on at one of the houses nearby. I sat there in my car, not in any particular hurry, enjoying the music and the night air. Finally, after around 40 minutes, a Belle Meade cop finally came by. I really didn't mind the wait as it was a tropical night, and I knew that a cop would be by sooner or later. If I'd been speeding, one would have no doubt shown up instantly. I explained the situation, he called Hillwood Wrecker Service and somebody came over with a floor jack and I was able to put on my spare tire and drive back home.

Another time, I was starting my usual nightly drive and was on Tyne, approaching Belle Meade Blvd. For some reason the car just stopped and wouldn't go in or out of gear…again. I had the car towed to Joe Robinson's and this time it turned out to be something minor, and I was back on the road again in a day or so.

One thing I especially liked about the Wraith was that the radiator shutters opened and closed (in theory) depending upon the engine temperature. Mine no longer worked automatically, but I could open the bonnet (as they call it), and move a single lever to open or shut them as much or as little as necessary. This was an important consideration since I regularly drove it in both hot and cold weather. As tall as the radiator is, a lot of air flows into it, and the closeable vanes are a good idea, especially in winter. As far as I know, all of the first generation Wraiths had a kneeling rather than standing `Flying Lady' as it's generally called, although technically it's named `The Spirit of Ecstasy' and was designed by British artist Charles Sykes in 1911.

Young Scotty at the Helm.

A country road on a summer day.

This had been my first experience with a Rolls-Royce. Other than the initial terror involving the gearbox, it was pretty much trouble free. Actually, it was a breeze compared to an E-Type Jaguar. I'd always wanted a classic Rolls and I think the original Wraiths are among the prettiest of all.

1958 Bentley One Saturday I was on the way to Chattanooga for a weekend trip with my girlfriend at the time. We were in my red 1969 Cadillac convertible with the top down, and as usual, had taken the old road from Murfreesboro through Manchester on the way. In Manchester, we passed a rather unusual used car lot with several semi-exotic cars for sale, one of which was a 1958 Bentley S-1. It was a beautiful gold over chocolate, not my favorite color combination, but very nice nonetheless. At this time I had a really nice 1962 Lincoln convertible, a 1964 Lincoln convertible, a 1975 Cadillac Fleetwood Brougham, another 1962 Lincoln convertible, a 1948 Rolls-Royce Wraith, and a bright 1969 red Cadillac convertible. None of them needed anything, which is rare for anybody who keeps and uses old cars regularly. Actually, I had what I considered the perfect fleet, and was satisfied with what I had, but then there it was, a beautiful Bentley S-1, generally, but not always recognizable as such by its single headlights.

At a used car lot in Manchester, Tennessee

I'd always wanted a Rolls-Royce Silver Cloud, or its Bentley equivalent as long as I could remember. Nobody can paint a car like the British, and many of these right hand drive cars were literally paint over rust, sent to the US market and sold to suckers who didn't know the difference, probably in delayed revenge for their defeats during Revolutionary War and the War of 1812, but as James Brown frequently said, "Don't start none, won't be none." A sure sign that an otherwise beautiful Rolls Cloud or Bentley S series is a rust bucket, is the telltale absence of the chrome strip beneath the doors on the sills at each side. They were present here. A magnet is a good thing to have as well in determining how much of any car is actually metal, especially right hand drive cars, given the climate from which they came. Of course the doors, hood, and trunk of these cars are aluminum. A look inside the trunk is a good thing as well, as there should be no rust in or on either of the two shelves. Nor should there be any rust on the frame or cross members beneath the body.

Several years earlier, country singer Tommy Overstreet had a beautiful right hand drive S-1 which was for sale. The Bentley S-1s all had a six-cylinder engine, and while I'd have preferred to have a V-8 in theory, I liked the sixes just as well, perhaps because six-cylinder Jaguar engines were so durable, despite their dissimilarities. The Rolls-Royce /Bentley V-8 debuted in 1959 and is a wonderful engine. I also thought at the time, the two S.U. carburetors placed as they were on top of the V-8s were a little strange, given their shape when compared to carburetors used on American V-8s. Anyway, I'd told Tommy that if my mechanic, Joe Robinson, gave it his approval we'd have a deal. Overstreet drove the beautiful black and silver Bentley over to Joe's shop and dropped it off for inspection. Later in the day Joe called and said I should come over. When I arrived he asked me to look in several places around and beneath this really beautiful car. The struts which supported the front fenders were completely rusted through, and there was rust in other places as well, so I sadly decided against it.

Anyway this 1958 I looked at appeared fine as far as rust was concerned, and the paint job was beautiful. Now for the bad news. The interior had been redone in a horrible burgundy crushed velvet or velour at some point, the same as was frequently found on 1970s Lincolns when new, and would shock you nearly every time you moved in or out of the car with a big jolt of static electricity. The distinctive interior vanity mirrors on each side of the rear roof quarter were missing as well, an unacceptable omission. Why?

On the way home from Chattanooga, we stopped and I took a few pictures of it. When I was young, I'd always heard that before you can get credit, you have to already have credit, meaning in reality that people who don't want or need a loan of any kind always have the ability to get one. Translated into automotive words, this means, 'You shouldn't buy an old Rolls or Bentley if you haven't already had one.' When I returned to my office on Monday, I called the car lot, spoke with the proprietor who told me what he wanted for it, and that it ran fine. An intelligent person would, especially given my recent experience with the Wraith, have made the short drive from Nashville to Manchester and checked the car out in person. For some reason, I didn't do this. I offered to trade him my 1964 Lincoln convertible and my 1969 Cadillac convertible. I described them, he said that was fine with him, that there wasn't much of a market for Bentleys in Manchester. In the late 1980s there were no ebay, craigslist, or any other outlets like we have now. He said he'd have a truck bring the Bentley to me and take my two cars back to Manchester. The title would be delivered with the car and I'd provide titles to both of my cars to his driver.

The truth is that by now I was a little tired of Lincolns. I'd had one or more since my early twenties. I was now 37. The same for Cadillac convertibles. I'd had a bunch of them in the last 11 years. The way I looked at it was that I'd refine and reduce my fleet, an idea that seemed logical at the time. With that in mind, we concluded the deal over the phone.

On delivery day, the truck arrived and dropped the Bentley off at my office. It ran fine, but it wouldn't shift out of first gear, although park, neutral, and reverse were fine. I limped home, made a few phone calls and found out that it needed to go to some dump on Gallatin Rd. This shop didn't look like it had ever seen a Bentley before, but in a week or so, they called and said that it was ready. In the late 1980s, there were still old-timers who actually knew how to work on older cars, and these guys knew what they were doing. I had somebody drop me off over there and I drove the car home. The transmission was fixed at a cost of $1,000, and the car ran great. I was wondering why so many of these places that competently worked on foreign cars were frequently in the wrong parts of town. I knew that the transmission was a GM, and that these people came highly recommended by Joe Robinson, someone I absolutely trusted. I did not yet know then that the car had an electric motor mounted on the side of the transmission which was activated through an electrical impulse, when you moved the gear shift lever, and actually shifted the gears. This, as opposed to a mechanical linkage like a Cadillac or Lincoln or any other American car. I couldn't help but wonder why the car had an electric gear actuator. The essence of anything great mechanically, is in my estimation, its ability to accomplish its intended function as simply as possible. The easier anything can be made to work, with the minimum of moving parts, the better the design.

Like my Wraith, the Bentley also had servo operated brakes which consisted of two rods attached to a wheel on each side of the transmission, one of which went to the front brakes and one to the rear brakes both port and starboard. This, in my estimation was needlessly complex and pointless. My experience with such brakes to date was that when I pressed down on the brake pedal, the car slowed to a point, and then if I actually wanted to stop, it was necessary to let off the brake pedal and then reapply it, harder the second time. It seemed to me that Rolls-Royce had gone out of its way to make inherently simple things much more complex than actually necessary. I concluded that there were most likely three plausible reasons for this: 1. Since you can probably get from the top of England to the bottom, that is, from north to south in one day, it would be theoretically more 'interesting' to make the machinery unnecessarily complex so that car owners would have something to talk about when comparing notes. 2. To create jobs for citizens. 3. Because they could. Who knows? I considered the servo-operated brakes, electric gear actuator, and later, a high pressure leveling system tied in with the brakes to be absurd. The British have done some strange things with automotive systems, many of which were over-engineered, and quite unnecessary.

Rolls-Royce had earned its reputation through achievement however, and its six-cylinder engines had plenty of power for normal use, and neither the Rolls or the Bentley ever overheated, and their oil pressure gauges did not drop at a stop light as had been the case with all of the E-Types I'd had. The S.U. carbs of the Bentley were familiar to me, and two were easier to tune than three as on the E-Types. I drove the Bentley regularly, and it was truly trouble free.

There was still one minor problem, however. The headlights didn't work at all, and I felt a bit like Cinderella in that I had to be home before midnight, well actually, before dark. Off the car went to Jag Cars, Ltd. where for $1,500, the headlights were fixed as good as new. Joe said that he thought the car might have had some electrical fire at some point, and I wouldn't have doubted it. Perhaps that explained the absence of the inside rear quarter vanity mirrors. The original fold-out picnic tables were absent as well.

As far as drivability was concerned, the car handled well enough as soon as I replaced the tires with 'radiums' as they are known in some circles, although it still bounced around like a jeep under normal usage, much in the same way as did my Wraith. It was at this point that I made another startling discovery. The entire differential of this Bentley had been replaced with that of a mid-'70s Chevrolet Monte Carlo. Why? I'd crawled beneath the car to check for rust and found none. The rods from the brake servo were in place and functioned as designed, and the car had the correct hubcaps all the way around. The rear hubcaps, as I subsequently discovered, were fastened with screws which had been welded to the back of the hubcaps and inserted through corresponding holes which had been drilled through the wheels. In other words, they could only be removed by unscrewing them in some manner from the back of the rear wheels. Somehow this worked, but thank God I never had to change a tire.

If you're going to have anything remotely out of the ordinary from an automotive standpoint, you'd better have one hell of a mechanic. Joe Robinson was a great mechanic, and the best Jaguar, Rolls, and Bentley mechanic in Nashville at the time (1980s). There wasn't anything he couldn't fix on any Rolls, Bentley, or Jaguar. He was that good.

One day, I realized that despite the number of cars I had, I didn't actually have a convertible I could take on a road trip. I still had two remaining 1962 Lincoln convertibles, at the time, but they were really impractical, as I've mentioned. After several years, the thrill was gone, to quote BB King. As had happened with Jaguars after ten years, I'd had the experience, and it had been wonderful. I now concluded that I might have been a bit rash getting rid of my 1969 Cadillac convertible after all. I'd wanted a classic Rolls or Bentley since I was a child, and now had enjoyed the experience and was ready to move on. I subsequently used both of them in trade for a really beautiful low-mileage 1976 Cadillac Eldorado convertible (see above).

There was one funny thing which happened regarding the Bentley. One night in the snow, a girlfriend and I rounded the corner from Harding Place to Belle Meade Blvd. Immediately a siren started blasting and we were pulled over by a Belle Meade cop for speeding. Hell, I couldn't have been speeding as I'd just rounded the corner from a complete stop and hadn't had time to really accelerate. "You were speeding before you got to the light," he said. He asked me what kind of car this was. It was a 1958 Bentley but had the wrong license plate for some reason. I don't remember now why, but it had the license plate from the 1948 Wraith. If he had to ask me, I reasoned that he probably didn't know the difference between a Rolls and a Bentley anyway, so I told him it was a 1948 Rolls. He didn't know the difference, checked the registration, which matched the Rolls, gave me a ticket, and I was on my way.

The funny part occurred when I went to traffic court at the Belle Meade city hall a few weeks later. The last time I'd been there was several months earlier for speeding in a Lincoln convertible, and the courtroom was almost empty then, so I expected the same thing this time. When I opened the door, to my surprise, the place was packed. There was only one unoccupied seat remaining and I told my girlfriend to take it which she did. Other than that, it was standing room only, with people lining the walls. I took a spot standing next to a tall black woman in her mid to late thirties, about my age at the time. She was obviously very perturbed and visibly as well as audibly agitated at having to be there at all. She stood there with her arms folded, her eyes constantly rolling, and her neck moving from side to side as she commented on everything the witness and judge said, loudly exclaiming such things as "Humph! Stupid bitch! Dumb ass!" or anything else that spontaneously applied to whatever witness stood before the judge. She occasionally looked at me as if seeking confirmation of her observations.

When Judge Haywood attempted to let one Volvo-driving yuppie housewife off the hook, the witness managed to persuade him not to do so, despite his best efforts. "Stupid bitch!" the woman standing next to me shouted loudly, as the judge looked up and all eyes turned toward her. The judge had a full docket and did his best to overlook her continued interruptions and outbursts. I expected her to be held in contempt of court and literally forcibly removed from the premises at any moment. I immediately began laughing like a hyena, silently biting my tongue as tears began rolling down my cheeks as my face turned bright red and my body trembled. People noticed and began looking at both of us, me and the black woman her cursing and me looking like I as weeping.

Saved by the bell! Not really. My name was called and I approached the bench, Judge Haywood, and old family friend of my parents, read the ticket, and looked up at me. It was all I could do not to scream loudly and run out of the room myself, overcome as I was with the hysterical laughter which had totally taken possession of me. He must have thought I was nuts, but it was all I could do to merely answer yes or no. I was ordered to pay a fine and managed to escape the courtroom, and that was that. As soon as I reached the parking lot I did scream and stood there laughing loudly for several minutes before I could even get in my car.

My mother casually mentioned a couple of weeks later that she'd seen Judge Haywood somewhere and he told her I'd recently been in his courtroom, and he'd tried to let me off the hook in every way he could but that I hadn't even offered any even slightly believable reason to do so.

Rolls-Royce Silver Spurs 1984-1988

1984 Silver Spur

I remember the first time I saw a Silver Spur, the car that replaced the long running Silver Shadow series cars. I was driving my black 1948 Rolls-Royce Wraith to work one morning when I chanced to see a brand new Spur coming up behind me in my side mirror. It pulled alongside and passed me as I headed down 16th Ave. South, Music Row. I watched as it passed, taking in every inch of its incredible presence. It was the most beautiful new car I'd ever seen. At the wheel was an acquaintance in the same business as myself. I caught him when we both stopped at the traffic light, and waved. Yes, my car was elegant with a handmade aluminum coachbuilt body, but his was new, fast, and powerful with a fuel injected V-8 and dual exhausts. From that moment forward I lusted after a Silver Spur, or its shorter wheelbase sister, the Silver Spirit. Before we look at these cars, it's necessary to examine their direct predecessors, the Rolls-Royce Silver Shadow, and its sister, the Bentley T-Series which had been designed to replace the long running Rolls Silver Cloud and Bentley S cars.

So, as the Germans like to phrase it, how would the Silver Shadow answer the question of "What should a new Rolls-Royce be for the (at the time) modern era?" First and foremost, it should be immediately recognizable as a Rolls-Royce. This was indeed a very tall order because when most people think of Rolls-Royce, the Silver Cloud still comes to mind, even now. A new Rolls or Bentley must also live up to the company's reputation as being the ultimate luxury car. It must also be `better' than any existing car, as well as any car likely to be produced by any other manufacturer in the foreseeable future, and its design must remain contemporary for at least a decade, and hopefully longer. Also, the car must be palatable to the U.S. market, which would be its biggest potential customer base. All of this was a lot to expect from what in automotive manufacturing circles, was a small company when compared to the U.S. `Big Three.' It should be remembered that during this time American cars that cars like Cadillacs, for example, were routinely completely re-bodied every two years.

At this time, cars were not designed using computers as they are now, and the development of any entirely new car from scratch, was a time consuming and expensive proposition. The first thing is the formulation of a project book, establishing the concept of what the new car has to be in terms of its intended its purpose, what it should cost to build and what its cost will be to the customer. This of course, depends on first determining where it should fit within the worldwide automotive market in general. What should it look like? How long, wide, and tall? What is the desired weight? The list is truly endless.

The exterior design of the era involved multiple design drawings submitted by various members of a design team, the construction and consideration of different scale models, and full-size clay models, before settling on a final exterior design. At the same time these designs are being worked out, it must be remembered all had to be considered within the context of various and often differing government regulations, some of which were subject to change (often without notice), by various government entities, especially within the U.S., the world's largest market. At the same time as exterior considerations are being worked out, other aspects of a car are being designed. Steering wheel, armrests, door panel facings, front and rear seats, instrument placement and layout, all of which must be made to fit within the final exterior. At some point working prototypes were produced and tested, often resulting in subsequent minor and even major changes.

Since Rolls-Royce and Bentley's have always been considered to be `expensive,' by the public in general, it is usually assumed that the company which manufactured them must be `rich.' The fact that these cars exist for a relatively small market means that the expense of design and retooling cannot be absorbed across a wide range of cars, trucks, and other commercial vehicles, which in total, sell millions of units annually, as with the U.S. Big Three.

The Shadows were indeed revolutionary cars for Rolls-Royce in a number of ways. For the first time, a standard production Rolls-Royce and Bentley were built with a monocoque, or unibody, meaning that there was no longer a body bolted to an underlying frame as had been the case with every previous car. Instead there was just a body with two subframes, one containing engine, transmission, and suspension at the front, and the other consisting of differential and aft suspension components at the rear. Also gone were the servo-operated brakes of the Silver Clouds, replaced with four-wheel disc brakes, the first ever for Rolls-Royce. In addition to these radical modernizations, there was a pressurized braking system combined with an automatic leveling system (which I shall mention later), and most importantly, for me at least, a multi-link fully independent rear suspension. Not only were the Shadows advanced for Rolls-Royce, they were advanced, period.

The development of the Silver Shadows, in addition, included convertibles and coupes for both brands which included essentially the same running gear as the sedans. The perhaps questionable tradition of basically sticking a Bentley grill on an otherwise Rolls-Royce body, which started with the Silver Dawn, had been done with the Silver Cloud and Bentley S Series, as well, and

was continued with the new Shadows and Bentley Ts. In time the Shadow-based convertible would be dubbed the Corniche. There was also a Corniche two-door coupe. The long-standing Bentley `Continental' name was soon resurrected yet again, and applied to the otherwise Corniche named convertible for Bentley. The Silver Spirit and Spur debuted as 1980 models in the U.S. and were both lower in profile and more fluid in appearance than their immediate predecessors, the Silver Shadows (1966-1979). Development of the new cars evolved as design progressed into a short wheelbase Spirit, and a longer wheelbase Spur. Both were powered by the same engine as their predecessors, basically an updated version of the Rolls-Royce V-8 which debuted in 1959. While the Silver Shadows and later, Wraiths were carbureted, the new range of cars destined for the US were fitted with Bosch fuel injection. They were essentially a re-bodied Silver Shadow, but with a much different outside appearance.

By 2007 used Spurs and Spirits were in the $25,000-$30,000 range with some priced higher and some lower. I determined that the time had come to get one, and that I would find the best one that I could find. The best place to start was on ebay, which I watched for several weeks until I found a couple of cars I could be happy with. For some reason, ebay would not let me bid in excess of $15,000 without my having to provide a bunch of additional information, which I was not inclined to do since my first ebay account had been hacked earlier. I was willing to buy the car through ebay, but didn't want to fool with all of that. I contacted the seller, a St. Louis dealer, directly, and agreed to their `buy it now' price of $20,000.

My banker at US Bank had been there for years and handled everything for me at no charge. The money was transferred, I received the title in the mail, and the car arrived one night, and was as described. Some people would think I was reckless at this point, if not downright stupid, in buying any car sight unseen, over the phone, and without the possible potential protection of ebay, especially in light of my previous experiences with the Wraith, which I'd seen and driven once at night; the Bentley, which I'd seen but not driven; and the 1970 Olds 442 convertible, which I hadn't seen or driven at all, but it turned out alright. The car was indeed as described.

On the night the car arrived, I met the car hauler a half mile away at a spot where he could unload it easily, which he did. Although it was dark, I thought that I should at least take it for a spin. It started right up, ran smoothly and quietly, and had plenty of power. I didn't take it too far in the event that it might catch on fire, (always a possibility with any British-made car), since I hadn't thought to bring an extinguisher, a flashlight, or any tools.

It took me a while to get used to the Spur since it was completely different from the `48 Wraith and the `58 Bentley. In the first place, it felt solid, and heavy, more like a Lincoln convertible than anything else. It also rode less like a truck than my first Rolls and Bentley, and it handled better, especially in corners. It was a bit strange knowing that the car literally had no brakes until the system was fully pressurized. What was stranger still was that the automatic leveling system and the brakes had been designed to work together. In other words, if a leak develops, or a loss of pressure anywhere in the levelling system, the brakes are compromised, not a good design in a car that weighs nearly three tons. It often seems that British engineers intentionally design what are routine automotive components in such a way that they are much more prone to failure, due to unnecessary complexity. The mechanical servo-brakes of the earlier Rolls and Bentleys were unnecessary, if not pointlessly complex. The 'evolution' of the braking systems with the subsequent Shadows and Spurs respectively, were even more complex and unnecessary. Large American cars and trucks had been easily stopped by so-called 'power brakes' since the 1950s, and possibly even earlier, and, for the most part worked fine. The arrival of disc brakes on large American cars, beginning with front wheels only for Cadillac in 1968 (and possibly others), brought braking systems fully into the modern era until the advent of antilock brakes.

I bought this car basically because I liked the way it looked, I mean specifically, the Spur and the Spirit, as opposed to the Silver Shadow. I knew that it had a V-8 which had been introduced in 1959. I also knew that it had a Bosch fuel injection system fairly similar to those found on earlier Porsche 928s and some Mercedes S and SL Class cars. I considered it to be a modern car technically, in that by now it probably didn't have servo-assisted brakes. I also knew that it had a fully independent rear suspension, as did its immediate predecessor the Silver Shadow. I assumed that it was both fast and cornered well. There were specific features I wanted on whatever Rolls I bought, including the flat European headlights, which had, for the US market at least, been fitted with a set of twin rectangular headlight clusters, identical in appearance to those used on Cadillacs beginning in 1975. While they looked good on a '76 Fleetwood, they didn't look as nice on a Rolls-Royce. I also wanted a dual exhaust system. Apart from that, I assumed that all of the Spirits and Spurs were pretty much the same beneath the skin, except that the Spirit had a shorter wheelbase, which probably meant that it handled slightly better.

I must take a moment to say something about the Silver Shadow (1966-1979), which replaced the classic Silver Clouds and Bentleys. Shadows weren't common in Nashville during their lengthy run although, there were a few around. I did see them from time to time in south Florida and found them interesting visually, but not attractive in the sense that the Silver Clouds were. I'd been managing late country singer Ray Price, who'd bought two new late model Silver Shadows in Dallas when the long wheel base models known as the `Wraiths' made their appearance later in their run. He didn't think very much of them, and told me that his wife had been subjected to complete brake failure one day without notice, and only by the grace of God, had managed to safely stop the car. He preferred his late 1970s Mercedes 450 SEL which had logged 285,000 miles and was still running fine, and only drove his Wraith when he had to. It has been my observation that the people I know who own, or have owned these cars, never use them as their daily driver. I think, and this is just my opinion, that most of them liked the idea of having one, more than the actuality involved. I think that most Rolls-Royce buyers, of any new or vintage vehicle like the impression ownership conveys, about themselves to themselves, as much as it does to others. Rolls-Royce and Bentleys will never be merely used cars, especially Rolls-Royces, given their relative rarity.

As regards my first Spur, I bought it in November, 2007 and still have it. It had its original plug wires when I bought it, which I replaced with a new set when I replaced the spark plugs. Needless to say, I replaced a couple of wires incorrectly and had to have Wurster's in Franklin fix things. The windows are temperamental and may or not work, depending on their mood sometimes. I had new tires put on the year before last. It ran hot and the electric fan in front of the radiator are thermostatically operated. I replaced the thermostat and bypassed the switch at the top of the housing altogether, connecting a 10 amp Mercedes fuse to the two wires, which solved the problem. As a rule, I prefer a manual electric fan switch over a thermostatically operated one. I always have several bottles of hydraulic mineral oil for the brakes on board in case the panel lights come on. As foolish as I think this system is, it has really been trouble free. The car slowly lifts at the rear, the panel lights go out and I'm good to go. The rear end stays up for a couple of weeks even if I don't drive it that often. Be that as it may, I don't tailgate anybody, making sure to leave plenty of distance for stopping.

My alternator belt recently broke. Nick Box at the parts department of the Rolls dealer, Carlock, in Franklin, said that there were two different alternators used on the Spur for the 1984 model year, unfortunately, the alternator on my car was not one of them, but rather a Delco-Remy. Since this engine had been used on the Spirits & Spurs, one would think that the decision to use a particular alternator would have been reached during the extensive development of the prototypes. Strangely, Rolls-Royce frequently made minor changes during the middle of an annual production run rather than logically incorporate them beginning with the next model year. For this and other reasons, anytime parts are needed, the vehicle identification number is required by the dealer's parts department.

I'm on my 14th year of ownership of this car and still enjoy driving it. Believe it or not I haven't had any real problems with anything other than the windows occasionally sticking, and some overheating which required a new fan clutch. The braking system has some leaks but stays pressurized for more the most part. I do check the brake fluid level before every drive, and top it up if necessary, as well as the oil level.

1985 Silver Spur

Dead at 16,000 miles!

Once again, I was looking through the cars for sale section of Nashville craigslist, and there was a Rolls-Royce Silver Spur for sale. It was listed as is `for parts or restore.' It looked all right, at least it warranted a closer look, and I could probably afford it. I drove to nearby Franklin, Tennessee and met the car's owner at some sort of multi-unit dwelling behind which the car was located. The car hadn't been moved in a couple of years, I was told. Apparently the car was given to my host in exchange for some construction work in Florida a few years earlier. It hadn't been running when he got it and he and his son got the engine to turn over but couldn't get it to start due to some electrical issues. In other words, as they say, `it ain't gettin' no fire.' Their apparent solution to this problem was to begin disassembling anything that could be unscrewed, who knows why? I imagined I could probably either fix it myself, or if worse came to worse, send it to Alex in Nashville, since he can literally fix anything on any car. I had shop manuals, wiring diagrams, etc. It would be fun to fool with and I could increase my knowledge of my current favorite car.

I agreed to his price, called Hillwood Wrecker Service, and had a wrecker follow me to the car where I paid the owner, received a title, and was on my way. A couple of days later I actually started looking at it. The trunk had been left open for about an inch for no telling how long, and the trunk key was missing, although I had the ignition key. There was a small bit of unnecessary rust in the center of the trunk floor but everything else was ok. The first thing I had to do before I could continue any further was to give the car a thorough cleaning, I removed everything from the trunk, the wet and dry-rotted carpet panels lining the floor, and inner wall panels of the trunk. I washed the car thoroughly and before long, it was quite presentable.

With the car cleaned inside and out I could finally fully assess the situation. The first thing to do was to stop the intrusion of water. Since the trunk was unlocked and partially open, I was able to disassemble the locking mechanism, clean and lubricate it, and then reinstall it, after which, I was able to fully open and close the trunk as designed. I'd never fooled with a Rolls trunk mechanism but it was fairly intuitively designed. I was surprised that the owner and his son hadn't fixed that to start with.

A closer inspection of the car showed the full extent of the abuse which had been inflicted on this nice car. Among the pointless indignities it had suffered in the hands of nincompoops were the following: Someone had removed the radiator shell, apparently to have a look at the two electric cooling fans. But being too stupid to unscrew it, somebody first tried unsuccessfully to pry it off the body at each side, thus damaging both sides. Eventually they found the screws behind it and removed the grill. They then removed one of the nuts holding the fan blade in place on one of the two fans. Then they replaced the radiator shell without replacing the nut on the fan blade. Why? Next, they removed the distributer cap with wires attached, and then just set it back on top of the distributor. Somebody had opened the door to the fuse panel, located just beneath the glove compartment door to see what they could see. "Man, look at all them wires. We're gonna hafta unhook the mounting bracket so as we can see what's behind that." So they removed the fuse panel and left it hanging with the fuse panel door fully opened. There might be some more wires inside that panel underneath the steering column. "Let's get after them too." And even though the courtesy light on the outside edge of the driver's door had nothing to do with starting the car, someone decided to pop it out of its housing, cut some wires and then stick it back where it goes. But why stop there? Inside the engine compartment against the starboard firewall they'd unscrewed the relay panel, I guess, `just for the halibut,' as they say in New England. Several hoses of garden size dimeter had been removed from one place or another, reconnected elsewhere, and covered with aluminum foil. There was absolutely no reason to leave the `battry' unmolested, so somebody had disconnected and removed the battery shut-off switch from its secure mounting on the starboard edge of the rear firewall, and disconnected and disposed of the ground wire altogether. The list of offenses continued.

In spite of the abuse and neglect this car had suffered there was an original reading of 16,000 miles on the odometer. Surprisingly the grey leather seats, door panels and headrests and headliner were in very good condition, as was the body, except for the minimal surface rust in the trunk. As much as I'd have liked to get this car going, my hopes eventually faded and I knew that my mechanic was really too busy to fool with it. He'd kept one of my 450 SLs for 14 months before even looking at it, and subsequently fixing whatever had been wrong with it in a couple of days. A beautiful black Spur sat there a year before he got around to fixing it. This is what happens with great mechanics. After they get a reputation, everybody wants to use them, and ultimately they become like every other high end auto mechanic. They have more work than they can handle. In his defense, if there is a problem with one of the cars I actually use on a regular basis, he will fix it immediately if I need it. He is a great mechanic and can literally fix anything having to do with any of the cars I have. He's that good, but if the Rolls was going to sit at his place for a year, it might as well sit in my driveway as a sculpture which I could at least enjoy viewing in passing. I kept it clean and polished awaiting that time when he would tell me to send it over. In Nashville or anywhere else, any car you may have is only as good as your mechanic.

I kept this car, basically as a sculpture and enjoyed looking at it, but when I found another one on Nashville craigslist, as I shall relate, I decided to let this one go. Believe it or not, the 1985 is classed in its own category by the Rolls-Royce Owners Club due to a number of reasons. Although it looks pretty much the same externally as any other Silver Spur or Spirit, there are a number of so-called 'improvements' to be found within the engine compartment and elsewhere. When I found another, later Silver Spur (1987) on Nashville's Craigslist, I decided it was time to send this one on its way, which I did. I kept the radiator shell and the flat European market headlights, as well as the two rear seat headrests and sold it to somebody on ebay, nobody near Tennessee, of course, but somebody in northern Michigan.

In the meantime, I bought the 1987 Spur sight unseen over the phone from somebody in Waynesboro, Tennessee. I sent him a deposit and he agreed to bring the car to me in Centerville at which time I'd pay him the balance in cash. This bought me several weeks of needed time for me to dispose of the black 1985, which to me, as I mentioned had now become a lost cause. I would have kept it as a parts car, but there were too many cars at my girlfriend's house already. She'd been understandably bitching about the black one sitting in the driveway for the past several months with increasing frequency. One day she told me she wanted it gone. "Funny you should mention that," I said, "because I've sold it on ebay and have bought another one which is truly beautiful." She had her reservations about that, but at least the black one would be gone.

I wanted the black one gone, and the new one delivered a day or two later. Of course it didn't turn out to be the seamless transition I'd hoped for, but then it seldom does. That would have been too easy. It took a couple of weeks before the buyer in Michigan found someone to pick it up in Tennessee and take it to northern Michigan. He already had a Spur so he was familiar with them. He didn't know whether he'd get mine running or use it for parts. He understood the car wasn't running and therefore would have to be winched onto a flatbed hauler. Additionally, the car had no brakes as the system has to be pressurized for the brakes to function at all. Also, the car weighs nearly three tons. I instructed him to make sure that whoever was picking it up fully understood these issues. The transport company was sending 'someone from Atlanta' I was told, and on that glorious day a foreigner showed up not in an over the road hauler with a flatbed, but instead with the same type of trailer a lawn service uses to carry a couple of riding lawnmowers.

We didn't like each other instantly. First of all there was the fact that he'd arrived totally unprepared. I'd spoken with the dispatcher several times and reiterated what equipment would be necessary. Then there was the language barrier. He could barely speak English. I don't know whether he was an Arab, a Russian, or whatever. Then there was the fact that he was mad at me that he wasn't prepared. He wanted me to turn the car around so that it could be driven onto his lawnmower trailer. When I told him that the car didn't run and that the dispatcher knew that, he said that `I'd need' to call a wrecker and have him turn the car around. By this time he should've had the car loaded and gone. I looked him straight in the eyes and said "I don't need to do shit. I didn't hire you and it isn't my problem. I didn't hire you and I'm not going to hire a wrecker. And I don't want to waste anymore time fooling with this. If you want to call a wrecker, it's your business." It was simple enough, in theory at least. He could back up his lawnmower trailer and use its winch to pull the car onto it. But of course, his winch didn't work. The situation was going from bad to worse. He was yelling angrily back and forth in Russian, or whatever, on his cell phone. I felt sorry for him, but I was angrier than I was sorry. I decided that I'd remove myself from the situation before it escalated, which was a definite possibility, given his belligerence and my sometimes volatile nature. I called the buyer and told him what happened and said I was going to dinner and when I got back I was going to have the car towed to a friend's place of business so that I didn't have to fool with it. I gave him the address where the car would be so he'd could inform whoever he'd made his arrangements with.

When we returned from dinner the man and his trailer were gone. I surmised that he'd correctly realized that he'd be unable to get that large three-ton car on that flimsy trailer, and had returned whence he came. I had the car towed to my friend's asphalt parking lot and that was that. The next morning I went over to check on the car, thinking that the dispatcher would have sent somebody with the proper equipment. The car was still there. As I looked at it, the driver and his trailer went flying by and he didn't even look in my direction. Perhaps he hadn't seen the car. I followed him to the top of the road to the Shell station, told him where the car was, and left. A few days later, the car was gone, and that was that.

And while on the subject of rotting Rolls-Royces, believe it or not, in a place as remote as Waverly, Tennessee, there is a burgundy 1974 Silver Shadow sinking into the driveway at a body shop there. When I first saw it several years ago, it was really beautiful. In the interim, it hasn't been moved or covered, a couple of the tires are now flat, and that nice leather has no doubt baked to a crisp. The man who owns the body shop said that he had the title in the drawer and that somebody had given the car to him. It ran, and drove to its likely demise under its own power. The man said that the car still runs fine, but I doubt that now. I would try to buy it from him, but to what end? And of course, "It's not for sale." I really have too many cars, finally. Still, its fate is similar to that of so many other cars throughout the world. One day the owner stops driving it for whatever reason, then the battery runs down. Then the gas putrefies. "I ought to get around to fixing it," but he never does. One day, it really is too late. In this instance, perhaps it's just a case of he doesn't want it, but he doesn't want anyone else to have it.

1987 Silver Spur

Almost as soon as the black car disappeared I had the royal blue 1987 Spur delivered. The man who'd sold it to me had done so for his employer. He'd charged me $250 to bring it to me from Waynesboro. I'd bought it sight unseen, as I said. My intuition is usually right, as it was in this case. Basically I'd sold the 1985 for $700 less than I paid for the 1988 and had picked up a $1000 pair of Euro headlights, a radiator shell, mascot, and a pair of leather rear seat headrests in the bargain.

I was pleased with my new purchase even though it didn't run, had a shredded vinyl top, and no keys. The few pictures he'd posted on Craigslist told me pretty much everything I needed to know. If it ran I'd be very happy. If it didn't, I could have it fixed or use it as a parts car for my `88 Spur. It had been transported and delivered at night to my friend's woodshop on what turned out to be one of the rainiest nights of the year. The trailer had a flat tire on the way here. The two guys who brought it had the title, a proper bill of sale, and the owner's manual and a couple of extra parts in the trunk, as well as the hubcaps which they'd placed there as well. I paid them, thanked them profusely, and sent them on their way.

The next morning the rain had cleared and I was over there bright and early to look at my new purchase. The beautiful tan leather with blue piping was almost as new without any visible wear, or cracks anywhere. The matching wood veneer was highly polished without any fading, peeling, or cracks. It literally looked brand new. The same for the door panels, the carpeting, and inside the trunk. The jack, spare, and original tool box were where they should be and undisturbed. The engine compartment was spotless and original, with everything in place. I immediately had it towed to the driveway. Now, all I needed were keys. I had a locksmith come over who was able to make me a door key but was unable to make an ignition key. At this point I called Nick Box, one of the parts guys at Carlock, the fairly new (at the time) Nashville Rolls dealer in Cool Springs (Franklin). I explained my dilemma, he did some research and said that he could order the correct keys from Bentley using the VIN, which I gave him over the phone. In the meantime, I'd bought some additional key blanks off ebay. When the keys arrived I drove to Cool Springs and picked them up. They worked perfectly. I soon changed the sparkplugs, distributor cap, and rotor and installed a new battery. The car turned over but wouldn't start. This was a good sign, not that it didn't start, but that the engine wasn't locked up.

I'd hoped Alex in Nashville would be able to take the car and fix whatever was wrong with it, but he still had a 450 SL there and said for me to let him finish with it first. In the meantime, my pal, songwriter Larry Weiss introduced me to David Blanks, his mechanic who, upon occasion, made house calls. He came all the way out to the house after work one night and literally had the Rolls running in less than ten minutes. "So we know it runs," he said but it's going to need a fuel filter, accumulator, and new fuel pump, which I ordered on the internet.

1988 Silver Spur

I already had a 1984 and a 1987 Rolls Spur, but checking Nashville Craigslist one day, there was a 1988 for sale. From the picture on craigslist it appeared that there was no vinyl top, a rarity if the car had been made that way. I personally dislike vinyl tops as they are breeding grounds for rust and they additionally interrupt the otherwise fluid lines of these cars. Although I've seen so-called Everflex tops applied to the shorter wheelbase Spirits, they are a rarity, and were only applied as an option to the Spirits while, as far as I know, they were standard on Spurs. There are many instances where the Everflex vinyl top has been removed after rotting, and the roof has been subsequently painted, usually to match the rest of the car. Vinyl, or `Everflex' as it is known in RR circles was liberally applied to Rolls-Royce cars beginning in earnest with the late Silver Shadows, and long wheelbase Wraiths, and continuing through the Spurs, and in some cases beyond. The idea has legitimate historical antecedents in early enclosed formal cars which often had leather tops applied to give them a more sedate appearance. By 1966 in the US vinyl tops were being regularly applied on everything from Cadillacs to Chevrolet Novas. These vinyl tops made sporty cars appear sportier and formal cars more distinguished. By the mid-1970s some car manufacturers were even padding them as on some Lincoln Town Cars and on the Cadillac Fleetwood Talisman. It was an amusing practice at first, but Rolls-Royce continued affixing these tops long beyond their fashionable period. Today, they are archaic, and troublesome in that they are rust magnets for any car that is or has been regularly left outside. Even cars which have never had anything but dry storage were often victims of rust at the bottom of the C pillar, usually because they were garaged after being regularly washed and then put back before the trim had thoroughly dried.

These days, vinyl tops are often removed, usually when they have become weathered. Removing a vinyl top, sanding away the residue and painting it does not necessarily cure the problem because the front and rear windshields were applied over the edges of the vinyl. Technically, the windshields should be removed, resealed and reinserted, otherwise water will sooner or later leak into the windshield as the remaining vinyl surrounding the front and rear windshields degrades. In comparing original cars equipped with vinyl to ones where the vinyl has been removed it's easy to see the differences between the windshield seals of each.

Excuse the detour. Anyway, there's always a way to do what you want to do, and if you haven't done so, it just means that you haven't figured out the way to do it yet. I met the `88 Spur's owner in Nashville near Vanderbilt University and took it for a drive. It ran well, didn't run especially hot, although it ran hotter than I would like, as did my 1984 at first. The car was found in the current owner's grandfather's garage after his demise, given a new battery, a new set of Michigans (Michelins) and was good to go. The money would be divided by the three grandchildren and he'd been empowered to sell it by the other two. He wanted to get rid of it as quickly as possible before something expensive went wrong, which in his studied estimation was just a matter of time. After my drive I decided I wanted the car, but I needed to get rid of something, specifically another car. I'd need to do it fairly quickly, before something else arrived. My girlfriend had, once again, understandably reached her limit.

To make a long story short when the transaction had been concluded, it was truly a deal out of Lil' Abner. The most expendable car from my fleet was my 1980 Mercedes 450 SL, since I still had another 450 SL. He'd always wanted one, drove mine, and liked it. I traded him that, a set of American Racing wheels which had been on the 1975 450 SL when I got it, several thousand dollars in cash, a Series 80 stainless 1911 Colt .45, and a cedar doghouse. I still have the Rolls several years later, and he still had my 450 SL until a year or so ago at which time he was rammed by an inattentive motorist after just having the entire front suspension and bushings replaced (see below).

As far as Rolls-Royce and Bentleys are concerned, I'd probably like to have a Bentley S-1. S-2, or S-3, a better one than the `58 S-1 I'd had the first time, more than thirty years ago. Both the six-cylinder and V-8 engines are fine with me. I also like the Bentley Azures, the recent Phantom VIIs, and the late Phantom Drophead. I'm not a fan of the revised radiator shells and consider their defacement on the current Wraiths, Ghosts, and recent Phantom

Dropheads, to be a real sacrilege as well as a disfigurement. The Phantom grill, at least, and as yet, hasn't been ruined by good intentions, and still befits the majesty of the Phantom sedan and short-lived Phantom Coupe, a courtesy which should have been equally extended to the Phantom Drophead. I think overall that the 2003 forward Phantoms are magnificent. They are unapologetically large cars, as they should be, and having driven one, can say that they are really wonderful. I do think that the current manufacturers of Rolls-Royce should finally stop recycling the names Wraith, Dawn, and Ghost, and come up with something new. For some reason, however, I think the title Phantom is a fitting continuation of its lineage as the top of the line.

Longtime friend Richard `Cadillac' Jett, beside his current Cadillac. He's also owned a Sedan DeVille D' Elegance, and a 1976 Talisman, and a beautiful `59 Chevrolet Impala coupe, among others.

My first company car, a `74 Fleetwood Talisman. Bard Selden at right. He still has his nearly fifty years later.

XVII.

1961-1963 Ramblers

1961 Rambler American

One spring afternoon in 1986 either myself or Bruce Shelton, who worked at my office, saw an ad in the paper or *Traders Post,* advertising two 1960s Rambler convertibles. Both were located at a residence on Hwy 96 in Franklin, thirty miles or so from Nashville. We made a phone call, and out we went. One was light blue with an automatic transmission. The other one was white, and better looking, but it had a column mounted manual transmission. Both had black convertible tops, and both had bodies which were in good shape with no dents or scrapes, and rust free. Our longtime friend Bard Selden from Hollywood, Mississippi had owned one of these cars for years, also a convertible, which he still has. In truth, if I wasn't well familiar with his, and hadn't regularly ridden to Boy Scout meetings in one, it wouldn't have been a car that would have appealed to me, not that I didn't find it interesting, just that I had other automotive priorities. But…here it was, I was president of the company, and we could afford them. I told the owner I'd call him the next day and let him know. I don't remember whether or not we took them for a test drive or not, though we probably did.

By the time we got back to the office, Bruce had talked me into buying one and letting 'the company' loan him the money to buy the other one. I'd already loaned him the money to buy a baby blue 1976 Fleetwood Talisman previously and he'd paid it back. I would have preferred to have the white one but didn't want to fool a column shifter. That suited him as he wanted the white one anyway. When we got back to the office, I called my benefactor Sherwood Cryer, who owned the famous Gilley's Club in Pasadena, Texas along with managing country singer Mickey Gilley, and asked him if I could buy the car. That was fine with him, so the next day we had somebody take us to Franklin and we drove both cars back to the office.

Bruce immediately went to work 'customizing' his car, attaching multiple curb feelers which looked like insect antennae, to all four corners of his car. The crown achievement of his 'improvements' was a transparent orange bug deflector with a propeller attached to its front, which he somehow affixed to the hood. One of us had found several new ones left over from the 1950s at the flea market. They were new in the box. As he drove, the propeller turned rapidly, slicing hapless insects into pieces and deflecting them from the windshield. With Bruce's brightly colored, and sometimes contrasting clothes augmented upon occasion, by multicolored shoes, he made quite a fashion

statement, although I'm not certain what it said.

My car was bland by contrast, and quite nondescript. Moreover, it had what I considered to be a strange front suspension, in that I was used to driving cars which were long, low and rakish, despite what in some cases, was their massive size. This car resembled a refrigerator, generally speaking, and felt like it was likely to overturn if I rounded a corner too quickly. Jeff Nunnally (AKA the Earl of Knuttsford), who also worked at In Concert, was so inspired by our cars and Bruce's colorful attire in particular, that he soon bought a 1959 Rambler sedan, which became his trademark. I kept mine for a couple of years and traded it to a friend of mine, but I must say, sometimes, I sort of miss it. As I look at pictures of these `61 and `62 Rambler convertibles now, I consider them to be both attractive and distinctive. In a perfect world, I'd still have one. In the meantime, if I want to ride in one or drive one, my friend Bard Selden still has his. In retrospect, my Rambler was a really wonderful experience, but at the time, I other convertibles which were larger and much faster.

Workmate Bruce Shelton and his Rambler. An arbiter of fashion, after a fashion. From the front the car sort of resembled a catfish.

At some point, Bruce bought this really exotic Studebaker Hawk GT with a supercharger. It was in wonderful shape with black bucket seats, but rattled like hell every time it hit any kind of bump, and I didn't think the build quality was that good. Still, it was a beautiful and exotic looking car. He didn't keep it long.

Coworker Jeff Nunnally, inspired by Bruce and me, sought out and found a 1959 which became his trademark for several years.

Jeff Nunnally, AKA, The Earl of Knuttsford, Kingston, Jamaica, is one suave...shut your mouth!

XVIII.

Porsche 928s

By the time the Porsche 928 debuted in 1977, I could have probably arranged a loan, but didn't want to put myself in that much debt for a car that I found interesting, but wasn't `in love' with. There were still too many cars I was in love with and enjoying at the time, specifically Lincoln and Cadillac convertibles, and E-Type Jaguars. But I, like every sports car enthusiast had read about the new front-engine Porsche 928, and how it was going to be the new flagship of the Porsche fleet, and represented the new direction of Porsche in general, that is away from rear-engine cars.

I'd never really gotten the Porsche thing anyway. The early ones looked to me an awful lot like prehistoric trilobites. Compared to Jaguars of the era, they were primitive (and ugly), and there was always the subconscious knowledge that a 356 Porsche was really a glorified VW, which it was. I've discussed the imbalance of a rear engine located behind the rear axle elsewhere, and need not repeat it here. Be that as it may, the racing successes of Porsche with rear engine cars could not be dismissed, but the 928 was something else entirely, and bore no relation visually, at least from any production Porsche predecessor. Above all, the 928 was the first Porsche finally free at last from the stigma of an all too obvious VW lineage.

The 928 was created as the Germans say, as 'an answer' to the question what should, and must be the future of a new sports car? I say must, because under the Carter administration's Draconian and constantly shifting safety and environmental regulations, Porsche, like other manufacturers, particularly those outside of America, had no idea what silly restrictions might be next. The EPA was not formed under Carter, as many believe, but was in fact a product of the Nixon administration. Carter, however, always the master of good intentions, was the first to really weaponize the EPA. He didn't like convertibles, noisy cars, air-cooled engines, and fast cars, speed or personal freedoms. He was concerned with air pollution (as we should all be), and after the so-called energy crisis, he wanted to 'save energy.'

What all of this meant for Porsche in particular, which, unlike most auto manufacturers, made only sports cars at the time, was that they'd better come up with something which could survive any and all future regulatory restrictions which did, would, or even might originate from the U.S., their largest market. It was doubtful that the Carter administration would attack the traditional front-engine, rear wheel drive platform, since that was the established formula for all American cars. A car with a noisy air-cooled rear engine, like the 911, was likely not to 'pass mustard' as they sometimes jokingly say in the military. Given Carter's well-known safety concerns about convertibles any new car from Porsche would of necessity be a closed car, a two-door coupe. The truth of the matter is that sports cars as they'd existed since their inception were on the way out. To this end, the 928 was the answer for Porsche. In the meantime, The 911 was still selling well, so while what would become the 928 was being developed, the 911 could still be sold, at least until it was regulated out of existence.

We may look briefly at the highly successful 914 and 924 elsewhere, but let it suffice to say that the new 928 would indeed, for a time, become the flagship for Porsche. It would replace the 911 as the top of the line. To that end everything was on the table for the Porsche engineers and designers. While much was considered, given the constantly shifting regulations and the high cost of creating a new car from scratch, whatever the 928 would ultimately be, it needed to remain in production for a long time in order to pay for itself. It was determined that front engine, rear wheel drive would be its layout. Instead of the transmission being affixed to the rear of its V-8 engine as is customarily done with front engine cars, the transmission would be placed at the rear of the car just ahead of the differential. There would be a driveshaft but it would not be the standard driveshaft with a universal joint at each end. Instead, the driveshaft would be housed within a rigid hollow tube which was bolted to the rear of the engine and the front of the transmission. As radical as this design seems at first glance, it was not a first. In fact, the Pontiac Tempest of 1961 had the same layout, nor was it the first either. It was interesting in that it formed a rigid and complete unit which was suspended beneath the monocoque body shell. Why would anybody do this? Well there are several advantages, the most significant of which is weight distribution. With the added weight at the rear of the car, rather than at the front, an almost 50/50 front to rear weight distribution was achieved, providing better balance, cornering, and road handling in general. The 928 also had an aluminum hood, front fenders, and doors. All of this was very interesting to me technologically, even though I had no intention of buying any new car during its first year of manufacture, before any potential bugs were discovered and corrected. The book `Project 928' was published almost concurrently with the release of the car and detailed the exhaustive development and testing involved in the creation of the 928.

1979 928 Euro

At some point I finally bought one, a 1979. Well, actually, I bought two of them, one of which was wrecked but all there, and one which no longer ran, although its owner allegedly didn't know why. As I recollect, they were cheap enough and would provide me an opportunity to see if I wanted to buy a really nice one. I'd followed this same policy with my first giant Lincoln Town Car, a 1979, which I'd bought and liked before getting a couple of really nice ones subsequently.

I had both cars towed to my house. As soon as they arrived I placed a fully charged battery in the one that didn't run. To my surprise, and having never had this happen before, when I connected the two battery cables to their respective terminals the battery became really hot very fast. It wasn't actually smoking, but given the inherently explosive nature of batteries in general, I didn't intend to wait around and see what might happen next. With that in mind I disconnected both cables as quickly as possible. Perhaps I'd inadvertently corrected the cables to the wrong terminals. No, I checked them and they'd been correctly connected.

I had the car towed to some Porsche repair place downtown which had been recommended to me by someone. They called me back a couple of days later and said that the engine was `locked up.' There is quite a difference between a car `not running' and a car whose engine is locked-up, but it was not the seller's fault, even if he knew the problem and didn't tell me. I should have at

least made certain the engine turned over before I bought it. I sold both of them on ebay as I recollect and was only out a couple of hundred dollars. I considered it money well spent. In retrospect, I suspect the timing belt slipped or broke and it was that which caused the damage. The 928 should never have had an engine timing belt to begin with, whether or not it had been the issue with this particular car. All engines should have timing chains, not timing belts. I soon bought the 8 or 9 volume set of 928 factory shop manuals off ebay in order to acquire a general knowledge of its construction and operation. This was indeed a far cry from the one-volume factory Jaguar E-Type shop manual.

1980 Euro 928

I next bought a faded red 1980 928 I'd seen parked in front of a German car repair facility on the old Highway in Manchester. It ran but wouldn't continue running. It had two fuel pumps, which is sort of like having two watches. I'd move it around the driveway from time to time and I liked it, but that so-called `op-art' interior was actually dizzying to look at. Additionally, it was fabric, with leather bolsters rather than all leather, and was therefore typical of the grey-market European models which sometimes made it to the U.S. before the more powerful 928 S hit our shores in 1983.

When I was working on a book about the 928 for Crowood Publishers in the U.K. I'd spoken with one of the people involved with the development and design of the 928. When I asked him about the strange interior, he seemed slightly perturbed that I didn't find it in keeping with the overall exotic nature of the car in general. "Leather was always an option" he told me dryly. The 928 was indeed exotic for its era in every respect, and there was a German tradition which embraced fabric seats for sports cars, as with the racing Mercedes 300 SLRs and even some production 300 SL models. British sports cars generally had leather seating to begin with, at least U.S. bound cars. American motorists preferred leather for sports cars, whether open or closed, despite some of the drawbacks associated with leather.

As to its appearance, the 928 was supposed to look like, that is, to be immediately recognizable as a Porsche, which to most enthusiasts, it was. Its pop-up headlights were clearly inspired by those of the earlier Lamborghini Miura, despite some denials to the contrary. They were kept visible, in their lowered position, as I was told, in order to decrease the visual length of the front end, by interrupting the otherwise unbroken lines at the top of the fenders. The front of the 928 looked long when compared to the stern which seemed 'bobbed' for lack of a better word, that is, shorter than the nose. Personally. I considered the 928, and still do, beautiful from any angle. Some people thought their appearance to be shark-like. I agreed, but also found it visually reminiscent of the first successful jet fighter, the German Messerschmitt ME-262. I genuinely like its looks from any angle, although it can't be considered as beautiful in the same sense as a Jaguar XK-E.

All 928's had alloy wheels, the earlier wheels were cast alloy while the latter, larger wheels of the 928 S were forged alloy. If Porsche did indeed copy, or was inspired by the headlights of the Lamborghini Miura, the compliment was fully returned by Lamborghini's blatant use of the 928's original wheel design on its Diablo. The 928's cast alloy wheels were extraordinary in that they were designed to draw one's eyes to the open spaces within the wheel as opposed to the wheel itself. The design worked and perfectly suited the car.

Another 1979

I soon got another 928, this time a metallic grey 1979 which I'd seen in the local Wheels & Deals. It was located in Tullahoma, Tennessee, not too far from Nashville and sort of on the way to Chattanooga, that is, off of I-24. It ran and was yet another European grey-market car, with both rear and front spoilers. I traded a 1993 Lincoln Town car for it. The Lincoln had been and was still a really great car but the automatic closing device on the trunk worked better sometimes than others, and the alarm was likely to go off without provocation. I fooled around with this 928 awhile and then sold it because I had other cars that I enjoyed more, and this one needed painting and interior work. Still, it had been fun messing around with and determined to buy a nice 1983-1985 at some point in the future.

1982 928

It ran well and looked good until the paint began to flake off of the places it didn't belong.

I bought a white 1982 928 off of Nashville's craigslist, and when I say white, I mean white. Some people had ideas during the mid-1990s that it might be cool to paint an entire car a particular color, even bumpers, chrome, rubber, and all. In fact, even Rolls-Royce and Bentley succumbed to this trend, to some degree. In the case of this 928, the choice of color was white. The previous owner had painted everything but the wheels white, including the black rear bumper guards, the rear spoiler, the side door guard strips, in short all of the exterior. This might be a good idea in theory except when surfaces which were never intended to be painted are generally painted without consideration of the ability of a particular paint to adhere to their surfaces. Invariably, this was the case here, as I expected, and the paint did start coming off places where it didn't ever belong soon enough. It looked nice when I bought it, so when the inevitable occurred I wasn't surprised or particularly disappointed.

It was a fairly presentable car for driving around out in Hickman County, which was about the only place I drove it. I liked its later forged alloy wheels and automatic transmission, and enjoyed it while I had it. I kept it for a year or so and sold on to somebody on ebay. I never had any trouble mechanically, it always started right up, and really was the best sounding car I've ever owned. That 4.5 liter engine had a loud rumble which satisfied my rusticity in a way no other car ever has before or since (except for Jaguar XK-Es, of course).

The pop-up headlights in their lowered position visually interrupted what would have otherwise been an exceptionally long front end.

As a final note regarding the 928, it never did replace the venerable and popular 911, as first intended, because the 911 was never taken out of production as feared, and continued adapting, evolving, and most importantly, selling. The 928 was a truly wonderful car despite some inherent problems. It was more or less a greenhouse, given its large amount of glass, and cars left in the sun often suffered interior damage including baked leather seats. My only complaint was that driving it was like watching television, from a visual standpoint at least, in that all I ever saw through the front windshield was the approaching scenery. I like to see a hood or some part of a car if for no other reason than as a point of reference.

Had the 928 been afforded the same considerations as the 911, it would doubtless have remained in production and would still be one of the best GT cars of all time. Regrettably it was never given a turbo, or produced as a convertible, like it should've been. Although the 924 debuted before the 928 as the first front engine Porsche, the 924 had originally been made as a VW for VW, though designed with working prototypes by Porsche. While there was some initial grumbling from rear engine Porsche purists at the debut of the 924, it was no challenge to the preeminence of the 911 as the top of the line Porsche. The 928, however, was indeed superior to the 911 in all respects, and could arguably be considered the first 'real' Porsche in that it did not descend from a Volkswagen. Its legacy, apart from its own intrinsic worth, might be that it paved the way for every front engine Porsche which followed, including the Cayenne, the Panamera, and the Macan. The 911 still reigns supreme, and is the car that comes immediately to mind when one hears the name Porsche, only now, there are many excellent alternatives from this great company. I still love the 928 and may buy a really excellent example someday, but having experienced the superiority of the 4-valve engine with the Mercedes S 420 & S 500s (see below), I'd probably pick a 1983 or 1984, even though the later 4-valve cars are probably 'better.' The 928 was truly a revolutionary car created by some of the best engineers and automotive designers in the world at the time, and some of its advanced technological features, such as the Weissach rear suspension developed specifically for the 928, were subsequently applied to the 911. In any case, the 928s are all great cars, and truly timeless, but they should have had a timing chain, not belt.

A giant spider hovers above the pre-4-valve engine. A front-mounted water cooled V-8 in a Porsche? Some detractors considered it a sacrilege, not me.

The stern looked blunt when compared to the long hood, but proportionally, it suited the car. Those who didn't like the 928 originally due to its water-cooled front engine, no longer have that as an excuse, since there have been many such Porsches by now, with more likely on the way in the foreseeable future, given the superior design.

Smile, you bastard! It's summer and nobody wants to be around anyone who's unpleasant.

Still ape-ing and clowning!

Brewster.

XIX.

Mercedes S Class 1995-1999

1996 S 500

I'd taken an oath sometime in either 2007 or 2008 not to buy any more cars for at least three years. I just had too many cars, all of them different marques and models. At some point, unless one has the resources of late casino magnate Bill Harrah, it would seem prudent to limit one's collecting to one series of one brand. But any great car I hadn't already had was a potential acquisition. By this point, I'd become `hog wild and pig crazy' as they say in Memphis. At the time of my self-restricting oath, I had a 1975 Fleetwood Brougham, a Jaguar V-12 coupe, a giant Lincoln sedan, a Porsche 928, a 1968 Cadillac Eldorado, a 1970 Cadillac DeVille convertible, a 1984 Jeep Grand Wagoneer, two 1980s Mercedes SLs, and a Rolls Silver Spur. The barn was full, so was the garage, I had a storage unit, and there were always at least three cars in the driveway. Enough was enough, at least for the moment. My oath excluded passenger cars however, should I perhaps need another one. After two and a half years of abstinence, I espied a 1996 S 500 parked in front of a business in nearby Dickson, Tennessee. I'd seen it parked there frequently in different spaces near the business. On a lark, I stopped by one summer afternoon merely to locate the car's owner and ask him what I should look for in terms of buying one.

I'd always liked these cars, I just couldn't afford a new one when they first appeared, and in truth, I was still preoccupied with large Cadillacs and Lincolns. I didn't know the difference then between any of these Mercedes sedans since they all looked pretty much the same. At first glance a 1993 500 SEL looks a lot like a 1999 S 600. The four-door S Class sedans were far less elegant visually than Jaguar sedans of the same era. The big Mercedes sedans looked more purposeful and `utilitarian' for lack of a better word than their contemporaries, and they are. The most significant improvement in the 1990s S Class over the previous S Class 1980's predecessors was the introduction of four-valve per cylinder engines. I'd had no previous experience with four-valve engines and considered them to be unnecessary. Two valves seemed simpler, and therefore `better.' I knew Porsche had introduced four-valve engines in the 928 as standard equipment beginning in 1985. I'd driven a new 1987 928 S-4 and it hauled ass, but I didn't attribute the 928's speed to the presence of additional valves.

Anyway, the owner of the S 500 said that his car was for sale if I wanted to buy it. It looked good to me and I could afford his asking price of $5000. He said that the air-conditioning didn't work, but that everything else did. It also had a rebuilt engine. A rebuilt engine in theory doesn't mean much to me as a rule, in that any rebuilt engine is only as good as the person doing the work. He said that the engine had been rebuilt by Euro Auto Body, some place off of Charlotte, across the street from Erol's Autobahn, a place that had once worked on my 450 SL. The car also needed new tires and brakes. We went for a spin and it drove fine and everything worked. I agreed to buy it at his asking price if he had the air conditioning repaired. I told him to call me when it was ready, and that was that.

In the meantime he called and said that the car was at Euro Auto Body having the AC repaired, and if I wanted, I should go there and talk to `Alex' since he had rebuilt the engine and serviced the car regularly. I stopped by the place and my future car was in one of the service bays. I met Alex and he said the car was in pretty good shape and that was that. I had no idea at this time that Alex Davidoff would play such an important part in my automotive future as far as Mercedes were concerned.

On the day I was to pick up the car in Dickson, I called its owner before I arrived and said that I wanted to take the car for a longer drive on the Interstate so I could see how it really ran in other than street travel. My best girl and I took it for a spin down 840 for about half an hour. I knew it needed tires so I really didn't push it much, but when I did step on it, it moved quickly and without hesitation. I almost didn't buy it because I realized that if I bought this car I'd be embarking in an entirely new automotive direction. I was still learning my away around my other cars and knew absolutely nothing about these cars.

By the time I made it back to Dickson, I'd decided, what the hell? I'd never had one of these, always liked the way they looked, and my friend Jay Page was a big wheel at the Mercedes dealer in Nashville, so if I needed help in the service department, he could see that I didn't get a full `Mercedes service welcome.' We returned to the owner's place of business, I paid him, left with the title and followed Katye back to her house. I had the brakes and rotors replaced, got new tires, and was on my way to Nashville a few days later.

The fact was that I needed another passenger car in addition to my Lincoln sedan for driving back and forth to Nashville. I could save the Lincoln for a trip car and use the S 500 as a daily driver. The first thing I noted was that the S 500 hauled ass, I mean really. It wasn't that its 5 liter engine was that big. The Cadillac's 500 cubic inch displacement translated to 8.2 liters or thereabouts, but the S 500 engine is just a hell of a lot more efficient.

I've had the car for ten years now, and still drive it regularly. The only trouble I've had with it happened recently. As I was on the way home from Nashville, windows down, stereo blasting, the car suddenly slowed and ultimately stopped. It was Friday afternoon rush hour traffic and I was on two-lane Hwy 100 heading west. Think fast! I called Alex, explained the situation, and asked him if I could bring it over. I could have waited several hours for AAA, but wanted it done now. I had Hillwood Wrecker Service pick it up and take it to Alex at Euro Auto Body. As soon as I'd made that call, I phoned a friend of mine Abner Dansby, who I knew was in Nashville. He was kind enough to drop what he was doing and cross the river to pick me up, and take me the 40 miles home, then turn around and drive back to Nashville. After a week or so I called to check on it and Mark, his long-time employee said that Alex had gone to Italy for three weeks. In the meantime I went to Mississippi for three weeks. When I returned I went to see Alex. The car now had 220,000 miles on it and I'd had it almost 10 years. Alex recommended that I not have it repaired, lest something else happen. I thought about it for a couple of days and decided to have it towed back to the garage and I'd deal with it later. I had no intention of giving it up and will have it fixed when I'm ready to start driving it again. In the meantime, I had another black S 500 in storage which only had 65,000 on its odometer which was licensed and insured and needed to be driven.

The 1995-1999 S Class Mercedes are in my opinion, the best passenger cars of the modern era, and possibly ever.

1999 S 420

When my 2000 Lincoln Town Car bit the dust (see above), I called my pal Jay Page at Mercedes of Nashville, which by this time had moved to Cool Springs, near Franklin. I told him that I was looking for a 1995-1999 Mercedes S 420 or S 500. He said that they didn't handle them anymore and that when one came in as a trade-in it was usually sold at auction. I knew that I didn't want a current (2000 forward) S Class sedan for several reasons. In the first place they were about the size of a Ford Taurus, possibly even smaller. I wanted the biggest Mercedes sedan I could find. Secondly, the newer S Class (beginning with the 2000 model year) in addition to being physically smaller, had plastic headlights. Aesthetically as well as practically, this was for me, a zero. The newer S class also lacked style. I stopped short of saying that it was ugly, but it was, in my opinion, close. The worst feature of any S Class, and possibly any Mercedes whatsoever after 1999, is its useless suspension. I'd see newer S Class sedans at repair shops or behind the Mercedes dealer or at other independent shops, basically sitting on the ground awaiting repair. At least with my Lincoln's air bags, when if ever they failed, the wheels still turned and the car was drivable.

Such was not the case with the newer Mercedes S Class suspensions, and like the suspension on the famous 6.9 when it conked, you weren't going

anywhere at all until it was fixed. Again more revenue for the dealership. No, as always, I knew exactly what I wanted.

Jay had earlier told me about a 1999 S 420 that one of his mechanics had inherited from his father in law. At that time the car was tied up in the estate which hadn't been settled yet. I asked him if it had been straightened out. He got the mechanic on the phone who said the car was finally available and for sale. I arranged to meet him a few days later at the dealer in Cool Springs and we took it for a drive. It was gold with tan leather, had been garage kept all of its life, and had logged 80,000 miles. It had a 4.2 liter, four valve V-8, the same displacement as a post `64 Series I Jaguar XK-E. That didn't seem to me to be enough engine for a large Mercedes sedan, but it was more than adequate, though lacking the power and response of my S 500. I knew as soon as I'd driven it less than five minutes that I was going to buy it. It was like new. He wanted $8,000. "I had wanted $8,500 but I'd take $8,000." I asked him if he'd let me think about it overnight. I still had around $5,000 from State Farm, for my destroyed 2000 Lincoln Town Car (see above) which I considered generous for a car showing nearly 140,000 miles.

I bought the car a couple of days later and was on my way. Alex had advised against getting an S 320 or an S Class in the pre-1995 140 series, not that the earlier S sedans weren't wonderful, but rather that the 1995-1999s were `better.' Personally, I think the earlier cars look better with their less encumbered belt line. In the case of the S 320, a six-cylinder car, Alex said that it was underpowered. The S Class sedans have now been redesigned three or four times since their 2000 Ford Taurus sized models. The owners of these nineties sedans are a small fraternity, generally speaking, and those who own them now have sought them specifically, and prefer them over anything newer. The idea of a newer, smaller, more expensive S Class with more than sixty computers, each of which will be out of warranty sooner or later, is not appealing, and again, given the plastic headlights, and high-tech though troublesome suspension, we prefer these larger and better 1990s sedans.

Once, en route from Holly Springs, Mississippi to a party in Memphis, the S 420 decided not to shift out of first gear. I had it towed back to Nashville, had Abner Dansby drive from Nashville to pick us up, and $1,100 later I was back on the road. Another time in Columbia, TN, we were visiting a friend of my wife's and suddenly, as we were ready to leave, the ignition key wasn't doing anything. It turned, but nothing happened. I had the car towed to Nashville and fixed. Another time, we were leaving Memphis at the beginning of November in the pouring rain, with the car absolutely loaded a German Shepherd in the back seat and a cat in a cage, when suddenly, in the cold pouring rain, the coffee which I'd spilled into the console thirty minutes or so earlier (for lack of a functional cup holder), began to work its magic, alerting me to its presence with an acrid smoke emanating from somewhere inside the console. I pulled over to the side of the road at a very busy intersection, turned off the engine immediately, and called my mechanic, Alex, in Nashville. I explained the situation, reached my own conclusion, started the car and drove back home without incident. Several months later, without any notice whatsoever, and after barely dodging a tornado, I stopped at Office Despot on Harding Road late on Friday afternoon, again in the pouring rain. I left my significant other in the car and entered the store. When I exited a few minutes later, I was greeted by the sound of the car's alarm system and her running toward the building shouting that the car was on fire. Actually, there were no flames per se, just a thick, electrical smoke emanating from somewhere inside the car and accompanied by a fairly slow but constant loud clicking sound. It was around 4:45 on a Friday night in a big storm. Crap like this invariably occurs in the worst places at the most inopportune time. I immediately called Alex, whose shop was less than a mile away. I almost called AAA but decided in light of the circumstances and the time factor I'd do better to call Hillwood Wrecker Service around the corner. I also had to find a way home forty-five miles away. I called State Farm, and they told me what I needed to do to get a rental car. Hillwood Wrecker picked the car up and towed it to their lot and deposited it at Alex's the next day. We managed to get to the nearest car rental place on Charlotte, just before closing. The Mercedes sat there at Euro Auto Body a week or so before the insurance adjuster came by. The car looked fine to him. Alex stripped the interior of the car, and I mean stripped it to the floor, removing both front seats, the entire rear seat, the console, all the carpeting and sound deadening insulation beneath it. He checked all of the wiring and started the car, letting it run nonstop for five or six hours and checking the wiring with a heat gun for anything unusual every so often. That this car could run in place for that

amount of time in May in Nashville, without even coming close to overheating is a testament to the build quality of the engine.

Alex finally determined that the driver's side mirror switch had shorted, and that was all that was wrong with it. He put it back together and it was good to go. I'd gotten off lucky and knew it, but then nobody knows these cars better than he does. He literally can fix anything.

It's my personal opinion that the 1995-1999 S Class Mercedes are the best cars that Mercedes has ever made in terms of pure utility. They may lack the elegance of some earlier passenger cars, but what they lack in pure physical beauty, they more than make up for with safety, performance, and reliability. I happen to prefer their looks to the often exaggerated and plastic appearance of some of their successors.

The stern, when compared to a Jaguar sedan of the same period, clearly lacks grace, but its `utilitarian' looks seem to suit the car.

1995 S 500

This beautiful 1995 Mercedes S Class sedan unexpectedly came to me by a strange and circuitous route as I shall relate. One day I pulled into the parking lot of the Green Hills US Bank on Abbott Martin Rd. in my black 1996 S 500. There was a woman seated in the driver's seat of some funky-looking white minivan. As I walked past her she said, "I have a car like that." I walked over to her and said that I was in a hurry to cash a check before the bank closed and told her that I'd love to talk to her and asked her if she'd mind waiting for a couple of minutes. When I exited the bank I went over and she introduced herself, as did I. She began reeling off a list of the cars in her possession: A Porsche turbo convertible, an Excalibur Phaeton, a Detomaso Pantera, A Mercedes S 500, and a Mercedes 560 SL. These cars sounded familiar to me, but I still didn't make the connection. Then, she mentioned her brother Glenn Ferguson, who was known to me personally as late country singer Johnny Paycheck's manager, back when I was in my mid-twenties working as an agent for the Lavender-Blake Agency which represented Paycheck at the time. (I would become Paycheck's exclusive agent later).

Her brother, Glenn had died, five years earlier, unbeknownst to me, and as She'd been his business manager, had been appointed trustee of his estate. Anyway Glenn Ferguson had grown up in the Music Row area of Nashville before it was ever known as such, and had won a hard-fought council race in

1959, his first time out, against Frank Melfi, an entrenched old school political figure. This election is still talked about today given the viciousness of the battle. Ferguson as councilman was a visionary, and in a highly controversial move, basically gave the land in his district at 16th & Division Street to the Country Music Association, as the site for the first Country Music Hall of Fame. He was also one of the prime movers in the establishment of what would become Music Row, as well as the formation of what we now know as `Metropolitan' Nashville, which replaced the separate city and county governments with one entity. He subsequently became Metro Trustee and systematically made the office more efficient than it had ever been.

Anyway, apart from his political work, Ferguson loved cars all of his life, and at one time had a 1957 or `58 Cadillac Eldorado Brougham, a 1969 Hurst Olds coupe, a Jaguar V-12 XJ-S convertible, a beautiful burgundy 1958 Cadillac Fleetwood 75 limousine, in addition to the cars he'd owned at the time of his demise: a Detomaso Pantera, a 1984 steel-bodied Porsche factory slant-nose convertible, an Excalibur Phaeton, a Mercedes 560 SL, a couple of Ford Rancheros, a Chrysler convertible, a Mercedes 380 limousine, and a 1979 Mercedes 450 SL Coupe.

After a couple of skipped meetings by Reba Ferguson, I met her at the property and looked at the cars. The 1984 Porsche convertible was black with red leather and sported a factory slant nose steel body with flared rear fenders. It resembled a turbo but wasn't. The Excalibur, being sort of a modernized copy of a 1930s Mercedes SSK or 540 K had a V-8, dual sidemounts and a removable hardtop. It was burgundy with tan leather, and had less than 7,000 miles on the odometer. Like all of the cars, it had been garage kept all of its life. The Pantera was white with black leather interior and missing ignition and door keys. There was also a 1995 Mercedes S 500. There were a couple of dead Ford Rancheros at the side of the driveway, with a partially assembled one in a garage bay. She asked me if I was interested in buying any of them, but I wasn't. I already had too many cars. I did, however, offer to sell them for her for 10%. She said that would be fine in that they'd been sitting there since her brother had died five years earlier.

We talked for awhile and knew many of the same people, both within and outside of the music business. She was incredibly intelligent and self-sufficient and we liked each other immediately. She said that she had a good feeling about me and that she trusted her intuition. I made it easy for her, and myself, by saying that I didn't want to handle any money. It would all be sent directly to her trust account, and when it had arrived and a car was paid for in full, she could pay me. This arrangement was a double win for me in that I got to fool with these interesting cars without having to actually own them or pay for their repairs. I got the Excalibur running myself and drove it around the property a couple of times and parked it back in the garage. I sold the Excalibur for $50,000 to some guy from California who'd seen it on ebay. He showed up, in a 1990s Mercedes E 500, a very rare car with a big engine for its size. I had him give her a deposit of $5,000, and he bankwired the rest of the money into her account before he had it picked up. It was a giant car with almost no outward visibility from the driver's standpoint. The frame extended  a couple of feet beyond the very tall grill, so it was difficult to know how far to pull the car forward while parking. The covered tires mounted ahead of the front door in each fender didn't help either. I never removed the detachable hardtop, but while it was affixed, rear and ¾ visibility were almost nonexistent. Still, it was a beautiful car and really, probably the best example of that model in existence.

In the meantime, the guy who'd bought the Excalibur also wanted to buy the Porsche. He was working for some high end used car dealership in Los Angeles and had been locating and buying cars for the dealership's owner. I felt like I had an obligation to Reba Ferguson and Glenn Ferguson, Jr. to get them as much money as possible, even though they didn't especially need it. When the buyer had shown up to pay the deposit on the Excalibur, he'd described the Pantera and the Porsche over the phone to his boss. They'd both wanted to buy the cars as they were, where they were, saying that they had their own mechanics in L.A. and would rather have them get them running. This was code for the fact that they were going to try to beat me up on the price. No dice. I knew they'd be saying crap like. "Well, we really don't know whether they run or not. We'd be taking a chance…etc. You'd just be wasting that woman's money fixing these cars up. You're not really being fair to her." I spoke to both of them and they tried to guilt me into selling them 'as is.' "Is fixing them really in her best interests?" I thought it was. A good running and driving car is infinitely more valuable than one that doesn't run.

By this time I had a good working relationship with Alex Davidoff at Nashville's Euro Auto Body. I asked him whether or not I should attempt to start the Porsche myself, but given its time in the garage unstarted, he suggested I send it over and let him fool with it. He had a nice red 930 Turbo and was familiar with rear engine Porsche cars, and I wasn't. Hillwood Wrecker picked it up and delivered it to him. He dropped the engine and its subframe, and got it running like new. In fact the car looked brand new. When it was ready, I drove it back over to the property and stuck it back in the garage. After a couple of no sale run-throughs on ebay, I sold it to the same guy who'd bought the Excalibur.

The 1974 Pantera wasn't running, mainly because it didn't have an ignition key. After several fruitless attempts to find one, I hired a locksmith, but for some reason, he was unable to make a key for it on site. I was anxious to have this car drivable so I could have some fun with it before I sold it, The Detomaso Pantera was always one of my favorite cars. In the tradition of the Facel Vega, the Jenson Healy, Bizzarrini, and Iso Grifo, it had a foreign designed body with an American engine, in this case, with a mid-engine from Ford. Theoretically, it represented the best of both worlds, especially since it was being sold and serviced through Lincoln-Mercury dealerships. At a price of approximately $12,000, when new, it was expensive, but not like a Ferrari.

It's interesting, how things come around, in that several years before Glenn had died, I'd sent him a Pantera sales catalog I'd found somewhere in my house. I knew he had a Pantera and I thought he might enjoy it.

I couldn't wait to hear the sound of that big V-8 through those four exhaust pipes, but I'd have to, as by this time, it was summer and I had to get to my house in Holly Springs, Mississippi. I figured I could deal with in November, when I was back in town, and that I could get running easily. The buyer of the other two cars kept bugging me to sell him the Pantera, even though it wasn't running. I decided to talk it over with Reba, which I did, and she said that I'd already gotten her the money she needed, so to do what I thought was best. The owner of the company in L.A. was nice at first, but a big-mouthed braggart, dismissively referring to the Porsche, Excalibur, and Pantera as `bread and butter' cars, saying that he regularly sold million dollar Ferraris. Again. I thought privately, `people who talk don't do, and people who do don't brag.' But I got the feeling that Reba just wanted to wrap all of this up so she could close her brother's estate. I reluctantly agreed to sell them the Pantera, but I was in Mississippi and wasn't coming home for awhile. I told them to wire the money to her account and gave them her account number again. "Here's the thing, I need a three day notice before you send somebody to pick it up, because I'm in

Mississippi," to which they agreed. About a week later, I received a call from the guy in L.A., saying that the truck was on its way to pick it up. I replied that wasn't our agreement. He basically told me, that was my problem and that the driver would need the key so he could drive it onto the truck. I reminded him that the car didn't run, and that it didn't have a key. He acted surprised, and angered. "You were the one who said you wanted to have your guys fix it," I told him. You knew that." He started raising hell like the ass hole he was so I told him I'd refund the money if he liked and that it didn't make a shit to me one way or the other. (Excuse my crass vulgarity). I meant to have said that it was of no excremental significance to me one way or the other. To make a long story short, I needlessly hauled ass home. If I hadn't been hired to take care of the details, I'd have told him that he could send a truck if he wanted, but that he wouldn't have access to the property until I was there, and that would require a three day notice as we'd agreed when we made the deal.

The driver showed up and had a difficult time extracting and loading it, but off he went, and the next day I returned to Mississippi. `Paid and played' as we used to say in the music business, meaning that the deal was successfully concluded. I was still sorry to have seen it go without ever having had the opportunity to play with it, but all's well that ends well, and I had enough cars already. The tale had an unexpectedly happy ending when I received a call from California from the person who'd first come by to buy the Excalibur. I excitedly asked him if they'd gotten the Pantera running, and he replied that they had. He'd called me however, to inform me that they wanted a partial refund, because the car was full of rust.

"How small a refund did you have in mind?" I asked him, not that I had any intention of paying him anything. He was thinking in terms of ten or fifteen thousand dollars. I told him that he'd personally examined the car when he examined the Porsche, and paid for the Excalibur. I reminded him that he'd kept beating me up to sell him the car and that he didn't want me to have my mechanic get it running. This was impossible for him to refute, but that didn't matter. "That money went into your account so we'll have to sue you," he told me, changing his tone. I knew that the money had not gone into my account, and I also knew that the late owner's sister had told him in my presence, that she didn't know anything about the Pantera other than that her brother seldom drove it, and she couldn't find the key. "Because the Excalibur and Porsche were in perfect shape, you assumed that the Pantera was as well. If I'd had it checked out and fixed by my mechanic, as I wanted to do, I'd have found any problems and had them repaired. You bought these cars as is where is. If in your haste to make a purchase you didn't do your due diligence, that's not my problem or the estate's. In the meantime, you can tell your boss, that he shouldn't brag so much. If he can't take a ten or fifteen thousand dollar hit, he shouldn't be in this business." That was the end of that. I'm still sorry that I didn't have a chance to enjoy that car. King Elvis supposedly shot his Pantera, and probably with good reason. I can't be sure, but I do understand him shooting televisions, and that was in the era before they listened to, watched and recorded us, as they do now.

Excuse the diversion. Back to this 1995 S 500. It had less than 60,000 miles when I acquired it, and doesn't have much more than that now. It is a work of art. I don't drive it that much because I want to keep it in its present condition as long as possible, even though I've had it for six or seven years now. By this time, I was fairly familiar with the 1995-1999 Mercedes S Class sedans. I didn't really need another one as I already had a 1996 S 500 and a 1999 S 420. While the S 420 was certainly not as fast off the line as the 500, it was fast enough. Like most high end cars, these expensive cars (when new) eventually passed on to second, third, etc. owners, each successive owner performing less and less of the necessary maintenance. I'd intended to sell this car as well, but thought that perhaps I should keep it after all. To that end, I made a deal with Reba Ferguson, the trustee of the estate in which in return for writing a biography of her late brother, she would give me this car. By the time I saw this car, it had been resting in a climate controlled garage along with the Excalibur, Pantera, and Porsche. It ran great and everything worked, but it would stall upon occasion when accelerating from a stop sign, or even on the highway. It would stop, and then after about thirty minutes, it would start up and run fine. The problem turned out to be its original spark plug wires, which along with its twin distributor caps and rotors, and some dry-rotted vacuum lines were replaced. Now it runs like the new car it basically is. That acquisition brought me up to three late 1990s S class sedans, which should have caused me to `throw in the trowel' as the Masons say. And I would have, except that the driver's side door mirror on my 1999 S 420 needed replacement. It flapped inside its housing, and its surface was obscured by some oil within, which has something to do with reducing headlight glare from cars behind you at night.

The 1995 S 500 is a wonderful car.

These cars have started showing up from time to time at Pull-A-Part. I checked their online inventory, and sure enough one had hit the lot two days earlier. I drove over there and both side door mirrors as well as the pump located beneath the back seat cushion had already been taken. This really pissed me off. These industrious Mexicans descend upon nearly everything that shows up there and strip them like locusts. I can't help but suspect they're being hired by parts houses who tell them what parts to get. The car had only been there for two days, and already had been stripped of the parts I needed. I did accompany my mechanic's assistant back there a few days later and retrieved the heater control unit, the console window switches, the radio/CD control unit and, strangely enough a perfect leather driver's seat which is an exact duplicate of my S 420's and in the same color. The problem, however still existed for my door rearview mirror. With this in mind, I called a couple of parts houses and was told that a new side mirror unit would cost $700. No, I don't think so. As I may have mentioned elsewhere, I expect a fair exchange when I buy anything. It isn't a question of whether I can afford something, it is the issue of `if I do this, how will I feel about myself in the morning?' I wouldn't feel good about myself at all if I paid $700 for a damn rearview mirror. As the great magician Eliphas Levi observed in the late 1800s, "To be able and to forbear is to be twice able," which in this instance means just buy a parts car while they're still available.

1999 S 420

With that in mind I bought an entire running 1999 S 420 for $700 I'd found on the Nashville craigslist, because it was available, and had it towed the fifty miles or so to a friend's garage in Nashville and parked it there. As with any car, especially something a bit out of the ordinary, it's always good to have a parts car. Believe it or not, this one was too good to use in that manner, so there it sits in the garage, awaiting recommissioning when needed. It had a problem in that it overheated quickly, so I spoke to the owner over the phone then arranged to drive to LaVergne where I paid him and received the title. Even the AC works. Although there is a problem with the engine temperature, it's ready to be put into service quickly should I suddenly need another one. It also has a wonderful leather interior and nice original black paint.

These are my favorite passenger cars of the modern era. Technically excellent, without unnecessary complexity, and combined with speed and excellent handling, make the 140 series the best of the bunch. The S 420s lack the acceleration of the S 500s, but they're definitely fast enough for my use as a daily driver. In short, I like the 420s just about as much as the S 500s.

1995 S 420. A running parts car to supply my other 1990s S Class sedans.

A few months after I bought this one, Mark, who works with Alex at Euro Auto Body in Nashville casually mentioned that his brother had another 1995 S 420 that he no longer wanted. I bought it sight unseen. It was not in as good shape as the one pictured above and has a transmission problem, but managed to make it from La Vergne to Alex's shop in Nashville under its own power. It has a wonderful engine which was rebuilt by Alex at Euro Auto Body. It paid for itself within three months by supplying the driver's door mirror ($700) and the highly-prized vacuum pump ($1100) which went out for the second time in the gold 1999 S 420. This gives me three excellent Mercedes W 140 series sedans which I drive with some regularity; the black `96 S 500, the gold `99 S 420, and the black `95 S 500, and a running parts car. Despite their overall excellence, these cars are not without their own unique problems, most notably in the 1997-1999 models, a functional cup holder.

In answer to the question which some of my friends ask, "Why do you always drive those twenty year old Mercedes? Why don't you just buy a new one?" My usual response is, `Because I can!' The 1995-1999 Mercedes S Class sedans are, in my opinion, perhaps the best passenger cars ever made by Mercedes-Benz, or anybody else, for that matter. As with the 1974-1976 Cadillac Fleetwoods, which I drove for more than twenty-five years (along with other cars), I intend to do the same with these Mercedes sedans. Their looks are even more striking now than they were when first introduced in 1993. Yes, they're expensive to maintain when a problem arises, but worth it, and you won't see five or six of them on any given day, day like you do many expensive but relatively common cars. They're fast, and agile, satisfying my need for safety, power, speed, and sports car handling. And they're both dependable and predictable. They're also large (by modern standards). I intend to always have several in use with additional parts cars for spare parts.

I'm not saying that I'll never get a new S Class Mercedes sedan, because I like them, but when and if I do, I'll lease it, since given their hi-tech operating systems, and dozens of computers, I wouldn't necessarily want to get stuck with one when the warranty expires, and forced into the dealership for repairs because nobody else will be able to fix it.

1978 450 SLC

XX.

The R 107 SLs & SLCs

1975 450 SL

The father of Randy Smith, one of my best friends then and now, was an early fan of SLs, and owned three of them simultaneously, a 230 SL, a 250 SL, and a 280 SL at a time when there probably weren't a combined total of a dozen SLs in the entire state of Tennessee. W.R. Smith, as he was named, was an interesting man in every respect. He'd earned an engineering degree at Vanderbilt and was financially successful. He enjoyed the company of his teen-aged son's friends, and in many ways was inspirational. He could go on and on about the merits of the SLs, and since we rode around in them, and were interested in cars in general, we'd sometimes have late night conversations with him about the merits and demerits of particular cars.

I can honestly say that were it not for him, I probably would never have had any Mercedes at all. In the first place, there weren't that many Mercedes of any kind in Nashville in the 1960s when we were in our teens. There were a few sedans in Belle Meade, where he lived, but not many, and to tell the truth, at least as far as sedans were concerned, Cadillacs and Lincolns were much better cars, and much larger, more elegant, and faster, especially Cadillacs. The Fleetwoods in particular had wood panels seemingly everywhere. A 1965 or 1966 Cadillac Fleetwood Brougham had been tested by one of the popular car models at the time and easily reached 120 miles mph. We were extremely impressed. Mercedes passenger cars were touted and considered to be some of the safest in the world, and perhaps they were. I do remember a young man of my age being burned alive on a sunny spring day in a late 1960s Mercedes sedan when he was hit head-on by a 1970s Chevrolet Monte Carlo on Woodmont Blvd. a residential thoroughfare at the time. I wasn't impressed by the outcome.

In addition to a few Mercedes sedans, there was a black 300 SL roadster and also a black 300 SL Gullwing coupe which I remember. Once, when I was eleven years old, I was hitch-hiking in my neighborhood and given a ride in a 300 SL roadster with its convertible top down on a bright summer day to Green Hills Shopping Center. I couldn't help but notice its 160 mph speedometer. Later, while in exile at Columbia Military Academy, I'd read car magazines with classifieds in the back. 300 SLs were plentiful then in the $1,500 range. Alas, I was only 16 years old.

There were a few 190 SLs around too. The 190 SL (1955-1963) was the less expensive production contemporary and successor to the magnificent 300 SL, and was similar in appearance. But a visual first impression is where any similarities ended. It did not have a tubular frame or a six-cylinder engine as did the 300 SL, but rather a four-cylinder single overhead cam engine, and as such, was in my estimation, underpowered. Although it lacked the exact appearance of the 300 SL, I think the average person didn't know the difference between the two, although automotive enthusiasts of the era certainly did. The 190 SL was a solidly built and beautiful car, with features which placed it on a higher level than many of its contemporaries. Glass side windows were standard as opposed to the detachable side window curtains of many of its rivals. The removable hardtop when in place, along with the glass side windows, effectively kept rain out of the interior and provided good visibility. The 190 SL was a logical next step to the 300 SL as an entry level open two-seat car, and as such, was successful, but a significant change was on the horizon for the Mercedes SL. In retrospect, I didn't like the 190 SL as much as I should have at the time, given its many wonderful features. For one thing, its steering wheel was also inordinately large and unwieldly, and probably more suited as the helm of an ocean liner. I was however, fully aware of its build quality and interior detail. I guess I unconsciously, and unfairly compared it to the 300 SL. I respected them then, and appreciate them now more than ever, but I was never passionate about them as I was about Jaguar XKs of the era. Today, the 190 SLs are highly desirable to Mercedes collectors and quite valuable, but regrettably, still severely underpowered.

My friend Clark Conn's parents bought him a beautiful 190 SL one summer which was white with blue leather seats, and we enjoyed riding around with the top down. When autumn came he went to law school in Atlanta and bought something more suited to everyday driving. Though he subsequently inherited a lot of money, other than a new Porsche 944, which he only kept a year or so, this was the last decent car he'd ever own, mainly because he was a cheapskate. He died rich, but he died, and by his own hand at his early 1800s Federal style mansion in the middle of nowhere, Kentucky. Contrary to the popular saying `the man who dies with the most toys wins,' is the reality that `the man who dies with the most toys dies!'

Anyway, Randy's father's fleet consisted of a white 230 SL, which the father called `White Bird,' a dark blue 280 SL which he called `Dark Bluebird,' and a light blue 250 SL which he called `Light Bluebird.' These cars have since become known as `Pagodas' due to the shape of the detachable hard top. They were crisp, visually striking, and beautiful, and as automotive works of art are considered by some, even more beautiful, than even the famed 300 SLs. Whether they were true to the original concept of a `super light' two-seat convertible coupe is debatable. They had a 94.5" wheelbase and an overall length of 168.7" with a curb weight right at 3,000 lbs. I enjoyed riding around town in them and occasionally got to drive one, an almost religious experience. At this point, I was 17 and didn't yet have my first car, although all of my friends did. Anyway, when the 1968 school year ended my friend Randy went to Ole Miss, and I went to the Navy to avoid being drafted.

A couple of years later, I was back and in college myself. Randy graduated from Ole Miss and returned home, and I was again in Nashville, this time for the summer, and we picked up where we'd left off. In the ensuing period, his father had shed the white 230 SL in favor of a new 350/450 SL which he bought from Madison Smith, the small local Mercedes dealer at the time. It was supposedly the first 350/450 SL sold in the state of Tennessee, and while we'd received many admiring glances in any of the other SLs, people stared in wonderment at the new car, a complete departure from the 230, 250, 280 series SLs. I was hooked. I had to have one. The problem was that I was 22 years old, and a student and with no money. Be that as it may, I knew that I'd have one (or more) someday, but it would probably be a while in the future.

The so-called R 107 was a long-running production car, (1971 through 1989), with constantly increasing prices and changing names (280, 350, 450, 380, 500, 560) as engine sizes increased or decreased, but keeping the same body except for the SLC (see below). The 450 SL (R 107) was entirely new SL, differing from its predecessors, not only in appearance, but underneath the skin as well. Like the earlier SL roadsters, it was a convertible coupe with a convertible soft top, and an optional detachable steel hard top. The 350/450 SL had been dubbed the 'panzerwagen' in house by the people who designed it, basically meaning 'tank' due to its considerable weight, which I considered a plus. At approximately 3,700 lbs., the super-light designation lost some of its meaning. To compensate for this it debuted in the U.S. with a 3.5 liter V-8, before almost immediately receiving a larger, 4.5 liter V-8, and being re-dubbed the 450 SL. While the car retained its visual roots, in that it was clearly a Mercedes SL, it appeared larger than the 230-250-280 SL series which immediately preceded it. For the U.S. Market, it now had four distinct round sealed beam headlights, two on each side as opposed to the flat single glass plates found on most, if not all, of the rest of the world cars. Those of the cars which made it to the U.S. market were fitted with floor-mounted automatic transmissions, as had been most of the 230-250-280 series SLs sold here. Vinyl bucket seats were available, as were fabric seats with leather bolsters, or optional full leather seats. For me, the most significant improvement was the introduction of a fully independent rear suspension as opposed to a swing-axle, which, in my humble opinion is almost less desirable than a solid live-axle, which is at least predictable and more stable in a hard corner. Two universal joints per axle on each side had debuted on the E-Type Jaguar in 1961. It wasn't until more than a decade later that Mercedes made the same logical leap with the 450 SL, even though Mercedes is credited with the first independent rear suspension of the swing-axle type, meaning in the case of the Mercedes at least, basically a hinge at the differential gear housing.

One day, many years later, I noticed a gold 450 SL at a high end used car lot on Harding Rd. In Belle Meade. It has been a gas station, a hardware store, and then a used car lot, and at the time of this writing is known as Global Motorsports. It was a 1975 and was in good shape. A friend of mine in Ft. Smith, Arkansas, Doug Parker, a surgeon, called me one day and asked me if I still had all of those African 'trophies,' as they were called, which I'd inherited from my Godfather, also a surgeon. "Yes I do, why do you ask?" Well, he'd restored this giant 1920s mansion on the main drag in Ft. Smith,

Arkansas and had walnut paneling brought over there from some castle in England and thought that they might look good in his den. I'd had the African trophies in my office for five years or so and now they were at my house. They were mainly shoulder mounts of various African animals.in good shape and had been prepared by Jonas Brothers, a Denver taxidermist. I specifically remember an Oryx, a Thompson's Gazelle, a Leopard rug with head, some sort of antelope, and some African spears. They were nice and I'd enjoyed them but I was familiar with my friend's house and I knew they would look great there.

There was also a shoulder mount African Cape Buffalo, a very large, cunning, and dangerous animal, and this particular one was the largest example I'd ever seen. Anyway, one day I was reading in an easy chair when I noticed my English bulldog attempting to come into the room with me. He appeared to be frozen in his tracks despite the fact that he was free to roam about the house and frequently came into the room where I was reading. On this occasion he noticed, apparently for the first time, the Cape Buffalo hanging on the wall in my room. What had scared him stiff was that now the head had a body, namely the large square grand piano on the other side of the wall. Try as I might, I couldn't persuade him to walk past the beast with the fearsome body and the menacing countenance. I got up and dragged him forcibly past the piano-bodied beast and into the room with me. After this process had been repeated several times, he finally decided that he was unlikely to be attacked by whatever it was, but he always passed it quietly and cautiously while looking at it fearfully.

Anyway, Doug sent a van and a driver up the next day along with a check. I cashed it and bought my first 450 SL which I enjoyed for the year and a half or two years I had it. Everything worked, including the air conditioning. It ran well and was very precise in its handling and didn't cause me any problems at all other than a fuel pump at some point. I considered it to be a beautiful car which like all of its SL predecessors looked good with the hard top affixed, and the convertible top either raised or lowered. The only strange thing was that when it rained, water would enter between the windshield and the underside of the hard top where it joined the top of the windshield, but the car didn't shake, rattle, or flex and felt solid.

The R 107 as the 350/450 SLs were known, had some general inherent faults which were minimal but should be mentioned. The sun visors, for example, were poorly designed and constructed. They were flimsy and attached to the windshield frame with weak plastic fasteners which invariably broke quickly causing owners to fabricate hooks made from paperclips or other flexible wire. For some reason, SL Coupes were fitted with much higher quality sun visors.

And speaking of Speaking of the 450 series, both sedans and sports cars, the early ones were often subject to spontaneous fires due largely to the eight individual short rubber fuel hoses descending from the fuel rail to each injector. These often develop cracks and subsequent leaks which are often undetected until it's too late. I suspect that in some cases these fires have been caused by fuel lines which have been replaced by rubber hoses rather than actual fuel lines by people who don't know the difference. For this reason if you smell gas around the engine in an earlier 350/450, it's always wise to examine each individual hose from top to bottom and all the way around. A wet spot usually indicates where the problem is. Actually, these hoses should be checked weekly.

One bright spring morning as I was driving to Nashville, I was delayed by some activity on the road ahead as I was motioned around a fire engine and a flatbed wrecker, which contained the still smoldering hulk of a 450 SL whose delightful top down journey had been permanently interrupted en route by an unexpected engine fire. Several years later, the highway is still scarred by the black spot where this unfortunate car met its Waterloo. This is another reason to always have a fire extinguisher on board.

Another problem with most R107s, at least over time, is that they have a pronounced tendency to roll forward or backward even though the transmission selector is clearly in `park.' Since this can happen without notice, it's always s wise to use the parking brake. Also, if your power antenna stops working, it should be disconnected from its electrical source and operated by hand as the motor housing can become hot enough to start a fire. Another problem which seems to plague all of the R 107 cars are fuel leaks around the fuel pump, located near the differential, My 1980 450 SL had to have it replaced, as did the 450 SLC, as did my 1985 380 SL in Holly Springs.

My girlfriend and I had been in Chattanooga one day and I espied a 1970 Cadillac convertible very similar to the one we were driving, parked in front of some beer joint. I went inside met its owner and we talked cars. He had several other cars, mostly Fords and Chevys. Somehow the conversation turned to Mercedes and I told him about mine. He asked if it was for sale and I told him that I really hadn't thought about it. I had, however been looking at a 1983 Porsche 928 S which was for sale by the son of its original owner. It was a nice burgundy and was in good condition with a nice tan leather interior. The current owner was asking $8,000 for the car. The man in Chattanooga offered me $8,000 sight unseen for my 450 SL if it was in good shape, which I told him, it was. When we returned home to Nashville, I sent him some photos, and he agreed to buy it. I'd decided to buy the Porsche 928, so it was basically an even trade.

When I took my girlfriend to see the 928, she said that it looked like something from `east Nashville,' and that she had no intention of ever setting foot inside it. She didn't like the way it looked, and hated its nice burgundy finish. In short, I decided that it was easier to get another car than endure any further uninformed bitching. It was, however, too late for me to keep the 450

SL as I'd already agreed to sell it. The buyer was excited about getting it and I intended to keep my word, but be that as it may, I had no intention of my automotive fleet being down a car. I'd find something else that I'd like. Like my 1970 442 Convertible, when the new buyer arrived to pick it up, I knew I'd made a big mistake. But to employ a twist of a popular phrase, 'The best way to get over one car is to get in another one.' With that in mind, I bought a 1968 Eldorado coupe (See Elsewhere).

1974 450 SL

Wurster's, an import repair shop in Franklin, TN, used to use the grass back yard of a building across the street as additional parking space for cars waiting to be either serviced or picked up. As I was frequently in the area, and had had my 1980 450 SL serviced there a couple of times, I'd occasionally drive back there and see what they had. Sometimes there were cars which had been left for servicing and never picked up. I asked the shop owner about a black 500 SL which had obviously been sitting back there for awhile, several years, to be exact. He said it had 'somehow fallen through the cracks' and gave me the owner's name and phone number. I called the owner who said that he'd never picked it up, but that it had driven there under its own power five years earlier, and had run well, but intermittently, and he never got around to checking up on it.

I told him that I didn't need any more cars, but that if the time came that he needed, or wanted to move it quickly, to call me. Several months went by and

I received a call from him saying that the building behind which it had been parked had been sold and the car needed to be moved within a couple of days. He had no place to put it and wasn't interested in fooling with it any further, and that it was his fault for not attending to it properly. I paid him $1,100 for it and had it towed out to the house and inserted into the barn, where it remained for almost fifteen years. I finally put a battery in it and the engine was locked tighter than an after-hours bank vault. I removed the spark plugs and inserted some transmission fluid in each of the eight cylinders and let it sit for awhile and that didn't help the situation so I added Marvel Mystery oil to that. That didn't do it so it became a parts car.

The 500 SL was sold in Europe, but not in the U.S., as the smaller engine 380 SL was being sold here from 1981 through 1985. The higher powered 500 SL had the same R-107 body and some of them made their way to the U.S. Actually, my car turned out to be a 450 SL rather than the rarer and to some enthusiasts, more desirable 500 SL, another case of somebody changing the lettering on the trunk to suggest that he has more of something than he actually does. In the meantime I'd bought another black hood for it which replaced the one seen here, and was the only place there was rust. I sold it to somebody in Alabama after I realized there was nothing I could do personally to fix it. I should have dealt with it within a week after I got it. I learned two important lessons from this experience, the first of which is to turn the engine over occasionally on every car I have, especially if I'm not going to use it for awhile. The second, has to do with the hard top. Believe it or not, it's easy to forget to lock the hard top down, especially if you're putting it back on for the winter, or cleaning the convertible top, and put it back on, thinking `I'll be taking it off an a few days, so there's no point in locking it down.' The next thing you know, you're driving down the road at 70 mph and then, suddenly, liftoff! No, this hasn't happened to me, but when the buyer of this 1974 450 SL sent someone to pick it up, he had this experience. The top lifted off unexpectedly and flew through the air but fortunately didn't hit another car or cause a multi-car accident. The driver called the car's new owner, told him what happened, and asked if he should `go back and get it.' The answer was a decided `No' since it was no doubt already irreparably damaged, and the police might be there by the time the driver got back to the scene. Oddly enough, a similar experience had previously happened to the buyer of this car. He'd sold a 450 SL to somebody and the hardtop had launched in transit, in the same manner. He was certain he'd locked it down. In thinking about the one I sold him, I can't help but think that I locked it down, but since there were none of the two levers used to lock it down in the car, and it wasn't going anywhere anyway, I may not have considered it necessary.

Also, the car came from the factory with two locking handles. They are meant to both be used at the same time, when the hardtop is being secured to the top of the windshield, one at each side. The metallic blue 1980 450 SL I bought (see below) had a cracked windshield when I bought it as a result of an improper lock down of the hardtop. I had the windshield replaced immediately, but it's best to generally lock them both down at the same time. This lessens the remote, but possible likelihood of cracking the windshield.

1980 450 SL

I had Alex apply the front spoiler from a 560 SL flood car.

I'd missed the gold 1975 450 SL and decided that I would get another one at some point. I kept seeing one parked behind Kaya's gas station in Belle

Meade. It had been there for several weeks and I asked Kaya what the situation was. He told me that it belonged to Dr. so and so's wife and that he thought it was for sale but didn't know the details. Since I was at his station frequently, I walked over and looked at it. Kaya had bought it new and I sort of remembered having seen it several years earlier. It was a nice metallic blue with grey leather seats and was in good physical shape. One day after a couple of months, it wasn't there anymore.

I asked Kaya about it and he said that the car's owner had it taken over to Erol's Autobahn to be fixed, if it needed anything, since she hadn't driven it in several years. Since that time, she'd bought a new SL 500 and no longer needed it. "You should go over there and have a look at it. Erol (Kaya's brother) can tell you what's wrong with it." I visited Erol and he said that it needed around $2,000 in repairs and showed me the list. He said that he wished the owner would have it fixed or pick it up, either one. He gave me her phone number and I offered to pay her $4,000, and to pay whatever the outstanding bill was, as well as the repairs it needed. She said she'd have to think about my offer, which I thought was fair. And that was that. The more I thought about it, the more I decided to go ahead and buy it. I called to offer her more money, but before I had a chance she said, "I've been meaning to call you. If you still want it at the price you offered me, you can have it. I'm really not going to use it anymore."

I paid her and asked Erol to do whatever was on the list. Several weeks went by and it was still sitting there. I called him on a Monday and said that I'd get it on Friday, ready or not. When Friday arrived I went over, paid him and drove it back to Centerville. It still needed a new water pump and there was a crack in the windshield, which had been there when I first looked at the car. The water pump leaked, but not much, so it was fine to drive around, but I wanted it fixed and drove it to Wurster's in Franklin and had it replaced. I then took it over to the glass repair place across the parking lot from Pull-A-Part in Nashville and had the front windshield replaced. I also got a set of Euro headlamps to replace the four round headlights. Now that I had it the way I wanted, I intended to keep it forever, but subsequently used it as partial trade on a Rolls Silver Spur (see below). It had been a wonderful car in the eight years or so that I'd owned it, and basically trouble free except that the driver's seatbelt had to be replaced and it leaked at the top of the windshield when it rained, even with the hard top in place. I still love the classic looks and the basic simplicity and dependability of these R 107 cars. I've personally known of several of them with more than 400,000 miles on the original engine.

An unfortunate end.

One night as I was looking on craigslist, I saw a car that I was certain was my former 1980. It was scraped and bent down the port side front to rear. I called Steve Howell, who I'd traded it to, several years earlier, and he told me that he'd no sooner had all of the front suspension bushings replaced than he was rammed as he rounded a corner. He'd been paid $12,500 by the insurance company of the at fault driver, and had just become aware that it was now for sale for $850 at some low end car lot on the wrong side of town. He said he was thinking about buying it and having it fixed up, but in a recent conversation he said it was too far gone to justify the expense of a repair.

1975 450 SL (2)

Another 1975

For most of one summer we'd return from Holly Springs to Nashville, through Jackson, TN., stopping for coffee and/or dinner before hitting I-40 East. I've always been interested in giant over the road trucks, especially Peterbilts, and would always look in the lot of a dealership as we'd drive by. One day I noticed among the giant brightly colored trucks with their gleaming chrome, a 1970s SL parked in the lot with a `for sale' sign in the window. We stopped to look at it and I spoke with a truck salesman who was selling it for a friend.

To make a long story short, my girlfriend bought it, and a friend followed us to Jackson where we picked it up, and followed us home down the old road from Jackson so if it conked out, I wouldn't be dangerously stranded on I-40 with cars and trucks whizzing buy. At Waverly, about forty or so miles from home, it began overheating. I stopped for gas and let it cool off. I literally made it home to the driveway before it stopped running of its own accord. I imagined the engine was ruined, with the cylinder heads warped, and no telling what else. After it cooled down, it started right up, but got hot again very quickly. My girlfriend didn't want to pay to have it fixed, didn't like the non-original wheels, didn't like the aftermarket vinyl racing seats, or the flat European headlights, or the aftermarket Momo wood steering wheel. In other words, she was sorry she bought it and wanted nothing to do with it. Furthermore, she would occasionally take up the subject without notice or provocation and start bitching about it. The firewall-mounted device which switched from heater to air conditioning had been removed altogether, and been somehow bypassed so that the AC was on all the time, not a good thing in the winter. The blower fan switch had also been somehow `transcended.'

I didn't especially like the wheels, or the aftermarket seats either, but it was a nice, low mileage car with its original manual and a bunch of receipts for work already done. I had it taken to Nashville to Euro Auto Body and had whatever was wrong with it fixed, which included new brakes, discs, and some incidentals. At least I thought I did. It sat in the back lot of the shop from

August 2015, when I had it towed over there until December 2016 at which time I was informed that it was ready. It was almost like getting a new car, except that it wasn't. There were fuses lying on the passenger floor and I was told that it was ready but had `electrical problems.' The car was drivable and ran great but didn't have any turn signals or dash lights, or starboard rear tail or brake lights. The air conditioning still couldn't be turned off at all. It did however have completely new brakes and it wasn't overheating.

I made it home without issue but for the reasons mentioned couldn't actually drive it anywhere other than to take off the trash. Even with its limited use, it was back at the shop the following November due to intermittent fuel delivery, where it had been sitting a couple of years. I couldn't complain overly since as recently as last week Alex replaced a coil pack on my S 420. The truth is that he's making a lot more money fooling with newer high end cars. There are always Ferraris, Mercedes, Aston Martins, and newer Bentleys at his shop for one thing or another, many brought by dealers due to his well known expertise. He really can fix anything.

1979 450 SL AMG

I was walking around Erol's Autobahn in Nashville one fall afternoon last year waiting while Alex was changing a coil pack on my S 420 at his shop across the street. There I espied a silver 450 SL which was obviously a parts car, even though it was complete except for two rear wheels which had been stolen. I asked Erol what he wanted for the euro flat headlights, since my 560 SL was missing headlights even though I had a set of the American spec headlight clusters. He casually replied, "Why don't you buy the whole thing?" He said he'd take $500 for it. I made a counter offer of $400 and he said OK.

It was absolutely too far gone to be anything other than a parts car. Despite its incredible amount of rust, it was an AMG, so I was able to get the front spoiler. I didn't like the AMG side rails, but I got the two chrome strips that go beneath each door. I also got the instrument cluster, the hood, the hardtop, starboard taillights, Euro bumpers, steering wheel, heater and AC controls, window switches, glovebox door, cold start valve, grill, and side trim strips for both sides. There were other parts I would like to have had, like the radiator, both doors, and indeed the entire engine and transmission. All of this had taken place over a couple of weeks, whenever I happened to be in town. Erol's patience was understandably wearing thin, and he wanted it gone, so I had it towed across the street to Euro Auto Body, where Mark stripped it of its Euro bumpers, hood, and hardtop.

The best thing apart from the headlights were the nearly perfect pair of dark blue leather seats. They were original to the car and were of the same dark blue as the interior of the white 1975 450 SL (see above). Given the severe rust and overall condition of the rest of the junk car, it was miraculous that the interior was in almost new condition, and just happened to match that of the white 1975 SL's original dark blue. Alex replaced the aftermarket vinyl seats of the white 450 SL with the correct seats from the rusty parts car. Erol even gave me the car's title, which now serves as a bookmark somewhere. There were other parts I should have kept but I was grateful for what I got.

1974 Mercedes 450 SLC

As far as I know, the 450 SL coupe or SLC was the first production SL coupe apart from the 300 SL gullwing coupe. For some reason Europeans are reputed to prefer the 2+2 over a plain two-seater, and as they say in Germany, the 450 SLC may have been the answer to the question `Can we make a GT coupe with a back seat and still retain the concept of the SL?' Americans, not so much. Perhaps the SLC is more practical in a place that is generally cold as hell. I don't know. What I do know is that Americans preferred the SL roadster in larger numbers. Jaguar had attempted to make a 2+2 coupe with the XK-E. It worked in that it was drivable and as trouble free as the standard coupe, (that's a joke, son), but what was the point? It was bulbous and elongated, but many were no doubt used to restore standard XK-E coupes and roadsters.

An unexpected gift from the gods.

Anyway, the 450 SLC was a fixed head coupe with a rear seat and an extended wheelbase. At its debut in America in 1972 as the 350 SLC, there were

many people, including a fair number of US buyers, intrigued by its concept and appearance. It was by no means a rare car, but SLs in Nashville of any kind in the early 1970s were quite rare indeed, and SLCs even more so.

One of my friends and early mentors in the music business was the late Louis Dunn, agent and close friend of country singing legend Marty Robbins. He was the first person I knew who bought a new SLC. His had the earlier 350 SL bumpers and was silver with black seats. It was exotic because it was unusual in appearance, but mostly because of its rarity. Back then in the early to mid-1970s, indeed throughout the 1970s, Nashville music executives still preferred large American cars like Lincolns and Cadillacs. Lincoln MK IVs and their successors the MK Vs were especially desirable. Behind the scenes on Music Row, there was a quiet departure by a few from the traditional big irons of Detroit. Chet Atkins had a new 450 SEL, and so did singer Don Gibson. Compared to a 1975 Cadillac Fleetwood, the Mercedes SEL seemed considerably less of a car to the average country music executive, and yet, it was expensive and different. Legendary record producer Fred Foster (Roy Orbison's producer) bought a Mercedes 6.9 when they debuted. I asked Louie why he hadn't bought an SL instead, since it had a removable top. He assured me that if he'd wanted one he would have gotten one. He thought the SLC was a better looking car than the SL. He also liked the extra space afforded by the longer wheelbase.

By the late 1970s Music Row had taken to Mercedes like it had to the early 1960s Lincoln four-door convertibles, 1967 Cadillac Eldorado, and the large Lincolns with their signature `opera windows.' Producers Billy Sherrill, and Tom Collins had SLs, as did singers Johnny Rodriguez, Lane Brody, Waylon Jennings, Rudy Gatlin, agent Jack McFadden, and others, and that's just off the top of my head.

Anyway, when I sold my house in Nashville and moved 40 miles west to a rural area, I would run to either Dickson, or Columbia, Tennessee at least once a week for lunch, the grocery, or whatever. For several years I kept seeing this particular yellow 450 SLC parked just behind the fence at the front of some towing service lot in Dickson. Other than its non-regulation yellow paint, it looked OK as I passed it while driving. There was always a `for sale' sign on the front windshield but I never stopped. One day it wasn't there and I surmised that somebody might have bought it. Good. A week or so later, I was leaving Dickson from another direction, and there it was on the back of the lot. I pulled in, on the spur of the moment, spoke with an employee who said that it was literally on the way to the scrapyard that very afternoon. "Well, what do you want for it?" I asked. After a call to `bossman' I was informed that it could be mine for $500 and delivered the thirty-five or so miles directly to my residence, but that if I didn't want it this very day, it was `a goner.' Apparently, `bossman' was tired of looking at it.

It looked fairly good, with no rust. The black seats had been redone in vinyl, but otherwise, it appeared in fairly good shape physically. I said, `wait here, while I go down the street to my bank and I'll be back in ten minutes.' Forty-five minutes later it was sitting on a concrete slab behind the garage. It had no title, only a bill of sale. What it did have was all of the original records and papers concerning its first purchase, as well as the right keys. The car had been special ordered by someone in a nearby small town and picked up in Germany, toured Europe, and then returned to its home in Tennessee. I know I'd have loved to have ordered my first car and picked it up in Europe and driven it around there for a couple of months.

I read over the service and maintenance records, read the original owner's manual, and wondered if perhaps the original owner was still alive and if so, did he know what became of his car, and finally, would he like to have it back? A week or so went by, and I called directory assistance for the owner's number, and to my surprise found it listed. I called and got the owner's grandson, and told him of my find. He said that his grandfather was dead, but that he'd ordered the car new, picked it up in Germany and then had it shipped back here. The grandson had been a child but fondly remembered the car and riding in it with his grandfather. "It was originally black," I was told, "but my grandfather had it painted yellow because it was `such a lemon.' It had to be in the shop constantly for electrical problems. He finally gave up on it and sold it to someone else. He thought that a new car that had cost as much as it had at the time, should have been able to be regularly driven without worrying from one minute to the next whether or not it would run, or even start." The grandson expressed no interest in the car so I thanked him and that was that. I still have it and it sits where it was parked two years ago on a concrete floor behind the garage. I haven't tried to start it or anything else, but at least it was immediately rescued from the scrapyard.

560 SL

OK, I really didn't need this car, but there it was. It had been inherited by my pal Glenn Ferguson, Jr. who didn't want it. Period. It had been under restoration by his father but had never been completed. It was intact, had been newly repainted its original red, and had perfect original tan leather seats. The dash cover had no cracks. It showed 125,000 miles on the odometer and ran well (after a new fuel distributor), although it quickly overheated. It was missing a few parts, such as its headlights, which had been removed prior to it having been repainted, and subsequently lost. I have several spare sets so no big deal. Same with the side trim pieces.

It's now five years later and I start it every once in awhile and drive it around the driveway loop so that the brakes won't lock up, but that's about it. Perhaps I'll get to it at some point. In the meantime it rests covered in a closed garage. The 560 SLs are the best of the bunch in my estimation, and seem to me to be considerably faster off the line than the earlier 450 and 380 SLs. I've never owned a 280 SL in the same body, but I did spend a couple of days driving around Branson, Missouri in an AMG version. I think all of them are fast enough, both for their era, and their intended purposes. I traded a two year old Omega Speedmaster Professional `Moonwatch' for this car, the fourth one of these watches I've had. I missed it and bought a new one last November. I got my first one when I was 18 at the Post Exchange in the Navy, in Newport, Rhode Island, and traded it for an antique pistol, and always seem to trade them for something or other.

1978 450 SLC

Glenn Ferguson, Jr. had also inherited a 450 SLC from his father and didn't want it since he already had a beautiful very low mileage 450 SL, and so I recently bought it from him. My mechanic had already gone over the car and got in proper working order. It's a nice rust-free example which has always been garaged. The odometer broke at some point so I don't know the actual mileage. Other than that, everything else does. It has a strange steering wheel and a factory rear spoiler, which leads me to suspect that it might be a grey market car, not that I especially care. It also has later, and larger 560 SL wheels, probably as an afterthought, and an aluminum hood. I had to have the steering coupler and tie rod ends replaced, but apart from that, it has been trouble free. I'd tried to sell it on ebay to help settle his late father's estate as well as in the Nashville Craigslist, but nobody had even inquired about it. It was in such good shape that I bought it. I've had it several years now, and the funny thing is that I've really grown to like it, almost as much as an SL. It's truly a beautiful car and I like the sunroof. Actually, it's one of my current favorite cars and I can't say enough good things about the SL coupes. They are undervalued and likely will remain so as they continue to be replaced by newer higher performance cars, but they are still beautiful, fun to drive, and reliable.

The rear window treatment is interesting and befitting the overall appearance of the car, and the rear windows can be lowered. The sun roof is also a plus. I've never seen another steering wheel like this on any Mercedes, and it prone upon occasion to honk without notice as I'm rounding a corner or making short turns in a parking lot.

At some point in this car's history it was retrofitted with the later 560 SL wheels, although I believe the aluminum hood, headlights, and rear spoiler to be original to this car.

1985 Mercedes 380 SL

Most cities have local weekly `throw away' cars for sale newspapers. We were in Holly Springs, Mississippi for the summer seven or eight years ago, and I espied a 1985 Mercedes 380 SL for sale for in one of them for $3,500. It was located about 60 miles South in Tupelo. It was worth a call, whereupon I was told that it was in nice original shape for its age. It had been a state of abandoned repose at a local repair facility for several years, but had recently had the engine rebuilt and was in good mechanical shape, in terms of running.

The white paint was presentable, the tires weren't great, and the blower motor for the heater and AC had conked out, been removed and was in the trunk. It's always a good idea to ask why the owner was selling the car, and how long he's had it. In this case, he'd had it for several years but didn't need it anymore because he'd recently bought a later 90s SL 500. Rust? Not in the car itself, but a bit on the detachable hardtop. It was worth a drive to Tupelo on a nice summer day.

When we arrived, the car was pretty much as described, so I took it for a spin. It was quiet with plenty of power, accelerating smoothly with good oil pressure, and didn't smoke. I told him we'd be gone awhile, which we were, since I wanted to make certain it didn't overheat. It didn't. It actually ran great. I had a 1980 450 SL at the time, back in Tennessee, and had never driven a 380, so I assumed that it would be much slower than it actually was, given its smaller 3.8 liter engine. I was pleasantly surprised to discover it had plenty of power. There were no oil or other fluid leaks beneath where it was parked. The transmission shifted smoothly and the brakes were fine. The windshield wipers didn't work, but that was no big deal. Perhaps it was a fuse, not that it especially mattered because I wouldn't be driving it in the rain anyway, and no further than Oxford, Mississippi, around thirty miles or so from Holly Springs. The windows were slow but worked well enough. The white paint was indeed `presentable' as described. The tan leather was dry, but I've owned worse. The convertible top was fine. The car even had the original owner's manual (usually a good sign). The chrome strips beneath the doors were missing, but otherwise everything was complete. I really didn't need another car, but when he dropped the price to $2000 before I even asked, he got my immediate attention. But…I just didn't want to be stuck on the side of the road because of one or more flat or dry-rotted tires. "I'll tell you what I'll do," I said. "If you'll drive it to Holly Springs, we'll take it."

"Deal."

On the way back home I was excited about getting a new toy. I've always loved Mercedes SLs, any and all of them. These cars had really been expensive when new, were well designed, and by 1985, the last year of the 380 SL, had been around since 1971 (as 350 SL), by which time most of the early bugs associated with them had long since been addressed and corrected. In the case of the 380 SL (1981-1985), the big problem had been the single rather than double row timing chain which had afflicted the 1981-1983 cars specifically, with the introduction of the new 3.8 liter V-8 engine, frequently resulting in expensive repairs to correct the manufacturing error. In fact, a colleague with an early 380 SL had an unexpected $5000 correction surprise several years earlier. For the 1984 & 1985 model years the original single timing chain was replaced with a proper double row chain. Earlier cars can be expensively retrofitted, but it's still cheaper than having valves potentially hit the pistons.

A couple of days later the car arrived at the house as agreed, followed by the owner's daughter in their 500 SL. It had arrived under its own power without incident. I paid him in cash and received the title. I looked at buying this car much the same as I used to consider buying old Jaguar roadsters when I was in my late twenties and early thirties. These are really wonderful cars, plentiful, with an abundance of parts available, and a loyal following. I had it insured the next day and it's still in Holly Springs. I got new tires, and bought new old stock chrome strips for beneath the doors, and a new blower motor for the heater which I've never installed since I don't drive it in the winter.

1985 Mercedes 380 SL (2)

I recently bought a 1985 Mercedes 380 SL. Why? Because I knew its history, and because it was also in great condition. I took it for a spin and it overheated fairly quickly, as I'd been told it would, but I suspected the problem was either the water pump, or a stuck thermostat. The owner, an amateur speculator, had bought it because he thought it was a 560 SL. Apparently, he didn't know the difference, and in his defense, it's an easy mistake to make at first glance. This 380 has the later 560 SL wheels. It does, however lack the distinctive front chin spoiler, a hallmark of the 560 SL. This car had also undergone what is referred to as a `ghetto upgrade' early in its career, having had the 380 SL lettering replaced with the later 560 SL badging, making it appear newer and more powerful to the original owner's friends.

I'd spoken to the car's current owner when the car had showed up on the

Nashville craigslist originally for $5,000 several months earlier, but had been too busy with other matters to fool with it. I'd already visited him several times at his place of business, before I actually saw the car, and he knew I had several old cars. When the car's owner dropped the price to $3,500, I went to see it and took it for a drive. It was in better shape than I imagined. The body was rust free, the dark grey paint was nice, the burgundy leather was in nice shape and everything worked. I asked him what his best price and he said "Don't beat me up. You said you'd give me $3,000." Actually the car was in such nice condition I was prepared to readily give him $3,500, and possibly more, but he said "You said you'd give me $3,000." I told him that would work for me and gave him a check for $3,000 as we'd discussed over the phone, although he had the option of cash if he wanted. The day I stopped by to pay him was the Sunday before Christmas (which fell on a Tuesday). I'd checked with my bank which would be open the next day, and told him he could cash the check tomorrow. I mentioned the day of the transaction for a reason, specifically because for the next week or so everybody would be more or less 'out of pocket' with Christmas and New Year's eve, etc. In the interim, I'd passed by his house on the way to Franklin a couple of days later and noticed as I drove by that he'd removed the car from his garage and parked it at the bottom of a steep, rutted gravel driveway in a three-car covered shed, out of his way. When I'd paid him he'd asked me when I wanted to pick up the car, and I'd said sometime in the next few days or week or so. I knew the car was in the shed, which had two other empty bays, and was out of his way. I called him at his place of business to ask him about another car he'd just gotten which was going to be for sale, at which time he told me he'd moved my car into the shed and the keys were on the floor along with the paperwork. It had been raining on and off almost every day since I'd bought the car. I'd stopped by his house one morning on the way to Franklin and retrieved the keys and the paperwork, and locked the car, since anyone could have driven away with it.

In the meantime, my girlfriend lost my cell phone. "It can't have wandered far," I told her. I had a land line in the interim so I wasn't worried about it. After three days I decided I needed to get another cell phone which I did. She misplaced that one as well. Then she found the first missing phone which had fallen into a boot. At this point I went to buy another phone for myself and gave my original phone to her. The point to all of this is that in terms of my cell phone, I was incommunicado for basically a week, or 'income-avocado' as it's spoken in certain circles.

The seller seemed happy to be rid of the 380 SL, as he'd said earlier, "Nobody wants anything but the 560s. The 380s aren't worth anything." These observations indicated his lack of knowledge about the R 107 series as the later ones regularly sell in the $5000-$10,000 range for one with low mileage in this condition. "I paid $5000, as you can see," he'd said as he handed me the paperwork. "I'm tired of fooling with it. I just want it out if here." I'd met him on several occasions, as I've mentioned, and I found him both likeable and interesting.

I'd called him a couple of times to ask for a few more days in light of the weather, and the fact that the car would have to be towed somewhere to be fixed as it would overheat within ten minutes, as I'd discovered on my first drive. He never answered his phone and his `mailbox' was full so I couldn't leave a message. The car was out of his way with two empty spaces beside it and he hadn't ever told me he wanted it out by any specific time. If we'd agreed on any specific date, it would've been gone by whatever time we'd mutually agreed upon. Besides, he'd been paid, cashed the check and given me a receipt for `paid in full' along with the necessary paper work.

I tried to call him several more times and couldn't leave a message because his mailbox was still full and wouldn't accept a message, and he wouldn't ever answer his phone. It's been my personal experience that anybody whose mailbox `hasn't been set up yet' or is always full is usually dodging creditors or other angry people. Anyway, on New Year's Eve I received a bitchy message when I returned home for the day saying that he was going to "drag my car up the steep driveway and haul it into the church parking lot down the street." This would have no doubt damaged the transmission, as the car was in park and the doors were locked. I immediately returned his call but he didn't answer the phone...again. I called several more times, and he didn't answer the phone.

Finally he did answer the phone and immediately began yelling at me calling me a fucking idiot and saying that he was tired of fooling with me and that he was going to give me my money back, and that I had too many cars already, and that I talked too much. I couldn't get a word in, literally. He just kept yelling. He hung up the phone. I called him right back and he started yelling again. I kept trying to ask him how long I had to get the car out of there, but he just kept yelling. Then he shouted "Now it's going to cost you $500 to get your car out of here." At that point, I said "My lawyer will be in touch." Then he started going on about how I didn't need the car anyway and that I had too many cars already, while continuing to curse me. I finally shouted, "Listen fucker! I sued Ford and won, I sued Blue Cross/Blue Shield, and won. You're next!" At that point, he said "You've got two days." Fine. Thanks.

I'm not as volatile as I once was, but after this, I was almost hoping he'd give me the opportunity to sue him. In reality, I wanted to kick his wormy little metro-sexual bitch ass, but I'd probably have more to lose than he would in the lawsuit which inevitably follows these days. I'm from the South and am used to looking someone in the eye, both of us making a specific agreement, shaking hands on it, and then backing it up in writing in case somebody legitimately forgets some aspect. He was a recent transplant from California,

334

Nevada, or somewhere out west. I noticed he wasn't saying this to my face, but over the phone, from a safe distance.

The next day, New Year's Day, was cold and overcast, and it looked like it might begin raining or snowing at any moment. I told my girlfriend that as much as I wanted to stay home today, we'd better go get the car now because it was parked in the shed at the bottom of that rutted, semi gravel hill, and if it started raining at all, I wouldn't be able to drive it up that fairly steep slope. By the time we arrived, my girlfriend had cooled me down to the point that it wouldn't have mattered what he said to me as long as I retrieved the car from his property. I parked in front of his house and saw him sitting at a desk or table, so I knew that he saw me. I walked calmly down the hill, started the car, and drove it up the semi-gravel driveway, onto, and down the street to the church parking lot. My girlfriend followed me the two miles or so to my sister's house a couple of miles away. I explained my situation to my sister and she said, sure, I could park it there, just make sure it's out of the way.

The 380 sat in my sister's driveway from January 1st to the first week of May. Part of the reason it stayed there so long was that I really didn't know where to take it. I still had my 450 SL which had spent the better part of almost five years at my main mechanic's place, and was still there, even though everything it needed could be fixed in less than an afternoon. When I decided to put the 380 SL in service, I figured it would make it to the main road, IE, Highway 96 before it overheated, which it did, but that was as far as it went. I called AAA, since I have `Premier' service. I got some imbecile on the line to arrange a wrecker to pick up the car and take it to Wurster's in Franklin. He called me back told me the wrecker would be there within an hour and a half to take it to the repair shop in Franklin. An hour and a half passed and I hadn't heard anything. I called the number he'd given me for the towing company and they said they'd told AAA that it had to be rerouted to another company because they were too busy to pick it up until the next day. I called AAA and told them that their service sucked and to cancel the order, I'd find somebody on my own, which I did. I called the Williamson County police department and made them aware of the car's location, then left it there on the side of the road and a wrecker picked up the car at a bit before 8:00 pm and delivered it to Wurster's, fifteen miles or so away in nearby Franklin, TN.

As it turned out, the car needed more than a thermostat. It needed a new radiator, the idle relay, a new steering coupler, and a couple of other things. It totaled $2,600 and change. I told them to fix it, which they did. I went by there, paid them on a Friday, and asked if I could pick it up the next week, which was fine with them. On that splendid, sunny day, I drove from Centerville to my sister's house and she was kind enough to take me to pick up my car. I got in and it started right up, and off I went. I'd driven less than three miles and the engine started sputtering and then stopped completely. I made it back to my sister's house in Leiper's Fork after it had died several times on the way. Then, a couple of weeks later, I actually managed to drive it back to Wurster's, after having stopped and restarted it two or three times. Every once and awhile I get an `automotive break,' a rare smile from the gods of transportation, and this had been one of them, that is, making it back to the shop without having to fool with a wrecker. It needed a new fuel pump, strainer, filter, and the fuel tank cleaned out. It was soon ready again, and everything works as it should, and I'm enjoying it now.

It's funny in a way, because as I looked over the paperwork I saw that it had belonged to Tennessee State Senator Peeler, a democrat from Waverly. He'd bought the car new and had been the one who put later 560 SL wheels as well as replaced the 380 SL badge with one from a 560 SL on the port side trunk lid, obviously in an attempt to impress somebody he most likely didn't even know. I was familiar with him and the car. In fact, it had sold at an auction at his house after his death for $12,500, and I'd been at the auction at the time.

The R-107 cars are in my estimation, the most preferable of the SLs, other than of course, the legendary 300 SL Gullwing coupes and roadsters, which are now very expensive, and thus too valuable to risk for everyday use, should one so desire. The subsequent SLs, beginning with the 300 SL and 500 SL of the 1990s are definitely `better' cars than the R-107s of the 1970s and 1980s, given their pop-up roll bars, better handling, anti-lock brakes, and 4-valve engines. They are, because of their upgraded performance, increased safety features, and creature comforts, infinitely more advanced, and therefore, more complex than their R-107 series predecessors. They're beautiful, to be sure, and certainly faster, but as they age, the potential for expensive, and often incompetent repairs increases exponentially. The pressurized suspension systems of the later cars in this series, and indeed all subsequent SLs are invariably doomed to failure at some point, much to the financial benefit of the authorized Mercedes dealer, but inversely so for their unfortunate owners after the warranty expires, as it always does.

The 107s are still plentiful as they were produced in greater numbers than their predecessors. Many have suffered at the hands of their subsequent owners due to improper or inadequate maintenance, as well as rust, which, by their introduction in 1971 shouldn't have been a problem anywhere. The matter of rust had successfully been addressed as early as 1964, and possibly earlier, by Ford with its Lincoln Continentals, so its continued presence on any high end car from any manufacturer, beyond that date is inexcusable. Prices on these SLs for low mileage models in excellent condition are rising. Should you buy one, check for rust, get what maintenance records may exist, and then I suggest buying a parts car preferably of the same model year, and above all find a competent and honest mechanic. It's also worthwhile to join the `Mercedes-Benz Club of America' and whatever local organizations may exist in your area. They are a great source of information and help with any questions or problems you might encounter. There are also many excellent online forums including benzworld.com and others.

Asking prices currently fluctuate on most of them anywhere from the $4000 range to $25,000 or higher for a really low mileage 560 SL. Asking prices for all models are generally more than they're worth in the actual market, and so many of them remain unsold. There are probably several reasons for the higher asking prices. I suspect that many of the people who currently own nice examples have had them for a decade or more now, and paid more for them then than they are actually worth now, and remember the sting. They were quite expensive when new, and they retained their resale value for a long time. That time has now, for the moment at least, run out. A really wonderful late `70s original 450 SL with approximately 50,000 original miles only brought less than $6,000 at one of the major auction houses this past year (2020). So, if you're thinking of buying one as an investment, I suggest you look for something else. There are just too many nice surviving examples out there. If on the other hand, you want something beautiful, classic, really fun to drive, and dependable, nothing says `old money' like a vintage Mercedes, and in that sense, the R107 SLs are the best of the bunch. I have personally known of several 450 SLs which had more than 400,000 miles on their original engines. I suggest avoiding any of the single timing chain 380 SLs because the repair will cost more than the car's worth.

My experiences with these cars have disclosed some inherent problems. Steering couplers tend to wear out, causing loose steering, and potential failure. Expect one of the fuel lines beneath the differential to rupture. This has happened to me on two 450 SLs and one 380 SL. The trunk seals frequently retain water, so it's best to open the trunk after a hard rain or washing to let the underside of the trunk lid dry. And speaking of trunk lids, I've had two that one day simply wouldn't unlock, for no apparent reason. The key turned the lock, it just wouldn't open.

The dashboard surface is subject to cracks and rifts. Some of them suffer from this affliction for no apparent reason while others don't. The model year seems to have nothing to do with this seemingly random phenomenon, nor do climate or temperature extremes. The good news is that one-piece aftermarket dash covers are readily available in different colors, inexpensive, and can be basically snapped on, and look original.

There are other shortcomings which seem strange in retrospect. The cheap, brittle, chrome-plated plastic pieces surrounding and covering the seat adjustment knobs and mechanisms should have been made of metal, not plastic, since they almost always break off, leaving the unattractive metal seat adjustment mechanism in plain sight.

And while on the subject of the 107 interiors, it's worth mentioning that cars destined for the US market originally were fitted with either leather seats (optional), or vinyl in approximately the same pattern. I generally prefer leather, but the standard vinyl seats are basically indistinguishable, and actually preferable in hot climates if one intends to leave the top down all the time.

The last concern is the detachable hard top. It's a wonderful design, and is made of steel rather than aluminum or fiberglass. It's easy enough to detach or reattach from the windshield with the two handles intended for that purpose usually found in the glovebox. Both sides should be both latched and unlatched simultaneously, that is, at the same time, since windshields have been known to crack if one isn't careful. This applies to the convertible top as well. These same handles lock the sides of the metal top in place on each side of the car, and do not necessarily need to be done simultaneously. The main problem with either top is the central lock post at the back center of both the hardtop and convertible top which requires the operation of two permanently attached concentrically mounted levers with round knobs located on the wall located behind the driver's seat. The manual isn't much help unless you happen to have a degree from M.I.T. Its A,B,C,D positions, arrows, etc. are confusing at best, and the smaller lever in some R 107s is made of plastic where it connects out of sight with whatever is beneath, and is easily broken. The hard tops may have been pretty much air tight when new, but aren't now, and subject to water intrusion while driving or just sitting, both at the front above the windshield, and at the base of the rear window. There are nylon circle inserts on the top of the windshield frame, one at each end which degrade over time. Replacing these sometimes helps the leaking at the top of the front windshield, but will do nothing about water intrusion at the rear.

These things having been done, the R-107s are truly wonderful cars, and represent the end of an era in that they have manually operated tops which won't fail to raise or lower due to some electronic or computer glitch. Their bodies are all steel, except as otherwise noted (in the case of aluminum engine hoods), and they're safe, solid, and dependable cars for everyday driving. These represent the last of a long line of classic Mercedes SLs, and make a personal statement unequaled by newer, 'better,' and more expensive Mercedes or other so-called sports or GT cars. Essentially, their statement at this point is 'old money,' and everything that implies.

When the newer 'battering ram' front and rear bumpers were mandated for all U.S. market cars in the early 1970s, I was appalled at the time by what I regarded as their hideous disruption of the Mercedes SL's otherwise beautiful lines. As strange as it seems to me now, I think I actually prefer the unwieldly U.S. market bumpers, and although I have a set of the European bumpers in the barn, I've never used them. I admit that the European bumpers definitely look better, I'm just used to the US bumpers.

Randy Smith and his current S 63. If not for my association with him, and subsequently his father, I probably would have liked Mercedes but never bought one.

Enough is Enough?

I think I finally have enough cars. My pal Bard Selden in Tunica recently offered me his 1977 Lincoln Town Car, which he'd taken somewhere a couple of years ago and never picked up for one reason or another. It's been sitting outside for all of that time but the leather interior is in perfect condition and there is no discernible rust. The gas tank will have to be removed and thoroughly cleaned, and then the car will have to be painted. And of course, it needs a new vinyl top. At this stage in my automotive journey, it's more than I want to fool with personally. I called one of my new car friends, Fred Harvey, Jr. and put him and Bard together and Fred drove to Tunica and picked it up. I'm glad it got a good home. It's one of my favorite cars.

I was recently in Franklin, TN. for lunch with some friends, and took a Rolls Phantom for a test drive at the wonderful dealership. The Phantom was black with tan leather, and huge. A Rolls-Royce is supposed to be big, and this one was. What became subsequently known as the Phantom VII debuted in 2003. This one was a 2012, which I thought was much better looking than its replacement which appeared in 2017. It had been bought new at the Nashville dealership (located in Cool Springs), but was now out of warranty. At an asking price of $212,000, as always, my thoughts immediately turned to what other automotive options that same amount of money would buy. Although it was truly a beautiful car, it would still depreciate quickly, and for the same amount of money, I could buy both a Phantom Drophead (convertible) and a Bentley (Azure), also a convertible. As I've mentioned, I'm concerned about newer cars' technical sophistication, and the expense, not to mention the damned inconvenience of having to something towed, or driving it to a repair shop, which in the case of the newer cars, for the most part, means the dealership. Then you have to have a friend, girlfriend, or spouse pick you up and take you home, and then back to pick the car up when it's ready. It's one thing if you live in town, it's another thing entirely to live sixty miles away from the dealership, as I do.

Bard Selden

I also know nothing about the new digital operating systems and dozens of computers which control every aspect of the newer cars, each of which are interconnected, and each of which, in upper end cars likely cost at least $1,000 or more. So, for example, "it will cost you just a bit under $8,000 to make your car drivable again, and that doesn't include XYZ, which you should probably have replaced while you are here, which including parts and labor, would make it just under $11,000." While a Bentley, Rolls-Royce, or an S or SL Class Mercedes have always been expensive to repair, even the well informed motorist is at the mercy of the mumbo-jumbo of the dealer's 'technical advisor' also frequently known in house, as a SALESMAN!

As much as I would love to have a Phantom VII, or a Phantom Drophead, I'm not inclined to have to fool with their technical sophistication, and all that implies in terms of money, but more importantly at this point in my life, the inconvenience and wasted time of fooling with the problems which are certain to arise. The Bentley Azure, on the other hand, is something I'm familiar with technically, (except for the problematic top), so perhaps?

I've used a number of mechanics during my automotive history, and after 50 years, these are who I've settled on. It's true that as one's tastes or preferences in cars changes, sometimes one must change mechanics accordingly. The folks I'm mentioning now do not work on Lincoln convertibles, or old Cadillacs, although they doubtless could, but we've reached the age of increasing specialization, and they basically work on German and other European `foreign' cars, and all of them are excellent at what they do. I mention them because the time when every gas station had two service bays with mechanics on hand who could fix basically any car are sadly gone forever. These are the people who allow me to enjoy my cars, without whom I simply couldn't.

Alex Davidoff and Mark Bowden at Nashville's Euro Auto Body. This company is primarily known for its auto bodywork, although technically Alex can fix anything mechanical. I met them in Late September, 2010 when I bought my first Mercedes S Class 140 series. I'd frequently seen a Mercedes 300 SL Gullwing at the small shop across the street from Erol's Autobahn on Leylette, when I'd have something done at Erol's or had come to Hillwood Wrecker Service around the corner to get something towed. There were other cars at Euro Auto body, of course, including Ferraris, Maseratis, and Mercedes of all types.

Alex's life story is interesting to say the least. He was born in Russia and studied automotive design there. When he graduated he worked as an exchange student for a year in Frankfort, Germany before starting work at Ital design in Turin, Italy from 1982-1989. He did not wish to return to the Soviet Union, and began applying for citizenship in various countries. The only countries interested were the US, Israel, and South Africa. He chose the US and after the required time, became a citizen. He opened Euro Auto Body in 1990 and has been in business there since 1990. Mark Bowden, pictured to the right of Alex, has been working there for almost 28 years.

Alex is a car aficionado and has a number of great cars including a 560 SL, a Porsche 930 Turbo, a Porsche 928, and a fleet of various Mercedes of all types, including a `60s SL with a manual shifter.

David Blanks

David Blanks runs TGC in Nashville I first met him through my friend legendary songwriter Larry Weiss, who knew David from the temple on Harding Road. I can honestly say that David Blanks is one of the most interesting people I've ever known. He's half Jewish and half Black to start with, reads and speaks Hebrew, and has been everywhere and done everything. He was born in Chicago and grew up there, and is one of those

people you like immediately. As pertains to cars, just like Alex Davidoff, he can literally fix anything and everything mechanical. Larry told him about me and said that I should call him, which I did. At that point there was something wrong with my `88 Rolls Spur and the 1984 Spur was running hot and slow to start after I'd parked it somewhere and was ready to leave. On his first trip out to the house, about sixty or so miles from his shop, and after a full day's work, he quickly determined that the `84 needed a new fan clutch. The `88 had a short somewhere (which he subsequently fixed). The reason my 1995 S 500 kept stalling was because the spark plug wires were original and needed to be replaced, which he did, as well as the two distributor caps and rotors, which he fixed on one of his Sunday afternoon visits.

David dropped out of T.S.U. his senior year, and enrolled in Nashville Auto Diesel College where he graduated. He was fortunate in that he was born with a high mechanical aptitude. He's always had bad knees and didn't run or walk much, so as a result of that, he built a go kart on a wooden frame with wheels from a baby buggy which he powered with the engine from his father's lawnmower. When it was time for his father to return home from work, David would replace the engine on the mower before his father got home.

David' first car was a red and white 1963 Mercury Meteor which he bought for $400. He rebuilt the engine from scratch in his upstairs bedroom but at the time didn't know anything about properly torqueing the cylinder heads, but learned after there was antifreeze in the cylinders. The car was really beautiful and though it was not for sale, per se, someone offered him $1600 for it and he sold it. Like most of us, it was a sale he regrets to this day. He currently has a number of interesting cars including a gigantic `67 Pontiac convertible, a beautiful red 1976 Corvette, a Mercedes SL 500, a triple black 1974 Lincoln Town Car, which he says is the longest production car ever made, as well as a bunch of other cars.

Erol (left), and Butch at Nashville's Erol's Autobahn: two more guys who can fix anything automotive. Be that as it may, they specialize in Mercedes and BMW, and that's basically all they want to fool with. Erol is a man of few words, and is precise in evaluating exactly what a car needs and what it will cost. In Nashville, his shop is well known to all Mercedes and BMW owners, and for most of them, is their first choice for service. They've been in business since 1989, and Butch has worked there for the past 30 years.

Last but not least is Wurster's in Franklin, a Nashville suburb. I first had them replace the water pump in my 1980 SL in 2007, mainly because they were there. I had originally thought they were just another foreign car repair shop, but they are much more than that. Although Mike Wurster was born in the US after World War II, his family were originally from Germany, and his grandfather Otto had worked as an engineer at Mercedes in Stuttgart for 25 years, after which time he was succeeded by Mike's father, Alfred Wurster who became Chief Engineer at Mercedes, and is credited with having designed the engine of the famed 300 SL Gullwing as well as having designed the CV axle for Mercedes.

After WWII the family immigrated to America and ended up in Nashville. Their first shop was located on Murfreesboro Road at Bell Road. Though originally working on Mercedes, they soon discovered that some Mercedes owners also had BMWs, and some BMW owners also had Volvos, and so on. For this reason they maintain the philosophy of serving their customer base by repairing whatever cars they might own in addition to Mercedes and BMWs. Soon they had more customers than they had room for and moved to Nashville suburb Franklin, in 1979, where they've been since.

Mike Wurster's own mechanical education, began with his father, but Mike also graduated from Nashville Auto Diesel College, one of the most respected automotive training schools in America. Wurster's mechanics are also equally well trained and are constantly receiving updates on the latest automotive technology at Wordpac. Since 2007 Wurster's repaired my botched tune-up on my `84 Silver Spur. They've also worked on the steering of my 450 SLC, basically mechanically restored my beautiful `85 380 SL, and recently replaced the fan clutch and fuel accumulator on my `84 Rolls.

What I especially like about Wurster's is that they still work on some cars that many mechanics won't work on at all, specifically, as pertains to me, older Rolls, Bentleys, and Mercedes. What I like best about Wurster's is that I know what it will cost to have my car fixed, in advance, and that when my car is taken in it is fixed right the first time, and doesn't sit there for weeks or months (or in some cases, years). Wurster's is a busy place with a large staff, all of whom are efficient in their respective jobs, on both the mechanical, and often overlooked but important areas of customer service and scheduling. Additionally, Mike Wurster is a car guy himself, and so are the people who work there.

Mike Wurster at his shop in Franklin, Tennessee.

Fomoco or Mofoco?

1984 Jeep Grand Waggoneer

My girlfriend had a Chevrolet Blazer when I met her which was my first experience with a so-called SUV. It was black with red fabric seats, and two doors. It also had, as I recollect a 2.0 liter engine. I was appalled by the small engine, and imagined that some motorcycles had larger engines. She'd bought the car new and I enjoyed driving it on occasion. It wasn't that big, but she'd bought it because she is, as Jackie Wilson said, `Reet Petit' meaning in this instance, short. Being higher off the street gave her better visibility of the surrounding area. By 1995, she'd decided to get a new car. To my surprise, she was able to sell a 200,000 mile car to a friend of hers for $4000. She decided on leasing a new 1995 Ford Explorer from Graham Ford in nearby Dickson, Tennessee. This was a good car, but she was limited to a certain amount of mileage annually, which didn't suit either of us. When it came time to turn it in, she bought a new 1997 Ford Explorer from Graham Ford. It was no sooner out of warranty than it began making a loud rattling sound somewhere within its engine. I didn't think she should drive it any further than to a Ford dealer to find out what was wrong. She took it to Performance Ford in Nashville and the service department told her that there was a problem with the timing chain tensioner and that the cost to repair it would be $4,000.

I distrusted their assessment, but being unfamiliar with these cars, other than driving them on occasion, I suggested we seek a second opinion. She was friends with the service department manager at the Ford Dealer in Columbia,

Tennessee. We took her car over there and left it overnight. The next day he gave us the same diagnosis as the other dealer in Nashville had. That being the case, I suggested that we return to Nashville and tell them to go ahead and fix it, which we did. To our surprise we were told that it couldn't be fixed at the moment because the dealer was unable to get the parts. Apparently it was some new six-cylinder overhead cam engine and parts were basically unavailable. "Well, when do you think you might be able to get the parts?" I asked with a bit of sarcasm. "We don't know." So, wait a minute, you mean the authorized Ford dealer can't get parts? That was the essence of it. "Oh yeah, one other thing, you shouldn't drive the car and further risk damaging the engine."

At this point I called Ford's national headquarters where I was informed after getting the runaround from a couple of people that I was S.O.L., since the car was out of warranty, though just barely. So basically she was unable to drive her car because it was broken as the result of an inherent design defect, which Ford was unable to fix. To make it worse, she still owed monthly payments. "She bought this car in good faith, and it is her second Ford Explorer, and in your advertisements for this particular car, the brochure said it wouldn't even require a tune up for the first 100,000 miles. And now you're telling me she can't drive it or get it fixed, but she still has to keep paying for it? I don't think so." The information was bad enough, but to add insult to injury, the woman on the line at Ford had a bad attitude, not who you want in customer service.

Since the car was out of warranty, there was little chance of winning a lawsuit. One would think that a company as large as Ford would just say, "Take it to your nearest Ford dealer and we'll fix it for you," if for no other reason than maintaining good customer relations, especially since two of our friends had bought new Ford Explorers based upon our recommendations, which I mentioned to Ford. But no. O.K., plan B. I called Jasper to see if I could get the engine rebuilt. No. Next, I called Grooms Engines in Nashville. No, they were familiar with these engines but had no source for parts either. This wasn't turning out well. It looked like all we could do was wait for some unspecified amount of time and hope the car could be fixed at some point in the near future.

In the meantime, she needed a car for the time being, so we went looking in the usual places, Gallatin and Dickerson Roads in east Nashville. There, we found a 1984 Jeep Grand Waggoneer, which we both liked. It was white, with tan fabric seats and was in great condition, and ran smoothly with its V-8. I think she paid $2,500 cash for it. One day, a month or so later, Katye said, "Why don't you call Grooms again and see if they can fix my car?" I told her that I'd already had this conversation in depth and they can't fix it. "No, I just have a feeling you should call. I thought it was pointless, but called anyway so she would drop the matter. I called Grooms once again and was told, "It's strange you should call because we just bought seven brand new ones on pallets." We asked each other some questions and I made an appointment to have the engine replaced with a brand new identical one in two weeks, the soonest they could get to it. I had no idea where they bought the engines and didn't care. Grooms had, and has an excellent reputation in Nashville, isn't part of some chain, and I knew their work would be exceptional, which it was. I wanted them to disassemble the original engine, document the problem, and take pictures so that I could sue Ford when the time came, which they did. It turned out to have been a problem of some sort with the timing chain tensioner, as best as I recollect. We paid the $5,500 and the car again ran great. Apparently the original problem had been corrected on these newer engines. We were both busy at the time and were just glad to have the car back since we really liked it. As I mentioned, it had been bought new. It was gold in color, had tan leather seats, a sunroof, and both a cassette and CD player. We loved the car. The upshot was that we'd eat the repair cost and that would be that. Life goes on.

But surprise, surprise. Good things come to those who wait. There was a form letter to Katye from Ford advising of a recall concerning the timing chain tensioner or something else related to it. We were advised to take her car to the nearest dealer and the problem would be fixed at no cost to her, (like it should have been to begin with). Not so fast, this letter indicated to me an admission of culpability on the part of Ford. I called my lawyer, J.P. Barfield, a well-known Nashville attorney who is not afraid of a courtroom. We met with him, gave him copies of the repair bill as well as of the cancelled check. He wrote a subtle but clearly threatening letter to Ford. They responded by sending us a check for the full amount of the repair bill, $5,500 or thereabouts. We paid $500 to J.P. and everybody was happy.

One day shortly thereafter, I received a call from some executive at Ford's headquarters asking why we hadn't just called Ford to begin with and explained the problem. I replied that I'd done exactly that at the outset after we'd been told by two separate Ford dealers that we couldn't get the car fixed and that we couldn't drive it. There was nothing he could say in rebuttal, and that was that. I've always liked Ford products and still do, and as Ralph Nader pointed out so succinctly in his landmark book `Unsafe at any Speed' automotive manufacturers do, upon occasion, make mistakes. The customer, however, should not have to pay for them. As a post script, I subsequently bought my girlfriend a 2004 Ford Explorer, which she still has, and she also owns a Mercury Mountaineer which she loves.

Now What? !

When I get obsessive and excessive about anything, as I'm known to do, I think about it, about why I do what I do. Sometimes it seems that I'm on autopilot in most everything. Maybe it's the way I'm wired. Eventually, however, I decide to rein myself in, to take corrective measures. Not strangely, such has finally become the case with cars, as it once was with some things, and still is with others. In the case of cars, I've become envious of those people who have a daily driver of new or recent vintage, and no more than one or two collector cars, and are happy and enjoy themselves and their cars. When I recognize that I'm basically out of control in any area of my life, I take an oath which stops the problem instantly. I think about exactly what I want this oath to accomplish, make some adjustments, and then formalize it by writing it down in my daily journal, so I remember it in case I'm tempted to slip. At this point, it's the issue of does it or does it not increase the quality of my daily life? As far as cars are concerned, the answer is probably not.

At some point, I must reluctantly ask myself, how many cars do I really need? Maybe there is an unconscious fear that perhaps downsizing is a sign of getting older, a step closer to my individual 'Night of Brahma,' or 'journey's end.' With that in mind I think I'll rephrase this concept as 'refining' my collection rather than 'downsizing.' But whatever I call it, it's still the same thing. Those I have now are obviously more cars than anybody normal reasonably needs. I've fortunately had pretty much every car I've ever wanted already. I've enjoyed each of them in its own way. I also remember them fondly as they relate to different times in my life, places I've been, friends I've known, and women I've loved. In other words, as the anonymous 'they' say, 'I'm good.'

Don't I want a Ferrari? If I wanted a Ferrari, I'd have owned one by now. A full classic like a Bugatti, a V-16 Cadillac, a V-12 Lincoln, or Packard, are certainly something I'd like to have in an ideal world, but as beautiful as they are, they're not from my era and don't have any personal significance to me apart from their functional beauty as art objects. And financially, I'm not in anywhere even remotely approaching the same league as the late casino magnate Bill Harrah, who had a full-time staff to restore and maintain what was at one time, the largest automotive collection in the world. There's always somebody with more money, and more and better, cars. I wish them well and applaud their success in their respective fields, as well as their efforts which help preserve these engineering masterpieces for future generations. They're an inspiration to us all. I'm thankful for what I've been given.

While the cars of the 1950s and 1960s were relevant to my generation, they won't mean as much to those who follow, mainly because our successors have no personal memories associated with them. But for the current crop of teens and college graduates entering the workforce, there are many options available, and hopefully, the cars they grew up with, and around, will have meaning for them in the future. I can't help but think however, that no subsequent generation will ever again have the freedoms we enjoyed. We drove everywhere we wanted without worrying about hooey, like manmade global warming, destroying the planet with carbon dioxide, and other equally absurd stuff. This isn't to say that manmade pollution, and carbon monoxide aren't a real problem, since they are. But carbon dioxide? No!

It was enough that we'd pool our money to buy gas for whoever's big brother had the family car when we were 12. Anybody could buy cigarettes, and beer was regularly sold to minors at different places with no questions asked. We shot at street signs with pistols our father's had brought home from World War II. And when we made any time with any girl we were proud of ourselves for having accomplished something worthwhile. In short, we lived off of the labor of our parents. Those who had grown up in the Depression, fought in and survived World War II, brought us fully into the modern era, with America, its products, freedoms, and lifestyle , the envy of the world. As Bard Selden once accurately observed, "We had the best music, schools, cars, and women." I couldn't agree more.

My friend Centerville, Tennessee native Abner Dansby and his `96 Mustang GT convertible.

My son's first car, a 1976 Cadillac Fleetwood Brougham. Speed, mass, and style.

These R 107 SLs are the perfect expression of their original purpose, and while I still love and miss Jaguar sports cars, I think these SLs are more suited to my current lifestyle .

Mercedes owner and enthusiast W.R Smith:

"The Zeus does not have an overhead cam engine. Somebody has to put you right and I'm just the man to do it!" He was right of course, but it did have a V-32 (see 3rd grader Salvatore `Sal, the pencil' Angelicola's excellent linear drawing below).

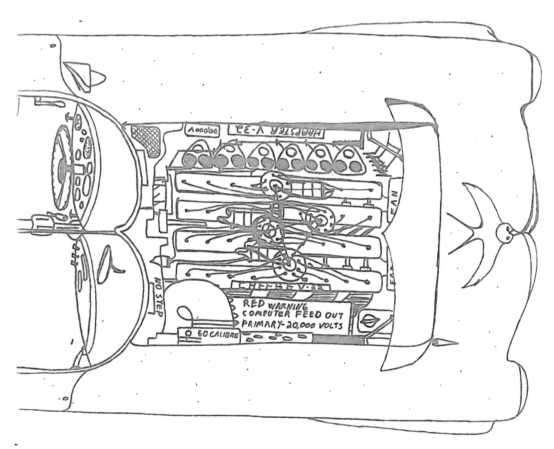

The Zeus.

**W.R. Smith and his 250 SL `Light Bluebird.** There were also a 280 SL dubbed `Dark Bluebird' and a 230 SL named `Whitebird.' "Remember, Randy, the monster walks at midnight." This meant that all of his friends had to beat it by 12:00 am.

W.R. Smith's son Randy in younger days. He had his father's Mercedes 280 SL at Ole Miss, a `69 BMW Bavaria, a 1963 Mercury Comet coupe, a Saab Turbo coupe, 1990s Mercedes S Class diesel, and currently, a Mercedes S-63

Our longtime friend Albert Marlowe with his 1965 Eldorado convertible. He's the first friend of mine who was as wild and as knowledgeable as I was about 1950s Eldorados. He's had two 1958 Biarritz convertibles and a 1959 Eldorado Seville, one of my favorite cars of all time. Cadillacs were truly magnificent cars through 1976, really, `The Standard of the World' as they billed themselves. Albert also had a Italian Ford, and a gold Rolls Silver Cloud I with black leather, which he kept for many years.

Tait Selden, Albert Marlowe, Hardface (Isaiah Ross) in Tunica. MS. Tait and Albert had stopped by to visit Hardface and to admire his car collection sometime during the late 1970s. Hardface had recorded on Memphis label Sun Records and was a car collector known for his sideways cap. He was also a well known gambler, and a veteran of World War II. This photo is taken from a plaque outside the Tunica Blues Museum, thus the cracks.

1993 Bentley Brooklands Just before publication of this

book I acquired a 1993 Bentley Brooklands as the result of a conversation with the guy who bought the black 1974 Mercedes SL (see above). He'd sent his driver, Donnell, up from Troy, Alabama to get it and we started talking. Donnell asked what I had in the garage, and I replied a couple of Rolls-Royce Spurs. He said his boss had a Bentley that looked just like the cars in the garage, which were parked nose first. Anyway, as it turned out, his boss and I hit it off over the phone and we ended up working out a trade over the phone. As it turned out he was really nuts over the early Mercedes 350/450 SLs and had quite a few of them, well, a lot of them actually, and was particularly fond of the SL coupes, as I had become. Basically, I traded him the red 560 SL in storage in Nashville, the 1978 450 SLC, the white 1975 450 SL, and a 450

SLC parts car. "Well," my girlfriend said when I told her about my trade, "you've still ended up with another car." I replied that I had indeed, but it was a net reduction of three cars. "I still want that blue car out of the driveway. It's been sitting there for at least two years. I want it gone." She had indeed been patient. "Yes dear. As soon as he picks up the red 560 SL in Nashville it can go in the garage in Nashville where the SL has been." That seemed to pacify her for the moment. Anyway, a month or so later, my new friend from Alabama, John Ferguson sent his driver back to pick up the 1975 450 SL. A couple of weeks later, the Bentley was brought up and John's driver Donnell arrived with the Bentley and left with the white 450 SL coupe.

Actually, John Ferguson should be the author of this book rather than me because he's had more and better cars than I have, and similar experiences, and some even more interesting than mine. On the day the Bentley arrived, I

asked Donnell to call me a half hour before he got here since he was going to be here early. The phone rang at 6:30 and he said he was already outside. I told him to give me 5 minutes and I'd be right out. When I got there, the Bentley was already in the driveway parked there and running quietly with the AC on full blast. It was as nice as I imagined, another car I'd acquired sight unseen. After Donnell left, I took it for a spin and filled it with gas. It ran great but the two front windows were off track, something I could fix myself since I could hear both motors running. The car had apparently been garaged all of its life and I am happy with it.

For more information on these, and upcoming books as well as cover pictures, reviews, and back cover comments, visit:

Deathcatmedia.com
Also by Scott Faragher:

Music City Babylon (Inside the World of Country Music)-Birch Lane, 1992, New York

The Branson, Missouri Scrapbook-Citadel, New York, 1994

The Complete Guide to Riverboat Gambling-Citadel. New York, 1994

Making it in Country Music-Citadel, New York 1996

Nashville, Gateway to the South-Cumberland House, Nashville 1998

New Orleans in Vintage Postcards-Arcadia, Charleston, S.C. 1999

Nashville in Vintage Postcards-Arcadia, Charleston, S.C. 1999

Memphis in Vintage Postcards (With Katherine Harrington)-Arcadia, Charleston, S.C. 2000

Beer Signs for the Collector-Schiffer. Atglen, PA., 2001

Chattanooga, Best of the Lookout City-Milton Publishing, Chattanooga 2001

Cameras for the Collector -Schiffer. Atglen, PA., 2002

The New South (contributing author)-Insight Guides. London, 2004

Porsche, the Ultimate Guide-K.P. Books. Iola, Wisconsin, 2005

The Peabody Hotel (With Katherine Harrington)-Arcadia-Charleston, S.C., 2006

The Hammond Organ-Scott Faragher Nashville, 2009

The Hammond Organ-Hal Leonard Milwaukee, Wisconsin, 2011

The Arlington Resort Hotel & Spa (With Katherine Harrington)-Deathcat Media-Nashville, 2017

Vignettes from the Modern Era-Deathcat Media-Nashville, 2017

The Peabody, The South's Grand Hotel (with Katherine Harrington)-Deathcat Media, Nashville 2017

Pilgrimage of Darkness-Deathcat Media, Nashville 2021

The Pigeon Drop-Deathcat Media-Nashville 2021

Glenn Ferguson, a Life of Public Service-Deathcat Media-Nashville, 2021

Porsche 928, An Introduction-Deathcat Media, Nashville, 2021

Wildman Tom Crockett and Richard `Cadillac' Jett on tour 1967.

Jim Leonard, Ed Fields, and Steve Cavanah. Ed is at the wheel of his 1928 Nash roadster. All three of us went to high school together.

With photographer William Eggleston's Bentley Continental. Memphis 1985.

Me, Kingsley Hooker, Bard Selden

Once ago. Summer 1970

NEXT !